HOSTAGES IN THE MIDDLE AGES

Hostages in the Middle Ages

ADAM J. KOSTO

OXFORD
UNIVERSITY PRESS

This book has been printed digitally and produced in a standard specification
in order to ensure its continuing availability

OXFORD
UNIVERSITY PRESS

Great Clarendon Street, Oxford OX2 6DP
United Kingdom

Oxford University Press is a department of the University of Oxford.
It furthers the University's objective of excellence in research, scholarship,
and education by publishing worldwide.

Oxford is a registered trade mark of Oxford University Press in the UK
and in certain other countries

© Adam J. Kosto 2012

The moral rights of the author have been asserted

Reprinted 2013

British Library Cataloguing in Publication Data
Data available

Library of Congress Cataloging in Publication Data
Data available

ISBN 978-0-19-965170-2

Acknowledgements

This book has been long in the making. It was John Boswell and Ralph Hexter who first suggested medieval hostages as a possible subject for an undergraduate thesis. I was fortunately sensible enough to figure out that the subject as I wanted to approach it was far, far too big for that purpose, and I ended up writing on Amazons of all things. I explored limited aspects of the hostages question for a master's thesis and a later seminar exercise, but when it came time to settle on a dissertation topic it still seemed too big, and the file went into a drawer for a decade; I worked instead on the archives of eleventh- and twelfth-century Catalonia. The occasional hostages I encountered in that project convinced me that this book was a good next step. In retrospect, there is another book I might have written first, but so it goes.

Because I wrote this book when I did and have been at it for so long, a comprehensive list of colleagues who have in some way contributed to this book would bear a striking resemblance to the International Directory of Medievalists. I list here, with thanks, simply those who made tangible contributions, however small, by providing references; confirming translations in languages way outside my strike zone (Arabic, Early Modern Hebrew, Syriac, Old Church Slavonic, etc.); sending unpublished material, images of documents or manuscripts, or photocopies of sources; or answering specific questions about particular episodes: David Armitage, Martin Aurell, Naby Avcioglu, Hannah Barker, Jenny Benham, Thomas Bisson, Paul Cobb, Susan Crane, Charles Donahue, Bruno Dumézil, Hélène Débax, Carmela Franklin, Jeffrey Fynn-Paul, Cecilia Gaposchkin, George Garnett, Patrick Geary, Jason Glenn, Jessica Goldberg, Ralph Griffiths, Valentina Izmirlieva, Ellen Joyce, Jessica Marglin, James Murray, Katherine Kornman, Laurent Macé, Michael McCormick, Laurent Morelle, Tom Noble, Michael Penman, Cosmin Popa-Gorjanu, Walter Prevenier, Ed Reno, Theo Riches, Jaume Riera, James Ross, Alexandr Rukavishnikov, Seth Schwartz, Bob Stacey, Robin Stacey, Dmitri Starostine, Henry Summerson, Fred Suppe, Kenneth Smail, Anna Trumbore, Marc Vandermaesen, Nicholas Vincent, Jeffrey Wayno, Bjorn Weiler, Gillian Weiss, Megan Williams, and John Witt (apologies to those I have surely omitted!). I am also happy to acknowledge the cheerful assistance of the staffs of Reid Hall, the libraries of Columbia University and the University of Pennsylvania, and the various European libraries and archives listed in the bibliography. The team at OUP—Christopher Wheeler, Stephanie Ireland, Emma Barber, Dorothy McCarthy—have been a model of efficiency and a pleasure to work with. Financial support at various points was provided by the United States Fulbright Commission and the Columbia University Faculty of Arts and Sciences. The maps are the work of Chris Henrick.

Seminar participants at Catholic, Columbia, Cornell, and Johns Hopkins Universities and the Universities of Minnesota, Paris, Oxford, Toulouse, and

Pennsylvania, as well as conference audiences in Atlanta, Ithaca, Seattle, and Washington, DC, helped me to refine my arguments. So too did a continuing conversation with the medieval historians at Columbia, notably Caroline Bynum, Robert Somerville, Joel Kaye, Neslihan Senocak, and Martha Howell; I feel extraordinarily fortunate in my colleagues. Martha Howell and John Gillingham, with the sort of scholarly generosity that can never be repaid directly, read an earlier version of the manuscript; the shape of the book and whatever clarity its arguments have is due to their tough and crucial advice, even if they would ultimately have made some different choices. The anonymous readers for OUP encouraged further refinements and saved me from not a few glaring errors of fact; Gale Kosto caught still more of language. That said, a project of this nature takes its author well beyond familiar terrain and guarantees more than the usual number of slips that specialists will find glaring. Particularly when venturing far afield, I have tried to confirm my readings of the sources by referring to contemporary scholarship, not all of which I have been able to cite. For those errors and misguided interpretations that surely remain, I of course take full responsibility.

Andrea Troxel has read pretty much every word at every stage and talked me through puzzle after puzzle, and the occasional crisis; Asa and Aviva can't quite wrap their heads around the idea of children being handed over as guarantees, but they have no worries on that front and seem to have made peace with the fact that Daddy spends far too much time reading big books in strange languages about really old stuff. For all that and much more that has nothing to do with scholarship, I dedicate this book to the three of them.

Bala Cynwyd

1 May 2012

Contents

List of Maps

List of Tables

Abbreviations

SOURCES

ACA	Barcelona, Arxiu de la Corona d'Aragó, Cancelleria [subseries Pergamins, unless otherwise noted]
ASC	*Two of the Saxon Chronicles Parallel*, ed. Charles Plummer and John Earle, 2 vols. (Oxford, 1892–9); trans. Dorothy Whitelock, David C. Douglas, and Susie I. Tucker, *The Anglo-Saxon Chronicle: A Revised Translation* (London 1961) [cited by year]
BnF	Paris, Bibliothèque nationale de France
CCCM	Corpus Christianorum, Continuatio mediaevalis (Turnhout, 1971–)
CFHB	Corpus fontium historiae Byzantinae (Berlin, 1967–)
CSHB	Corpus scriptorum historiae Byzantinae, 50 vols. (Bonn, 1828–97)
CTH	Collection de textes pour servir à l'étude et à l'enseignement de l'histoire, 51 vols. (Paris, 1886–1929)
Froissart	Jean Froissart, *Chroniques*, ed. S. Luce et al., 15 vols., SHF (1869–75) [other editions cited where used]
JE/JL	*Regesta pontificum romanorum ab condita ecclesia ad annum post Christum natum MCXCVIII*, ed. Philipp Jaffé, 2nd edn., ed. S. Loewenfeld, F. Kaltenbrunner, and P. Ewald, 2 vols. (Leipzig, 1885–8) [JE for 590–882; JL for 882–1198, cited by register number]
MGH	Monumenta Germaniae historica (Hanover, etc., 1826–)
AA	Auctores antiquissimi
Capit.	Capitularia regum Francorum
Const.	Constitutiones et acta publica imperatorum et regum
DD	Diplomata
F I	Friderici I. (= Diplomata regum et imperatorum Germaniae 10)
Kar.	Karolinorum
Epp.	Epistolae (in Quarto)
SrG	Scriptores rerum Germanicarum in usum scholarum separatim editi
SrG ns	Scriptores rerum Germanicarum, nova series
SrL	Scriptores rerum Langobardicarum et Italicarum
SrM	Scriptores rerum Merovingicarum
SS	Scriptores (in Folio)
Monstrelet	Enguerrand de Monstrelet, *Chronique*, ed. L. Douët-d'Arcq, 6 vols., SHF (1857–62)
OMT	Oxford Medieval Texts (Oxford, 1967–)
PL	*Patrologia cursus completus*, series Latina, 221 vols. (Paris, 1841–64)
Potthast	*Regesta pontificum romanorum inde ab a. post Christum natum MXCXVIII ad a. MCCCIV*, ed. August Potthast, 2 vols. (Berlin, 1874–5) [cited by register number]

RHC	*Recueil des historiens des croisades*, 16 vols. (Paris, 1841–1906)
RHF	*Recueil des historiens des Gaules et de la France*, 24 vols. in 25 (Paris, 1738–1904)
RI	Regesta imperii, new edn. (Graz, 1950–); www.regesta-imperii.de
RIS[2]	Rerum italicarum scriptores, 25 vols. in 28 (Milan, 1723–51); 2nd edn., 34 vols. in 109 (Città di Castello, 1900–75)
RS	Rerum Britannicarum medii ævi scriptores (Rolls Series), 99 vols. in 253 (London, 1858–96)
SC	Sources chrétiennes (Paris, 1941–)
SHF	Société de l'histoire de France (Paris, 1835–)

Classical authors and legal texts (Ammianus Marcellinus, Aurelius Victor, Eunapius, Jerome, Julius Caesar, Livy, Malchus, Procopius, Sozomen, Tacitus) are cited with standard abbreviations as in the *Oxford Classical Dictionary*, 3rd edn. (Oxford, 1996), and omitted from the list of works cited; translations, when used, are noted and included in the list of works cited. References to Roman and canon law similarly employ standard abbreviations.

STUDIES

Allen, *Hostages*	Joel Allen, *Hostages and Hostage-Taking in the Roman Empire* (Cambridge, 2006).
Benham, *Peacemaking*	Jenny Benham, *Peacemaking in the Middle Ages: Principles and Practice* (Manchester, 2001).
Bossuat, 'Châteauvillain'	André Bossuat, 'Les prisonniers de guerre au XVe siècle: La rançon de Guillaume, seigneur de Châteauvillain', *Annales de Bourgogne*, 23 (1951), 7–35.
Claustre, *Geôles*	Julie Claustre, *Dans les geôles du roi: L'emprisonnement pour dette à Paris à la fin du Moyen Âge* (Paris, 2007).
Friedman, *Encounter*	Yvonne Friedman, *Encounter between Enemies: Captivity and Ransom in the Latin Kingdom of Jerusalem* (Leiden, 2002).
GCA	Pierre-Clément Timbal, *La Guerre de Cent Ans vue à travers les registres du Parlement (1337–1369)* (Paris, 1961).
HGL	Cl. de Vic and J. Vaissete, *Histoire générale de Languedoc avec des notes et les pièces justificatives*, 15 vols. (Toulouse, 1872–93).
Kershaw, *Peaceful Kings*	Paul J. E. Kershaw, *Peaceful Kings: Peace, Power, and the Early Medieval Political Imagination* (Oxford, 2011).
Kosto, 'Carolingian'	Adam J. Kosto, 'Hostages in the Carolingian World (714–840)', *Early Medieval Europe*, 11 (2002), 123–47.
Kosto, 'Crusades'	Adam J. Kosto, 'Hostages during the First Century of the Crusades', *Medieval Encounters*, 9 (2003), 3–31.
Kosto, 'Late Antiquity'	Adam J. Kosto, 'Hostages in Late Antiquity' (unpublished paper).

Lavelle, 'Use and Abuse'	Ryan Lavelle, 'The Use and Abuse of Hostages in Later Anglo-Saxon England', *Early Medieval Europe,* 14 (2006), 269–96.
Lecoy, *René*	A. Lecoy de la Marche, *Le roi René: Sa vie, son administration, ses travaux artistiques et littéraires, d'après les documents inédits des archives de France et d'Italie,* 2 vols. (Paris, 1875).
Les prisonniers	Sylvie Caucanas, Rémy Cazals, and Pascal Payen, eds., *Les prisonniers de guerre dans l'histoire: Contacts entre peuples et cultures* (Toulouse, 2003).
Lutteroth, *Der Geisel*	Ascan Lutteroth, *Der Geisel im Rechtsleben: Ein Beitrag zur allgemeinen Rechtsgeschichte und dem geltenden Völkerrecht* (Breslau, 1922).
Niermeyer, *Lexicon*	J. F. Niermeyer, *Mediae latinitatis lexicon minus* (Leiden, 1993).
Pugh, *Imprisonment*	Ralph B. Pugh, *Imprisonment in Medieval England* (Cambridge, 1968).
Reynolds, *Fiefs*	Susan Reynolds, *Fiefs and Vassals: The Medieval Evidence Reinterpreted* (Oxford, 2001).
SP	*Les sûretés personnelles,* 3 vols., Recueils de la Société Jean Bodin pour l'histoire comparative des institutions 28–30 (Brussels, 1969–74).
Stacey, *Road*	Robin Chapman Stacey, *The Road to Judgment: From Custom to Court in Medieval Ireland and Wales* (Philadelphia, 1994).
Walker, 'Hostages'	Cheryl L. Walker, 'Hostages in Republican Rome', PhD dissertation, University of North Carolina–Chapel Hill, 1980; chs.harvard.edu/publications.sec/online_print_books.ssp (Washington, DC, 2005).
Walliser, *Bürgschaftsrecht*	Peter R. Walliser, *Das Bürgschaftsrecht in historischer Sicht dargestellt im Zusammenhang mit der Entwicklung des Schuldrechts in den schweizerischen Kantonen Waadt, Bern und Solothurn bis zum 19. Jahrhundert* (Basel, 1974).

Note on Citations

With the exception of the few titles included in the list of abbreviations, I have referred to primary sources throughout with modified short titles (easily locatable in the list of works cited), balancing demands of space with a desire to make the particular editions used easily identifiable at each occurrence. For narrative and legal sources, edition and page location are noted in parentheses; for documentary sources, page location appears first, with document number, when available, in parentheses and identified as such. Throughout, book/chapter volume/number divisions are separated with a full stop, volume and page of the edition with a colon. Thus 'Malaspina, *Die Chronik*, 4.6 (MGH SS 35:186–7)' is book 4, chapter 6 of the chronicle, as edited in volume 35 of the MGH series at pages 186–7; '*Preußisches Urkundenbuch*, 1.1:100–2 (no. 134)' is document 134, found in volume 1, part 1, pages 100–2 of the edition. Secondary sources are cited according to the customary system: full citation at the first instance in each chapter, followed by short titles. Where I have worked from a translation or quoted a translation directly, that is noted in the citation (trans. rather than ed.); for my own translations, I usually provide the original text in the notes, although considerations of space did not allow for absolute consistency.

1

Hostages in the Middle Ages: Problems and Perspectives

A thirteenth-century biography relates that William Marshal, one of the most famous knights of his day, almost didn't survive childhood. In 1152, William's father, John Marshal, whose men were besieged in the castle of Newbury, handed his son over voluntarily to King Stephen to convince the king that he would abide by a truce. When John instead used the period of respite to reinforce his defences, the king's advisors recommended that he execute the boy. When John learned of this, he called their bluff: 'I still have the hammers and anvils with which to forge better sons', he boasted. The king, furious, ordered the boy executed, but could not bring himself to follow through. William Marshal was what the medieval sources call a hostage. John had handed him over as a guarantee of an agreement: if the agreement were kept, he would be returned; if not, his life was forfeit. John promptly violated the agreement, knowingly putting his son's life at risk, but the king did not carry out his threat and eventually released William.[1]

William Marshal does not fit the modern understanding of the hostage: the victim of a kidnapping, often by terrorists, often politically motivated. The first task of this book, then, is to explain what a hostage was in the Middle Ages: who served, to what ends, and how. That the last of those questions—how?—will prove the most interesting is hinted at by the case of William Marshal: not only did the agreement collapse, the hostage (and thus the one who granted him) did not suffer for that collapse. That is, the hostage was completely ineffective as a guarantee, but the hostage-holder did not follow through on what was seemingly the only course of action that justified accepting the hostage in the first place. This puzzle points to the fact that hostages were not simply a legal institution in the Middle Ages. They were also a political institution.

Hostages substituted for or represented actors in a wide range of transactions. There was no single way in which hostages performed their roles, which differed depending on the parties involved, on the nature of the business at hand, and, crucially, on the particular period in question. For even confining ourselves to the medieval period, it is clear that hostages have a history. Tracing that history, and its significance for our understanding of medieval history generally, is the second task

---

[1] *History of William Marshal*, 467–714 (ed. Holden, 1:24–36) ('Mais il dist ke ne li chaleit/Les enclumes e les marteals/Dunt forgereit de plus beals'); David Crouch, *William Marshal: Knighthood, War and Chivalry, 1147–1219*, 2nd edn. (London, 2002), 1–11.

of this book. A study of the way people employed hostages over time illuminates the changing ways people settled conflicts and made agreements in a legal and political environment very different from our own, and, on a very basic level, the changing ways medieval societies assigned importance and value to relationships and people.

In the chapters that follow, I make three central claims. First, medieval hostage-ship is best understood as a guarantee; such an approach ties together and renders more comprehensible the histories of a number of interrelated practices that have generally been considered separately. Hostageship is rarely, however, simply a guar-antee, and in that fact lies the institution's political power and utility. Second, medieval hostageship changed in the course of the eleventh and twelfth centuries, alongside well-studied changes in society. Third, the persistence of hostageship through the later Middle Ages and its decline thereafter suggests that hostageship in its various forms is characteristic of medieval political life: despite developments in governance, bureaucracy, and law, conditions arose frequently enough—whether absence of a common superior capable of enforcing agreements, or simply of a shared customary framework—that physical control over people remained crucial.

A VERY SHORT HISTORY OF HOSTAGES

This book focuses on hostages in medieval Europe and its neighbours, but hostages are by no means solely a medieval institution. The hostage as guarantee is a very widespread, if not a universal, practice in human history. It is not, however, a time-less practice, as a brief historical survey shows. In the Hebrew Bible, when Joseph sent his brothers back to Canaan to retrieve Benjamin, he kept Simeon in Egypt, to guarantee their return. Reuben later told his father, Jacob, that if the brothers failed to bring Benjamin back from Egypt, 'Thou shalt slay my two sons'.[2] What-ever their reaction to Joseph's manipulations of family loyalties, the audience for these tales would have found nothing remarkable in the idea of hostageship, which appears scattered throughout other Ancient Near Eastern sources, as it does in the earliest sources from China.[3] The context of the hostages of Genesis was, however, different from that of most ancient hostages for which we have evidence, namely military and diplomatic affairs. If Homer himself was not a hostage of this sort,[4] from the fifth century BCE evidence for hostages becomes common in the Greek world, not only in the histories of Herodotus and Thucydides, but also in drama and inscriptions. Certain historical episodes stand out—the Aeginetan hostages

[2] Gen. 42.16–20, 37; Scott Morschauser, '"Hospitality", Hostiles and Hostages: On the Legal Background to Genesis 19.1–9', *Journal for the Study of the Old Testament*, 27 (2003), 476. Cf. Gen. 43.9 (ערב as unspecified surety), 44.33 (no underlying agreement).
[3] *SP* 1:155–231; Antonio Forte, *The Hostage: An Shigao and His Offspring* (Kyoto, 1995); below, p. 207, n. 35.
[4] Holger Thesleff, 'Notes on the Name of Homer and the Homeric Question', in *Studia in honorem Iiro Kajanto* (Helsinki, 1985), 293–314, dismisses the idea.

during the Persian war, or the stay of Philip of Macedon as a hostage at Thebes—but they were a regular feature of both the internal and external relations of the Greek city-states and the Hellenistic kingdoms.[5]

Hostages appear early in Roman history, figuring in some of Rome's founding legends, such as the cases of the heroine Cloelia and the Battle of the Caudine Forks, and Rome did receive some hostages during the early phases of its expansion on the peninsula. But it is with the Punic Wars that the institution appears to become a regular instrument of diplomatic policy. It was Julius Caesar who was the most active Roman trafficker in hostages, receiving thousands from various tribes in Gaul and Britain during his long campaigns.[6] Cheryl Walker has catalogued over 140 such hostage episodes for the second and first centuries BCE; in two-thirds of the cases Rome, or a Roman party, was the recipient.[7]

Over the course of Roman history, however, hostageship changed. First, in the transition from peninsular republic to world empire, and in moving from dealing with local oligarchic city-states to overseas kingdoms, Rome was presented with the opportunity to receive princely hostages; these often acquired an education in and sympathy for Roman customs and were used by Rome to influence the internal politics of allies or client states. A second shift that accompanied the spread of Roman influence in the Mediterranean world concerns the growing role of Roman hostages as a means of political communication: public display of hostages in triumphs, their inclusion in public entertainments, their role in cultural diplomacy, and their use as pawns in political battles. Third, after the death of Augustus (14 CE), there was a marked decline in cases of Rome receiving hostages, which lasted through the third century, although the few traces of hostageship in the writings of imperial jurists hint that high-status hostages remained a numerous enough category in the late second and third centuries to raise legal issues.[8]

Rome's experience with hostages in Late Antiquity represents another change, as the empire was faced on the one hand with a Persian counterpart that it had to treat as an equal, and on the other hand with frontier tribes that, while seen as inferior, nevertheless started winning military victories. In both cases, Rome found itself in the unaccustomed position of delivering, instead of receiving, hostages, and increasingly employing hostages in the day-to-day management of warfare, diplomacy, and also domestic affairs. Hostageship became less a given than something subject to negotiation, and the outcome of hostage transactions was

[5] The only general studies are: M. Amit, 'Hostages in Ancient Greece', *Rivista di filologia e di istruzione classica*, 3rd ser., 98 (1970), 129–47; Raoul Lonis, 'Les otages dans les relations internationales en Grèce classique: Insuffisances et ambiguïtés d'une garantie', in *Mélanges offerts à Léopold Sédar Senghor: Langues–littérature–histoire anciennes* (Dakar, 1977), 215–34; Andreas Panagopoulos, *Captives and Hostages in the Peloponnesian War* (Amsterdam, 1989 [1978]).

[6] M. James Moscovich, '*Obsidibus traditis*: Hostages in Caesar's *De bello Gallico*', *Classical Journal*, 75 (1979–80), 122–8.

[7] Walker, 'Hostages', 214–44. Other general studies: A. Matthei, 'Das Geiselwesen bei den Römern', *Philologus*, 64 (1905), 224–47; Stephan Elbern, 'Geiseln in Rom', *Athenaeum*, 78 (1990), 97–140; Saliou Ndiaye, 'Le recours aux otages à Rome sous la République', *Dialogues d'histoire ancienne*, 21 (1995), 149–65; Allen, *Hostages*.

[8] Allen, *Hostages*; Elbern, 'Geiseln im Rom'. On Roman law, see below, pp. 212–13.

consequently less predictable. Finally, in the late imperial period, hostages increasingly are found in agreements not directly involving rulers: hostageship was now decentred. This more complex institution was inherited by the successor kingdoms of the West and the early Byzantine state, where the new Islamic empire fitted easily into the great-power role formerly occupied by Persia. Although hostages are absent from the Qurʾān, there is ample evidence that Islamic traditions surrounding hostageship absorbed not simply Roman and Persian antecedents, but also those of pre-Islamic Arabia.[9]

In the sweep of European history, the period on which this book focuses represents a high point for hostages. They feature in nearly every major politico-military development or event between the fifth and fifteenth centuries: the collapse of Roman rule in the West, the rise of the Carolingians, the Viking invasions, the Peace and Truce of God, the Norman conquest of England, the Investiture Contest, the Iberian Reconquista, the Crusades in all their manifestations, Magna Carta, Bouvines, the Peasants' Revolt, Crécy and Agincourt, the capitulation of Granada... But they also feature in major financial deals and in countless lesser transactions with only local import. The shifts in hostageship in this period will be the subject of later chapters; it is worth noting at this point that while strong echoes may be found of Roman practice, particularly under the Carolingians, the much more polyfocal nature of political life during these years supported correspondingly different varieties of the institution.

As will be discussed in Chapter 7, hostageship looks still different starting in the sixteenth century, when the number of parties that could legitimately grant and receive hostages shrank with the formation of nation-states, and the hostage as a mode of surety outside of high-level diplomacy all but disappears. In the eighteenth century, while even high-level hostageship among European powers fades away—the last case is generally considered to be the Treaty of Aix-la-Chapelle in 1748—a new sort of hostage emerges: the individual seized during wartime to force certain behaviour. It was this type of hostage that was discussed at the Nuremberg War Crimes Tribunals. The older variety of hostage re-emerges in the colonial context, persisting there again into the twentieth century. The current idea of the hostage as terrorist victim is a later development still, datable only to the last third of the twentieth century, and enshrined in the International Convention against the Taking of Hostages of 1979: 'Any person who seizes or detains and threatens to kill, to injure or to continue to detain another person (hereinafter referred to as the "hostage") in order to compel a third party, namely, a State, an

---

[9] In the Qurʾān, the root *rhn* refers once to real surety (2.283) and twice metaphorically to persons or souls (52.21, 74.38). See Jonas C. Greenfield, 'Kullu nafsin bimā kasabat rahīnā: The Use of *rhn* in Aramaic and Arabic', in Alan Jones, ed., *Arabicus Felix: Luminosus Britannicus: Essays in Honor of A. F. L. Beeston on his Eightieth Birthday* (Oxford, 1991), 224–5; Joseph Schacht, 'Foreign Elements in Ancient Islamic Law (I)', *Mémoires de l'Académie internationale de droit comparé*, 3.4 (1955), 137–8; *Encyclopedia of Islam*, 2nd edn., 13 vols. (Leiden, 1960–2005), s.vv. *Rahn, Dāhis, Salūl* 1; and below, p. 64, n. 50. Sources, e.g.: *Sabaean Inscriptions*, 67–8, 318–19 (no. 576.2); 'Inscriptions sud-arabes: Dixième série', 278, 283–4, 285, 291–2 (nos. 506.7–8, 507.6–7); *Corpus inscriptionum semiticarum*, 4.2.3:280, 284, 289, 294 (no. 541.52); *The Book of the Himyarites*, 48 (ed. and trans. Moberg, 56, cxliii).

international intergovernmental organization, a natural or juridical person, or a group of persons, to do or abstain from doing any act as an explicit or implicit condition for release of the hostage commits the offence of taking hostages ("hostage-taking") within the meaning of this Convention.'[10]

HOSTAGES AND HISTORIANS

The medieval hostage is obviously related to this modern hostage, and not only in name, but it is not the same. Nor is the medieval hostage precisely the same as its ancient predecessors or early modern successors. Indeed, hostageship is not a fixed institution even within the medieval period. Previous scholarship on hostages has tended to collapse these various distinctions, ignoring both the peculiarities of the medieval institution and its development over time. The most comprehensive analysis of hostageship in history remains the broad study of Ascan Lutteroth, *Der Geisel im Rechtsleben* (1922).[11] His work is constructed around two binaries common in the literature: a distinction between hostages by agreement and unilateral hostages (*vertragsmässige* and *einseitige Geiselschaft*), and a distinction between hostages within societies and hostages in 'international law'. Both of these distinctions cause problems when dealing with the European Middle Ages.

The division between hostages by agreement and unilateral hostages distinguishes between hostages given and hostages taken. As Lutteroth himself notes, the separation of these two categories is a product of modern international law.[12] As will be seen, the language of the medieval sources does not distinguish clearly between these ideas, highlighting the notion of giving even when compulsion is evident. Such a view is more consonant with current understandings of the gift in the Middle Ages, which explain well the obligations underlying and created by grants and donations of all sorts.[13] Compulsion is thus never entirely absent, even in the most apparently pacific transfers of hostages. The fact that the sources adhere to the notion of giving, however, makes it possible to separate for analytical purposes historical hostageship from the modern form of kidnapping that goes by the same name. In the present study, hostages are always given—but given in complex ways.

The second distinction, between international and domestic law, overlaps with a distinction between private and public law, and, by extension, is relevant to attempts to identify a coherent set of medieval 'laws of war'. While these categories have firmer historical roots, they too fit uncomfortably with the medieval evidence. As the events of the early twenty-first century are making increasingly clear,

---

[10] *International Convention*, art. 1.1 (ed. 1316:207).
[11] Lutteroth, *Der Geisel*. Helmut R. Hoppe, 'Die Geiselschaft: Ihre Entwicklung und Bedeutung', Dr. iur. dissertation, Georg-August-Universität Göttingen, 1953, adds little.
[12] Lutteroth, *Der Geisel*, 15–16; see below, p. 223.
[13] Gadi Algazi, Valentin Groebner, and Bernhard Jussen, eds., *Negotiating the Gift: Pre-Modern Figurations of Exchange* (Göttingen, 2003); see Marcel Mauss, *The Gift: The Form and Reason for Exchange in Archaic Societies*, trans. W. D. Halls (New York, 1990 [1950]), 60, 122 (n. 206).

modern international law relies on the notion of nations, or states.[14] Classical
Roman law does seem to distinguish between treaty-hostages arising from conflicts
between Rome and its neighbours, on the one hand, and hostages arising from
personal obligations on the other, despite the apparent rarity of this later type.[15] In
the medieval sources, as will be seen, such a division is absent.[16] Furthermore, even
before Late Antiquity, Romans used hostages in their dealings with people whom
their law did not formally recognize as states.

The utility of the concept of 'state' for discussions of medieval history is itself a
vexed question, but for the present purposes, it is difficult to draw the line between
medieval political structures that merit the term and those that do not.[17] At a certain point, transactions between two individuals each at the head of 'an organization of human society within a more or less fixed area', each of whom 'more or less
successfully controls the legitimate use of physical force'—to use one sensible
definition of the state[18]—descend to a level where the term is a distraction. Because a category of 'international' is hard to isolate for the Middle Ages, it is not
useful to think about hostageship as part of 'international law' in that period.
Similar arguments apply to distinctions between public and private law. As for the
'laws of war', in addition to the problem of distinguishing a state of war in which
such laws apply from other states of violence in which they do not, there was no
medieval equivalent of the Geneva Conventions—no formal law code to which
historians can turn for help. In this study I use 'international', 'private', and 'laws
of war' as useful shorthands in situations where their meaning should be clear;
they are not, however, useful analytical frameworks for the study of hostageship in
the Middle Ages.

On a more general level, Lutteroth's study, like almost all previous scholarship,
treats hostages narrowly as a species of the legal-historical category of surety. This
is a concept that fits much more easily with the medieval evidence, which is re-
plete with guarantors and guarantees of all types, and the language and categories of suretyship provide very useful tools for discussing hostageship in the
Middle Ages. The legal trio of debtor/creditor/guarantor is a convenient abstrac-
tion for discussion of relationships between the grantor of the hostage whose
promise is being guaranteed, the receiver of the hostage, and the hostage. Legal
historians also distinguish between real and personal surety, between things and

---

[14] In fact, the Hostage Convention of 1979 is an early example of attempts to address the problems
of this conception of international law: it extends protection from states to any 'international
intergovernmental organization, a natural or juridical person, or a group of persons'. See below,
p. 225.

[15] Nov. 134.7, a sixth-century law of the emperor Justinian that prohibits the use of free individuals
as captive guarantors for debts, employs the term *pignus* instead of *obses*. See Kosto, 'Carolingian',
128–9, and below, p. 213. On Roman suretyship and its later influence generally, see *SP* 1:295–325.

[16] A point recognized with respect to Scandinavian hostageship by Karl von Amira, *Nordgermanisches Obligationenrecht*, vol. 2: *Westnordisches Obligationenrecht* (Leipzig, 1895), 177.

[17] Rees Davies, 'The Medieval State: The Tyranny of a Concept', *Journal of Historical Sociology*, 16
(2003), 280–300.

[18] Susan Reynolds, 'The Historiography of the Medieval State', in Michael Bently, ed., *Companion
to Historiography* (London, 1997), 110.

people used as guarantees. Hostages have been understood as a mixture of the two: they are people, but from a legal standpoint they are treated as things (not unlike slaves). While the medieval vocabulary of guarantee does not, as will be seen, consistently maintain a distinction between real and personal sureties, deciding whether a given guarantee is a person or an object is an essential starting point in an investigation of hostageship. In addition, the concept of suretyship highlights the connections between true hostageship, in which the hostage is handed over immediately, and conditional hostageship, in which such a transfer is only promised—a connection that is not self-evident and that plays an important role in the story told in this book. Finally, legal historians have created a useful typology of personal surety: the *hostage*, who is deprived of liberty as a means of exercising pressure on the debtor to perform; the *influencing guarantor*, who uses various forms of persuasion to ensure performance; the *executory guarantor*, who forces performance, as by seizing real surety promised by the debtor; the *amending guarantor*, who compensates the creditor for a loss; or the *paying* or *performing guarantor*, who undertakes independently the action promised by the debtor himself.[19]

If this legal-historical vocabulary is useful, however, suretyship as a conceptual framework has limitations. First, the scholarship on personal surety marginalizes hostages topically, treating them as a bizarre variation on the main theme, and chronologically, by treating the medieval period as a brief, because relatively poorly documented, chapter in the long history from antiquity to the modern period.[20] The present study, in contrast, makes medieval hostageship its central focus. Second, the principal concern of legal historians has been to find the place of hostageship, normally viewed as the most archaic form of guarantee, in a teleological genealogy of modern suretyship; hostageship is even viewed by thinkers as influential as Max Weber and Oliver Wendell Holmes as at the origin of the idea of contract itself.[21] Thus an earlier tradition, enshrined in the work of Otto von Gierke, saw all sureties as 'ideal hostages', while more recent work tends to support the theory of Franz Beyerle that sees hostageship and other forms of surety as practices that developed separately.[22] The present study is more concerned with the historical contexts for hostageship than with tracing institutional genealogies; by not viewing hostageship as a primitive practice, it is able to explore the persistence of hostageship alongside other 'more advanced' forms of surety. Third, the suretyship framework allows for the idea of the debtor acting as his own surety; in the present context, this would mean acting as a hostage for oneself. Historically, debt

---

[19] *SP* 1:50–2.

[20] *SP*.

[21] Raoul Berger, 'From Hostage to Contract', *Illinois Law Review*, 35 (1940), 154–74, 281–92; Oliver Wendell Holmes, *The Common Law* (Boston, 1881), 247–50; Max Weber, *Economy and Society: An Outline of Interpretative Sociology*, ed. Guenther Roth and Claus Wittich, 2 vols. (Berkeley, 1987), 2:679–80.

[22] Otto von Gierke, *Schuld und Haftung im älteren deutschen Recht: Insbesondere die Form der Schuld- und Haftungsgeschäfte* (Breslau, 1910), esp. 56; Franz Beyerle, 'Der Ursprung der Bürgschaft: Ein Deutungsversuch vom germanischen Rechte her', *Zeitschrift der Savigny-Stiftung für Rechtsgeschichte*, Germanistische Abteilung, 47 (1927), 567–645.

slavery is a good example of this phenomenon, and in some medieval situations, terms for hostage are applied to the 'debtor'.[23] Generally, however, combining this phenomenon with third-party hostageship would be to be led by words away from the historical practice of interest. Finally, a narrow focus on hostageship as a form of personal surety isolates the institution from a wide variety of other practices, and it is these other practices that provide the historical contexts within which hostageship is best understood.

Social history, rather than legal history, provides a third conceptual framework relevant to the study of hostages, namely 'captivity', the broadest understanding of which would include not only captives arising from war and prisoners arising from judicial or quasi-judicial processes, but also victims of kidnapping (in the modern sense) and slaves, as well as hostages.[24] From a legal-historical perspective, slavery and hostageship are in fact closely linked: debt-slavery, whether of the debtor or of a third party, is part of the history of credit and suretyship, while hostages of all sorts could become slaves in case of violation of an agreement. Scholars have tended, however, to treat slaves as a category distinct from captives and prisoners.[25] Whether they distinguish between wartime captives and judicial prisoners depends mostly on the period and region studied; the medieval sources do not seem to make such a distinction regularly, although that is a claim that needs to be tested.[26] Many studies that focus on imprisonment draw on sociological scholarship that identifies custodial, punitive, and coercive types of confinement, while recognizing that these categories tended to overlap in the Middle Ages.[27] From that perspective, hostageship is a particular form of coercive confinement, one in which the person coerced is not the person in custody (a status shared with victims of kidnapping). Michel Foucault's *Surveiller et punir* is a touchstone of all this recent literature on imprisonment, and its framing of the subject as part of the history of power remains influential. To the extent that the present study argues that the practice of hostageship in the Middle Ages is best understood in the context of shifting structures of power, it owes a debt to that work. Scholarship that focuses on prisoners of war, in contrast, makes very different contributions to the study of hostageship, particularly in its analyses of the economic aspects of captivity, the chronology of the development of the laws of

---

[23] e.g. Heinrich Taube von Selbach, *Chronica*, s.a. 1295 (MGH SrG ns 1:2): 'in obstagio pro se'. See also Claustre, *Geôles*, 43–4, 321 (*ostagium*); Eduard Feliu, 'Mots catalans en textos hebreus medievals: Els dictàmens de Salamó ben Adret', *Calls* (Tàrrega), 3 (1988), 65–6 (*ostages* [אוצגייש]); and below pp. 134, 161n. 129.

[24] Martin Kitzinger, 'Geiseln und Gefangene im Mittelalter: Zur Entwicklung eines politischen Instruments', in Andreas Gestrich, Gerhard Hirschfeld, and Holger Sonnabend, eds., *Ausweisung und Deportation: Formen der Zwangsmigration in der Geschichte* (Stuttgart, 1995), 41–59; Elizabeth Lawn, *'Gefangenschaft': Aspekt und Symbol sozialer Bindung im Mittelalter, dargestellt an chronikalischen und poetischen Quellen* (Frankfurt am Main, 1977).

[25] Jean Dunbabin, *Captivity and Imprisonment in Medieval Europe, 1000–1300* (Basingstoke, 2002), 8; Lawn, *'Gefangenschaft'*, 117–22.

[26] Dunbabin, *Captivity*, 8–11.

[27] e.g. Pugh, *Imprisonment*, 1 n. 4; Guy Geltner, *The Medieval Prison: A Social History* (Princeton, 2008), 30; Dunbabin, *Captivity*, 3; Roger Grand, 'La prison et la notion d'emprisonnement dans l'ancien droit', *Revue historique de droit français et étranger*, 4th ser., 19–20 (1940–1), 58–87.

war, and the nature of cross-cultural transmission.[28] But as with surety and international law, captivity is an inadequate framework for an analysis of hostageship in the Middle Ages.

Many hostages shared with prisoners and captives the experience of confinement (not all, because conditional hostages did not necessarily do so), and confinement was central to the logic of hostageship. As in the cases of prisoners and captives, however, the confinement of hostages encompassed a wide range of physical experience, from the life-threateningly harsh to the luxuriously light (and in the case of conditional hostages, the merely hypothetical). As I will demonstrate in Chapter 2, conditions of confinement were not strictly determined by contractual status. This range, alongside the difficulty of generalizing from the relatively sparse evidence for the treatment of hostages, limits the potential gains of studying hostageship principally as a form of captivity or imprisonment.

In short, while elements of these various conceptual frameworks—public/private law, suretyship, captivity—are useful and make appearances in the present study, my own approach is more idiosyncratic. I have tried instead to maintain a focus on a distinct historical practice, broadly conceived: the handing over of third parties as guarantees for agreements.

FINDING HOSTAGES IN THE MEDIEVAL SOURCES

The definition of hostageship employed in the present study, developed from European and Mediterranean sources from the fifth to the fifteenth centuries, includes the following elements. First, the hostage is a *guarantor of an agreement*, and thus distinct from the captive, prisoner, or prisoner of war. Second, and consequently, a hostage is *not subject to ransom* (although a hostage may serve to guarantee the payment of a ransom for a prisoner). Third, the hostage is a *third party*—not, that is, one of the individuals whose performance is being guaranteed. Fourth, the hostage is *actually or potentially subject to loss of physical liberty*, and thus distinct from a wide variety of other forms of personal surety. Finally, the hostage is—at least in theory—*given rather than taken*; hostages may be handed over under duress, but without acknowledgement of their standing as hostages by both parties, they could not serve their function as guarantors.

Even this broad definition differs distinctly from the modern one, and the difference means that several medieval historical figures commonly described in modern terms as hostages, in medieval terms are not. It is crucial not to read back our contemporary understanding onto past events. Thus Richard the Lionheart was not taken hostage by Henry VI on his return from the Crusades, although hostages were granted to the emperor for the king's ransom.[29] The 'Burghers of

---

[28] e.g. Friedman, *Encounter*; *Les prisonniers*; Françoise Bériac-Lainé and Chris Given-Wilson, *Les prisonniers de la bataille de Poitiers* (Paris, 2002); Jarbel Rodriguez, *Captives and Their Saviors in the Medieval Crown of Aragon* (Washington, DC, 2007); Linda Colley, *Captives: Britain, Empire and the World, 1600–1850* (New York, 2004).

[29] Below, pp. 171–6.

Calais', who famously surrendered to Edward III after the capitulation of that town, were not hostages,[30] although hostages were a regular part of agreements to end sieges. The poet Charles of Orléans was not a hostage, although his younger brother, held in nearly identical circumstances, was. Galla Placidia, captured by the Visigoths and married off to their future king, was not; Aetius, her general, who also spent time among the Visigoths, was. Djem-Sultan, the fifteenth-century Turkish prince who spent time at various European courts was not; Manuel II, a fourteenth-century Byzantine prince at some of those same courts, was.[31]

Because what medieval people called a hostage was so different from the contemporary understanding, it is all the more important to be clear about the historical practices under investigation and the terms and concepts—both modern and medieval—used to describe and discuss those practices.[32] Medieval institutional historians always run the risk of turning the words in the sources on which they rely into coherent practices, by, for example, narrowing a wide semantic field to focus on a 'core meaning', or by distinguishing between technical and lay uses of words to make the evidence fit a particular pattern, or by overlooking the possibility of semantic and institutional change over time or space. Nevertheless, a historian who chooses to begin with written sources—as opposed to archaeological sources or various types of abstract models about the way the world works—must by definition begin from words, while keeping in mind the interpretative pitfalls.

In the case of the word 'hostage' and its equivalents in many languages, it is precisely the apparent disjunction between modern and earlier significations that invites attention. The modern signification as enshrined in the 1979 Convention focuses on the use of force—the 'taking' of the hostage—and on compulsion as a goal, principally in the context of international terrorism. When medieval sources use the terms that refer in modern languages to hostages, context makes clear that they do not mean hostages in the modern sense, even if we set aside concepts that might be challenged as anachronistic, such as state, international, and terrorism; relying on context is to argue for that difference, rather than to assume it. What exactly do terms for hostage mean in the medieval sources, and do they seem to be used in a consistent enough fashion that they may be relied upon as indicators of a coherent set of practices or an institution? The answer to the second of those questions is yes. The definition of hostageship given above, developed from the medieval sources, focuses not on force and compulsion, but instead on the

---

[30] Froissart 1.311–12 (4:53–62); cf. Theodor Meron, *Henry's Wars and Shakespeare's Laws: Perspectives on the Law of War in the Later Middle Ages* (Oxford, 1993), 81–4. They do not become 'hostages' until the nineteenth century; see Jean-Marie Moeglin, *Les bourgeois de Calais: Essai sur un mythe historique* (Paris, 2002), 315 n. 1 (reference from 1894).

[31] Lucy De Angulo, 'Charles and Jean d'Orléans: An Attempt to Trace the Contacts between Them during Their Captivity in England', in *Miscellanea di studi e ricerche sul quattrocento francese* (Turin, 1967), 61–92; Stewart Irvin Oost, *Galla Placidia: A Biographical Essay* (Chicago, 1968), 93–141; Nicolas Vatin, *Sultan Djem: Un prince ottoman dans l'Europe du XVᵉ siècle d'après deux sources contemporaines: Vâkʾiat-i Sultân Cem, Œuvres de Guillaume Caoursin* (Ankara, 1997); John W. Barker, *Manuel II Palaeologus (1391–1425): A Study in Late Byzantine Statesmanship* (New Brunswick, 1969), 4–20; Oskar Halecki, *Un empereur de Byzance à Rome* (Warsaw, 1930), 33–4, 62, 135, 192.

[32] Reynolds, *Fiefs*, 12–14.

contractual role of the hostage: a hostage is a form of surety, a person (potentially) deprived of liberty by a second person in order to guarantee an undertaking by a third person.[33] The hostage is thus distinct on the one hand from the captive, who is deprived of liberty, but is not a surety, and on the other from the guarantor, who is a surety, but is not deprived of liberty.

The most common Latin designation for hostage is the classical term *obses* (<*obsideo*, 'remain near'); Greek sources employ ὅμηρος. Romance language terms such as *ostaggio* and *(h)ostage* derive from the Vulgar Latin *o(b)stagium* (<*obsidaticum*), the Spanish term *rehén* from the Arabic root *rhn*; the Germanic term is *gisal* (Ger. *Geisel*).[34] Etymological discussions from nineteenth-century philologists to Derrida explore the links between the concepts of hostage and enemy (*hostis*), hostage and host (*hospes*), or hostage and guest (also *hospes*).[35] The last of those is in fact a connection that repays historical investigation, but fortunately the evidence speaks loudly enough for us to set aside speculations and examine the relationship between the words used in the medieval sources and the phenomena they seem to describe. With remarkable if not absolute consistency, the sources distinguish between hostages and captives. Authors rarely use terms for hostage to refer to captives and prisoners, employing instead words derived from roots indicating seizure (Lat. *captivus*; Fr. *prisonnier<prendre*; Ger. *Gefangene<fangen*). The philological line between hostages and other forms of surety is less clearly maintained, but the evidence does reveal distinct practices.

One way to explore these distinctions is by examining the vocabulary of individual authors. Thus the same source that describes William Marshal as a hostage (*ostage*) at Newbury does not use that term when William is years later seized by a mercenary trying to recover a debt owed by William's lord.[36] But sources that refer to hostages and captives with distinct functions in the same episode offer the best positive evidence for the use of separate sets of terms to refer to separate historical practices, one concerned with forcible seizure and the other with guarantee. The Treaty of Brétigny offers perhaps the clearest illustration. In the early years of the Hundred Years War, John II of France (1350–64) was captured by English forces at the Battle of Poitiers. The royal prisoner was finally released in 1360 against a

---

[33] Cf. the definitions, equally historically grounded, of Lutteroth (*Der Geisel*, 25: 'ein zur Sicherheit eines Anspruchs in die Gewalt des Berechtigten gegebener Mensch') and Gilissen (*SP* 1:52: 'un garant qui est privé de sa liberté pour assurer un comportement déterminé ou l'exécution d'une obligation par le garant au profit du bénéficiaire').

[34] *Novum glossarium mediae latinitatis ab anno DCCC usque ad annum MCC* (Copenhagen, 1957–), s.vv. *obses, ostagium, ostagius*; Pierre Chantraine, *Dictionnaire étymologique de la langue grecque: Histoire des mots* (Paris, 1984–90), 797; Adolf Tobler and Erhard Lommasch, *Altfranzösisches Wörterbuch* (Berlin, 1925–), s.v. *ostage*; Walther von Wartburg, *Französisches etymologisches Wörterbuch* (Bonn, 1928–), s.v. *hospes*; Elias Steinmeyer, *Althochdeutsches Wörterbuch* (Berlin, 1952–), s.v. *gisal*; Joan Corominas and José A. Pascual, *Diccionario crítico etimológico castellano e hispánico* (Madrid, 1991–2), s.v. *rehén*. The second-century etymology of Pompeius Festus (*obsides<ob fides*) was current in Charlemagne's day: Kershaw, *Peaceful Kings*, 17–18.

[35] Adolf Tobler, 'Romanische Etymologien', *Zeitschrift für romanische Philologie*, 3 (1879), 568–71; Georges Gougenheim, 'La fausse étymologie savante', *Romance Philology*, 1 (1947–8), 284–6; Maurice Tournier, 'De hôte à otage: comment en est-on venu là?', *Mots: Les langages du politique*, 25 (1990), 95–8; Jacques Derrida, *Apories: Mourir—s'attendre aux 'limites de la vérité'* (Paris, 1996), 112.

[36] *History of William Marshal*, 7003–156 (ed. Holden, 1:356–64).

promise of a ransom of 3,000,000 *écus* over a six-year period, 600,000 immediately, with the rest guaranteed by hostages, eighty-three in all.[37] Sixteen of the total of eighty-three hostages had originally been captured at Poitiers: they were prisoners of war whose ransoms were being negotiated. By the terms of the treaty their ransoms were cancelled—they were no longer captives—but they were to remain in English control as hostages. The treaty specifies that the *prisonniers* are to be 'released from their prisons'.[38] The remaining sixty-seven hostages were deprived of liberty only by the terms of the treaty: they were granted, not taken, as guarantees for the king's, not their own, ransom. In 1369, when open warfare resumed, those hostages that remained once again became prisoners. A court case concerning Jacques Capelet from 1383 reports that while serving as a hostage (*obses*) in England, he was captured (*captus*) by the English and held prisoner (*retentus prisionarius*) there; in addition, he was at that point assigned his own ransom.[39] For the individuals who composed these documents, hostage and prisoner were distinct categories.

A thousand years before Brétigny, this same distinction was articulated in an account of an agreement between the emperor Julian (360–3) and the Chamavi. Eunapius reports that Julian:

> granted peace, demanding hostages (ὅμηρα) as a pledge. When they said that those whom the Romans had captured (αἰχμαλώτους) were sufficient, Julian replied that he held them as a result of the fighting, not by agreement: now he was seeking their best men, lest they use deceit in respect of the peace-agreement. They agreed and begged him to name whom he wished. In reply he demanded the king's son, whom he held as a prisoner (αἰχμάλωτον), pretending that he did not have him.

Julian, moved by pity, ultimately revealed the boy to the Chamavi and proposed to keep him as a hostage, but Eunapius has the emperor clarify that because he was 'not handed over by you under agreement, but taken in war' and 'not received from you as a pledge of peace, but whom I hold as proof of our bravery against you', the boy would not be subject to punishment in case of violation of the agreement. Furthermore, in the end only the king's mother served as a hostage. The same author tells of the dealings between Julian and Vadomar: 'when he had handed over his son as hostage (ὅμηρον... δεδωχὼς) until he returned the captives whom he had taken in his raid (αἰχμαλώτους... συνηρπασμένους), he demanded the return of the hostage even though he had not restored the captives, making many threats if this were not done. Julian returned the son to Vadomar, adding only that in his eyes one youth was not a worthwhile hostage for so many better-born persons.'[40] This last example employs another verbal distinction that helps to separate

---

[37] Below, pp. 163–5.

[38] *Les grands traités de la Guerre de Cent Ans*, 2.15 (CTH 7:51–2): 'Item est accordé que les dessus diz seze prisonniers, qui venront demourer en hostage pour le Roi de France, comme dit est, seront parmi ce delivrés de leurs prisons, sanz paier aucunes raencons pour le temps passé.'

[39] GCA 428–32; L. de Lauwereyns de Roosendaele, *Les otages de Saint-Omer, 1360–1371: Épisode de la Paix de Brétigny* (Saint-Omer, 1879), 71–2.

[40] Eunap. fr. 18.6, 19 (trans. Blockley, 2:25–7, 29). Similarly, *Annales de Saint-Bertin*, s.a. 862 (SHF 88–9).

practices: captives are taken, hostages are given. Thus in Carolingian narrative sources, the most common verbs associated with hostages are *dare* (give), *accipere* (accept), and *recipere* (receive). Anglo-Saxon uses *sellan* (give). In later French language sources one finds the term *bailler* (give). To indicate the force that could lie behind such grants, authors might add that debtors were ordered to make them, as in Roger of Wendover's description of a Welsh grant to Harold Godwinson: 'compelled by necessity, they granted hostages to him'.[41] But Harold did not 'seize hostages'. The conceptual distinction between a hostage granted and a captive seized is maintained.[42]

The administrative register of Philip II Augustus of France (1180–1223) also distinguishes between hostages and captives. It contains both a list of hostages (*hostagii*) granted by Flemish towns in 1213 and a list of prisoners (*prisones*) taken at the Battle of Bouvines in 1214. The former are mentioned as hostages (*obsides*) in contemporary chronicle entries. Additionally, the latter text includes a list of those prisoners who had been returned or released against sureties (*hostagiati*).[43] The same distinction appears in the text of a treaty of 1196 between Philip and Richard I of England ('captives and the hostages of captives'), and in a memorandum of receipt issued by John of England in 1214 that carefully separates the statuses of five hostages and four prisoners, all of whom had been in the custody of the same individual.[44] Episodes where hostages are exchanged for prisoners, as between the German emperor Frederic I (1155–90) and the Milanese, also highlight this difference.[45]

As both the Treaty of Brétigny and the story of Julian and the Chamavi show, captives could become hostages.[46] Conversely, hostages could become captives, as when sometime after 1431 the castle where the guarantors for the ransom of Guillaume de Châteauvillain were being held was seized; as a later complaint to the royal court of Parlement reveals, they were themselves treated as prisoners of war and put to ransom.[47] At about the same time, a French source describes

[41] Roger of Wendover, *Flores historiarum*, s.a. 1063 (ed. Coxe, 1:503): 'necessitate compulsi, obsides illi dederunt'. Similarly, John of Worcester, *Chronicle*, s.a. 934 (OMT 2:390).

[42] Kosto, 'Carolingian', 131. Sources do occasionally refer to the taking or seizure or holding of hostages, although this is not the norm; e.g.: *Historia Francorum Senonensis* (MGH SS 9:365); *Chronicon Sancti Petri Vivi* (ed. Bautier and Gilles, 70); *Annales S. Columbae Senonensis*, s.a. 911 (MGH SS 1:104); *Chronique de Saint-Pierre de Bèze*, s.a. 911 (ed. Garnier, 280); *Gesta Stephani* 105 (OMT 200); *Chronica regia Coloniensis*, s.a. 1162 (MGH SrG 18:113); Richard of San Germano, *Chronica*, s.a. 1191 (MGH SrG 53:9); *Annales Casinenses*, s.a. 1191 (MGH SS 19:315); Morigia, *Chronicon Modoetiense*, 3.39 (RIS 12:1155); *HGL* 8:463–5 (no. 103), 10:616–20 (no. 223); Monstrelet 2.17 (4:186); *GCA* 69; etc.

[43] *Les registres de Philippe Auguste*, 1:558–66 (Miscellanea 12–13); *Histoire des ducs de Normandie et des rois d'Angleterre* (SHF 126, 136); Sigebert of Gembloux, *Chronica*, cont. Bergensis (MGH SS 6:439). *Hostagiati* probably refers to conditional hostages. On 1213, see below, pp. 92–3.

[44] *Diplomatic Documents*, 18 (no. 6) ('prisones et hostagii prisonum'); *Foedera*, 1.1:120.

[45] *Gesta Federici I. imperatoris in Lombardia* (MGH SrG 27:46); perhaps also *Annales Fuldenses*, s.a. 871 (MGH SrG 7:74).

[46] Similarly, Alpert of Metz, *De diversitate temporum*, 2.21 (MGH SS 4:720); John of Trokelowe, *Annales*, s.a. 1317 (RS 28.3:101).

[47] Bossuat, 'Châteauvillain', 24; similarly, *GCA* 442–55.

how the Burgundians 'gave hostages' to the duke of Alençon, but then 'seized and retained prisoners...in order to recover their hostages'.[48] The Arabic and Latin sources for Richard I's infamous massacre of the Muslim garrison after the siege of Acre (1191) seem inconsistent in their descriptions, but that inconsistency is grounded in the polemical nature of the sources, which exploit precisely the distinction between hostages and captives: if the garrison were hostages rather than captives, Richard was perfectly justified in killing them, for Saladin had violated his agreement.[49] The exact meaning of many references to *obsides* remains ambiguous, but rarely is a term usually reserved for hostages clearly applied to captives.[50] The reverse—terms usually reserved for prisoners or captives applied to hostages—is more common, especially to describe their *condition* (for example, *in captionem* or *tenere prisonum*) rather than their *status* (*captivus, prisonarius*), but even this is unusual.[51] In general, the language of the medieval sources distinguishes between the historical phenomena of hostageship and captivity.[52]

The philological line between hostages and other forms of personal surety, which were much more common in most contexts throughout the medieval period, is less clearly drawn than the one between hostages and captives. Here words alone are a less secure indicator of historical practice. Terms that normally refer to sureties other than hostages are only rarely used independently to indicate individuals actually or potentially in captivity. When this occurs, it may simply be a stylistic choice, for example as a way to vary vocabulary. William of Malmesbury, describing the mechanics of the prisoner exchange involving King Stephen and Robert of Gloucester in 1140, refers to the queen, prince, and magnates left to ensure Robert's safety as *vades* (pledges) for the earl's release, while a few lines later Robert's son, who served a precisely parallel function, is (twice) *in obsidatu*.[53] On the other hand, *obses* and particularly *(h)ostage* and its cognates do appear in reference to individuals acting as sureties of various sorts but whose liberty was never at risk, as is made explicit in some charters: an *obses* who promises to seize compensation from the debtor's goods in case of violation, and *obsides* who are to make amends for a violation; a *fideiussor et obses* who undertakes to 'provide compensation from his own land'; and more dramatically, a count of Namur labelled both *obses et fideiussor* and *testis et ostagius ac fideiussor* who will, if necessary, defend in battle with his sword a

[48] *Chronique de la Pucelle*, 54 (ed. Vallet de Viriville, 309–10): 'donnèrent aucuns hostages ès mains du duc d'Alençon...prindrent et retindrent prisonniers aucuns des gens dudict duc d'Alençon, pour recouvrer leurs hostages'.

[49] Kosto, 'Crusades', 21–4.

[50] Middle High German literature, where *gisl* often indicates a prisoner, is a notable exception: e.g. *Kudrun*, 15.804, 30.1600, 1610 (ed. Bartsch, 170, 339, 341); *Das Nibelungenlied*, 4.190, 217, 236, 238, 250, 15.878, 36.2105, 38.2297, 39.2337, 2351, 2364 (ed. Bartsch and Boor, 38, 42, 45, 47, 148, 329, 359, 365, 367, 369). See Lawn, *'Gefangenschaft'*, 297–8.

[51] e.g. *GCA* 309, 329, 401, 443; Monstrelet 2.245 (5:407); *Royal and Other Historical Letters*, 475 (RS 27.2:72–4); *Foedera*, 1.1:67–8. See also Kosto, 'Carolingian', 131–4.

[52] Although see below, pp. 68–9.

[53] William of Malmesbury, *Historia Novella*, 57 (OMT 106). See also Monstrelet 1.262 ('plèges...lesquelz pour seureté de ce obligèrent corps et biens'), 2.11 (*plaiges*), 2.17 (*seuretez*) (4:97, 169, 186); *HGL* 10:619 (no. 223) (*pleiges*).

donation by one of his men.[54] When King Henry II of England declared himself a *hostagius* for the customs granted by the count of Eu to the burghers of that town, nobody imagined that he would be entering anyone's custody.[55] On occasion, *ostagius* and *obses* even refer to property rather than persons.[56] The fact that terminology might vary within the same documentary context, coupled with the dizzyingly complex and constantly evolving nature of suretyship in the Middle Ages, adds a further layer of difficulty.[57] To complicate matters even more, theological discussion of the Eucharist or the figure of Christ himself as a pledge (*pignus*), or of relics as pledges (again, *pignus*), certainly coloured the vocabulary choices of many clerical authors and scribes.[58] Bernard of Clairvaux labels Christ an *obses* in one sermon, while John of Salisbury describes someone swearing an oath as giving 'God and, as they say, his Christianity as *obsides*'.[59] Finally, the integral study in this book of both sureties handed over at the formation of an agreement (true hostages) and sureties to be handed over after violation of an agreement (conditional hostages) means that evidence that a given individual is not in custody does not allow the conclusion that we are not dealing with a hostage.[60]

The area in which it is most difficult to determine the precise role of sureties is that of judicial (or arbitrational) procedure: guarantors for appearance at a tribunal or adherence to its judgment. The *bons pleges* of the *Chanson de Roland*—the thirty relatives handed over by Ganelon—are the most famous case, if a problematic one. They are clearly in custody: Charlemagne orders them held and ultimately executes them. What is not clear is whether they are guarantors of an undertaking; they are killed as a result of Pinabel's loss of the duel—proof of Ganelon's treachery—not because Ganelon or they failed to do something related to the trial. Similarly, in *Raoul de Cambrai*, Bernier grants his father to the king before a duel, but the king has requested a hostage because *he* himself has agreed to stand as a guarantor of Bernier's oath.[61] 'Hostages' for appearance and for adherence to judgments or

---

[54] *Cartulaire de Sainte-Croix d'Orléans*, 111–12 (no. 58); *Cartulaire de l'abbaye de Savigny*, 1:421 (Savigny, no. 804); *Cartulaire de l'abbaye de Saint-Aubin d'Angers*, 1:181 (no. 155) ('idem de propria terra excambium rectum persolvet'); *Actes des comtes de Namur*, 50–1 (no. 20).

[55] BnF, ms. lat. 13904, fols. 1v–2r. In a previous agreement (fol. 1v, fragmentary), the king was termed a *plegius*. See *Calendar of Documents Preserved in France*, 524 (no. 1418). Cf. royals as *obsides* in *Recueil…Louis VI*, 2:297–300, 479–81, 3:88 (no. 380; ap. 3, no. 4; Interventions de Louis VI, no. 15).

[56] *Regula Magistri*, 87.125 (SC 106:366); *Recueil…Philippe Auguste*, 2:96 (no. 546); *Foedera*, 1.1:451–2, 454 (Mise of Lewes, a. 1265; the same text refers to a human *obses*); Amalio Marichalar and Cayetano Manrique, *Historia de la legislacion y recitaciones del derecho civil de España*, vol. 5 (Madrid, 1862), 35–6, 38–9 (Aragonese Privilege of Union, a. 1287); William of Newburgh, *Historia rerum Anglicarum*, 2.38 (RS 82.1:198) (Treaty of Falaise, a. 1174).

[57] See e.g. *Layettes*, 1:400, 2:90–1, 93 (nos. 1069, 1796–9, 1804), all documents concerning the counts of Comminges: in the first (a. 1214), *obses* refers to a hostage; in the rest (a. 1226), it seems to refer to simple guarantors. On medieval suretyship generally: Walliser, *Bürgschaftsrecht*; *SP*; Stacey, *Road*.

[58] Niermeyer, *Lexicon*, s.v. *pignus* 3.

[59] Bernard of Clairvaux, *Sermones in nativitate Domini*, 5.1 (ed. LeClerq and Rochais, 4:266); John of Salisbury, *Letters*, 298 (OMT 2:694) ('primo Deum et [ut dici solet] Christianitatem suam obsidem dabat'); cf. *La vie de Seint Auban*, 292–3 (ed. Harden, 9); *Charters of Saint Paul's, London*, 221–2 (ap. 1).

[60] Below, Chapter 5; similar cautions at *SP* 2:315–16, 497–8.

[61] *The Song of Roland*, 278.3846–9, 288.3947–59 (ed. Brault, 2:234, 240); *Raoul de Cambrai*, 228.4748–51 (ed. Kay, 294); cf. Albert of Aachen, *Historia Ierosolimitana*, 4.45 (OMT 318).

arbitrations do appear in later medieval records. For example, hostages were turned over to Lothar III for his arbitration of the contested papal election of 1133 *pro servando iudicio*, while in a dispute between the counts of Forcalquier and Provence, mediated by Peter II of Aragon in 1204, the parties named at the outset of the notice as hostages to abide by the king's *mandatum* are identical to the conditional hostages named at the end of the document, who promise to enter into the king's custody in case of a future dispute. These are both clear cases of hostages for performance.[62] Rebels from Bordeaux arrested in England in 1249 were released to stand trial back in Gascony only after they had granted true hostages to the king to 'submit to the justice of our court'. These are plausibly hostages for appearance.[63] But in the majority of cases involving judicial procedure, it is simply impossible to determine if the pledge has entered or is promising to enter into custody.[64] Furthermore, even in cases where pledges were explicitly liable with their bodies—to be put in prison if the defendant did not appear, for example—this obligation seems rarely to have been enforced; monetary fines were more likely.[65] The procedural hostage thus plays less of a role than might be expected in the present study.

Given the slipperiness of the vocabulary of personal surety, how should we proceed? Consider the following passage recording the text of the peace settlement of 1174 between Henry II of England and his sons after their rebellion:

> Prisoners (*prisones*) who made a pact with the lord king before the peace made with the lord king—namely the king of Scotland, and the earl of Leicester, and the earl of Chester, and Ralph de Fougères, and their hostages (*obsides*)—and the hostages of other prisoners whom he had held (*habuerat*) before that time, shall be excluded from this agreement. Other prisoners on each side ought to be released, that is, the king will accept hostages (*obsides accipiet*) from those of his prisoners from whom he wishes to have (*habere*) them and who are able to give (*dare*) them; and from the others he will have security (*securitatem*) by their faith and oath and that of their friends.[66]

Prisoners grant hostages to guarantee the terms of their release. Ralph de Fougères had in fact granted his sons for his release ('dedit obsides') after his capture in the

---

[62] MGH Const. 1:166–7 (no. 114); Guy de Tournadre, *Histoire du Comté de Forcalquier (XIIème siècle)* (Paris, 1930), 231–40 (no. 7). Cf. Schacht, 'Foreign Elements', 137.

[63] *Foedera*, 1.1:271 ('stabunt judicio curiæ nostræ'); cf. 275–6. See also below, p. 111.

[64] *SP* 2:282–8, 501–25; although various authors cite examples of conditional procedural hostages (507 n. 74, 519 n. 102, 522 n. 115, 523 n. 117, 524 n. 118), true hostages appear only at 524 n. 121. See however R. C. Van Caenegem, *Geschiedenis van het strafrecht in Vlaanderen van de XIe tot de XIVe eeuw* (Brussels, 1954), 264–80; Kosto, 'Crusades', 14–15; and below, pp. 122, 141, 142, 143, 144, 211. Cf. in a different context MGH Leges (in Folio) 4:225 (c. 28), with Huguette Taviani-Carozzi, *La principauté lombarde de Salerne (IXe–XIe siècle): Pouvoir et société en Italie lombarde méridionale*, 2 vols. (Rome, 1991), 1:245.

[65] *SP* 1:72–3, 2:57–81.

[66] Roger of Howden, *Chronica*, s.a. (RS 51.2:68) [*Foedera*, 1.1:30]: 'Prisones vero qui cum domino rege finem fecerunt ante factam pacem cum domino rege, videlicet rex Scotiæ, et comes Leicestriæ, et comes Cestriæ, et Radulfus de Fulgeriis, et obsides eorum, et obsides aliorum prisonum quos prius habuerat, sint extra conventionem istam. Alii autem prisones ex utraque parte deliberari debent, ita scilicet quod dominus rex obsdies accipiet de prisonibus suis de quibus habere voluerit, et qui dare poterunt. Et de aliis habebit securitatem per fidem et sacramentum suum et amicorum suorum.' See W. L. Warren, *Henry II* (Berkeley, 1978), 136–9.

previous year.[67] As we will see, the use of sons is a first indication that we are dealing here with custodial hostages rather than non-captive guarantors, although it is not proof. The Treaty of Falaise by which William I of Scotland was freed against hostages was not concluded formally until after this settlement, but the terms may already have been on the table. Here too, then, an independent text supports the interpretation that hostages are in custody: the verb used to refer to them in the treaty is *liberare*.[68] The earls of Leicester and Chester were kept in captivity, and thus never provided hostages, although the first mention of hostages in this passage need not refer to all four figures. In the absence of hostages, prisoners could also be released on their honour, supported by oaths of their friends acting as non-captive guarantors. We can be fairly confident in this case that the word *obsides* indicates the phenomenon of custodial hostageship.

Contrast with this a passage from a roughly contemporary charter, recording a sale to the abbey of Silvanès in the Rouèrgue in 1151. A group of vendors transferred a plot of land to the abbey in return for 350 *s*. Two of the vendors were under-age, so they promised that when they reached the age of majority, they would confirm the sale. They supported this undertaking with guarantees:

> we have given as primary sureties (*fideijussores*) to you [seven names are listed] who have all given their faith in the hand of lord Peter, bishop of Rodez, that they will serve as hostages (*ostatgue*) without deceit when they are ordered to do so by the bishop or the abbot or their successors, either by themselves or by their representatives, until the aforesaid sale has been conceded and confirmed by us. We have also given as secondary sureties (*manulevatores*) [two names are listed] who have similarly said in the hand of the aforesaid bishop that they will serve as hostages (*ostatgue*) without deceit if the primary sureties (*fideijussores*) fail—let it not happen—to fulfil their promises.[69]

Fideiussores and *manulevatores* are common enough labels for sureties in documents from Southern Francia, as is the recourse to multiple layers of guarantee. The reference to service as hostages when warned is plausibly a reference to a promise to enter into the custody of the bishop—conditional hostageship of the sort that is described more precisely in contemporary documents from this region. The fact that the grant of land is relatively substantial, and that major local figures are involved in the transaction, could support such an argument. On the other hand, in other documents, references of this sort to 'hostageship' are clearly to routine, non-custodial surety. It is simply impossible to say with confidence whether or not

---

[67] Robert of Torigni, *Chronica*, s.a. 1173 (RS 82.4:261).

[68] *Anglo-Scottish Relations*, 3–4 (no. 1).

[69] *Cartulaire de l'abbaye de Silvanès*, 48–50 (no. 61): 'Et est sciendum quod nos duo fratres, Arnaldus et Raimundus, promisimus in manu domni Petri, Rutenensis episcopi, domino Deo et tibi Guiraldo, abbati, quod, cum majores annis scilicet XXV erimus, predictam vendicionem tibi predicto Guiraldo, abbati, vel tuis successoribus laudabimus et confirmabimus; de quo fideijussores tibi dedimus...qui omnes fidem suam dederunt in manu domni Petri, Rutenensis episcopi, se tenere ostatgue sine dolo cum commoniti fuerint ab ipso episcopo vel abbate vel ab eorum successoribus vel per se vel per nuncios suos, donec a nobis concessa et confirmata sit predicta vendicio. Dedimus autem manulevatores...qui similiter in manu predicti episcopi dixerunt se tenere ostatgue sine dolo, si fideijussores, quod absit, mentirentur.'

these *fideiussores* and *manulevatores* who promise to serve in *ostatgue* are promising to enter into custody.

These two examples represent the extremes of an interpretative grey area: we cannot be certain, as we can in some cases, that the sureties in question conform to the definition of hostage used in this study; on the other hand, we cannot be certain, as we can in some cases, that they do not conform to that definition. Given the geographical and chronological range as well as the generic variety of the sources examined in this study, there is no fixed rule to follow when attempting to move from the words used in the sources to an understanding of historical practice. In the face of these challenges, I have tried to maintain a conservative approach, identifying individuals as hostages only where context or an independent source makes likely the fact of or potential for physical custody—when the evidence is closer to the treaty of Henry II than to the charter of Silvanès. What emerges from such a reading of the sources is that in general, across time and space, the personal surety subject to loss of personal liberty, rather than solely to financial or some other sort of liability, receives a separate designation: hostage.

In addition to the challenge of determining what historical practice lies behind a given word, there is the problem of the trustworthiness of the sources.[70] Even if we can be confident that in a particular case *obses* means hostage, how can we be certain that the incident described in fact happened—that a particular individual served or was offered as a hostage? Leaving aside problems of transmission (are the words we read today the words that were written by the medieval author or scribe, or have they been altered by later copyists or editors?[71]), any given document might be a forgery or contain a meaningless fossilized formula, and even the simplest chronicle cannot be trusted as a neutral source. The anonymous *Deeds of the Hungarians* (*c.*1200), for example, record numerous cases of the Árpád rulers receiving hostages during their conquest of Transylvania in the tenth century. Much of this history, however, is thought to be fabricated, and the descriptions of hostages are likely an attempt to model early Hungarian history on Carolingian and Roman precedents: receiving hostages is simply something that conquerors did, therefore the Árpáds must have done so, too.[72] Students of hagiography (the study of saints' lives) have established that while the main stories are often tropes rather than specific to the saint in question, the incidental details are likely to be appropriate to the time and place of composition.[73] Saint Benedict may or may not have miraculously caused a fountain to appear on Monte Cassino, but if there was no fountain on Monte Cassino (Gregory the Great wrote that it runs 'even to this day'), the

---

[70] See also Kosto, 'Carolingian', 126–7.

[71] See e.g. below, p. 49 (a. 876).

[72] *Die 'Gesta Hungarorum' des anonymen Notars*, 9–12, 18, 20–1, 29, 33, 37, 42, 44–5, 59–62 (ed. Veszprémy and Silagi, 46, 48, 50, 52, 66, 68, 70, 72, 80, 86, 90, 100, 104, 106, 114, 116, 120).

[73] Friedrich Lotter, 'Methodisches zur Gewinnung historischer Erkenntnisse aus hagiographischen Quellen', *Historische Zeitschrift*, 229 (1979), 298–356; Paul Fouracre, 'Merovingian History and Merovingian Hagiography', *Past & Present*, 127 (1990), 3–38; although note the cautions of Timothy Reuter, *Medieval Polities and Modern Mentalities*, ed. Janet L. Nelson (Cambridge, 2006), 96–7. See also in a very different context William Ian Miller, *Audun and the Polar Bear: Luck, Law, and Largesse in a Medieval Tale of Risky Business* (Leiden, 2008), 15–21.

audience would have taken note. More to the point, Saint Leonard may or may not have miraculously freed chained prisoners from dungeons in eleventh-century Southern Francia, but if there were no prisoners, no chains, and no dungeons, the stories would have no resonance.[74]

The same approach may be taken, I argue, with the sources of institutional history. The chronicler Enguerrand de Monstrelet's description of the breakdown of the agreement for the surrender of Senlis in 1418 during the Hundred Years War may present a pro-Burgundian account of the events. One might even hypothesize that his story of the killing of the hostages there is a fabrication.[75] But if hostages were not given for these sorts of arrangements, the particular story would raise questions in the minds of Monstrelet's audience about his account. Furthermore, the dozens of similar accounts in Monstrelet would call into question the entire work. Likewise, unless the intention of the forger of a charter was to misrepresent the nature of the guarantees, rather than who owned what and when, an inaccurate description of those guarantees would call into question the charter as a whole, undercutting the deception. Similarly, the fact that an author draws directly on biblical language in describing hostages does not necessarily diminish the value of a source.[76] The hostageship of William Marshal in 1152 is known only from a verse biography composed shortly after his death in 1219, and thus only from memories of an old man's tales of his youth, or stories then circulating among his men. The poet erred throughout the work in details and indulged in pure fiction.[77] None of that, however, reduces the historical value of the story and its utility as a point of entry into the study of medieval hostageship. As this study is interested in the institution itself, rather than in its role in particular episodes, a generalized approach is valid: proving any individual source inaccurate—and I am certain that, given the range of sources used, this is possible—does little to change the overall picture and argument.

OUTLINE

Medieval hostages were fundamentally guarantees for agreements, but they were often much more. It is precisely in the ways that hostageship fits into broader social, legal, and political frameworks that the development of the institution may be followed. Hostageship thus offers a novel way to trace the evolution of medieval

---

[74] Gregory I, *Dialogues*, 2.5.3 (SC 260:154) ('ut nunc usque ubertim defluat'); Pierre Bonnassie, 'Hagiographie et Paix de Dieu dans le Sud-Ouest de la France (Xe–début XIIe siècle)', in Bonnassie, *Les sociétés de l'an mil: Un monde entre deux âges* (Brussels, 2001), 325–36; for release miracles of St Germanus concerning actual hostages, see *Historia Selebiensis monasterii*, 2.12–14 (ed. Fowler, [38]–[39]).

[75] In this case, however, a pro-French account confirms the story; below, pp. 108–9. See also Kosto, 'Carolingian', 126–7.

[76] Particularly 1 Mc 9:53 ('accipit filios principum regionis obsides') and 11:62 ('dedit illis dextram et accipit filios eorum obsides'); e.g. Helmold, *Cronica Slavorum*, 2.106 (MGH SrG 32:208), and below, pp. 70–1 (*obsides* and *dextras*).

[77] Crouch, *William Marshal*, 1–11; *History of William Marshal*, 3:26–41.

societies. The point of the ambitious chronological and geographical scope of this book is not to allow a fruitless hunt for institutional origins, but rather to render visible important and large-scale changes. The story told is not strikingly new: Rome still falls, something big still happens in the eleventh century, and the rise of the early modern nation-state still matters. But if the story of hostageship does not challenge traditional chronologies—in fact, it reinforces them—it does help us understand better the ways agreements were made and kept, and how those with power ruled and those without it responded.

Chapter 2 expands on some of the material in this introductory chapter, presenting the variety of forms of medieval hostageship from across the whole period. I show that in terms of the subject of the agreements for which hostages were granted and their structure, as well as the identity and treatment of the hostages themselves, there was no 'typical' medieval hostage. Nonetheless, certain core questions concerning hostageship remain important throughout the Middle Ages, allowing for a general exploration of the logic of hostageship.

Chapter 3 surveys hostageship in the early Middle Ages. I show how, in the context of the break-up of Carolingian hegemony, the symbolic and communicative aspects of this sort of hostageship were as, if not more, important than its guaranteeing function, and how the political significance of hostages extended well beyond the interests of the grantor and the receiver. Hostageship in the early Middle Ages emerges as deeply embedded in structures of family and practices of alliance that shaped the contemporary political landscape.

For the period before 1000, my geographical net is cast very widely—focused on the Carolingian and post-Carolingian evidence, but touching on regions from Russia and Central Asia in the east to the Celtic and Scandinavian borderlands in the west and north. I have also, for this period, aimed at comprehensiveness; while I have surely not identified every hostage in the sources from the first millennium, I have tried to do so.[78]

Such a comprehensive approach becomes impossible after the millennium, principally because of an explosion in the amount of evidence and a diversification of the institution of hostageship itself. There is a danger, of course, that these two reasons are connected—that we see more and different kinds of hostages simply because there are more and different kinds of evidence. The attempt at comprehensive coverage for the earlier period is in part an attempt to address this problem, but concerns about dramatic evidentiary change masking underlying historical continuity should be assuaged, if not eliminated, by other factors. First, convincing arguments have been made for changes in some of the broader frameworks in which I see hostageship as embedded, for example the conduct of warfare, or the commercialization of society. These arguments could be just as wrong, and for the same reasons, but I think it is much more likely that they are independent checks on the proposed chronology of hostageship than the building blocks of a circular argument. Second, the development of hostageship is in some contexts linked to the development of the institutions that produced the documentation; in other

[78] There are some 325 cases between 500 and 1000; not all are cited here.

words, the existence of more evidence is not a neutral fact but a comprehensible historical phenomenon.

Instead of attempting to provide a comprehensive picture of hostageship from the eleventh to the fifteenth century, Chapters 4 to 6 concentrate on what changes, at the expense of the many aspects of hostageship that do continue from the earlier period. The most striking change, which offers the key to understanding all the others, is the reappearance of female hostages, or rather women who are *designated* as hostages. The Greeks explicitly used women as hostages, but the Romans did not, and although Tacitus claims that the 'Germans' did, there is no good evidence for it. Only a handful of examples, far-flung and of questionable value, survive from Late Antiquity and fewer still from the eighth to the tenth centuries; by 1200 they are routine. I argue that the appearance of female hostages marks a shift of hostageship out of the framework of family and alliance that predominated in the early Middle Ages and into one that was at once more de-individualized, commercialized, and bureaucratic.

Chapter 4 goes on to examine how hostages become important not as individuals, but as representatives of larger groups; how they developed new roles in the conduct of warfare, particularly concerning ransom and conditional respite; and finally how they spread from the realm of war, politics, and diplomacy into the world of simple financial transactions. Chapter 5 studies the early history of an entirely new form of hostageship in which the human pledge is not handed over immediately but simply promised. In examining this history, I show that what has been interpreted as a tangential development in the history of law is very much a part of the story of hostageship in the Middle Ages. Conditional hostages play important roles in the spread of hostageship to financial transactions, with crucial implications for our interpretation of the relationship between the worlds of lordship and commerce, and are a key to understanding the earliest written political treaties.

Chapter 6 builds on the superb documentation for some of the most well-known cases of hostageship in the Middle Ages, namely hostages granted for the ransom and release of captive kings: Baldwin II of Jerusalem and Richard I of England in the twelfth century, Louis IX of France and Charles II of Naples in the thirteenth, David II of Scotland in the fourteenth, and James I of Scotland in the fifteenth. While tying together themes from the previous two chapters, these case studies offer a density of detail that is often missing in other contexts, allowing for a careful reconstruction of the social, political, and financial networks that underlay royal authority, and on which opponents knew how to draw in shaping guarantees. In postponing the discussion of these cases, I aim to avoid placing too much weight on them in developing my arguments about hostageship generally. The bulk of the evidence adduced in this study does concern elites, but, as Chapters 4 and 5 show, that category extends well beyond the royal milieux examined in these particular cases.

The later medieval chapters are less wide-ranging than the earlier ones, principally because of the gravitational pull of rich bodies of evidence. In choosing areas to explore, I have tried to match well evidence to themes; English and French sources for the Hundred Years War, for example, put a particularly strong stamp on the discussions of hostages in warfare in Chapter 4. Nonetheless, I also devote substantial sections there and elsewhere to evidence from the Low Countries, Italy, Iberia, and the Crusader States. If there is less on the core lands of the German Empire, and less still on Scandinavia, eastern Europe, Byzantium and various regions of the Islamic world, that is a result of the state of the sources and my own expertise, linguistic and otherwise. I hope that the occasional consideration of these 'peripheral' areas strengthens the argument, and that what was set aside—and there was a lot of it—would not have changed the overall picture in significant ways. Similarly, the history of hostages related in the pages that follow touches on so many themes and subjects that it has been impossible to do more than gesture at the implications of hostageship for some of them; my hope is that readers can follow those gestures if so inclined, and that they will see other connections that I have not noted or even imagined.

Chapters 2 to 6 interpret medieval hostageship for the modern reader. The arguments presented there do help to understand how medieval people thought of the institution, but only in an indirect sense. Chapter 7 begins by gathering the limited direct evidence for the medieval understanding of hostageship. How did people react when a king received or granted hostages? Or when they themselves were called upon to serve? Or when a hostage was executed? Stray remarks of chroniclers offer some answers. I also examine more closely the words and deeds of the papacy, which provide the closest thing to an interpretation that was meant to be pan-European. The answers in both cases are varied: there was no single understanding. Certain words and deeds of the popes, however, those that were included in the basic texts of canon law and were much discussed by medieval commentators, prove to be at the root of our modern understanding of hostages.

I am conscious of the fact that the geographical and chronological range of the evidence adduced—particularly in Chapters 2 and 7, where I discuss side by side cases separated by hundreds of years and thousands of miles—has drawbacks. The first is to downplay the very real differences among societies and historical contexts. For the purposes of arguing that hostageship was characteristic of medieval political life, this concern is outweighed by the benefits of highlighting commonalities. On the one hand, the use of a person as a pledge is a very basic human institution, found in societies throughout history and notably in interactions *between* different peoples.[79] On the other, it is increasingly apparent that from early on the medieval world was interconnected in surprising ways. For both of these reasons, events far removed in time and space can prove mutually illuminating. The second drawback is to undercut the chronological aspects of my argument. The non-chronological approach in Chapter 2 is deliberate, as there I aim to provide the reader with an institutional and conceptual vocabulary with which to understand the evidence discussed in the rest of the book. In the first half of Chapter 7, it is instead the limited nature of the evidence that necessitates the approach; there, too, however, the findings are broadly applicable to what has come before. As for

[79] *SP.*

the rest, the chronological progressions will be clear, whether between Chapters 3 and 4, or within Chapters 5 and 6.

Chronology returns at the end, as Chapter 7 and the book close by tracing briefly hostageship and its interpretations through early modern writers on international law to the Nuremberg War Crimes Tribunals and the International Convention of 1979. Readers will find that the institution of hostageship and views on it changed considerably after the medieval period that is the focus of this study. That later history shows why the story of William Marshal, which would have been perfectly comprehensible until quite recently, now requires explanation.

2

Varieties and Logics of Medieval Hostageship

A medieval hostage was a personal surety subject to loss of physical liberty—an individual subject to confinement as a guarantee for the obligations or undertakings of a second person or group to a third person or group. In principle, the hostage as guarantor (like any sort of guarantor) could be useful in any sort of transaction that created an obligation or duty for one or both parties—in other words, where a promise of future behaviour was involved. In practice, hostages are found as guarantors in the medieval period in particular sorts of agreements. Similarly, in principle, any third party could serve as a hostage, as long as the detention of that person could affect the future action or behaviour of one of the parties to the agreement; in practice, particular categories of individuals served as hostages. In principle, hostages were to be kept in honourable custody until the violation of an agreement removed all restraints; in practice, their treatment in the medieval period varied widely. Finally, hostage agreements might be structured in a wide variety of ways, for example unilaterally (one-sided grant) or bilaterally (exchange), and with differently constituted deadlines or means of fulfilling the guaranteed obligation. Thus in terms of the subject of the underlying agreement, its structure, and the identity and treatment of the guarantor, there is no 'typical' medieval hostage. The first task of the present chapter is to survey the variety of medieval hostage agreements. The approach here is synchronic, with examples drawn from a broad chronological and geographical range. Subsequent chapters will put this picture in motion, as the identities of hostages, the sorts of agreements for which they were granted, and the way those agreements were structured change over time. What remains fairly constant, however, is a set of problems surrounding the use of hostages: how hostages could function as guarantees, and whether or not they were effective. An exploration of the *logic* of hostageship, the second goal of the present chapter, will help us to interpret its history.

VARIETIES OF HOSTAGESHIP

The previous chapter has already introduced a number of different kinds of agreements secured by hostages. The case of William Marshal, like the surrender of Senlis in 1418, involved a promise to surrender a castle. The cases of Richard the Lionheart and the Treaty of Brétigny involved promises to pay a ransom. The 1174 agreement between the kings of England and Scotland referred to hostages for release from captivity, presumably to guarantee promises of good behaviour. The hostages requested by the emperor Julian from the Chamavi were related to their promise not to violate a peace treaty. What ties all of these situations together is the presence of a promise. In the absence of a promise—an undertaking to act or not act in the future—there is nothing to guarantee, hence no need for any kind of guarantor, let alone a hostage. Focus on this time-element offers a convenient way to analyse the variety of hostage transactions.

A promise may be indefinite, with no end in sight. In an *open-ended agreement* of this sort, the behaviour or action guaranteed by the hostage is meant to be ongoing. The party granting the hostage may do something to violate the agreement and thus forfeit the hostage; but there is no way that the party granting the hostage can end his or her obligation by the performance of a specific action—the action must be repeated—thus there is no fixed point built into the agreement at which the hostage is to be released. Likewise, an open-ended agreement does not set a specific date at which the agreement will be considered over and the hostage returned or forfeited. Alternatively, an agreement may have a definite endpoint. A *finite agreement* involves a chronological deadline before which a particular action must be performed or a particular behaviour must be maintained, lest the hostage be forfeited; it may also involve a particular action that, once performed, fulfils the obligation and leads to the release of the hostage.

The most common type of *open-ended agreement* guaranteed by hostages in the medieval sources was submission following military defeat. Hostages, granted unilaterally, guaranteed the defeated party's undertaking, whether implicit or explicit, not to revolt against its conqueror. Such submissions had no deadline: there was no future point at which it would become permissible for the defeated to revolt. For example, following the Battle of Hastings in 1066, William of Normandy received hostages from Dover and then London; following his coronation, he took a group of the most powerful nobles back to Normandy 'like hostages'. Returning to England at the end of 1067, he proceeded to enforce the submission of other regions of the country: Exeter granted hostages in early 1068, as did York—where the Northumbrian noble Archill submitted, too, granting his son as a hostage—and then Lindsay.[1] These are not the only places that submitted to William in the years following 1066,[2] but even if we ignore the possibility of additional hostages, their role in the submission of the English to their new Norman rulers is clear. William remained in England establishing control until 1072. Only one of the hostages granted is named in the sources, and he is the only one whose fate is known: he was in custody—from which he escaped—as late as 1074, that is at least six years after being granted. The influential hostages brought back to Normandy may have gained their freedom earlier, but not because the submission of the English to William was no longer required. After a certain time, a conquest may become a fait accompli; a certain degree of trust develops between conquerors and the conquered,

---

[1] William of Poitiers, *Gesta Guillelmi*, 2.28, 38 (OMT 144, 146, 168); Orderic Vitalis, *Historia ecclesiastica*, 3, 4 (OMT 2:180–2, 196, 212, 218); Simeon of Durham, *Historia regum*, 161, s.a. 1074 (RS 75.2:202). The first two use the phrase *velut obsides*.

[2] David C. Douglas, *William the Conqueror: The Norman Impact upon England* (Berkeley, 1964), 204–44.

or at least the former cease to see the latter as a threat. At that point, the sort of guarantee provided by hostages might be deemed unnecessary and they might be released, but the agreement for which they had been granted essentially remained in force.

The same sorts of unilateral, open-ended agreements operated at the level of individuals rather than communities in many cases of release from captivity. The hostage or hostages substituted for the captive, allowing for his freedom, but guaranteeing the continued good behaviour of that individual, as well as of his retainers, supporters, or army; this sort of transaction was embedded in the 1174 Anglo-Scottish agreement. But captivity did not only result on the battlefield. In 1267 in Rome, for example, Henry of Castile, recently elected senator, moved against many of the Guelph nobles in the city, inviting them to a meeting, arresting them, and imprisoning them in various strongholds. Alone among the group, Giovanni Savelli was considered safe to release, but not before turning over his son, Luca, as a hostage. (That Savelli was found in the army that defeated the Hohenstaufen forces in the following year indicates that this guarantee was ineffective; Luca's fate is unknown.)[3] The pervasiveness of this practice of substitution is demonstrated by the fact that it worked its way into hagiographical literature not as a subject, but as an incidental detail. One of the miracles of Gerald of Aurillac involved his appearance in a dream of Raimond II, count of Toulouse. Raimond had captured Gerald's nephew, who was freed when the prisoner's brother presented himself as a hostage. Gerald's image threatened the count with ill fortune if he did not release his hostage, which he promptly did. The message is reinforced later in the tale where the saint himself releases a prisoner without demanding a hostage in exchange.[4]

The release of high-status captives against hostages with these sorts of openended agreements made sense, as Gero, archbishop of Magdeburg, argued to Emperor Henry II in 1014. In that year, the duke of Bohemia had imprisoned Miesko, son of Duke Boleslaw of Poland, who had approached him about an anti-imperial alliance. Boleslaw appealed to the emperor to free his son. Perhaps if the emperor had intervened earlier to free the prince, the seizure could have been ignored, but now, the archbishop warned, on account of Boleslaw's anger at the length of his son's detention, 'I fear that if you send him back *without hostages* or other guarantees, *in the future* you will be deprived of the faithful service of both of them'.[5] As in the case of submissions, that future was indefinite.

Even when it was not a question of conquest or captivity, rulers often had good reason to feel threatened by those whom they ruled, and we see similar unilateral,

---

[3] Malaspina, *Die Chronik*, 4.6 (MGH SS 35:186–7). Luca is cited at 186 n. 40 as the podestà of Viterbo in 1271, but this does not seem to be the case: Norbert Kamp, 'Konsuln und Podestà, *balivus comunis* und Volkskapitän in Viterbo im 12. und 13. Jahrhundert, mit einem Verzeichnis der Konsuln, Podestà, *balivi comunis* und Volkskapitäne 1099–1300)', in Augusto Pepponi, ed., *Biblioteca degli ardenti della città di Viterbo: Studi e ricerche nel 150° della fonadazione* (Viterbo, 1960), 122.

[4] Odo of Cluny, *De vita S. Geraldi comitis*, 2.28 (*PL* 133:685).

[5] Thietmar of Merseberg, *Chronicon*, 7.12 (MGH SrG ns 9:410): 'vereor, si hunc sine obsidibus aut aliis confirmationibus remittitis, ut in posterum fidelis servitii in ambobus careatis'.

open-ended grants of hostages to ensure the loyalty of acknowledged subordinates. To take another English example from a century and a half after the Conquest, King John needed to worry not about a recently conquered population, but instead about the behaviour of his 'own' nobles. William Marshal himself, now one of the most powerful barons in England, granted his own sons to John during times of tension between the two in 1205 and 1207, and then, in 1210, he granted five of his knights as hostages.[6] William was far from alone in this treatment, as dozens of lords less powerful than he handed over hostages to the king throughout his reign, though in greater numbers at various crisis points, such as following a plot against John in 1212, during the war of 1215–16, and perhaps following the Interdict. John's consistent use of hostages as a means of control of his realm explains Magna Carta c. 49: 'We will restore at once all hostages and charters delivered to us by Englishmen as securities for peace or faithful service.'[7] In the 1210 case, the king was forced to release his hostages; William Marshal's knights were freed because the king needed William's military support. But neither then nor earlier had the promise of 'peace and faithful service' for which he had granted hostages expired.

Alliances, whether or not inscribed in a formal treaty, are a fourth variety of open-ended agreement often secured by hostages. Again in England, following Cnut of Denmark's victory over the English army of Edmund Ironside at Ashington in 1016, the kings met on an island in the Severn and negotiated the partition of England, settled the amount of tribute payments owed to the Danes, and sealed an alliance. Although the parties exchanged hostages, the agreement quickly collapsed—Edmund died and Cnut succeeded to his territories—but the initial agreement was nonetheless open-ended.[8] Similarly, Gregory of Tours reports that Childebert I of Neustria and Theuderic I of Austrasia sealed their non-aggression pact of around 530 with an exchange of hostages; here, too, the agreement quickly collapsed and the hostages were enslaved, but there is no indication that a specific end to the alliance was foreseen.[9] General alliances of this type secured by hostages are in fact uncommon in the Middle Ages. As will be seen, the *exchange* of hostages in this period is a rarity, and in cases of unilateral grants to secure alliances, it is more likely than not a case of submission or subordination of the sort described above.[10] More importantly, it is often possible to identify an implicit finite goal in these agreements. For example, the exchange of hostages between Chilperic I of Neustria and Childebert II of Austrasia in their treaty of 583, while on the surface parallel to the treaty of 530, is in fact clearly directed at

---

[6] *History of William Marshal*, 13271–6, 13362–419, 14319–486 (ed. Holden, 2:164, 168–72, 216–24); *Rotuli litterarum clausarum*, 1:118b, 132b.

[7] Ed. and trans. J. C. Holt, *Magna Carta*, 2nd edn. (Cambridge, 1992), 464–5 ('Omnes obsides et cartas statim reddemus que liberate fuerunt nobis ab Anglicis in securitatem pacis vel fidelis servicii'); Roger of Wendover, *Flores historiarum*, s.a. 1212 (RS 84.2:61–2), with Holt, *Magna Carta*, 82 n. 35; William Sharp McKechnie, *Magna Carta: A Commentary on the Great Charter of King John with an Historical Introduction*, 2nd edn. (Glasgow, 1914), 441–4.

[8] *ASC*, s.a. 1016; *Encomium Emmae Reginae*, 13–14 (ed. Campbell, 28–30).

[9] Gregory of Tours, *Historiae*, 3.15 (MGH SrM 1.1:112).

[10] On exchanges, see below, pp. 46–7.

a short-term goal: guaranteeing the kings' mutual loyalty in a campaign against their brother and uncle, Guntram.[11]

The range of open-ended agreements for which hostages might be granted was thus fairly limited. What explicit motives could there be for indefinite detention of hostages other than permanent loyalty or good behaviour? In the short term, however, the mechanism of hostages was flexible enough for it to be applied in pretty much any situation, to guarantee any sort of finite promise—either a promise with a specific deadline, or a promise to perform a specific action that would fulfil the obligation.

If open-ended agreements guaranteed by hostages often followed on the end of violent conflict, the course of the conflict itself presented many different occasions for finite agreements involving hostages. The truce—a time-delimited suspension of hostilities—is a paradigmatic example of an agreement with a deadline: as long as the truce was not broken, at the end of the truce the hostages were in principle to be returned. In 939, in the midst of the wars of late Carolingian Francia, Louis IV and Hugh the Great agreed to a truce, secured by hostages, until the following 1 June; three years later, they exchanged hostages for a truce from mid-September to mid-November.[12] The hostage for a time-limited truce is found already in Byzantine relations with the Persians and the Goths in the sixth century, and well before that in Roman wars.[13]

The role of hostages in these truces was to guarantee a formal and complete cessation of hostilities between two armies. More limited pauses in conflict relied on the same type of guarantee. The case of William Marshal at Newbury in 1152 is an example of the institution of conditional respite, which involved a truce for a fixed period between besiegers and besieged: if help did not come, the besieged fortress was supposed to surrender; if it failed to do so, the hostages were forfeit. As will be demonstrated in Chapter 4, although there are a few isolated early medieval cases, these transactions become routine only in the course of the twelfth century, and are ubiquitous in the sources for the Hundred Years War.[14] Hostages might also guarantee more straightforward terms of surrender, as when the garrison of Saint-Vaast bought themselves time to evacuate by granting hostages to Charles the Simple in 899 to guarantee a promise not to continue resistance, or a few years earlier when Charles, himself trapped in Reims, refused to surrender until he received hostages from Robert of Neustria for his safe exit.[15]

The latter example shades into another category of finite agreement often secured by hostages, namely safe passage. This was a different sort of truce, in that violence was prohibited not for a fixed amount of time, but rather against a certain individual while in a particular place. This sort of transaction proved useful in the

[11] Gregory of Tours, *Historiae*, 6.31 (MGH SrM 1.1:299); similarly, *Ajbar machmuā* (trans. Lafuente y Alcántara, 49).

[12] Flodoard, *Annales*, s.aa. 939, 942 (CTH 39:71, 85).

[13] Malalas, *Chronographia*, 18.69 (CFHB 35:393–4); Procop. *Goth.* 6.6.36, 6.7.13; Stephan Elbern, 'Geiseln in Rom', *Athenaeum*, 78 (1990), 100, 140 (ap. D).

[14] On conditional respite, see below, pp. 99–110.

[15] *Annales Vedastini*, s.aa. 899, 894 (MGH SrG 12:81, 74).

thick of battle, as when envoys were sent to negotiate with the enemy: for example, when Otto I decided to try to arrange an end to his unsuccessful two-month-long siege of Mainz, his cousin Ekbert was sent into the town as a hostage to guarantee the safety of his rebellious son and son-in-law, who safely entered and exited the royal camp.[16] But hostages for safe passage might be demanded whenever someone feared for his or her safety. In 1416, Henry V of England granted his brother, the duke of Gloucester, as a hostage to guarantee the safety of John II of Burgundy at a peace conference at Calais. John was at the time a neutral party, but was suspicious of Henry nonetheless. The English and Burgundians met at the stream separating Calais from Saint-Omer; while the armed retinues remained on the banks, the two dukes crossed simultaneously, enjoying a chat midstream before continuing on their way, Burgundy to the conference, and Gloucester to honourable and comfortable detention in Saint-Omer; after the conference, they returned in the same way.[17]

Hostages for release from captivity appear not only in the open-ended agreements described above, but also in finite agreements. The action guaranteed in such cases might simply be the return of the captive to custody. René of Anjou was captured at the Battle of Bulgnéville in 1431 and transferred to Philip III of Burgundy. Granted a one-year release in May 1432 to deal with the various crises in his territories, he left his two sons as hostages with the duke. Philip let him overstay his release while it was politically convenient, but recalled him in December 1434. René duly re-entered captivity, but the duke only released one of the hostages; the second had to await the intervention of a Milanese ambassador in October 1435. René was released once again in 1436, again against the re-entry of a son into hostageship.[18] Other prisoners were temporarily released against hostages for such diverse reasons as illness, serving as an emissary, and fencing practice.[19]

Captives might also be released against hostages when it was *not* expected that they would return, as after the Battle of Vlaardingen (1018), at which Godfrey of Lorraine and his men were captured by the count of Holland: the duke was released while his men were kept in chains until such time as he could negotiate an agreement between the count and the emperor.[20] But far and away the most common transaction that did not foresee the return of the captive was the ransom agreement, wherein the specific action guaranteed by the hostage was a monetary payment. The cases of the Treaty of Brétigny and Richard the Lionheart have already been noted. Structurally, hostages in a ransom agreement guaranteed not a particular behaviour or action (submission, loyalty, surrender, return to prison...), as in most of the types of agreements described above, but the transfer of property from

---

[16] Widukind of Corvey, *Res gestae Saxonicae*, 3.18–19 (MGH SrG 60:113–14); cf. Thietmar of Merseberg, *Chronicon*, 2.3 (MGH SrG ns 9:44–5).

[17] *Chronique des Cordeliers*, s.a. 1417 (SHF 235); cf. Monstrelet 1.161 (3:162–3).

[18] Lecoy, *René*, 1:92–136; the 1436 agreement is Augustin Calmet, *Histoire ecclésiastique et civile de Lorraine*, vol. 3 (Nancy, 1728), preuves, cols. cxxx–cxxxii. Documents assembled as BnF, Coll. Lorraine 238–9 (e.g. safe conducts for the hostages at 238, nos. 4 and 5).

[19] Below, pp. 111–14.

[20] Alpert of Metz, *De diversitate temporum*, 2.21 (MGH SS 4:720).

debtor to creditor. While there are examples of hostages guaranteeing the transfer of real property,[21] normally territory or fortifications, the most common such property in question was simply money: hostages guaranteed debts ranging from those of kings to those of simple knights. Hostages for ransom and for financial transactions generally will be addressed in great detail in Chapters 4 to 6, as their emergence is one of the most striking and characteristic aspects of the history of medieval hostageship.

Apart from the open-ended/finite distinction, medieval hostageship exhibits a second time-based division, not with respect to the point at which the obligation guaranteed by a hostage comes to an end, but rather to the point at which the hostage guaranteeing the obligation enters custody. In the case of William Marshal, and most of the examples just surveyed, the hostage was turned over at the *formation* of the agreement, that is when the promise guaranteed was made. It was also possible for the parties to agree, however, that the hostage would only be handed over on *violation* of the agreement, that is when the promise made was broken. I refer to this form of guarantee as *conditional* hostageship, distinguishing it from *true* hostageship.

Conditional hostages appear, for example, in the Treaty of Sahagún of 1170. By the terms of the treaty, Alfonso VIII of Castile promised Alfons I of Barcelona that the ruler of Murcia and Valencia, Ibn Mardanīsh, would pay to him a tribute of 40,000 *morabetins* a year for five years and would submit to arbitration concerning certain disputes between them. Alfonso named three of his nobles, who were to swear an oath and do homage to Alfons that these terms would be kept. If the agreement were violated, the three were to 'come as hostages into your hands until all of these things are fulfilled, and are in no way to depart without your permission'. Alfons, in turn, promised Alfonso that he would keep the peace with Ibn Mardanīsh for five years, and submit to arbitration if the latter had any complaints against him. Alfons, too, offered three nobles who were to enter into Alfonso's control in case of violation. The tribute payments dried up at Ibn Mardanīsh's death in 1172. There is no evidence that the hostages, referred to as *obsides*, were ever handed over, but the agreement clearly foresaw that they might be.[22] Conditional hostages do not only appear in treaties. In around the same year, Alfons contracted with a merchant concerning the financing of a voyage to Constantinople. If the merchant were not paid by Christmas, six barons were to serve as hostages (*tenebunt ostaticum*) at Marseille until the debt was fulfilled. There was no question of the merchant going to war against Alfons, but once again, the entry of the hostages into custody was not immediate—it was conditional on violation of the agreement.[23] Conditional hostage agreements thus include two levels of

---

[21] e.g. *Liber pontificalis*, Hadrianus, 30/310 (ed. Duschesne, 1:495); *Annales qui dicuntur Einhardi*, s.aa. 755, 756, 760, 761 (MGH SrG 6:13, 19); *Codex Carolinus*, 64 (MGH Epp. 3:591); Asser, *Life of King Alfred*, 46 (ed. Stevenson, 35); *Annales Fuldenses*, s.a. 873 (MGH SrG 7:80–1).

[22] Julio González, *El Reino de Castilla en la época de Alfonso VIII*, 3 vols. (Madrid, 1960), 2:239–41 (no. 139): 'ipsi ueniant obsides in manu uestra de potestate uestra quousque compleantur preter uoluntatem uestram nullatenus egresuri'.

[23] Below, pp. 159–60.

guarantees. Before violation, non-hostage guarantees, real or personal, guarantee both the promise to abide by the terms of the agreement *and* the promise to deliver named hostages if a deadline has passed without the terms being kept; after the violation and delivery of the hostages, the hostages themselves act as guarantees of the terms of the agreement. If hostages are seen as the strongest form of guarantee, then a conditional hostage agreement paradoxically involves a weaker set of sureties guaranteeing the delivery of a stronger set. Conditional hostages, too, form a central part of the history of medieval hostageship, and are treated in Chapter 5 below.

The variety of medieval hostageship is found not only in the subjects of agreements guaranteed by hostages and the way they were structured, but also in the identity of the hostages themselves. A hostage had to have some importance to the person granting the hostage to be seen as a desirable form of guarantee; in the absence of such importance, the potential fate of the hostage could not have any impact on the decision of the grantor whether to adhere to the terms of the agreement. The fact that the hostage must be of some value to the debtor requires a pre-existing personal or institutional relationship between the hostage and the grantor of the hostage that underlies that value.[24] Medieval sources, particularly chronicles, that describe grants of hostages often fail to identify the individuals serving in that capacity, either by name or by status. When they do, however, it is usually quite simple to determine the relationship between hostage and grantor/debtor that makes the hostage worthwhile to the creditor.

William Marshal's connection, of course, was that he was John Marshal's son, and indeed the impression given by the sources is that sons were by far the most common form of hostage. Simply in the examples cited above of the varieties of hostage agreements, we have seen sons handed over by Archill, Giovanni Savelli, René of Anjou, and John Marshal. Service as a hostage was almost a standard element in the curriculum vitae of a medieval prince: Charles of Lorraine (son of Louis IV of West Francia); Grimoald of Benevento (son of Arichis II); Theodo of Bavaria (son of Tassilo III); Cacatius of Carinthia (son of Boruth); Romanos and Boris of Bulgaria (sons of Peter I); Boleslaw of Poland (son of Miesko I); Odo of Vienne (son of Heribert II of Vermandois); Bagrat of Georgia (son of George I); Duncan of Scotland (son of Malcolm III); Edward of England (son of Henry III); and many, many others.[25] For the period from 300 to 700, this anecdotal assertion

---

[24] While one can imagine a general humanistic impulse exercising a degree of pressure on someone (give me £10,000 or I will kill this random bystander), such an individual would not provide a plausible guarantee for a creditor, even if a debtor could 'grant' such an individual.

[25] *Annales regni Francorum*, s.aa. 787, 809 (MGH SrG 6:74, 128); *Conversio Bagoariorum et Carantanorum*, 4 (MGH Studien und Texte 15:104); Flodoard, *Annales*, s.aa. 928, 946 (CTH 39:41, 99); *Annales Altahenses maiores*, s.a. 973 (MGH SrG 4:11); Skylitzes, *Synopsis historiarum*, Boris and Constantine, 5 (CFHB 5:255); Zonaras, *Epitoma historiarum*, 16.23 (CSHB 3:495); *Georgian Chronicles* (Armenian) (trans. Thomson, 283–5); *ASC*, s.a. 1093; William of Newburgh, *Historia rerum Anglicarum*, cont., s.a. 1264 (RS 82.2:544). See also sons of: Valdemar II of Denmark (below, p. 164, n. 3); Charles II of Naples (below, pp. 177–82); John II of France (below, pp. 163–5); James of Cyprus (below, p. 164, n. 3); Emperor John V (above, p. 10; below, p. 79, n. 9). Additional cases: *Annales regni Francorum*, s.a. 809 (MGH SrG 6:128) (Thrasco, duke of the Obodrites); *Chronicon Moissiacense*, s.a. 805 (MGH SS 1:307) (Semela, king of the Sorbs); *Annales Fuldenses*, s.a. 862 (MGH SrG

may be quantified: 71 of 109 hostage episodes from the period give some indication about the identity of the hostages; of those, 48 (68 per cent, or 44 per cent of all episodes) involved the grant of a son, alone or with others—leaving, therefore, a substantial fraction who were *not* sons. William Marshal was John Marshal's *fourth* son, and while we do not know if his brothers were available to be offered as hostages, in other cases we see that which son served as a hostage could be a subject of negotiation. There is, however, no consistent pattern. To free Louis IV of West Francia from the Northmen, Queen Gerberga sent her younger child (Charles), but refused to part with the older one (Lothar). Charlemagne, meanwhile, declined to treat the older son of Arichis of Benevento as a hostage, accepting on those terms only the younger one. While an eldest son might in some frameworks enjoy a better claim to an inheritance, that did not necessarily make the eldest son the most valuable to the father, and thus the most valuable hostage for the creditor.[26]

Other close relatives do appear as hostages in the medieval evidence: a father, brother, uncle, nephew, cousin, mother, wife, or daughter.[27] But there is a marked preference for sons. Thietmar of Merseburg's vivid account of his brush with hostageship provides the most informative discussion of which relatives were considered worthwhile hostages. In 994, Vikings captured two of his uncles on his mother's side, Henry and Siegfried, along with a certain Count Adalgar, and demanded a ransom. When the bulk of the ransom had been paid, they accepted hostages for the remainder from Henry (his only son, along with two others) and from Adalgar (his uncle and his aunt's son). Siegfried had no sons, so he asked his sister (Thietmar's mother) if one of her sons would serve as his hostage. When Thietmar's brother's abbot refused to release him for this service, Thietmar himself was prepared for the mission.[28] Our inability to identify Adalgar and the other two hostages for Henry (another account refers to them only as *milites*[29]) is disappointing,

---

7:56) (Tabomuizl, duke of the Obodrites); Erchempert, *Historia Langobardorum Beneventanorum*, 35–6 (MGH SrL 248) (Waifer, prince of Salerno, a. 872); Regino of Prüm, *Chronicon*, s.a. 890 (MGH SrG 50:134) (Zwentibold, King of Moravia); John of Worcester, *Chronicle*, s.a. 934 (OMT 2:390) (Constantine II, king of Scotland); *Annales Altahenses maiores*, s.a. 974 (MGH SrG 4:12) (Harald Bluetooth, king of Denmark); Froissart 1.154 (ed. Sauvage, 1:177) (John II of France, a. 1354); Froissart 1.654 (7:224–5) (Charles II of Navarre); Galíndez de Carvajal, *Crónica de Enrique IV*, 10 (ed. Torres Fontes, 91) (Abū Naṣr Sa'd of Granada, a. 1454); William of Tyre, *Chronicon*, 2.11–12 (CCCM 63:174–6) and *Die Kreuzzugsbriefe aus den Jahren 1088–1100*, 154 (no. 12.3) (Emperor Alexius I). Rejected proposals: *Codex Carolinus*, 83 (MGH Epp. 3:617) (Arichis, duke of Benevento); Richer, *Historiae*, 4.49 (MGH SS 38:262) (Charles, duke of Lorraine); Benzo of Alba, *Ad Heinricum IV. Imperatorem*, 2.12 (MGH SrG 65:226) (Emperor Constantine X, a possible forgery); *Annalista Saxo*, s.a. 1137 (MGH SS 37:608) (Roger II of Sicily); *Historia peregrinorum* (MGH SrG ns 5:140) (Emperor Frederic I); RI 5.2.3:7024a (Emperor Frederic II).

[26] Flodoard, *Annales*, s.a. 946 (CTH 39:99); *Annales regni Francorum*, s.a. 787 (MGH SrG 6:74); see below, pp. 42–3.

[27] Daughters, wives, mothers: see below, pp. 83–92. Father: Salimbene de Adam, *Cronica*, s.a. 1285 (CCCM 125A:910). Uncle and cousins: below, p. 164, n. 3 (James of Cyprus). Brother: Monstrelet 1.97 (2:303–4). Nephew: Skylitzes, *Synopsis historiarum*, 20 (CFHB 5:464); 'Nuova serie di documenti sulle relazione di Genova coll'impero Bizantino', 472–3 (no. 16); *Royal and Other Historical Letters*, 61 (RS 27.1:73).

[28] Thietmar of Merseburg, *Chronicon*, 4.23–4 (MGH SrG ns 9:158–63).

[29] *Annales Altahenses maiores*, s.a. 994 (MGH SrG 4:15).

but even with those gaps this account reflects a preference for sons—Henry grants his only son, and Siegfried is at first kept because he has no son—but a willingness to accept other relatives within two degrees. This preference was still in place at the time of the Treaty of Falaise (1174), when hostages granted by the king of Scotland could be released only after providing a substitute, 'a legitimate son, if they have one, and from others their nephews or nearest heirs'.[30] The pattern is confirmed in other sources that show relatives other than sons *alongside* sons. The son and *nepos* of Harald, king of Denmark, found at the court of Louis the Pious in the 820s, may have been hostages.[31] Around the same time, Stephen III of Naples offered his mother and sons in his ruse to defend the city from the Beneventans. Brothers appear alongside sons twice in cases involving Muslim Spain: Charlemagne, according to one account, received the brother and son of Abu Taher of Huesca in 778, while Alfonso III took from Abuhalit not only his son but also two of his brothers and a cousin.[32] In the absence of any sons, as Thietmar's case indicates, nephews may have been the preferred substitute. Gilbert of Lorraine provided his brother's sons to Berenguer of Namur, Landulf of Capua the sons of his *cognatus* to Louis II, and the castellan of Coucy his nephews (*nepotes*) to Lothar.[33]

Two other facts about William Marshal are worth comment. First, his age: he was perhaps 5 years old when he was handed over. As will be seen, in some periods the age of hostages does turn out to be quite significant, but the sources rarely divulge this information; it is usually discernible only when, as in the case of William, the hostage becomes an important historical figure later in life.[34] Hostages identified only as children of the grantor may be understood to be 'young' children—too young to have an independent reputation or political importance that would make their names recognizable—but what that means varies from situation to situation: Charles, son of Louis IV, was probably a newborn;[35] Duncan of Scotland was around 13; Edward, son of Henry III, was 25. Second, William Marshal was a son, not a daughter. As noted, women—mothers, daughters, wives—do appear as hostages, but in addition to being less common, they are the subject of one of the more remarkable shifts in the history of medieval hostageship, a shift that, again, will be addressed in detail below.

Given that hostageship must be grounded in some sort of connection to the grantor, it makes sense that many hostages are relatives. But not all hostages are relatives, as family ties are not the only connections that could ground a guarantee. Friends and followers—to use the other two elements of Gerd Althoff's triad[36]—

---

[30] Ed. and trans. *Anglo-Scottish Relations*, 4 (no. 1).

[31] Ermoldus Nigellus, *Poème sur Louis le Pieux*, 4.2510–11 (ed. Faral, 190). See RIS 2.2:75 n. 66.

[32] Erchempert, *Historia Langobardorum Beneventanorum*, 10 (MGH SrL 238); *Chronicon Moissiacense*, s.a. 778 (MGH SS 1:296); *Crónica Albeldense*, 15.12 (ed. Gil Fernández, 177).

[33] Flodoard, *Annales*, s.aa. 924, 958 (CTH 39:21, 145); Erchempert, *Historia Langobardorum Beneventanorum*, 36 (MGH SrL 248).

[34] Walker, 'Hostages', 36, has 60 per cent of Roman cases involving youths, alone or along with adults.

[35] Philippe Lauer, *Le règne de Louis IV d'Outre-mer* (Paris, 1900), 135 n. 4.

[36] Gerd Althoff, *Family, Friends, and Followers: Political and Social Bonds in Medieval Europe*, trans. Christopher Carroll (Cambridge, 2004 [1990]).

were another rich source. The newborn son of Louis IV was accompanied into hostageship by the bishop of Soissons, perhaps along with the bishop of Beauvais and a great number of warriors.[37] The conditional hostages on each side in the Treaty of Sahagún, mentioned above, are another example of hostages with no close family connection to the grantor: three counts from the Castilian side; three of the most powerful Catalan barons from the other.[38] Followers and subordinates of this sort might be valuable to the grantor for several reasons: affective ties, customary or legal obligations of lords, and, in the case of numerous warriors, simple military strength—by entering into the custody of the enemy, soldiers became unavailable to fight against them. Like family, friends and followers are connected to individuals as grantors. But what if the grantor is not an individual but a group, with or without a formal corporate existence: a people, or a social class, or a town, or a guild? The family, friends, and followers of the leaders or members of such communities might be useful hostages, but, as I will argue in Chapter 4, the ties that make certain individuals good hostages from the perspective of the creditor might also be grounded in connections akin to representation. Changes in who precisely is able to stand in for another as a hostage mean that the study of hostageship in all its variety becomes, too, a study of the structures of power in the European Middle Ages.

THE LOGICS OF HOSTAGESHIP

The logic of hostageship seems self-evident. By handing over a human being as a guarantee, a debtor puts the hostage's treatment and ultimately life entirely in the hands of a creditor or enemy. The threat of mistreatment or death increases the likelihood that the debtor will adhere to the agreement for which the hostage was given.[39] Hostages should initially be treated well by their custodians, as the possibility of a change in circumstances (short of execution) provides the creditor with further means of increasing pressure on the debtor—in addition to making it more plausible that a hostage would be handed over in the first place, even under duress. Family, friends, and followers are common hostages because they have value to the debtor, and indeed more value than any conceivable real surety; they are thus that much more of an inducement to performance of a promise. Sons are among the most common hostages because that bond is plausibly the strongest.

On occasion, the medieval sources describe hostageship as working in precisely this manner. The Astronomer writes that the Franks respected the safe passage they had granted to the Basque leader Adalric because of the sureties they had handed

[37] Flodoard, *Annales*, s.a. 945 (CTH 39:99).
[38] Above, p. 30.
[39] Rare explicit statement of this at the formation of the agreement, rather than as a later threat: *Annales Altahenses maiores*, s.a. 1043 (MGH SrG 4:33) ('in festo Andreae his perfectis reciperentur aut infectis perderentur'); Ansbert, *Historia de expeditione Friderici imperatoris*, 7 (MGH SrG ns 5:88) ('capitalem excipietis sententiam'); Gerald of Wales, *Expugnatio Hibernica*, 1.17 (RS 21.5:257) ('præcisum tibi filii tui caput proculdubio remittemus').

over: 'he suffered nothing because of the danger to those same hostages'.[40] Flodoard reports that Lotharingian bishops refrained from defecting to Louis IV of West Francia 'because King Otto [III, of Germany] was keeping their hostages'.[41] According to the *Ágrip*, Cnut of Denmark's rule over Norway was eased by the fact that 'men dared not rise up for the sake of their sons who were held hostage', just as Magnus I of Norway was able to take power in Denmark 'without opposition, because the sons of the most important men were held hostage'.[42] One response of the justiciar Hubert Walter to the threats posed by the activity of the London populist leader William fitz Osbert in 1196 was to convince the townsmen to grant hostages 'for fidelity to the lord king and the keeping of peace'. When he finally decided to move against William, it was when 'the people were behaving more quietly *out of fear for the hostages*', and when William took refuge in a church, the people did not rush to his aid 'both out of fear of the knights *and out of respect for the hostages*'.[43] Similarly, in 1252, Brancaleone del Andalo insisted on hostages from the Roman nobility to guarantee his personal safety while serving as senator; captured and imprisoned during two revolts in 1255, he was spared on both occasions because of the hostages. Matthew Paris writes that the Bolognese who had custody of the hostages refused to release them despite pressure, for 'they knew for certain that if they were handed back, Brancaleone would quickly be killed'.[44]

Conversely, when the Welsh rebelled against King John a year after granting twenty-four noble youths as guarantees of their fidelity, he executed the hostages 'as punishment for the abovementioned offense'.[45] And when in 1148 the town of Faro failed to deliver promised payments to the besieging Crusader army, forty hostages they had handed over were hanged.[46]

As for treatment, we know that in 1348 the infante Ferdinand of Portugal and his substantial entourage were taken from their comfortable surroundings at Asilah and clapped in irons at Fez when the Portuguese failed to evacuate Ceuta—the promise for which they were serving as hostages.[47] Similarly, when the squire for whom he was serving as a hostage failed to return on schedule in 1358, Ancelin de Pommelain found himself thrown in irons weighing fifty pounds and placed on a bread and water diet; when he was in such a sorry state that his toenails and finger-

---

[40] Astronomer, *Vita Hludowici imperatoris*, 5 (MGH SrG 64:298): 'Sed eorundem obsidum periculo nichil passus'.

[41] Flodoard, *Annales*, s.a 939 (MGH SS 3:386): 'quoniam rex Otho eorum secum detinebat obsidatum'.

[42] *Ágrip af Nóregskonungasogum*, 30, 36 (ed. and trans. Driscoll, 42–3, 48–9); cf., however, c. 31 (pp. 42–3), where hostages are a pretext for rebellion.

[43] William of Newburgh, *Historia rerum Anglicarum*, 5.20 (RS 82.2:469–70): 'populus propter periculum obsidum quietius ageret... tamen vel respectu obsidum vel metu loricatæ'.

[44] Paris, *Chronica majora* (RS 57.5:358, 547, 563–4): 'Sciebant enim proculdubio, quod si redderentur, Brancaleo festine morti traderetur.'

[45] Roger of Wendover, *Flores historiarum*, s.a. 1212 (ed. Coxe, 3:239): 'in ulitionem jam dictæ transgressionis'.

[46] *Annales Elmarenses*, s.a. (ed. Grierson, 111–12).

[47] Álvares, *Trautado*, 15, 21ff. (ed. Almeida Calado, 1:26, 42ff.); Pina, *Crónicas*, Duarte, 42 (ed. Lopes de Almeida, 570); António Joaquim Dinis, 'Carta do Infante Santo ao regente D. Pedro, datada da masmorra de Fez a 12 de junho de 1441', *Anais da Academia Portuguesa da História*, 2nd ser., 13 (1965), 164–71.

nails began to fall off, he was finally released on parole. Jacques Capelet, a hostage from the town of Reims for the Treaty of Brétigny, was held in irons and chains in dungeons after the resumption of Anglo-French hostilities in 1369.[48] And in 1376x7, the wives of two hostages for a failed agreement at Brest in 1373 complained that their husbands were 'harshly imprisoned and often at the brink of death'.[49]

In theory, then, it should be possible to quantify the utility of hostages generally, or of certain types of hostages, as guarantees in various situations by determining how often agreements secured by hostages were kept or were violated, and whether in cases of violation the hostages were mistreated or killed. In practice, however, more often than not the sources do not reveal the outcome of the agreement, or, even when the outcome is known, the fate of the hostages. When we know the names of the hostages and they appear later not as hostages, obviously they survived. But even when their fate is known, their stories often fail to follow this simple script.

Consider first the question of treatment before the violation of an agreement. The image of William Marshal playing happily with his royal custodian and the clause from the Treaty of Brétigny indicating that the prisoners-turned-hostages were to be released from their prisons support an argument that hostages were treated well, and in fact better than prisoners—a distinction that goes back as far as Livy.[50] Freedom of movement and temporary release were common; violation of parole, bribery of guards, and even outright escape were always risks.[51] But the possibilities for the good treatment of hostages had few limits. In the fifth century, Peter the Iberian was brought up and loved 'like a son' by the Roman emperor, as was Aetius by the Gothic ruler Alaric: 'in name he calls him son', as Merobaudes writes. Duncan of Scotland was knighted upon his release by the English king.[52] The sons of Charles of Salerno established a household in their Catalan residence, with a *major domus*, a physician, a chamberlain, esquires, a cook, and valets—for themselves but also for the forty noble hostages who accompanied them. A move to Barcelona in 1293 afforded more opportunity for direct contact with the outside world, and we find one of the sons—Louis, the

---

[48] *GCA* 361–6, 428–32.

[49] London, National Archives, SC 8/261/13046 ('en dure prisone et souent en point de perdre leur vies'). See below, pp. 105, 109. Similarly, *Vita S. Laurentii archiepiscopi Dublinensis*, 2–3 (ed. Plummer, 129–30); Machairas, *Chronikon Kyprou* (ed. Miller and Sathas, 308–10) (James of Cyprus); Paris, *Chronica majora* (RS 57.5:547, 564); *Ajbar machmuã* (trans. Lafuente y Alcántara, 91); *History of William Marshal*, 11457–8 (ed. Holden, 2:224); *Raoul de Cambrai*, 41.695 (ed. Kay, 52).

[50] Livy 32.26.

[51] Freedom of movement: *HGL* 10:616–20 (no. 223). Bribery: Simeon of Durham, *Historia regum*, 161 (RS 75.2:202). Escape: Procop. *Goth.* 5.26.1–2; Thietmar of Merseberg, *Chronicon*, 4.24 (MGH SrG ns 9:160–2); Albert of Aachen, *Historia Ierosolimitana*, 7.1 (OMT 486); Michael the Syrian, *Chronique*, 15.10 (trans. Chabot, 3:195–6); William of Tyre, *Chronicon*, 11.8 (CCCM 63:506); *Foedera*, 1.2:969, 2.1:437, 3.1:281–2, 372–4; *Mémoires...Bretagne*, 1:1568; *The Acts of Welsh Rulers, 1120–1283*, 799 (no. 604); *Liber Eliensis*, 3.96 (ed. Blake, 332–3); *Chronica monasterii Casinensis*, 2.63 (MGH SS 34:292); *Le Assise di Ariano*, 18/12 (ed. Zecchino, 40, 78). Violation of parole: below, p. 163.

[52] *Vita Petri Iberi* (trans. Raabe, 23); Flavius Merobaudes, *Panegyricus II*, 140–1 (MGH AA 14:16; trans. Clover, 15); John of Worcester, *Chronicle*, s.a. 1087 (OMT 3:48).

future bishop of Toulouse and saint—ministering to the poor from his apartments and attending the Franciscan provincial chapter of 1294.[53] John of Angoulême was more isolated from his fellow hostages, but nevertheless enjoyed at various times the service of chaplain, a tutor,[54] two domestic servants, and a scribe. Messengers travelled back and forth to France, bringing reports from home but also supplies: good French wine, luxury toiletries, and linens from his châteaux. John's principal diversions were books, to which he had extensive access, and the harp; he did not permit himself, we are told, the distractions of dice and cards.[55] In the latter, he was unlike one of the hostages of Brétigny, Louis of Bourbon, who passed his days gambling with the queen.[56]

These were not simply Western European customs. The tenth-century Byzantine emperor Constantine VII recommended that Pecheneg hostages in Constantinople 'enjoy all imperial benefits and gifts suitable for the emperor to bestow'. He later notes with disdain that hostages in Cherson 'are shameless in their demands for generous gifts, the hostages demanding this for themselves and that for their wives'.[57] Constantine's policy in such matters appears to have been effective, as his own hostages in Islamic lands were permitted to visit the shrine of Saint Thomas at Edessa and leave imperial donations there.[58] And in eighth-century Muslim Iberia, the emir 'Abd al-Rahmān I promised to treat hostages received from a rival honourably, holding them 'only in comfortable confinement with him in the palace of Córdoba'.[59] The precise terms of hostages' 'confinement' were subject to negotiation and specified in treaties and auxiliary documents; the cost was often imposed on the debtor or even the hostage.[60] Later variations on conditional hostageship in fact *required* lavish expenditure, so as to place further pressure on the debtor.[61] Records of litigation over the expenses of hostages and financial accounts survive to document their potential resources.[62]

The problems with generalizing from these cases are twofold. First, the same sort of evidence could be assembled to demonstrate the condition not of hostages, but of prisoners or captives being held in 'honourable captivity'. To the present day, conditions of confinement vary widely according to the social status of the

---

[53] Margaret Toynbee, *S. Louis of Toulouse and the Process of Canonisation in the Fourteenth Century* (Manchester, 1929), 60–3, 70–2. Similarly: Galíndez de Carvajal, *Crónica de Enrique IV*, 10 (ed. Torres Fontes, 91); Álvares, *Trautado*, 15, 21ff. (ed. Almeida Calado, 1:26, 42ff.).

[54] Cf. *Rotuli litterarum clausarum*, 1:123b; Ibn al-Qūṭīya, *History* (trans. James, 121).

[55] Gustave Dupont-Ferrier, 'La captivité de Jean d'Orléans, comte d'Angoulême (1412–1445)', *Revue historique*, 62 (1896), 50–5.

[56] Orville, *La chronique du bon duc Loys de Bourbon*, 1 (SHF 4–5); below, pp. 164–5. Similarly: *Foedera*, 3.2:772, 773; Monstrelet 1.161 (3:162–3); *HGL* 10:616–20 (no. 223).

[57] Constantine VII, *De administrando imperio*, 1, 7 (CFHB 1:48, 54; trans. CFHB 1:49, 55); cf. 49 (1:230) (ὡς ὁμήρους).

[58] *Theophanes Continuatus*, 6.32 (CSHB 455).

[59] *Ajbar machmuá* (trans. Lafuente y Alcántara, 89).

[60] e.g.: *Foedera*, 1.2:694; *The Treaty of Bayonne*, 14, 22, 33, 45, 58–9 (various versions of article 20); *Rotuli litterarum clausarum*, 1:132b; but cf. Pugh, *Imprisonment*, 315.

[61] Below, Chapter 5.

[62] *GCA* 329–31, 404–7, 409–26; Michael Jones, 'The Ransom of Jean de Bretagne, Count of Penthièvre', *Bulletin of the Institute of Historical Research*, 45 (1972), 12 and n. 2; Bossuat, 'Châteauvillain', 22.

prisoner,[63] and good treatment of one's captives became a centrepiece of the chivalric ethos.[64] Because of the nature of the sources, particularly for earlier periods, most of the hostages we know about were either noble or wealthy enough to merit (or negotiate) good treatment. Furthermore, many hostages of lower status were handed over pursuant to agreements negotiated by powerful people and thus the conditions of their confinement reflected their patrons' influence. Where hostages are treated well, in other words, it is as likely to be because of who they were as because of their status as hostages.

The second and more serious problem with an argument for the comfortable lifestyle of hostages before any possible violation of an agreement is that it is equally possible to marshal evidence for their mistreatment. References to hostages as 'in prison' do not necessarily refer to a physical location; mentions of places, such as castles, or guardians, such as bishops or abbots, alone say nothing about the particular conditions of confinement.[65] But there are hostages described as kept in chains (*vincula, compedes*), and not only in Ireland, where tradition held that 'he is not a king who does not have hostages in fetters'.[66] Many of the scandalous tales of mutilation or sexual abuse of hostages come from sources concerning eleventh- and twelfth-century England and Normandy, which raises questions both about the extent of such activity elsewhere and indeed the veracity of the reports themselves.[67] But not all of them do, and mistreatment was not limited to such abuses. Then there are the reports of hostages who *died* while in confinement, such as the son of Godfrey III of Lorraine; the brother and nephew of the Byzantine merchant Symon Musonus; the son of Azzo III of Este; Jean Rabache de Hengest, one of the hostages for John II; Noiseux de Sailly, a hostage for payments

---

[63] Jean Dunbabin, *Captivity and Imprisonment in Medieval Europe, 1000–1300* (Basingstoke, 2002), 114–29; Guy Geltner, *The Medieval Prison: A Social History* (Princeton, 2008), 57–81.

[64] As with the Black Prince's treatment of John II after his capture: Froissart 1.397 (5:63–4).

[65] Castles: Pierre des Vaux-de-Cernay, *Hystoria Albigensis*, 585 (SHF 2:278); Gislebert of Mons, *Chronique*, 209 (ed. Vanderkindere, 294); Galbert of Bruges, *De multro*, 117 (CCCM 131:163); *Book of Prests*, 76, 141; and below, p. 127, n. 195. Ecclesiastical households: below, pp. 67–8; *Vita S. Laurentii archiepiscopi Dublinensis*, 2–3 (ed. Plummer, 129–30). References to *carcer* are even rarer: Gislebert of Mons, *Chronique*, 209 (ed. Vanderkindere, 294); Salimbene de Adam, *Cronica*, s.a. 1250 (CCCM 125A:554); *Royal and Other Historical Letters*, 475 (RS 27.2:72); 'Nuova serie di documenti sulle relazione di Genova coll'impero Bizantino', 473 (no. 16); *Vita S. Caelestini V* (*Acta sanctorum*, Maii IV 448), a poetic description.

[66] Alpert of Metz, *De diversitate temporum*, 2.21 (MGH SS 4:720); Galbert of Bruges, *De multro*, 117 (CCCM 131:163); Fulcher of Chartres, *Historia Hierosolymitana*, 3.44.2 (ed. Hagenmeyer, 770); Salimbene de Adam, *Cronica*, s.aa. 1192, 1240, 1285, 1287 (CCCM 125:26, 257, 125A:910, 972); *Royal and Other Historical Letters*, 475 (RS 27.2:72); *Brut y Tywysogyon*, s.a. 1165 (trans. Jones, 147); Álvares, *Trautado*, 24 (ed. Almeida Calado, 1:47); cf. *Vita S. Laurentii archiepiscopi Dublinensis*, 3 (ed. Plummer, 130); *Corpus iuris Hibernici*, 219.5, 570.26; Fergus Kelly, *A Guide to Early Irish Law* (Dublin, 1988), 173–6. Of course these same Irish sources include hostages in seating charts for royal banquets.

[67] William of Malmesbury, *Gesta regum Anglorum*, 5.398 (OMT 1:724); Orderic Vitalis, *Historia ecclesiastica*, 8, 12.8, 12.10 (OMT 4:294, 6:207, 210–12); Roger of Howden, *Chronica*, s.a. 1165 (RS 51.1:240); John of Salisbury, *Letters*, 279 (OMT 2:602); *Hemingi chartularium*, 1:259; *ASC*, s.a. 1014; *Annales Cambriae*, s.a. 1166 (RS 20:50); Thietmar of Merseberg, *Chronicon*, 4.24, 7.41 (MGH SrG ns 9:160–2, 448); *Historia Selebiensis monasterii*, 2.13–14 (ed. Fowler, [38]–[39]). See also John of Fordun, *Chronica gentis Scotorum*, Gesta annalia, 22 (ed. Skene, 275); *Annals of the Four Masters*, s.aa. 1250, 1259 (trans. O'Donovan, 3:341, 373). For sexual abuse, below, p. 85.

due from the town of Lihons to the English; or the infante Ferdinand of Portugal.[68] The townsmen of Monza who expressed their fear at being delivered up as hostages to the prince of Teck in 1329 were not being unreasonable; nor was Edward I of England in ordering on behalf of his hostages in Aragon in 1288 prayers 'customarily offered in church for captives'.[69]

So the treatment of hostages did not always correspond to what might be expected given the status of an agreement. The same is true for the more specific question of execution. It is undeniable that many agreements guaranteed by hostages were not kept; many such examples have already been cited, starting with the case of William Marshal. But William was not killed, and in that he had a lot of company among medieval hostages. In fact, among the over 1,500 cases surveyed for the present study, I have identified fewer than thirty episodes of the execution of hostages between 500 and 1500.[70] Some of these are straightforward: the hostages are killed because the agreement for which they were granted was violated. The examples of Faro in 1148 and the Welsh hostages of King John in 1212 were cited above. There are a few others where links between violation and execution are quite clear. In 536, the Ostrogothic king, Witigis, took with him from Rome to Ravenna the greater part of the senators as hostages to guarantee the loyalty of the city. When the city later welcomed Belisarius, Witigis besieged Rome and ordered the hostages killed; at least two escaped, but most perished.[71] In the 1160s, the Irish lord Diarmait of Leinster granted hostages including his son, Conchobhar, to Ruadri of Connacht, as part of his submission to the latter's lordship. When Diarmait rebelled, reports Gerald of Wales, Ruadri sent messengers accusing him of violating their agreement and having no pity for the hostage he had given; if he did not desist, Ruadri would send him his son's head. When Diarmait replied with defiance, the boy was killed.[72] And when in 1427 the duke of Bedford arrived before the castle of La Gravelle and demanded that the French garrison surrender according the terms of a conditional agreement guaranteed by hostages, he found that those who had made the agreement had apparently been displaced and the new commanders refused to yield. 'Thus', reports the chronicler, 'he had the hostages decapitated.'[73]

---

[68] Sigebert of Gembloux, *Chronica*, s.a. 1045 (MGH SS 6:358); Salimbene de Adam, *Cronica*, s.a. 1250 (CCCM 125A:554); Paul Roger, *Noblesse et chevalerie du comté de Flandre, d'Artois et de Picardie* (Amiens, 1843), 196–7; Monstrelet 2.245 (5:407); 'Nuova serie di documenti sulle relazione di Genova coll'impero Bizantino', 472–3 (no. 16); Álvares, *Tratuado*, 41 (ed. Almeida Calado, 1:90). See also Theophanes Confessor, *Chronographia*, s.aa. 5998, 6142, 6144 (ed. Boor, 1:148, 344–5); *Chronicle of Zuqnīn*, 4, s.a. 1063 (trans. Harrak, 189); *History of William Marshal*, 14459–62 (ed. Holden, 2:224); Bossuat, 'Châteauvillain', 24; below, p. 183.

[69] Morigia, *Chronicon Modoetiense*, 3.39 (RIS 12:1155); *Foedera*, 1.2:697 ('in ecclesiâ consuetis, pro captivis offerri').

[70] Appendix. In compiling this list, I have omitted some victims characterized by other scholars as hostages but who do not fit my definition of that status, e.g. Benham, *Peacemaking*, 164.

[71] Procop. *Goth.* 5.11.26, 5.26.1–2.

[72] Gerald of Wales, *Expugnatio Hibernica*, 1.10, 17 (RS 21.5:244, 257–8); *Annals of Ulster*, s.aa. 1166, 1170 (trans. Hennessey and MacCarthy, 2:153, 163–5); *Annals of the Four Masters*, s.aa. 1169, 1170; cf. a. 1246 (trans. O'Donovan, 2:1173, 1177–9; 3:317–19).

[73] *Chronique de la Pucelle*, 25 (ed. Vallet de Viriville, 249) ('pour ce fist-il couper la teste aux hostages'); see below, p. 109.

But most of the other episodes of execution are not so simple. The conflicting Latin and Arabic accounts of the massacre following the siege of Acre were mentioned in the previous chapter; in that case the question is whether or not the individuals executed were in fact hostages. Hostages for the town of Liège to the duke of Burgundy who were executed in 1467 did not lose their lives because of the violation of the treaty for which they had been granted; when it was broken the hostages were released. They were instead executed because upon release they had promised the duke not to take up arms again—that is, they were executed not for the violation of an undertaking of the town, but rather for their *own* undertaking. Here the question is not the status of the people killed, but the precise agreement whose violation led to the execution.[74] A different sort of problem is presented by Flodoard's account of the execution of the son of Count Odelric in 960. Bruno, archbishop of Cologne, besieged Robert of Troyes at Dijon and received from him two hostages, whom he handed over to King Lothar. The king proceeded to execute Odelric's son after he was determined to be the traitor responsible for handing over the royal castle to Robert in the first place. Here the execution of the hostage had nothing to do with any agreement.[75] Such ambiguities apply to most of the cases of execution I have identified. Even if we assume, however, that in all ambiguous cases, hostages were executed because of direct violation of the agreement for which they had been granted, and even if we assume that there other examples of executions that have not been adduced (as there surely are), the fact remains that in the medieval sources, execution of hostages is a rarity.[76]

In addition to the rarity of executions, there are other unexpected outcomes, where the result of the agreement and the fate of the hostages seem at odds. In 1162, Frederic Barbarossa, despite continued conflict, returned 300 of the 400 hostages he held from Milan. Around 1184, Bohemond III of Antioch, 'moved by piety', simply set free hostages for the ransom of Isaac Comnenus of Cyprus when he realized that he would never be paid. In 1437, ambassadors from Bruges left hostages with the forces of Ghent as a guarantee that the town would ratify the treaty they had negotiated; Bruges refused, but the hostages were nonetheless released.[77] The simple model introduced above fails to explain these results.

The basic question of whether hostages were effective guarantees, whether an agreement fortified by hostages was more likely to work than one that was not, cannot be answered in a systematic fashion, for, as noted, the data are woefully incomplete. It has been suggested that hostages are taken for granted by the narrative sources and only mentioned when something bad happened to them.[78] This is clearly not the case, as examples of the sort surveyed above of mistreatment and

[74] Below, pp. 204–6.
[75] Flodoard, *Annales*, s.a. (CTH 39:148–9); cf. Richer, *Historiae*, 3.12 (MGH SS 38:176–7).
[76] As it was in late Republican and early Imperial Rome: Allen, *Hostages*, 52–4.
[77] *Gesta Federici I. imperatoris in Lombardia* (MGH SrG 27:55); Roger of Howden, *Chronica*, s.a. 1180 (RS 51.2:204) ('pietate commotus'); Monstrelet 2.224 (5:329).
[78] Christopher Holdsworth, 'Peacemaking in the Twelfth Century', *Anglo-Norman Studies*, 19 (1996), 5 and n. 22. Cf. Kay Peter Jankrift, 'Aus der Heimat in die Fremde: Geiseln und Kriegsgefangene im frühen Mittelalter', in Hardy Eidam and Gudrun Noll, eds., *Radegunde: Ein Frauenschicksal zwischen Mord und Askese* (Erfurt, 2006), 53.

execution, let alone examples of good treatment—are vastly outnumbered by references to hostages where absolutely nothing is said about their treatment or fate.
My impression is that it is precisely the *treatment* and *fate* of hostages, rather than
their mere use, that is more likely to be mentioned when something bad happened.
Given the state of the evidence, such an argument is not susceptible to proof.

HOSTAGES AND THE THEORY OF CONTRACTS

If we cannot perform a quantitative analysis of the outcomes of hostage agreements, the evidence does permit further exploration of the logic of hostageship,
logic that, as shown, cannot correspond to the intuitive model described above.
The story of William Marshal reveals the problems. King Stephen accepted a hostage to guarantee a truce requested by the elder Marshal to appeal to his superior
for aid. Normally, such agreements included a promise on the part of the defenders
not to reinforce the castle during the truce and, if aid were not forthcoming within
a certain period, to surrender the castle without a fight; the besieging force made a
complementary, but unsecured, promise to allow the garrison to surrender peacefully. In this case, no sooner had the besieging forces withdrawn than the Marshal
used the opportunity to shore up his defences, violating the first part of the agreement. This action alone indicated to the king that he had been deceived. Nonetheless, he waited until the appointed term before doing anything; when the garrison
failed to surrender, the second part of the agreement had also been violated. The
king could now act on the threat implied in the initial agreement: that in case of
violation, he would kill the hostage. But he did not kill William, and his failure to
carry out the threat to kill his hostage seems to undercut the rationale of asking for
the hostage in the first place. Just as the Marshal's actions (and words) declared that
the hostage was worthless to him, the king's failure to act declared that the hostage
was also worthless from his perspective. Or was it?

Recent work in the theory of contracts has turned to the notion of the hostage
given as one way to increase the security of agreements in the context of 'private
ordering' and 'self-enforcing agreements', that is, the way parties structure agreements outside of the norms of positive contract law that might be enforced by the
state. The absence of an external enforcement mechanism, let alone a state, obviously applies to many if not most interactions in medieval European society, particularly before the very end of the period. The hostages adduced and studied by
this literature rarely resemble the medieval variety. For example, a buyer might
make specific investments in physical plant that would be useless to it if it failed to
follow through on a promised order to a supplier. Or a buyer might purchase private equity stakes in the seller's company, creating a disincentive to harm the company financially by failing to adhere to an agreement.[79] These 'hostages'—physical

---

[79] Oliver E. Williamson, 'Credible Commitments: Using Hostages to Support Exchange', *American
Economic Review*, 73 (1983), 519–40, developing an idea of Thomas C. Schelling, 'An Essay on Bargaining', *American Economic Review*, 46 (1956), 300 n. 17; Beth V. Yarbrough and Robert M. Yarbrough,

plant, private equity stakes—are real rather than personal sureties. Despite this fundamental difference, however, some of the more abstract findings of this scholarship illuminate the puzzling case of William Marshal and the problems of medieval hostageship generally.

Anthony Kronman proposes a typology of mechanisms that attempt to reduce the risk inherent in transactions in the absence of (and even in the presence of) external enforcement: hostages, collateral, hands-tying, and union. A 'hostage' is something of value to the debtor (independent of its value to the creditor, which may be nothing) handed over to the creditor, to be returned on performance. 'Collateral' is something handed over that has a value to the creditor. 'Hands-tying' involves the creation by the debtor of a self-executing punishment: a 'hostage' who is 'killed' without any affirmative action on the part of the creditor. 'Union' involves an arrangement that 'seeks to reduce divergence by promoting a spirit of identification or fellow-feeling between the parties'.[80] The third of these terms, hands-tying, in fact encompasses many of the modern applications of hostage theory, such as sunk costs,[81] but is all but irrelevant to medieval hostageship, in which the decision about what to do with the hostage was nearly always in the hands of the creditor: it was up to King Stephen, not some third party, whether or not to kill young William. In the few cases where hostages do seem to be in the hands of a third party, it is someone with ties of lordship to the debtor and/or the creditor, or a direct interest in the outcome of the agreement.[82]

The questions of the relative value of the pledge to the creditor and the debtor implicit in the distinction between 'hostage' and 'collateral', and the notion of 'union', are, by contrast, central. From the standpoint of the debtor, the ideal 'hostage' has no value to the creditor or anyone else: the debtor runs no risk that the creditor will keep the 'hostage' instead of (or in addition to) enforcing the agreement. But it is precisely the creditor who runs the risk that he has evaluated incorrectly the value of the 'hostage' to the debtor,[83] as apparently happened with King Stephen. If the creditor guesses wrong, he is left with a worthless pledge. It is thus in the interest of the debtor to dissimulate, as the town of La Rochelle was said to

'Reciprocity, Bilateralism, and Economic "Hostages": Self-Enforcing Agreements in International Trade', *International Studies Quarterly*, 30 (1986), 7–21; Robert E. Scott, 'A Relational Theory of Secured Financing', *Columbia Law Review*, 86 (1986), 901–77; Christina Ahmadijan and Joanne Oxley, 'Using Hostages to Support Exchange: Dependence and Partial Equity Stakes in Japanese Automotive Supply Relationships', *Journal of Law, Economics, and Organization*, 22 (2005), 213–33. Paul B. de Laat, 'Dangerous Liaisons: Sharing Knowledge within Research and Development Alliances', in Anna Grandori, ed., *Interfirm Networks: Organization and Industrial Competitiveness* (London, 1999), 208–33, engages with history more than most of this literature.

[80] Anthony T. Kronman, 'Contract Law and the State of Nature', *Journal of Law, Economics, and Organization*, 1 (1985), 5–32. The author presents these as ideal types that in fact overlap in practice.

[81] Williamson, 'Credible Commitments', 522–3.

[82] *Layettes*, 2:92 (no. 1800); *Foedera*, 1.1:31–2; *Brut y Tywysogyon*, s.a. 1241 (trans. Jones, 237); Wavrin, *Recueil des croniques*, 5.6.14–15 (RS 39.4:355–62); below, p. 62; Flodoard, *Annales*, s.a. 960 (CTH 39:148–9); Guy de Tournadre, *Histoire du Comté de Forcalquier (XII`ème` siècle)* (Paris, 1930), 231–40 (no. 7); Froissart 1.670 (8.2:6).

[83] Cf. Kronman, 'Contract Law', 14.

have done when faced with demands for hostages from Louis VIII: 'hostages, whom they took care to choose from among the least important people (*vili de plebe*), wishing thus to trick the illustrious king'.[84] The citizens of Mainz tried the same in negotiations with their archbishop in 1160, offering 'low-born and common boys' (*plebeios et ignobiles pueros*), a ploy that led to the collapse of the agreement.[85] Conversely, it is in the interest of the creditor to exercise due diligence: in a ransom agreement with John of England in 1208, his prisoner had to prove that his hostages were in fact his relatives.[86]

In the case of William Marshal, why did Stephen get it wrong? William Marshal was, as the account reports, a younger son, but the elder Marshal's boast—repeated in more graphic fashion by Caterina Sforza at the siege of Forli, at least in Machiavelli's account—suggests that any child would have been abandoned.[87] Yet these and other cases of child hostages should not be used to generalize about the weakness of affective feelings of parents for their children. The fact that despite cases such as this, children, and particularly sons, along with other relatives, remain common sources of hostages throughout the Middle Ages suggests that family ties were thought of as particularly strong. Indeed, William Marshal's mother sent a spy to check up on him, and she and his brothers were said to have suffered greatly in his absence.[88] In one of the rare cases where a hostage was killed, the act had the desired effect precisely because of such ties: after the execution of the son of Alexander Seton at Berwick in 1333, the town renewed the surrender agreement under dispute 'out of affection (*tendresce*) for their children, who were hostages'. Likewise, Orderic Vitalis describes a hostage granted to Henry I of England as useful 'because he was the brother-in-law of the aforesaid knight, and linked to him by a heavy obligation (*tanta necessitudine*)'.[89] The deception at the heart of Saxo's account of the siege of Søborg in 1161 relies on the garrison finding it equally plausible that their lord could 'care more for his castle than his grandson', but that he could then change his mind, declaring that he 'had more love (*caritas*) for his grandson than for his castle'.[90] A debtor's willingness to abandon a child, or any hostage, to a creditor, and perhaps to death, simply indicates that in a particular situation heavy obligation, or affection, or love was outweighed by other factors.

From the standpoint of the creditor, the other problem with Kronman's ideal 'hostage' is that 'killing' the 'hostage' means destroying the only means of leverage over the debtor: the creditor can exert pressure on the debtor by threatening to 'kill' the 'hostage', but once 'killed' the hostage has no value, and the creditor has no

---

[84] Nicolas de Brai, *Gesta Ludovici VIII, Francorum regis*, 1738–9 (*RHF* 17:342) ('Obsidibus primis, vili de plebe creatis,/Missis: egregium voluerunt fallere Regem'); cf. Allen, *Hostages*, 144–6.

[85] *Vita Arnoldi archiepiscopi Moguntini* (ed. Jaffé, 3:655).

[86] *Foedera*, 1.1:98. Similarly, below, p. 193, n. 112.

[87] Machiavelli, *Discorsi*, 3.6.18 (ed. Vivanti, 1:440). Similarly, Procop. *Vand.* 4.11.13.

[88] *History of William Marshal*, 620–8, 704–8 (ed. Holden, 1:32, 36).

[89] Gray, *Scalacronia* (ed. Stevenson, 163) ('Cest ostage mort a la maner, lez autres dedenz la vile par tendresce de lour enfauntz, qestoient ostages'); Orderic Vitalis, *Historia ecclesiastica*, 12.17 (OMT 6:228–30) ('quia prefati militis erat sororius, tantaque necessitudine confœderatus').

[90] Saxo Grammaticus, *Gesta Danorum*, 16.26.9–13 (ed. Olrik and Ræder, 1:436–7) ('maiorem se urbis quam nepotum sollicitudinem gerere...maiore Eskillum nepotis quam urbis caritate teneri').

leverage.[91] The debtor knows this, and thus is in an advantageous bargaining position, able to negotiate a level of performance less than what the 'hostage' was originally granted to guarantee.[92] At Newbury, for example, even after the elder Marshal made clear that he was willing to sacrifice his son rather than surrender the castle and the king failed to kill the boy, the parties might have negotiated the return of the hostage for something short of the original goal, such as a monetary payment.

'Killing' a 'hostage' only benefits a creditor when the transaction is considered as part of a series rather than as an isolated occurrence. Here, the value in killing the hostage comes from the establishment of a reputation for being willing to follow through on a threat to kill a hostage: it has no effect on the present agreement, but may have an effect on a subsequent agreement, an 'advertising function', and not only with respect to the same debtor.[93] Of course even effective advertising could backfire: after Frederic Barbarossa executed a hostage before Susa in 1168, the inhabitants attacked him and freed other hostages, thinking that acquiescence would be viewed as weakness.[94] In the case of William Marshal, the king's advisors—'deceivers' (*losengier*), to the author—who urged him to kill the hostage had a reasonable position. The king was in the midst of a war, and this was unlikely to be the last hostage agreement. Still, killing a human being—even in the midst of a war—could never be the same as destroying an heirloom, or liquidating an inventory, and a reputation for leniency might also have value. Saxo Grammaticus, for example, makes it clear that Valdemar I's threat to hang a hostage at Søborg in 1161 was a ruse (*simulabat*).[95] The degree to which there was a moral impediment to killing hostages is difficult to measure; I address the evidence in Chapter 7. By the later Middle Ages, the high status of some hostages—rather than any moral strictures—may have put them beyond the threat of execution.[96] But the structure of hostageship alone—the fact that once the debtor has violated the agreement, the hostage loses its value—goes a long way toward explaining the rarity of executed hostages in the sources.

Still more important, however, is the fact that Kronman's ideal 'hostage'—distinguished from 'collateral' by having no value outside the immediate context of the agreement[97] to anyone but the debtor—is very much an ideal type. Hostage transactions existed not only within a series—which could create, as just seen, an incentive to kill the hostage—but also in history, which exercised a countervailing force. In most conceivable situations, the two parties involved in a hostage

---

[91] Kronman, 'Contract Law', 17.

[92] Kronman, 'Contract Law', 14–15.

[93] Scott, 'A Relational Theory', 958 n. 210. Kronman, 'Contract Law', 18–19, describes reputation effects as a sort of hands-tying. Medieval hostage situations could conceivably be analysed from the perspective of game theory: e.g. Reuben Miller, 'Game Theory and Hostage-Taking Incidents: A Case Study of the Munich Olympic Games', *Conflict Quarterly*, 10 (1990), 12–33.

[94] John of Salisbury, *Letters*, 272 (OMT 2:558).

[95] Saxo Grammaticus, *Gesta Danorum*, 14.26.12 (ed. Olrik and Ræder, 1:437).

[96] J. R. Maddicott, *Simon de Montfort* (Cambridge, 1996), 284; Lavelle, 'Use and Abuse', 293 n. 102.

[97] 'Outside the context of the immediate agreement' needs to be added to Kronman's definition, for within the context of the agreement the 'hostage' always has value to the creditor as the object of threatened destruction; it has no value only after its destruction.

transaction could expect to be linked by circumstance—war, trade, alliance, marriage—at some point in the future, and the publicity value of killing a hostage would need to be balanced against the costs of such an action with respect to later transactions. In 1152, Stephen was fourteen years into a civil war that would end in the next year with the Treaty of Winchester. He was going to have to deal with John Marshal, as with his family, friends, and followers, even if he were victorious. So, too, were his successors: as noted, many years later, William himself granted his own sons to a different English king.[98] Killing William would sour relations not just with his father (whatever his boast), but to a greater or lesser degree with an extended network of potential negotiating partners. Reputation cut both ways. In this sense, parties in the real world are always and naturally embedded in the fourth of Kronman's strategies: union.

In fact, as will be seen in the next chapter, hostage transactions regularly *contributed* to the creation of 'fellow-feeling' between parties that is the defining characteristic of the strategy of 'union'. And as the sixth-century Roman official Cassiodorus recognized, such common interest was a much better guarantee: 'For what hostages will ensure good faith, if it cannot be entrusted to the affections?'[99] With respect to the creditor and debtor, keeping the hostage alive maintains a relationship that would be broken if the hostage were killed. This is true even in the context of a finite agreement such as the one proposed at Newbury. Keeping the hostage alive, even after the failure to surrender on schedule, keeps open the possibility for negotiation and communication. Common interest is, however, more evident in the case of hostages serving for open-ended agreements at noble courts. Here the presence of the hostages establishes a long-term link between parties. Furthermore, there is the strong possibility—and in some cases a clear intent—for the development of affective ties between the creditor and the *hostage*. William Marshal's biographer describes the beginnings of such ties between the hostage and the king, who referred to the boy as 'my dear friend' (*beals ami chers*) while playing games with him.[100] The possibilities of this bond were cut short by Stephen's death in 1154.

Such ties between hostage and creditor could be of lasting political value to the creditor, or rather to the creditor's polity. Ammianus Marcellinus, on a reconnaissance mission in Persia in 359, makes contact with the satrap Jovinianus, who was a hostage in Roman Syria during his youth and maintained an affection for Roman culture; he recognizes the Syrian Ammianus and gives him logistical support.[101] Gothic hostages spared by Narses at Lucca praise the Byzantine general and argue for the surrender of the town to him.[102] Duncan of Scotland remains at the English court after his knighting, and seven years later seizes the Scottish throne with English support.[103] Hywel, son of the Welsh prince Rhys ap Gruffudd of Deheubarth, serves

---

[98] Above, p. 27.
[99] Cassiodorus, *Variae*, 3.4 (MGH AA 12:80–1; trans. Barnish, 48).
[100] *History of William Marshal*, 613 (ed. Holden, 1:32).
[101] Amm. Marc. 18.6.20–1; cf. 18.7.1.
[102] Agathias, *Historiae*, 1.12–13, 18 (CFHB 2:24–7, 33); see below, p. 203.
[103] John of Worcester, *Chronicle*, s.a. 1087 (OMT 3:48); Simeon of Durham, *Historia regum*, 174 (RS 75.2:222).

thirteen years as a hostage at the court of Henry II of England and later returns as an ambassador; the extent to which he had taken on the culture of his hosts was reflected in his sobriquet—'Sais', or Englishman—and one chronicle noted that he was always faithful to the English king.[104] This was part of the logic behind the Roman use of hostages with client states.[105] It remained an important aspect of hostageship throughout the Middle Ages. Precisely because real-life hostages (as opposed to the ideal types of legal theory) were human beings with lives (extension in time), homelands (extension in space), and families (extension in social networks), they always had potential value for the creditor who held them, value that went beyond the strictly mechanical function of a pledge to be threatened with destruction.

The hostage metaphor in law and economics originated in a consideration of how to create incentives for *each* party to an agreement—in other words, *exchange*.[106] Hostages were granted by both sides in the Middle Ages in a variety of contexts: to secure a truce or peace treaty, as between the Danes and English in 1016; to guarantee safe passage, as was prescribed for Byzantine relations with the Pechenegs in the tenth-century manual *De administrando imperio*; or to facilitate the transfer of a town after a siege, as at Tyre in 1124.[107] The number of clear examples, however, is quite limited (more may be concealed behind phrases such as *datis obsidibus*, or by chroniclers whose subjects were on the short end of an encounter trying to make it seem more decisive than it was[108]), and most refer to precisely the geographical contexts just mentioned: the Byzantine East (following upon late Roman practice), relations between the Vikings and Northern Europe, and the Crusades—all cross-cultural frameworks. Chronologically, most fall in the tenth, eleventh, and twelfth centuries.[109] In other words, exchange

---

[104] ' "Cronica de Wallia" ', 41. See Adam J. Kosto, 'L'otage, comme vecteur d'échange culturel du IVe au XVe siècle', in *Les prisonniers*, 175–6.

[105] Allen, *Hostages*, 149–77.

[106] Schelling, 'An Essay on Bargaining', 300 n. 17; Williamson, 'Credible Commitments', esp. 530–3.

[107] *ASC*, s.a. 1016; Fulcher of Chartres, *Historia Hierosolymitana*, 3.34.2 (ed. Hagenmeyer, 734); Constantine VII, *De administrando imperio*, 8 (CFHB 1:56); also *Annales de Saint-Bertin*, s.a. 862 (SHF 89).

[108] See e.g. Lavelle, 'Use and Abuse', 283, and below, pp. 56–7.

[109] Byzantium/Russia: Symeon Logothetes, *Chronicon*, 136.29, 34 (CFHB 44:321, 323), a. 913; *Russian Primary Chronicle*, s.aa. 6505, 6609 (trans. Cross, 123, 199), aa. 997, 1101; Constantine VII, *De administrando imperio*, 8 (CFHB 1:54–6), s. 10; Comnena, *Alexiade*, 8.6.4, 9.1.6 (ed. Leib, 2:146, 160), aa. 1091, 1092. Northmen: *Annales Vedastini*, s.aa. 884, 885 (MGH SrG 12:55, 58); Flodoard, *Annales*, s.a. 944 (CTH 39:91); *Annales Fuldenses*, s.aa. 882 (MGH SrG 7:98); *ASC*, s.aa. 1016, (C) 1023; *Ágrip af Nóregskonungasogum*, 36 (ed. Driscoll, 48–9) (Denmark and Norway). Crusades: Albert of Aachen, *Historia Ierosolimitana*, 6.53 (OMT 474); Fulcher of Chartres, *Historia Hierosolymitana*, 3.34.2 (ed. Hagenmeyer, 734), a. 1124; Oliver of Paderborn, *Historia Damiatina*, 79, ap. (ed. Hoogeweg, 275–6, 280), a. 1222. Late Rome: Philostorgius, *Kirchengeschichte*, 12.14 (ed. Bidez and Winkelmann, 150), a. 425; Pseudo-Joshua the Stylite, *Chronicle*, 97 (trans. Twombley and Watt, 114), a. 506; Procop. *Goth.* 6.6.36, 6.7.13, 7.37.18, 39.27, aa. 537, 550. Other examples: Gregory of Tours, *Historiae*, 3.15, 6.31 (MGH SrM 1.1:112, 299), aa. 533, 583; Regino of Prüm, *Chronicon*, s.a. 863 (MGH SrG 50:80); Thietmar of Merseburg, *Chronicon*, 2.3 (MGH SrG ns 9:44), a. 953; *Chronica monasterii Casinensis*, 4.37 (MGH SS 34:503), a. 1111; Orderic Vitalis, *Historia ecclesiastica*, 12.10 (OMT 6:210), a. 1119; *Recueil...Jean IV*, 1:88–9 (no. 30), a. 1363; *Monumenta Henricina*, 6:210–12 (no. 64), a. 1437. Cf. proposals at: Lambert of Hersfeld, *Annales*, s.a. 1073 (MGH SrG 38:162); Galbert of Bruges, *De multro*, 95, 99 (CCCM 131:143, 146), s.a. 1128; Falco of Benevento, *Chronicon Beneventanum*, s.a. 1132 (ed. D'Angelo, 126); Saxo Grammaticus, *Gesta Danorum*, 14.25.2 (ed. Olrik and Ræder, 1:426), a. 1160.

played only a minor role in the history of medieval hostageship: hostages normally came into play where there was a substantial difference in power or leverage between the parties.[110]

Finally, the literature on contract theory considers hostageship as a *contractual* tactic—a mechanism used in structuring an agreement acceptable to both sides. But hostages could also be a *negotiating* tactic. If, as appears to be the case, the elder Marshal never intended to surrender the castle, he was not in fact trying to reach an agreement: the offer of a hostage was simply a ruse that allowed him to reinforce the castle.[111] On the other hand, it is not precisely true that the king failed in his goal. The castle ultimately submitted, and the demand for a hostage, acceptance of a hostage, and repeated unfulfilled threats to execute the hostage must be considered as part of the process that led to that conclusion rather than simply as aspects of a failed guarantee. It is far from safe to assume that the king did not know that the Marshal was likely to renege, or even that he would not be able to bring himself to execute an innocent child. It is possible to imagine that even with this knowledge, at that particular moment in the siege, the king saw the charade as it eventually played out as a means to an end.

The function of hostages as a negotiating tactic is evident not simply in those cases where hostages are repudiated. Froissart, for example, reports how John IV of Brittany sent his son as a hostage to Olivier de Clisson in the midst of negotiations; Clisson, who had already rejected the offer of three barons to remain as hostages, was so impressed by the duke's humility that he sent the boy back and made peace with his rival.[112] Hostages were among the guarantees (oaths, *fideiussores*, and real surety) offered by Walter of Palearia in his attempt to regain Innocent III's favour in 1202; the pope rejected the offer, telling Walter that he preferred to see spontaneous proof of Walter's loyalty.[113] In both of these cases, the mere offer of hostages led to an agreement. In 1213, the town of Toulouse haggled with the leaders of the Albigensian crusade over the number of hostages they would hand over: the bishops demanded 200, the town said they would only give 60, the bishops called their bluff and agreed, the town refused to hand any over, and a final settlement was delayed for almost a full year before Toulouse ultimately delivered 120.[114] Avignon followed suit in 1226, offering certain hostages to guarantee Louis VIII's passage through the town, then not handing over either the total number or the individuals promised, and barring the king's entry.[115] Similarly, the capitulation of Rouen was held up for twelve days in 1449 until the English agreed to hand over Lord Talbot as a hostage, during which time they managed to improve the terms of

[110] See also Benham, *Peacemaking*, 162–5. Allen, *Hostages*, 76–9, finds exchange even more rare in late Republican and early Imperial Rome.

[111] Cf. *The Song of Roland*, 3.40–6, 4.56–61, 43.572–3, 51.646, 54.679 (ed. Brault, 2:4, 36, 42, 44).

[112] Froissart 4 (ed. Kervyn de Lettenhove, 15:210–12).

[113] *Die Register Innocenz' III.*, 6:98–100 (no. 6.71) [Potthast 1923].

[114] Pierre des Vaux-de-Cernay, *Hystoria Albigensis*, 484, 507 (SHF 2:177–8, 201); *HGL* 8:647–51 (no. 174).

[115] *Layettes*, 2:85–6, 87–9 (nos. 1787, 1789); *Gesta Ludovici VIII* (*RHF* 17:309–10).

surrender.[116] In these cases, hostages were the cause of extended negotiations, with benefits to one of the parties.

The parties in these negotiations could use offers and refusals of hostages tactically precisely because they were both operating within the same framework. King Stephen and the elder Marshal had different ends in mind, but their tactical use of hostages rested on a common understanding of the way hostages were supposed to work. In a cross-cultural context, however, there was a strong possibility that hostages were understood in a very different fashion by the two sides—a possibility that may explain the frequent repudiation of hostages granted, for example, by the Saxons to Charlemagne in the late eighth century, or Procopius's characterization of North African Moors in the sixth: 'they care not either for oaths or for hostages, even though the hostages chance to be the children or brothers of their leaders'.[117] In such situations, hostages are part of a broad set of potentially ambiguous acts involved in cross-cultural peacemaking, such as oaths, baptism, fictive kinship, homage, and the use of writing. Differing interpretations are precisely what make short-term agreement possible, but they lay the groundwork for future disputes. That hostages can play such a role confirms their status as a very basic element of the grammar of interaction between peoples, and people.[118]

There is, then, no single logic to hostageship. Two parties to a hostage transaction may or may not view their acts in the same way, either with respect to the meaning or to goals. The way hostageship worked was specific to the context of, and the parties involved in, each grant. Success or failure of a guarantee as determined by whether or not an agreement secured by hostages was kept is thus a poor metric for understanding the institution, even in those cases—a minority, as noted—where outcomes are known. The logic, or better, logics of medieval hostageship must encompass such varied situations as the ransom of Valdemar II of Denmark, whose hostages were granted with a ten-year time limit, or the treaty between the emperor Otto IV and Ludwig of Bavaria, whose hostages could leave after two.[119] Or Henry III of England's distribution of hostages to barons who had themselves given him hostages on the same day. Or Edward I's return of ten hostages to Llewelyn, prince of Wales, after just a year.[120]

It is the historical context of individual episodes that renders explicable the variety of hostageship in question and the apparent underlying logic. It is to those contexts that we now turn.

---

[116] Du Clercq, *Mémoires*, 1.19 (ed. Reiffenberg, 1:345–6).

[117] Kosto, 'Carolingian', 123–4; Procop. *Vand.* 4.8.10 (trans. Dewing, 2:275).

[118] Richard Abels, 'Paying the Danegeld: Anglo-Saxon Peacemaking with the Vikings', in Philip de Souza and John France, eds., *War and Peace in Ancient and Medieval History* (Cambridge, 2008), 173–92; Stéphane Coviaux, 'Baptême et conversion des chefs scandinaves du IXᵉ au XIᵉ siècle', in Pierre Bauduin, ed., *Les fondations scandinaves en Occident et les débuts du duché de Normandie* (Caen, 2005), 67–80; Kershaw, *Peaceful Kings*, 17. A similar culturally conditioned slippage of meaning may be evident on the Franks Casket, where prisoners from the siege of Jerusalem are labelled *gisl*: Carol Neuman de Vegvar, 'Images of Women in Anglo-Saxon Art: I. Hostages: Women in the "Titus" Scene on the Franks Casket', *Old English Newsletter*, 24 (1990), 44–5.

[119] Arnold of Lübeck, *Chronica Slavorum*, 6.17 (MGH SrG 14:239); MGH Const. 2:49–50 (no. 40). These are the only two cases of time-limited hostageship that I have encountered.

[120] *Close Rolls . . . 1231–1234*, 312–13; *Foedera*, 1.2:562.

APPENDIX: EXECUTION OF HOSTAGES

This list does not include hostages who are said to have died in custody (see above, pp. 38–9), or hostages who are mutilated or otherwise mistreated. Although there are a few straightforward cases (536, 902, 1148, c.1160, 1212, 1427…) in which hostages are killed because the agreement for which they were granted was violated, most are more ambiguous.

*c.*530, Francia (Gregory of Tours, *Historiae*, 3.7 [MGH SrM 1.1:104]). Thuringians execute hostages granted at time of alliance with Theoderic. Gregory presents this as simple treachery, rather than response to a violation on the part of the Franks.

536, Rome (Procop. *Goth.* 5.11.26). Witigis executes senatorial hostages from Rome after the town welcomes Belisarius.

756, Iberia (*Ajbar machmuā* [trans. Lafuente y Alcántara, 89, 94]). ʿAbd al-Rahmān I receives two sons of Yūsuf al-Fihrī as hostages, then kills one and imprisons the other for life, but only after Yūsuf has already been killed for revolting.

902, Iberia (Ibn al-Qūtīya, *History* [trans. James], 137). ʿAbdallāh receives hostages from Ibrāhīm ibn Hajjāj and Ibn Hafsun; some are executed after a revolt.

876, England (Asser, *Life of King Alfred*, 49 [ed. Stevenson, 37; trans. Keynes and Lapidge, 83]). Keynes and Lapidge (246 n. 91, 249 n. 108) propose a textual emendation (*obsides* for *equites*) that would have the Vikings kill hostages exchanged with Alfred, out of treachery rather than a violation of an agreement.

884, West Francia (*Annales Fuldenses*, s.a. [MGH SrG 7:101–2]; *Annales Vedastini*, s.a. [MGH SrG 12:55]; Regino of Prüm, *Chronicon*, s.a. [MGH SrG 50:121–2]). Vikings kill hostages after the death of Carloman. These are presumably hostages exchanged to secure a truce earlier in the year, granted to allow the Franks time to raise 12,000 l. If the Franks had not paid, they would have been in violation, but the payment seems to have been made. Regino suggests that when the Vikings returned, the Franks accused them of violating the agreement; they replied that since there was a new king, another 12,000 l. was due. This is a possible source of a perceived Frankish violation. See Timothy Reuter, trans., *Annals of Fulda* (Manchester, 1992), 97 n. 10.

960, East Francia (Flodoard, *Annales*, s.a. [CTH 39:148–9]). Bruno, archbishop of Cologne, receives two hostages from Robert, count of Troyes; these are handed over to the king, who executes one of them—a son of Count Odelric—for treason. The hostage is thus not killed for anything that Robert has done.

1016, London (Thietmar of Merseberg, *Chronicon*, 7.40–1 [MGH SrG ns 9:448–9]). Emma of England grants Harald, Cnut, and Thorkell of Denmark 300 hostages to raise siege of London. After an English counterattack and reinforcement of the town, the Danes either kill or mutilate the hostages (*truncatis obsidibus*). Thietmar earlier (4.24 [9:160–2]) uses *truncare* to refer to mutilation. The 1016 agreement had called for Emma's sons to be killed, and they were not, so the English were in violation. In addition to the question of the translation of *truncatis*, the event is not attested independently and may be conflated with an earlier case of mutilation. See Lavelle, 'Use and Abuse', 293.

1049, Ireland (*Annals of the Four Masters*, s.aa. 1048, 1049 [trans. O'Donovan, 2:855–7]). Hostages granted for release of Gairbhith Ua Cathasaigh are put to death by Conchobhar Ua Maeleachlainn in the face of an attempt to recover them.

1092, Normandy (Orderic Vitalis, *Historia ecclesiastica*, 8 [OMT 4:294]). Robert of Bellême poisons the son of Robert Giroie. Context unknown.

1111, Aleppo (Albert of Aachen, *Historia Hierosolymitana*, 11.39 [OMT 812]; cf. Ibn al-Athīr, *Chronicle* [trans. Richards, 1:156–7]). Ridwan of Aleppo refuses aid to Mawdud of Mosul, but grants his son as a hostage to guarantee a promise not to intervene in Mawdud's conflict with Tancred. Mawdud later breaks the agreement and threatens to execute the hostage if Ridwan does not render aid. Mawdud executes the hostage. Note that here the violation is on the part of the *creditor*.

1124, Ireland (*Annals of the Four Masters*, s.aa. 1123, 1124 [trans. O'Donovan, 2:1017, 1021]; *Annals of Ulster*, s.a. 1124 [trans. Hennessy and MacCarthy, 2:11]). Hostages of Desmond granted in 1123 killed by Toirdhealbhach, king of Connacht.

1148, Faro (*Annales Elmarenses*, s.a. [ed. Grierson, 111–12]). Faro hands over forty hostages to guarantee payment to besieging Crusader force; when they fail to pay, the hostages are hanged.

1159, Crema (Rahewin of Freising, *Gesta Friderici I. imperatoris*, 4.56–7 [MGH SrG 46:294]; cf. *Gesta Federici I. imperatoris in Lombardia* [MGH SrG 27:37]). Barbarossa executes forty hostages at the siege of Crema and has others tied to siege engines. It is not clear when the hostages were granted. Crema may have entered into an agreement at the same time as Milan, Pavia, Cremona, and Piacenza, in 1158 (see RI 4.2.2:607); the *Gesta Federici* state that hostages from *Cremona*, along with prisoners from Milan, were the victims. See below, pp. 93–6.

1170, Ireland (Gerald of Wales, *Expugnatio Hibernica*, 1.10, 17 [RS 21.5:244, 257–8]; *Annals of the Four Masters*, s.aa. 1166, 1167, 1169, 1170 [trans. O'Donovan, 2:1161, 1167, 1173, 1177–9]). Diarmait of Leinster grants son, grandson, and the son of his foster-brother, as part of a submission to the overlordship of Ruadri of Connacht. Diarmait rebels; Ruadri executes the hostages on the advice of Tighearnan Ua Ruairc, who also kills his own hostages from East Meath.

1168, Italy (Otto of Saint-Blasien, *Chronica*, 20 [MGH SrG 47:27]; Obertus, *Annales*, s.a. [MGH SS 18:75]); John of Salisbury, *Letters*, 272 [OMT 2:554–60]; *Gesta Federici I. Imperatoris in Lombardia*, s.a. [MGH SrG 27:62]; *Annales Brixiensis*, s.a. [MGH SS 18:813]). Barbarossa hangs Zilius de Prando, a hostage from Brescia, before the walls of Susa. The *Gesta Federici* say that it was in response to an attack on Biandrate in which Brescia participated. John of Salisbury says that this was because of his personal participation in a conspiracy against the emperor. Otto of Saint-Blasien claims that Barbarossa executed all the hostages received from Milan, while Obertus says it was some of the Lombard hostages. See below, pp. 93–6.

1190, Iconium (Dietrich of Nieheim, *Cronica* [MGH Staatsschriften des späteren Mittelalters 5.2:271]). Writing in the fourteenth century, Dietrich claims that Frederic executed some hostages granted by Qilij Arslan, sultan of Iconium, although contemporary sources say merely that they were kept as captives after violation of the agreement. See Kosto, 'Crusades', 12.

1191, Acre (Roger of Howden, *Gesta Henrici II et Ricardi I* [RS 49.2:185–90]; Ibn al-Athīr, *Chronicle* [trans. Richards, 2:388–90]; etc.). Richard I massacres Muslim troops after fall of Acre. The precise status of the victims is not clear. See Kosto, 'Crusades', 21–4.

1196, Scotland (John of Fordun, *Chronica gentis Scotorum*, Gesta annalia, 22 [ed. Skene, 275]). Harald Maddadsson, earl of Orkney, is captured by William I of Scotland, imprisoned, and released against the hostageship of his son, Thorfinn. When Harald rebels again, Thorfinn is mutilated and dies in captivity.

1212, Wales (Roger of Wendover, *Flores historiarum*, s.a. [RS 84.2:61]; Gervase of Canterbury, *Gesta regum*, cont., s.a. [RS 73.2:107]; *Barnwell Chronicle* [RS 58.2:207]). In response to Welsh rebellion, John of England executes (twenty-eight) hostages received at the time of Llewelyn's submission the previous year. The execution of the son of Maelgwyn ap Rhys by Robert de Vieuxpont in the same year is probably connected to this episode (*Brut*, s.a. [trans. Jones, 195]). Of the many accounts of the treatment of Welsh hostages in 1165, only the *Annales monasterii de Waverleia*, s.a. (RS 36.2:239) might be interpreted as describing execution rather than mutilation: 'perdidit obsides'.

1237, Ireland (*Annals of the Four Masters*, s.a. [trans. O'Donovan, 3:293]). Hostages of Conor, son of Cormac, executed by Felim, son of Cathal Crobderg. Context undetermined.

*c.*1240, Ravenna (Salimbene de Adam, *Cronica*, s.a. 1285 [CCCM 125A:910]). Father of Guido da Polenta, a hostage from Ravenna, is executed by Frederic II due to the machinations of Guido Malabocca—and thus not for anything that Ravenna did to violate the agreement.

*c.*1240, Ravenna (Salimbene de Adam, *Cronica*, s.aa. 1240, 1250 [CCCM 125:261, 125A:554]). Frederic II burns alive Aica, daughter of Paul Traversario, podestà of Ravenna, out of anger at the father for switching allegiance of the town to the papacy. See RI 5.1.1:2449b.

1246, Sligo (*Annals of the Four Masters*, s.a. 1246 [trans. O'Donovan, 317–19]). Maurice Fitzgerald receives two hostages from Melaghlin O'Donnell and leaves them in the castle of Sligo; O'Donnell attacks Sligo; the garrison hangs the hostages.

1333, Berwick (Gray, *Scalacronica* [ed. Stevenson, 163]). English execute the son of Alexander Seton after the town refuses to abide by conditional surrender agreement. Town claims that they had in fact been relieved. See below, p. 108.

1373, Derval (Froissart 1.742 [8.2:158–9]). French execute two knights and two squires after town refuses to abide by conditional surrender agreement. Robert Knollys claims that his captains had no right to make the agreement in the first place. See below, p. 108.

1418, Senlis (Pintoin, *Chronique du religieux de Saint-Denys*, 38 [ed. Bellaguet, 6:194–7]; Monstrelet 1.186 [3:252–3]). French execute four hostages after town refuses to abide by conditional surrender agreement. Town disputes violation. See below, pp. 108–9.

1427, La Gravelle (*Chronique de la Pucelle*, 25 [ed. Vallet de Viriville, 249]). Hostages executed for failure to abide by a conditional surrender agreement. See below, p. 109.

1467, Liège (Commynes, *Mémoires*, 2.1–3 [SHF 1:118–37]). Hostages granted by Liège are freed, even though the town is in clear violation of the agreement. Some are later executed, not for the town's violation of the original agreement, but because they returned to the fighting in violation of a promise made when they were released. See below, pp. 204–6.

3

Hostages in the Early Middle Ages:
Communication, Conversion,
and Structures of Alliance

In the year 772, Charlemagne mustered his troops at Worms and crossed for the first time into Saxon territory. His army proceeded to Eresburg, where it seized a fortification, and then looted and destroyed the nearby pagan sanctuary. Continuing downstream, the army reached the River Weser, where Charlemagne 'held a meeting with the Saxons, and received twelve hostages, and returned to Francia'. These were hostages for submission: guarantees that the Saxons would accept Carolingian overlordship. The submission did not last long, as in the following year Saxons invaded Frankish territory, attacking the Christian sanctuary at Fritzlar. Charlemagne had been in Italy, but upon his return, in 774, he sent armies again into Saxony, and then again in 775. In that year, after defeating a Saxon army at the Weser, Charlemagne received the submission of a group of Saxons identified as the Eastphalians, who 'gave hostages according to his wishes and swore oaths to the effect that they would be faithful to the said lord King Charles'. They were followed in their submission by a second group, the Angrarii, who also gave hostages, and then, after another battle, by the Westphalians, who 'gave hostages just like those other Saxons'. Again, however, these submissions were short-lived. In the next year, 776, a messenger appeared at court reporting that the Saxons were in rebellion: 'they had abandoned all their hostages and violated their oaths'. Another campaign led to a swift Frankish victory and another submission with hostages. In the following year, they rebelled again. The Saxons granted and abandoned their hostages again in 779, and then in each year from 794 to 798.[1]

Charlemagne's Saxons are perhaps the most familiar hostages of the early Middle Ages, because of their repeated appearance in the *Royal Frankish Annals*, whose narrative has long provided the foundation for standard accounts of Carolingian history. And in fact hostages for submission are the most common type of early medieval variety. But, as the Saxons' history of repeated betrayal suggests, submission in this period was not always straightforward.[2] Neither was the use of hostages.

---

[1] *Annales regni Francorum*, s.aa. 772, 775, 776, 779, 795, 797, 798 (MGH SrG 6:34, 40, 42, 46, 50, 96, 100, 104); *Annales qui dicuntur Einhardi*, s.aa. 794, 795 (MGH SrG 6:97); *Annales Petaviani*, s.a. 796 (MGH SS 1:18). Cf. Einhard, *Vita Karoli Magni*, 7 (MGH SrG 25:10).

[2] Benham, *Peacemaking*, 160–1, offers parallels to later Welsh and Slav hostage giving.

The sources for the sixth and seventh centuries are famously sparse, and only the work of Gregory of Tours offers more than one or two mentions of hostageship in the post-Roman West.[3] When with the rise of the Carolingians in the eighth century the sources become more dense, we find hostageship almost entirely limited to the realms of warfare and diplomacy. Open-ended grants predominate, although finite agreements do appear more frequently toward the end of the period. And, when identified, the hostages are most frequently sons. In other words, early medieval hostageship draws on a fairly limited range of the possible varieties of medieval hostageship surveyed in the previous chapter.

Limited, but not static. In the later Roman Empire, one of the signal developments in hostageship was its decentring. The pattern, normal for the Republic and the early Empire, that saw hostages delivered to the Roman emperor in the wake of conquest was broken. As Rome's power relative to its neighbours in the east and the north declined, it occasionally found itself in the position of granting, rather than receiving hostages. When receiving hostages, it was increasingly not just from enemies, but also from subordinates. Furthermore, hostageship became less a given than something subject to negotiation.[4] The political dominance of the Franks in the early Middle Ages, and the consequent preponderance of sources focused on the Franks, gives the eighth-, ninth-, and tenth-century evidence a similar trajectory: sources that show the Carolingians collecting hostages from their enemies, such as the Saxons, as they consolidated their power over much of Western Europe give way to sources that show the Carolingians and their successors 'exporting' rather than 'importing' hostages, and hostages being used in a variety of finite arrangements that reflect the Carolingians' weakened position. And as the Saxon history suggests, the extent of their strength even at its height should not be exaggerated. In such a world, hostages were crucial both as a mechanism of politics and as a symbol of power, but in ways that do not always seem to correspond.

The present chapter begins by examining more closely hostages for submission and then other hostage agreements, open-ended and finite, that run counter to a triumphalist view of Carolingian history. In this period the symbolic role of hostages, beyond any guaranteeing function, appears crucial. A brief analysis of the use of hostages in Frankish–Papal–Lombard relations shows in addition how the use of hostages was not simply a form of political communication, but could implicate directly the interests of parties beyond a hostage's grantor and the custodian. I then examine three documents that provide rare evidence for the *fate* of hostages in the early Middle Ages, the last of which leads back into a consideration of the symbolic and communicative role of hostages in the context of conversion. Early medieval hostages, I argue, must be understood as a manifestation of the structures of family and alliance that defined early medieval political action.[5]

[3] Gregory of Tours, *Historiae*, 2.8, 2.9, 3.7, 3.15, 3.23, 5.26, 6.26, 6.31, 7.39, 10.9 (MGH SrM 1.1:51, 54, 104, 112, 122, 232, 293, 299, 362, 493); *Liber in gloria martyrum*, 83 (MGH SrM 1.2:544). See generally Kosto, 'Late Antiquity'.
[4] Kosto, 'Late Antiquity'.
[5] Kosto, 'Carolingian', is an earlier attempt to address this question, with fuller references in places. See also Kershaw, *Peaceful Kings*, esp. 17–19.

HOSTAGES AND POLITICAL COMMUNICATION

Charlemagne was not the first Carolingian king to receive hostages from the Saxons, nor were the Saxons the only group that submitted to Carolingian rule via hostages. Carolingian rulers also accepted hostages at various points from the Lombards, Bavarians, Alamannians, Aquitanians, Basques, Bretons, Danes, Norse, Frisians, Iberian Muslims, various Slavic groups (Sorbs, Veletians, Obodrites, Siusli, Linones), Moravians, and Bohemians. Nor were hostages a purely Carolingian institution in the early Middle Ages. The emperors at Constantinople, Islamic emirs, doges of Venice, and kings of England,[6] Sweden, and Lombardy received hostages from their enemies as well. Hostageship was even employed by these 'subject' peoples to guarantee and mark submission. Thus the Danish king, Godfrid, received the son of the Obodrite ruler in 809. Then when Godfrid's sons rose up against his successor, Harald, Louis the Pious commanded the Saxons and Obodrites to come to Harald's aid and attack the Norse of Silendi, from whom they received forty hostages. In 839, the Saxons defeated a tribe of Sorbs, killed their king, and received hostages from the new one they set up in his place.[7]

In most cases, the actual reason for the grant of hostages remains implicit: the annals state that hostages are granted after a conquest that suggests submission, that is, after the victors subjugate, defeat, conquer, overcome, or make tributaries of their enemies.[8] In a few cases, what is merely suggested elsewhere is made clear. Hostages are described as given to guarantee promises not to rebel (Bavarians, a. 747; Lombards, a. 756), or to remain loyal or faithful (Basques a. 768; Angrarii, a. 775), or to serve the emperor (Sorbs, a. 806).[9] Noteworthy in this respect is the statement of the royal annals that in 797 Charlemagne accepted the surrender (*deditio*) of the Saxons 'by means of hostages' (*per obsides*).[10]

Yet while the historical contexts of the conquests of Lombardy and Saxony, for example, are reasonably well understood, in many cases what exactly 'submission' entailed is open to discussion. It is clear that the sources often simplify and even distort complex situations, and it is necessary to read between the lines to determine the precise relationship between any given parties. Hostages played a central role in defining such relationships. For example, the quite consistent descriptions of hostages as granted rather than taken might make what was in fact a straightforward submission look more like an agreement between equally positioned opponents, but the chroniclers occasionally let slip that such grants were made under duress. The garrison of Saint-Vaast gave (*dederunt*) hostages to the king of West Francia,

[6] Lavelle, 'Use and Abuse'.

[7] *Annales regni Francorum*, s.aa. 809, 815 (MGH SrG 6:128, 142); *Annales de Saint-Bertin*, s.a. 839 (SHF 35).

[8] e.g. *Annales Mettenses priores*, s.aa. 734, 738 (MGH SrG 10:27, 30); Fredegar, *Chronica*, cont., 25 (MGH SrM 2:180); *Annales regni Francorum*, s.a. 779 (MGH SrG 6:50); *Annales Laureshamenses*, s.a. 788 (MGH SS 1:34).

[9] Fredegar, *Chronica*, cont., 32, 38, 51 (MGH SrM 2:182, 185, 191); *Annales Mettenses priores*, s.a. 775 (MGH SrG 10:63); *Chronicon Moissiacense*, s.a. 806 (MGH SS 1:308).

[10] *Annales regni Francorum*, s.a. (MGH SrG 6:100).

'but not willingly' (*non voluntarie*). The duke of the Slavs sent (*mittit*) his son to Otto I because he was 'terrified' (*terrore compulsus*). The duke of Moravia gave hostages to Louis the German, 'forced by necessity' (*necessitate coactus*), which-ever and however many Louis the German wanted; Robert, count of Troyes, acted under similar compulsion faced with the troops of Bruno of Cologne and King Lothar in 960 (*Coactusque*); Alfred of Wessex, likewise, forced the North-umbrians and East Saxons to offer hostages (*compellens*). Further to the south, Adalchis of Benevento was forced (*coactata*) to pay tribute and grant hostages to Sawdan, emir of Bari.[11] This language suggests open-ended grants of hostages after defeat or subjection to guarantee the positive obligation of continued fidelity.

The language of force and the transfer of hostages might therefore reveal the differences in power between parties to an agreement. Conversely, the language of agreement might, in combination with the grant of hostages, serve to mask such differences.[12] There are several examples of this in Frankish dealings with the Vikings, where what the Frankish sources describe looks more like settlement than defeat. Charles the Simple's cession of Normandy to Rollo in 911 is the most famous case: 'the aforesaid Charles, having received hostages, handed over to them Neustria'. With similar words, Flodoard describes Robert's concession of Brittany and the county of Nantes in 921. Hostages in these cases marked submission, but in the broader context of territorial compromises that are best viewed as strategic defeats.[13] Similarly, *exchanges* of hostages, which would logically only occur between parties of equal strength, might also cloak power differentials, or reflect the sources struggling to come to terms with the fact that their subjects had become exporters rather than importers of hostages. When Charles the Fat and the Viking chieftain Godfrid exchanged hostages to seal their shaky peace in 882, for example, equality was definitely not maintained, as the deal involved tribute payments and the Vikings sailing off with 200 captives.[14] Later, according to Flodoard, it was with an exchange of hostages that Hugh and Heribert 'conceded' the county of Nantes to the Northmen in 927.[15] In both this case and the earlier unilateral grant of hos-tages in 921, the settlement and cession occur after what Flodoard describes as extended sieges of the Vikings by the Franks, the first of five months, the second of five weeks. Flodoard thus depicts the Vikings—who in each case depart signifi-cantly richer—as on the defensive; the grants of hostages are an element in that depiction. When we read that Hugh the Great and the Vikings in 944

---

[11] *Annales Vedastini*, s.a. 899 (MGH SrG 12:81); *Annales Altahenses maiores*, s.a. 973 (MGH SrG 4:11, emended); *Annales Fuldenses*, s.a. 864 (MGH SrG 7:62); Richer, *Historiae*, 3.12 (MGH SS 38:177); William of Malmesbury, *Gesta regum Anglorum*, 2.121 (OMT 1:184); Erchempert, *Historia Langobardorum Beneventanorum*, 29 (MGH SrL 245); See also *Annales de Saint-Bertin*, s.a. 871 (SHF178–9); *Annales Fuldenses*, s.aa. 848, 862 (MGH SrG 7:38, 56).

[12] Benham, *Peacemaking*, is particularly attentive to this issue generally.

[13] *Genealogia ducum Northmannorum* (ed. Duchesne): 'Karolus prædictus acceptis obsidibus, eis Neustriam tradidit'); Flodoard, *Annales*, s.a. (CTH 39:6).

[14] *Annales Fuldenses*, s.a. (MGH SrG 7:98–9); cf. cont. Ratisbonensis, s.a. (7:108).

[15] Flodoard, *Annales*, s.a. (CTH 39:38): 'datis acceptisque obsidibus et concesso sibi pago'.

confirmed a treaty by the exchange of hostages, then, we are probably not looking at a straightforward agreement between equals.[16] The receipt of hostages by the Frankish kings in these cases may have helped contemporaries swallow the bitter pill of territorial concession by making a defeat look more like the formation of a relationship of subordination. Hostages remained a marker of power, whether or not that power was a political reality.

This loss of relative power on the part of the Franks echoes the Roman experience, where after centuries of being only on the receiving end of hostage transactions—there are no certain Roman hostages in foreign hands between 107 BCE and 405 CE[17]—the emperors found themselves handing over hostages to Persians and barbarian rulers alike. And as in the later Roman Empire, the decentring of early medieval hostageship is also seen in open-ended grants for the submission not of the vanquished, but of one's own subordinates. For example, in 872, the emperor Louis II received as hostages for good conduct the sons of Waifer, prince of Salerno. Louis had apparently taken this action on the advice of Waifer's enemy, Landulf, bishop of Capua, who had become one of the emperor's closest advisors. When Louis returned to the north, leaving the empress Engelberge in charge in Capua, Landulf seized Waifer and accused him of treachery before the empress. When the charges fell through, Engelberge accepted hostages from Landulf himself. Here hostages were used not to guarantee the submission of a defeated enemy, but the fidelity of a potentially rebellious underling. Hostages were also wisely requested from one's troops.[18] Richer reports that Duke Gilbert of Lorraine judged at one point that his knights might defect if he did not require an oath from them, so he 'accepted fidelity from all of them by means of oaths but also whatever hostages he wished'.[19]

Finally, the decentring of hostageship is reflected in the increasing evidence for its use in a variety of short-term undertakings, mostly associated with the day-to-day conduct of warfare: truces,[20] or agreements for the return of property[21] or the release of captives.[22] Again, it is possible that the shift is an illusion created by the nature of the sources, by chroniclers paying more attention to the details of

---

[16] Flodoard, *Annales*, s.a. (CTH 39:6, 38, 91).

[17] Kosto, 'Late Antiquity'.

[18] *Chronicon Salernitanum*, 119 (ed. Westerbergh, 133); Erchempert, *Historia Langobardorum Beneventanorum*, 35–6 (MGH SrL 248). Ottonian examples: *Translatio S. Alexandri* (MGH SS 30.2:955); Orestes of Jerusalem, *De historia et laudibus Sabae et Macarii Siculorum*, 46 (ed. Cozza-Luzi, 317); *Catalogus comitum Capuae*, cont. (MGH SrL 501); Flodoard, *Annales*, s.a. 939 (CTH 39:72). Non-Frankish examples: *Russian Primary Chronicle*, s.a. 6452 (trans. Cross, 72); Ibn 'Abd Rabbih, *al-'Iqd al-farīd*, 190 (trans. Monroe, 96); *Crónica Albeldense*, 15.13 (ed. Gil Fernández, 179).

[19] Richer, *Historiae*, 1.40 (MGH SS 38:75) ('fidem ab omnibus ex iureiurando, sed et obsides quos vult accipit').

[20] Flodoard, *Annales*, s.aa. 939, 942 (CTH 39:71, 85); *Annales Vedastini*, s.a. 884 (MGH SrG 12:55); Flodoard, *Annales*, s.a. 959 (CTH 39:146); Richer, *Historiae*, 2.28 (MGH SS 38:118). *Alfred and Guthrum*, 5 (ed. Liebermann, 1:128), on the surface about commercial transactions, probably conceals the establishment of temporary truces on these occasions; see Asser, *Life of King Alfred* (trans. Keynes and Lapidge, 312–13 [n. 7]); cf. Æthelweard, *Chronicon*, 4.3 (ed. Campbell, 44).

[21] *Liber pontificalis*, Hadrianus, 30/310 (ed. Duchesne, 1:495); *Annales qui dicuntur Einhardi*, s. aa. 755, 756, 760, 761 (MGH SrG 6:13, 19); *Codex Carolinus*, 64 (MGH Epp. 3:591); Asser, *Life of King Alfred*, 46 (ed. Stevenson, 35); *Annales Fuldenses*, s.a. 873 (MGH SrG 7:80–1).

[22] *Annales de Saint-Bertin*, s.a. 862 (SHF 88–9).

conflicts, but there are two reasons for thinking that this is not the case. First, as I will demonstrate in the following chapter, the growth of short-term hostage agreements in the ninth and especially tenth centuries lays the groundwork well for institutional developments in subsequent centuries. Second, the nature of both the conflict with the Vikings and the break-up of Carolingian hegemony presented a very different military and political context, one in which the subjects of our sources had to use hostages in different ways.

Hostages to guarantee safe passage appear to have been the most pressing concern. The logic of such transactions may be self-evident, but sources do occasionally state it. In a letter of 775 to Charlemagne, Pope Hadrian relates that Hildebrand, duke of Spoleto, proposed presenting himself before the pope if the pope sent hostages, 'on account of his doubts'. Tassilo of Bavaria refused to travel to meet Charlemagne at Worms in 781 without a grant of hostages 'who would make it unnecessary for him to doubt his safety'. Most explicitly, the *Deeds of the Bishops of Cambrai* reports that in 978 Otto II offered to meet Lothar of West Francia for single combat, but that he would only come if hostages had been given lest he be ambushed on the way there.[23]

The most common situation that called for hostages for safe passage—at least in the sources that dominate this period—was a negotiation to end military conflict. Parties did not always attempt to arrange for general truces for fixed periods, but rather looked to mechanisms that would guarantee the safety of the negotiators simply for as long as they were at risk. In the spring of 867, Charles the Bald announced a campaign against Salomon of Brittany to follow an assembly at Chartres on 1 August. Mediators managed to arrange for negotiations at Compiègne at the start of August, with the date for the assembly of the host put off, if necessary, until 25 August. Charles granted hostages to Salomon for the safety of his negotiator, who met Charles in Compiègne as planned on 1 August. The negotiations were successful, and Charles cancelled the campaign. When the West Frankish nobility met a few years later to settle on new leadership for the realm, they are said to have come together *jure obsidum*. Under similar agreements Ragenald, count of Roucy, entered Reims on behalf of Louis IV to treat with Duke Hugh, and Odo of Blois negotiated with the garrison of Melun. One account of the meeting of the Viking chieftain Godfrid and the emperor Charles the Fat in 882 has Godfrid travel six miles outside his fortress to meet the king, but only after he had received hostages.[24]

The particular concern for the safety of negotiators, and the role of hostages in establishing that safety, may be seen in the events leading up to the Treaty of

---

[23] *Codex Carolinus*, 57 (MGH Epp. 3:582) ('pro sua dubitatione'); *Annales qui dicuntur Einhardi*, s.a. 781 (MGH SrG 6:59) ('sub quibus de sua salute dubitare nulla sit necessitas'); *Gesta episcoporum Cameracensium*, 1.98 (MGH SS 7:441).

[24] *Annales de Saint-Bertin*, s.a. 867 (SHF 136–7); Richer, *Historiae*, 1.4, 2.45, 4.75 (MGH SS 38:41, 130–1, 284); cf. Flodoard, *Annales*, s.a. 945 (CTH 39:97); *Annales Fuldenses*, s.a. 882 (MGH SrG 7:98–9) (see RI 1.1:1639b). Richer, *Historiae*, 2.28 (MGH SS 38:118) repeats the phrase *iure obsidum*. See also above, pp. 28–9.

Verdun of 843, the famous division of the Carolingian lands among Charlemagne's grandsons: Charles the Bald, Louis the German, and Lothar. The brothers had agreed that their representatives, forty each, would meet at Metz on 1 October 842, but when Charles was passing through the area on 30 September, he discovered Lothar and his forces camped at nearby Thionville, while his own and Louis's forces were based in Worms, some 120 miles away. Fearful for the safety of his (and Louis's) men were they to meet for the negotiations in Metz in the shadow of Lothar's army, Charles presented Lothar with the following choices. If he wanted the conference to take place at Metz as originally planned, he either had to offer hostages for the safety of the participants or agree that all the parties would encamp at an equal distance from the town. Alternatively, the conference could take place at Worms, and Louis and Charles would provide whatever hostages he wished. Or they could all move their camps to locations equidistant from Metz, or hold the conference at a different location—the ultimate solution.[25] What is particularly striking here is that Charles and Louis could believe that a grant of hostages would in fact secure the safety of such a large number of their most important men, for the commissioners were not mere clerks but rather men 'pre-eminent in nobility'. Charles and Louis were ready to trust Lothar not to trade the lives of his hostages for the opportunity to cripple if not his brothers' military strength, then at least their administrative capabilities. Rational choice theory would lead to the sacrifice of the hostages to gain control of the more 'valuable' commissioners. In the context of medieval politics, however, hostages had a 'value' beyond their worth in comparison to the thing guaranteed. In this case, a grant of hostages communicated good faith in ways that words could not.

Hostages for safe passage might thus play the same complex symbolic and communicative role as hostages for submission. When principals rather than delegates appeared under the protection of hostages, it was more likely than not to be a case of submission rather than of negotiations between equals. Hostages might also be granted by the weaker party as a sign of submission, but these appear distinct from the hostages granted for safe passage by the stronger party to the weaker one. Charlemagne, for example, granted hostages to Tassilo of Bavaria in 781 so that he would appear at Worms to acknowledge his fidelity. He did the same for the Saxon nobles Widukind and Abbio in 785, in advance of their baptism at Attigny; they did not view a royal promise as sufficient, and so requested hostages for their safety. Other Carolingian rulers and their successors followed suit. Herispoius of Brittany submitted to the rule of Charles the Bald after an exchange of hostages and oaths, while the Danish prince Roric came to Louis the German to enter into his lordship only after a grant of hostages. Boso, besieged in *Durofostum* by Henry I of Germany, exited under a grant of hostages and met with the king to swear oaths and promise to return lands he had seized.[26] In each of these cases, the victor—or

[25] Nithard, *Histoire des fils de Louis le Pieux*, 4.4 (ed. Lauer, 134): 'nobilitate praestantes'.
[26] *Annales regni Francorum*, s.aa. 781, 785 (MGH SrG 6:59, 70); Regino of Prüm, *Chronicon*, s.a. 863 [sic] (MGH SrG 50:80); *Annales Fuldenses*, s.a. 873 (MGH SrG 7:78); *Annales Xantenses*, s.a. 873 (MGH SrG 12:32); Flodoard, *Annales*, s.a. 928 (CTH 39:40).

at least the stronger party—felt it important enough that the vanquished be personally present to submit that he was willing to grant hostages; conversely, the supplicant maintained respect by being able to appear on his terms.

Other cases suggest that—as seen in the discussion of hostages granted for submissions themselves—these submissions may not have been so straightforward. When in 789 Louis, king of Aquitaine, summoned the Basque rebel Adalric to an assembly, he refused to come without hostages, and then left well supplied with gifts and having apparently effected an exchange of prisoners.[27] Similarly, Rollo received hostages from Charles the Simple before going to their meeting in 911.[28] In 994 it was, arguably, Olaf Tryggvason of Norway who had the upper hand in his dealings with Æthelred II, as the latter was forced to promise a payment of 16,000 l. silver in addition to supplies as a way to halt the Viking attacks. But Æthelred convinced Olaf to meet him at Andover, where the king sponsored Olaf's Christian confirmation and showered him with additional gifts in return for a promise never again to invade England. Olaf's appearance at Andover was secured by hostages.[29] In short, the sources, most written from the perspective of the stronger party in these encounters, understandably report events in a way that favours their subjects; what appears to be a submission may in fact be closer to a negotiated settlement, and the grant of hostages for safe passage communicates that this was the case.

It is tempting, at least where kings are involved, to posit a connection between these grants of safe passage and a more general notion of royal protection.[30] If it were possible to trace punishments for violation of safe passage—and thus to compare them to punishments for other violations of royal protection—we could test this hypothesis. The evidence of normative sources is, unfortunately, too thin. The term *obses* appears only once in the law codes of the Germanic kingdoms: the Frisian code establishes a ninefold composition payment for the killing of a hostage. The Frisian law recalls a passage of the Digest in which such an action was defined as treasonable, but its fuller context is not entirely clear.[31] What is more, descriptive evidence is also lacking, because grants for safe passage were inevitably described as successful. Some were mere offers, never carried out: the negotiations among Charles, Louis, and Lothar were in the end held without hostages, for example. But I know of no case when an explicit grant of safe passage was violated. Nonetheless, like the frequently abandoned hostages for submission, hostages for safe passage were part of a symbolic discourse in which the *way* in which political acts were undertaken was as significant as the acts themselves.

---

[27] Astronomer, *Vita Hludowici imperatoris*, 5 (MGH SrG 64:298).

[28] Dudo of Saint-Quentin, *De moribus et actis primorum Normanniæ ducum*, 2.28 (ed. Lair, 168).

[29] *ASC*, s.a. The presence of gifts here and in the case of Adalric above links hostages to the sort of political communication via ritual examined by Gerd Althoff, *Spielregeln der Politik im Mittelalter: Kommunikation in Frieden und Fehde* (Darmstadt, 1997). In Dudo, too, Normandy is referred to as a *donum*.

[30] A complex subject in its own right; see recently e.g. Maurizio Lupoi, *The Origins of the European Legal Order*, trans. Adrian Belton (Cambridge, 2000 [1994]), 374–81.

[31] *Lex Frisionum*, 20.1 (MGH Fontes iuris Germanici antiqui in usum scholarum separatim editi 12:64); D. 48.4.1; see H. Siems, *Studien zur Lex Frisionum* (Ebelsbach, 1980), 321–2.

THE WIDER IMPACT OF HOSTAGE AGREEMENTS

Because of this symbolic role, hostages implicated parties beyond those directly involved in the agreement for which they were granted: the audience for the political communication they embodied. Third parties were also implicated in a direct way, however, taking an active interest in what in principle was a guarantee mechanism for a bilateral agreement. This aspect of hostageship is best seen in the comparatively rich and varied evidence for Carolingian involvement in the Italian peninsula, in which chronicle sources can be supplemented with letters between the Frankish kings and the popes.

As part of the 'First Peace of Pavia' agreed between the Frankish king Pippin, the Lombard king Aistulf, and Pope Stephen II in the late summer of 755, Aistulf granted to Pippin forty hostages. The various accounts differ as to the function of the hostages: the revised royal annals, echoing in substance the royal annals, say that they were received 'for returning the rights (*iustitia*) of the holy church of Rome', while the continuator of Fredegar claims it was 'never to withdraw from Frankish overlordship, and never again to enter with troops within the territories of the Holy See or the Empire'.[32] In either case, hostages are granted to Pippin by Aistulf at least in part to protect not his own, but *papal* interests. When Aistulf refused to fulfil his obligations, Pope Stephen wrote twice to Pippin in late 755 to encourage him to enforce the terms of the Pavia treaty. In a curious line in the second letter, the pope requests: 'quickly and without delay return those things that you promised to Saint Peter through your grant (*donatio*): the towns and the other places and all the hostages and captives (*obsides et captivos*), and everything contained in that grant'.[33] The *donatio* in question is most likely the Pavia treaty, but the identity of the hostages is a puzzle. Various interpretations have been proposed: the forty hostages received by Pippin from Aistulf; Roman hostages in the hands of the Lombards; or hostages received from the cities promised in the Pavia treaty to guarantee their transfer.[34] Whatever the precise explanation, the hostages are out of the hands of the party whose rights are in question. Similarly in 756, Pippin's emissary Fulrad accepted hostages from the towns of the Pentapolis as guarantees of their subjection not to Pippin, but to Rome. Pippin did receive further hostages from Aistulf in that year for his own purposes;[35] these, combined with the forty from the previous year, were the subject of two letters of Pope Paul I to Pippin in 758. In the first, the pope reported to Pippin that Desiderius

---

[32] *Annales qui dicuntur Einhardi*, s.a. (MGH SrG 6:13): 'pro reddenda sanctae Romanae ecclesiae iustitia' (cf. *Annales regni Francorum*, s.a. [MGH SrG 6:14]). Fredegar, *Chronica*, cont., 37 (MGH SrM 2:184): 'ut numquam a Francorum ditiones se abstraheret et ulterius ad sedem apostolicam Romanam et rem publicam hostiliter numquam accederet'.

[33] *Codex Carolinus*, 7 (MGH Epp. 3:493): 'velociter et sine ullo inpedimento, quod beato Petro promisistis per donationem vestram, civitates et loca atque omnes obsides et captivos beato Petro reddite vel omnia, quae ipsa donatio continet'. Cf. 6 (MGH Epp. 3:488–90).

[34] Kosto, 'Carolingian', 139 n. 77.

[35] *Liber pontificalis*, Stephanus II, 47/253 (ed. Duschesne, 1:454); Fredegar, *Chronica*, cont., 38 (MGH SrM 2:185).

proposed returning to papal hands the city of Imola, on the condition that Pippin return Desiderius's hostages and establish a peace between the Franks and Lombards. In the second, Paul revoked his request in the first, apparently written under duress, and encouraged Pippin to hold on to the hostages.[36] Here it was the pope involving himself in a hostage transaction between Pippin and Desiderius.

This pattern continues under Charlemagne. During the final campaign against Desiderius in 773, according to the *Liber pontificalis*, Charlemagne offered to accept three sons of Lombard judges as a guarantee that the Lombard king would return long-disputed towns to papal control; Desiderius refused this offer, and Pavia fell soon thereafter. In 780, Pope Hadrian requested fifteen hostages from the Neapolitans as part of a deal to return to them the town of Terracino; he then wrote to Charlemagne that he had no intention of returning the hostages without the king's approval, for it had been done 'in [the king's] service'.[37] In 787, Charlemagne marched into Italy and at the instigation of Pope Hadrian invaded Benevento. To forestall the invasion, the duke of Benevento sent a party headed by his two sons, Grimoald and Romuald, to Charlemagne and offered them as hostages. Charlemagne kept only the younger son, Grimoald, along with twelve others; he sent Romuald back.[38] Soon thereafter, the duke of Benevento died, and Charlemagne made a deal with Grimoald to put him in power. At this point the episode starts appearing in correspondence between Charlemagne and Pope Hadrian. In a series of letters from 787 and 788, the pope begs Charlemagne not to send Grimoald back to Benevento, but rather to invade it himself.[39] Even though Hadrian was not a party to the original agreement, he was extremely interested in its guarantee mechanism. In each of these cases, hostages were at root guarantees for a bilateral agreement, but in a broader sense pawns in a multilateral political game whose players extended well beyond the principals of the agreement.

THE FATE OF HOSTAGES: THREE EPISODES

The overwhelming majority of early medieval hostages are not identified. The terse annal accounts simply state that hostages were given. When the sources are more forthcoming, they provide two types of information: social status and family relationships.[40] In general, status indications are biased toward the

---

[36] *Codex Carolinus*, 16, 17 (MGH Epp. 3:513–14).

[37] *Liber pontificalis*, Hadrianus, 30/310 (ed. Duschesne, 1:495); *Codex Carolinus*, 64 (MGH Epp. 3:591) ('pro vestro servitio').

[38] *Annales regni Francorum*, s.a. 787 (MGH SrG 6:74).

[39] *Codex Carolinus*, 80, 83, 84 (MGH Epp. 3:611–14, 616–20).

[40] *Annales qui dicuntur Einhardi*, s.a. 786 (MGH SrG 6:73); *Annales regni Francorum*, s.a. 815 (MGH SrG 6:142); *Annales Lauresbamenses*, s.a. 780 (MGH SS 1:31); *Chronicon Moissiacense*, s.a. 780 (MGH SS 1:296); *Annales Mosellani*, s.a. 780 (MGH SS 16:497).

nobility.[41] As for family relationships to the grantor, sons were preferred, and relatives over non-relatives. Similarly, the norm is for the sources to remain silent about the treatment and ultimate fate of hostages in the early Middle Ages. We must rely for an understanding of customary treatment of hostages on the few passages where the chroniclers depart from their usual habits.

A first hint is that hostages were escorted; distinguished escorts may indicate honourable treatment. When Charlemagne sent hostages to the Saxon nobles Widukind and Abbio for their safe passage, they were accompanied by one of his courtiers, Amalwinus. When a few years earlier he had accepted twelve hostages at Worms from Tassilo of Bavaria, they were sent to Quierzy with Sinbert, bishop of Regensburg; the annals report they were received there 'from the hand' of the bishop.[42]

Quierzy was a royal villa, which was a logical place to keep a royal hostage. Corroboration of this practice comes from an opaque passage in the capitulary *De villis*, in which judges on royal estates are forbidden from 'commending' hostages.[43] Quierzy is some 400km from Worms, and in the opposite direction from the Bavarian homeland of the hostages, roughly the same as the distance from Nîmes to Barcelona, which is where the wālī Ambasa ibn Suhaym al-Kalbi sent his hostages after the sack of the Aquitanian town.[44] Again, it was logical that hostages would be kept far from their homes, although it would be difficult to prove that it was typical. The Saxon hostages recorded in the *Indiculus obsidum* of 805x6 (see below) were sent to ecclesiastical and secular noble households in distant Alamannia and Bavaria. But another Saxon hostage, Hauthumar, travelled only as far as Würzburg, and the Carinthian prince Cheitmar was held at Chiemsee, fairly close to his border.[45] In encounters with the Vikings, Frankish hostages could find themselves held on ships, as was the case with the hostages for the safe passage of Roric in 873; ships were also the recommended holding place for Pecheneg hostages received by Byzantine fleets in Bulgaria.[46]

We occasionally learn that hostages returned safely, especially in the cases of short-term agreements, such as for safe passage; these short-term agreements were,

---

[41] *Annales qui dicuntur Einhardi*, s.a. 760 (MGH SrG 6:19); Flodoard, *Historia Remensis ecclesiae*, 2.18 (MGH SS 36:173); *ASC*, s.a. 876 (cf. Henry of Huntingdon, *Historia Anglorum*, 5.7 [OMT 286]); *Codex Carolinus*, 64 (MGH Epp. 3:591); *Liber pontificalis*, Hadrianus, 30/310 (ed. Duschesne, 1:495); Andreas of Bergamo, *Historia*, 7 (MGH SS 3:234); Richer, *Historiae*, 4.4 (MGH SS 38:234). In contrast, I would follow Thomas Charles-Edwards, 'Alliances, Godfathers, Treaties and Boundaries', in Mark A. S. Blackburn and D. N. Dumville, eds., *Kings, Currency, and Alliances: History and Coinage of Southern England in the Ninth Century* (Woodbridge, 1998), 47 n. 4, in seeing the *foregislas* of *ASC*, s.a. 878 as a reference to procedure rather than status (cf. Asser, *Life of King Alfred*, 56 [ed. Stevenson, 46; trans. Keynes and Lapidge, 85]: 'distinguished hostages').

[42] *Annales regni Francorum*, s.aa. 785, 781 (MGH SrG 6:70, 58): 'de manu'.

[43] MGH Capit. 1:84 (no. 32.12): 'Ut nullus iudex obsidem nostrum in villa nostra commendare faciat'.

[44] *Chronicon Moissiacense*, s.a. 715 (MGH SS 1:290).

[45] See below, pp. 66–8.

[46] *Annales Xantenses*, s.a. (MGH SrG 12:32); Constantine VII, *De administrando imperio*, 8 (CFHB 1:54–6).

as noted, perhaps more likely to succeed.[47] In three prominent cases, hostages were returned after the death of the person who had granted them. Acceding to a request of the Beneventans (and ignoring the pleas of the pope), Charlemagne sent back Grimoald to take up his father's throne after the latter died. Cacatius and Cheitmar were likewise released from their hostageship after Boruth's death, and the Bulgarian hostage-princes Romanos and Boris were returned after the death of their father, Peter.[48] When agreements failed, however, as they often did, there is little evidence that it was the hostages who suffered for it. Of course evidence for the positive treatment of hostages in this period is not that much more common.

In two well-known and interesting cases from Anglo-Saxon England, a hostage is found fighting alongside his custodians. The first is from the *Anglo-Saxon Chronicle*'s account of the killing of Cynewulf of Wessex by Cyneheard. The sole survivor of the attack is a 'British' (i.e. Welsh) hostage. The second is from *The Poem of the Battle of Maldon*, where a Northumbrian hostage, Æscfrith son of Ecglaf, is singled out for his military prowess in the battle between the English and the Vikings.[49] On the one hand, these cases show the trust placed in the hostages and the honourable positions they are given fighting alongside their holders. On the other hand, both of these figures suffer: the British hostage was gravely wounded, and if Æscfrith's exact fate is unknown, he was fighting on the side that was badly defeated. These cases are tantalizing echoes of the late antique association between hostages and military recruits, as in the case of the Tervingi in the service of the Romans in 378, who may have been hostages, or the presence in pre-Islamic Arabia of a regiment in the army of al-Hīra called the *raha'īn*—literally, 'hostages'. The regiment comprised 500 youths from neighbouring subject tribes, rotated through every six months.[50] And the success of the general Aetius against the Visigoths in the fifth century may be linked precisely to military training received years before when he was a hostage among them. The panegyrist Flavius Merobaudes makes just this point:

> After admiring the fearsome dignity of the boy and the eyes indicating his destiny, the king himself had given him his first quiver to wear, and praised him as he poised his

---

[47] *Annales Fuldenses*, s.a. 873 (MGH SrG 7:80–1); Erchempert, *Historia Langobardorum Beneventanorum*, 65 (MGH SrL 260); *Annales Fuldenses*, cont. Ratisbonensis, s.a. 882 (MGH SrG 7:108); Flodoard, *Annales*, s.a. 945 (CTH 39:97); Astronomer, *Vita Hludovici imperatoris*, 5 (MGH SrG 64:298).

[48] Erchempert, *Historia Langobardorum Beneventanorum*, 4 (MGH SrL 236) (cf. *Codex Carolinus*, 80, 84 [MGH Epp. 3:611–14, 619–20]); *Conversio Bagoariorum et Carantanorum* 4 (MGH Studien und Texte 15:104); Skylitzes, *Synopsis historiarum*, Basil and Constantine, 5 (CFHB 5:255); Zonaras, *Epitoma historiarum*, 16.23 (CSHB 3:495); Alice Leroy-Molinghen, 'Les fils de Pierre de Bulgarie', *Byzantion*, 42 (1972), 405–19. There are strictly legal grounds for such a return, based in the intransmissability of obligations, but it is doubtful that they were in play. Later examples: David II of Scotland (below, p. 188); *The Acts of Welsh Rulers, 1120–1283*, 453 (no. 284).

[49] *ASC*, s.a. 757; *The Battle of Maldon*, 265 (ed. Scragg, 65); Kershaw, *Peaceful Kings*, 19.

[50] Eunap. fr. 42; M. J. Kister, 'Al-Hīra: Some Notes on Its Relations with Arabia', *Arabica*, 15 (1968), 167; Kosto, 'Late Antiquity'. For hostages serving as troops in eighteenth-century Dutch Suriname, see Richard Price, *Alabi's World* (Baltimore, 1990), 404 (n. 70).

arms and carried the spear, forgetting that he was one of us. Oh the heart of the king, ignorant of what danger it would be for savage peoples that he teaches the Roman leader the art of war![51]

Three documentary records provide specific information and more detail on the fate of Carolingian hostages. The first is an original diploma from 808, a confirmation of lands granted by the emperor. At some point after the final conquest of the Lombard kingdom, Pippin, king of Italy, asked his father to allow the hostages he had collected to return to their homeland and to restore to them their properties, which had been confiscated. One of these hostages, originally from Reggio, requested the confirmation from Charlemagne in advance of his return.[52] Unfortunately, the name of the petitioner is lost. We also do not know when this hostage was granted, for no other contemporary source describes Lombards received from Italy by Charlemagne as hostages. Still, the document shows the fate of the lands of hostages, as well as the fact that they remained hostages for many years, in this case perhaps as many as thirty-five.[53] It is proof that open-ended agreements could be very long-term indeed.

The second is another royal diploma, preserved in a formula-book. In 823, a man named Lambert from the castle of Turenne in the Périgord presented himself before the court of Louis the Pious and related the following tale. During the time of Pippin, hostages were requested from and given by the inhabitants of that region, in order to maintain peace. Among these hostages was Lambert himself, granted by his father, Aganus, likely the castellan of Turenne, and by the count, Ermenric. At some time shortly thereafter, the hostages were released, but Lambert himself was reduced to servitude by a new count and his patrimony was seized. Lambert requested that he be freed and that his patrimony be restored; the emperor granted his request.[54] This case is most interesting, perhaps, because of the amount of time involved. Lambert would have become a hostage at the time of Pippin's conquest of Aquitaine, at the latest in 768. He was petitioning the emperor no earlier than 823, a gap of at least fifty-five years. Add to this that Lambert must have been beyond infancy to have been worthwhile as a hostage, and we are dealing with an individual who was living with the consequences of his father's actions well into his sixties. That is not to say that he remained a hostage well into his sixties. Confiscation of property and servile status were not incidents of hostageship,

---

[51] Merobaudes, *Panegyricus II*, 134–40 (MGH AA 14:16; trans. Clover, 14–15): 'rex ipse verendum/miratus pueri decus et prodentia fatum/lumina primaevas dederat gestare pharetras/laudabatque manus librantem et tela gerentem/oblitus quod noster erat. pro nescia regis/corda, feris quanto populis discrimine constet/quod Latium docet arma ducem!' Ibn al-Qūṭīya, *History* (trans. James, 121) reports a tale of a minister in ninth-century Córdoba insisting that young hostages not be taught 'heroic odes', but rather 'drinking songs': 'You have gone to demons who have sorely grieved the emirs and taught them poetry, which will give them an insight into real courage!'

[52] MGH DD Kar. 1:278–9 (no. 208). That these are hostages and not captives is demonstrated by the phrase 'pro credentiis', which echoes MGH Capit. 1:129 (no. 45.13). Bruno Dumézil suggested to me that the time period may be linked to the thirty-year rule for prescriptive possession.

[53] See also the case of Trasarius: Kosto, 'Carolingian', 141.

[54] *Formulae imperiales*, no. 53 (MGH Formulae Merowingici et Karolini aevi 325–6).

but the condition of hostageship might subject someone to such treatment.[55] Lambert did not become a slave, nor were his lands confiscated, when he became a hostage; this only occurred when he returned. Still, the fact that Lambert prefaced his complaint with a description of hostageship implies that there is a direct connection between the hostageship and the servitude. We may speculate that at Pippin's death, or at the time of the foundation of the kingdom of Aquitaine in 778, the hostages were not simply set free, but they were returned to the then count of the Périgord, the successor of the individual who had provided the hostages in the first place. The count freed most of them, but took advantage of having Lambert under his control to reduce him to servitude, for some unknown reason. If so, then the release of hostages was mediated through the count. The case of Lambert again highlights the significance of the involvement of individuals beyond the narrow trio of debtor–creditor–hostage.

The third document is a remarkable survival, the so-called *Indiculus obsidum Saxonum Moguntiam deducendorum* ('List of Saxon hostages to be led to Mainz'). It is a single folio of parchment in an early ninth-century hand, tucked into the back of a Carolingian canon law manuscript.[56] The title was bestowed by the nineteenth-century editor.[57] The text itself, apparently fragmentary, begins with the rubric: 'Let Bishop Hatto and Count Hitto receive these from the Westphalians'. There follows a list of ten individuals; in each case the father's name is given, and in all but the first the name of the person who 'held' the individual is also provided: 'Bishop Aino held Adalrad, son of Marcrad'. There follows another rubric—'From the Eastphalians'—and a list of fifteen names, presented similarly, and then a third rubric—'From the Angrarii'—and twelve more names.[58] The list is followed by the accurate notation, 'there are thirty-seven in total'. The fragment closes with one last rubric: 'Let these come to Mainz at mid-Lent'. Although the individuals on the list are not explicitly labelled as hostages, the number involved, the fact that all are identified as sons of other individuals, and the fact that all are 'held' supports this conclusion.

[55] Gregory of Tours, *Historiae*, 3.15 (MGH SrM 1.1:112) (a. 530); although see Walter Goffart, 'Roman Taxation to Mediaeval Seigneurie: Three Notes (Part I)', *Speculum*, 47 (1972), 187 n. 106. Islamic cases: al-Ṭabarī, *History*, s.a. 56 (trans. Rosenthal et al., 18:189–90) (a. 676) (cf. al-Balādhurī, *Origins of the Islamic State*, 19.2 [trans. Hitti and Murgotten, 2:175]); William of Tyre, *Chronicon*, 4.4–5 (CCCM 63:237–9) (a. 1098).

[56] Sankt Paul im Lavanttal, Stiftsbibliothek, cod. 6/1 (olim 25.4.12, olim XXV.a.6), fols. 191v–192r.

[57] MGH Capit. 1:233–4 (no. 115). For further details, see Kosto, 'Carolingian', 142–4; Heinrich Tiefenbach, 'Sprachliches zum Namenverzeichnis in der Handschrift St Paul 6/1', in Uwe Ludwig and Thomas Schilp, eds., *Nomen et fraternitas: Festschrift für Dieter Geuenich zum 65. Geburtstag* (Berlin, 2008), 115–29; Janet L. Nelson, 'Charlemagne and Empire', in Jennifer R. Davis and Michael McCormick, eds., *The Long Morning of Medieval Europe: New Directions in Early Medieval Studies* (Aldershot, 2008), 224–8, 233–4.

[58] On the nature of these designations, see Ian Wood, 'Beyond Satraps and Ostriches: Political and Social Structures of the Saxons in the Early Carolingian Period', in D. H. Green and Frank Siegmund, *The Continental Saxons from the Migration Period to the Tenth Century: An Ethnographic Perspective* (Woodbridge, 2003), 271–98.

It has been proposed that this document was drawn up by a commander in the field at the time of the receipt of these Saxon hostages.[59] This cannot be the context, for the *Indiculus* is a list of individuals *already held*, rather than a distribution list for hostages received. Although undated, the document may be assigned on prosopographical grounds to 805x6 (which agrees with the palaeographical dating[60]), a full year, at least, after the final defeat of the Saxons. The gathering of these scattered hostages may in fact be a prelude to their return to Saxony; as just seen, Charlemagne did allow Lombard hostages to return home during these years. Alternatively, as Janet Nelson has suggested, the gathering may be a prelude to the redistribution of the hostages within Charlemagne's empire, as part of a system of hostage holding for which she sees evidence in passages of the capitulary *De villis* and the *Divisio regnorum* of 806.[61] We are in the unfortunate position of not being able to trace the ultimate fate of the hostages. Although the Saxon names are useful for studying onomastic patterns, none of the seventy-two individuals listed (the hostages and their fathers) has been identified.

In the *Indiculus* the questions of the identity of hostages and their fate come together. For while the hostages themselves have not been identified, most of their hosts have been,[62] and this leads in more promising directions. The roughly two dozen names include, in addition to Alamannic lay magnates, three well-known ecclesiastical figures: Egino, bishop of Constance; Sinbert, bishop of Augsburg; and Waldo, abbot of Reichenau. The housing of hostages in ecclesiastical households is attested elsewhere. Flodoard writes of Archbishop Wulfar of Rheims (803–14): 'That Emperor Charlemagne put a great deal of trust in him is proven by the fact that he committed to his safekeeping fifteen noble hostages of the Saxons whom he had brought back from Saxony'.[63] Why were hostages sent to these ecclesiastical households? Other hosts in the *Indiculus* are designated counts, and the ecclesiastical lords may simply have been other trustworthy magnates whom Charlemagne wished to honour with this responsibility. But youthful hostages at cathedrals or abbeys were in a perfect position to receive instruction in the Christian faith.

The link between hostages and conversion may date back to the reign of Pippin. The *Conversio Bagoariorum et Carantanorum* (870x1) reports that in the early 740s the Slavic prince Boruth asked that his son Cacatius and nephew Cheitmar, whom he had granted to Pippin as hostages, be 'educated in the Christian manner and made Christian'; Cheitmar was sent to Chiemsee.[64] One of the earliest mentions of

---

[59] François Louis Ganshof, 'The Use of the Written Word in Charlemagne's Administration', in Ganshof, *The Carolingians and the Frankish Monarchy: Studies in Carolingian History*, trans. J. Sondheimer (Ithaca, 1971), 132.

[60] Bernhard Zeller, personal communication. Cf. Nelson, 'Charlemagne', 224 n. 11, citing David Ganz.

[61] Nelson, 'Charlemagne', 227–8; see above, p. 63, and below, p. 69.

[62] Nelson, 'Charlemagne', 225–6.

[63] Flodoard, *Historia Remensis ecclesiae*, 2.18 (MGH SS 36:172–3): 'Cui valde credidisse Karolus imperator Magnus ex eo probatur, quod illustres Saxonum obsides XV, quos adduxit de Saxonia, ipsius fidei custodiendos conmisit'.

[64] *Conversio Bagoariorum et Carantanorum*, 4 (MGH Studien und Texte 15:104): 'quem pater eius more christiano nutrire rogavit et christianum facere'.

hostages received from the Saxons, dating from Pippin's Saxon campaign of 753, also draws a connection between hostages and conversion. One account records that they were granted to guarantee the safety of missionaries, another that they secured a promise that the Saxons would become Christians.[65] The *Miracles of Saint Wandregisil* tell of a Saxon named Abbo, sent to the abbey of Saint-Wandrille, where he was baptized.[66]

The conversion of the Saxons (and others) was principally the work of missionaries, but giving a religious education to Saxon youth would have been a wise investment in the long-term success of the endeavour. Hostages, in most cases children from influential families, were the perfect instruments. Whether at this early point there was an intention that they be returned to instruct their countrymen is not known, but this certainly happened later. Cacatius and Cheitmar, now both 'made Christian', returned to their homeland as rulers, where they wielded significant influence over the official conversion of their people.[67] More striking is the case of Hauthumar, the first bishop of the Saxon diocese of Paderborn. He was granted as a boy to Charlemagne as a hostage, entered the monastic community at Würzburg, and then returned to his native land as a bishop.[68] In fact, there is a contemporary statement of this policy: the *Translation of Saint Vitus* reports that Charlemagne, concerned about the state of monasticism in Saxony, ordered that Saxons 'whom he had led back as hostages and captives at the time of the conflict be distributed throughout the monasteries of the Franks so that they might be instructed in scripture and monastic rules'.[69] Just as Charlemagne brought Lombard scholars to his court and then returned them to Italy where they were in a position to 'introduce Frankish perspectives',[70] so he and other rulers brought Saxons to Frankish ecclesiastical institutions and then sent them back home as a means of introducing Christianity. The old Roman practice of cultural diplomacy via hostageship[71] had merged with the imperial Christian mission.

EARLY MEDIEVAL HOSTAGESHIP IN CONTEXT

As the *Translation of Saint Vitus* shows, hostages were not the only individuals who were subject to this campaign of conversion: there they are grouped together with captives. As I have argued, the sources are normally quite careful to distinguish

---

[65] *Annales Mettenses priores*, s.a. (MGH SrG 10:44); *Annales Lobienses*, s.a. (MGH SS 13: 228). Cf. *Annales S. Amandi*, s.a. 776 (MGH SS 1:12); *Annales regni Francorum*, s.a. 776 (MGH SrG 6:46); *Annales qui dicuntur Einhardi*, s.a. 776 (MGH SrG 6:47).

[66] *Miracula S. Wandregisili abbatis*, 1.4–5 (*Acta sanctorum*, Julii V 282).

[67] *Conversio Bagoariorum et Carantanorum*, 4 (MGH Studien und Texte 15:104): 'iam christianum factum'; 'christianus factus'.

[68] *Translatio S. Liborii*, 5 (MGH SS 4:151).

[69] *Translatio S. Viti* (ed. Jaffé, 1:6–7): 'quos obsides et captivos tempore conflictionis adduxerat, per monasteria Francorum distribuit, ad legem quoque sanctam atque monasticam disciplinam institui praecepit'.

[70] Rosamond McKitterick, 'Paul the Deacon and the Franks', *Early Medieval Europe*, 8 (1999), 323.

[71] Above, p. 3.

among captives and hostages, but the two statuses were related and could function in very similar ways. The sister of Khan Boris of Bulgaria, for example, was converted to Christianity while a captive, rather than a hostage, but like other eastern European hostages, she contributed to the conversion of her home country when she returned.[72] In other cases, however, it is sometimes difficult to tell from the sources if an individual was a hostage. For example, historians have at times referred to the Lombard scholars just mentioned as hostages, although this is impossible to prove.[73] This difficulty is telling, for hostageship overlaps not only with captivity, but with a broad range of other early medieval institutions.[74] Examining hostageship in the context of these other institutions helps to clarify its social and political role in the early Middle Ages.

One such institution is exile. The blurring of boundaries between hostages and exiles is facilitated by the fact that they are both objects of 'political compulsion'.[75] It is noteworthy that one of the few normative texts to refer to hostages, the *Divisio regnorum* of 806, lumps these two categories together: both hostages and exiles are not to be sent from one subkingdom to another without permission.[76] They travelled together, as on the Byzantine fleet that carried to Constantinople hostages, but also two Venetian nobles whom the emperor had exiled.[77] Ambassadors might also be added to the mix. Waifer of Salerno sent his *cognatus* Peter and his son Waimar to the emperor as *legati*; the emperor, on the advice of a certain Landulf, seized them and ordered that they be sent into exile (*exilio*); he later received two other sons as hostages (*obsides*) and sent them to Lombardy. The distinction between hostages and exiles in this account breaks down in the subsequent description of the nephews of Landulf, whom he gave to the empress Engelberge as hostages (*obsides*), and whom she sent into 'exile' at Ravenna (*exilio*). Each of these three sets of individuals probably travelled together with the empress on her return to the north. Constantine VII also conflates hostages and ambassadors in his account of the dealings with the Pechenegs: when Byzantine ambassadors are sent into Pecheneg territory, he writes, the Byzantines should 'take from their side sureties (ὁμήρους), that is, hostages (ὄψιδας) and a diplomatic agent, who shall be collected together under charge of the competent minister in this

---

[72] *Theophanes continuatus*, 4.14 (CSHB 162–3); Zonaras, *Epitoma historiarum*, 16.2 (CSHB 3:387–9).

[73] Kosto, 'Carolingian', 131–2.

[74] On overlap: Michael McCormick, *Origins of the European Economy: Communications and Commerce, A.D. 300–900* (Cambridge, 2001), 274; Philippe Depreux, 'Princes, princesses et nobles étrangers à la cour des rois mérovingiens et carolingiens: Alliés, hôtes ou otages?', in *L'étranger au Moyen Âge: XXXᵉ congrès de la Société des historiens médiévistes de l'enseignement supérieur (Göttingen, juin 1999)* (Paris, 2000), 133–54; Jonathan Shepard, 'Manners Maketh Romans? Young Barbarians at the Emperor's Court', in Elizabeth Jeffreys, ed., *Byzantine Style, Religion and Civilization: In Honour of Sir Steven Runciman* (Cambridge, 2006), 135–58; Allen, *Hostages*; Llinos Beverley Smith, 'Fosterage, Adoption, and God-Parenthood: Ritual and Fictive Kinship in Medieval Wales', *Welsh History Review*, 16 (1992), 18.

[75] McCormick, *Origins*, 254–61.

[76] MGH Capit. 1:129 (no. 45.13); repeated MGH Capit. 2:22–3 (no. 194.9).

[77] *Chronicon Venetum* (MGH SS 7:14); McCormick, *Origins*, 274, 893.

city'.[78] If the precise legal statuses of all of these figures were different, their lived experience may have been very much the same.

I have argued that hostages for submission possessed symbolic value, but it was not a constant value. It is not always the case that equals exchanged hostages while a unilateral grant indicated submission. The role of hostages in a submission agreement is rarely such a simple indicator, because it is never the sole indicator. Like any relationship, submission is marked by multiple rituals, including words, physical gestures, and legal actions.[79] The grant of hostages is often paired with an oath (*sacramentum, iuramentum, promissio*), sometimes unspecified, but sometimes explicitly an oath of fidelity.[80] The gestures that accompanied these oaths are the hardest to see, although they were perhaps the most important and memorable at the time. One account of the submission of the Saxons in 779 notes that they offered not oaths, but their right hands (*dextras*) along with the hostages. A different source makes the same statement about the Wilzi in 812.[81] These may be simple metonymic expressions, but association of pledging and promising with the right hand is ancient. Hostages might also accompany offerings of an inanimate form—called 'gifts', but equally open to the possibility of being given under duress. The Obodrites, threatened by Louis the German's army in Saxony, sent gifts (*munera*) and hostages to forestall an attack; years later, Louis subdued other Slavic tribes 'without war', accepting 'many hostages, and not a few gifts'. In Italy, Berengar used hostages and gifts (*dona*) to encourage the Magyars to leave the peninsula.[82] Repeated 'gifts' of money were defined as tribute, which is also often found paired with hostages. The emir of Bari, for example, extorted a *pensio* from the prince of Benevento, along with the hostages that he received. These elements could be combined in various ways. The Bavarians, faced with attack from Pippin, sent legates with gifts (*munera*), swore oaths, and gave hostages. Similarly, Charlemagne received from the duke of Benevento hostages, but also gifts (*munera*) and oaths. Olaf of Sweden at Seeburg accepted *dextras*, along with current tribute

---

[78] Erchempert, *Historia Langobardorum Beneventanorum*, 35–6 (MGH SrL 248); Constantine VII, *De administrando imperio*, 1 (CFHB 1:48; trans. CFHB 1:49).

[79] Geoffrey Koziol, *Begging Pardon and Favor: Ritual and Political Order in Early Medieval France* (Ithaca, 1992), 16, 59, 110–11; Verena Epp, *Amicitia: Zur Geschichte personaler, sozialer, politischer und geistlicher Beziehungen im frühen Mittelalter* (Stuttgart, 1999), 62–97, 218–29; Kershaw, *Peaceful Kings*, 17–22.

[80] *Sacramenta*: *Annales regni Francorum*, s.aa. 755, 761, 775, 779, 781, 788, 789 (MGH SrG 6:14, 18, 40–2, 54, 58, 80, 86); *Annales qui dicuntur Einhardi*, s.aa. 786, 795 (MGH SrG 6:75, 97); *Annales Mettenses priores*, s.aa. 744, 753, 755 (MGH SrG 10:36, 44, 49); Fredegar, *Chronica*, cont., 32, 38, 51 (MGH SrM 2:182, 185, 191); *Liber pontificalis*, Gregorius II, 22/186 (ed. Duschesne, 1:407–8). *Promittere/promissum*: Fredegar, *Chronica*, cont., 25 (MGH SrM 2:180); *Annales qui dicuntur Einhardi*, s.a. 755 (MGH SrG 6:13); *Chronicon Moissiacense*, s.aa. 806, 812 (MGH SS 1:308, 309). *Polliceri*: Einhard, *Vita Karoli Magni*, 10 (MGH SrG 25:13); *Annales de Saint-Bertin*, s.a. 837 (SHF 22). *Iusiurare*: *Annales qui dicuntur Einhardi*, s.a. 794 (MGH SrG 6:97).

[81] *Annales Mosellani*, s.a. 779 (MGH SS 16:497); *Annales Laureshamenses*, s.a. 779 (MGH SS 1:31); *Chronicon Moissiacense*, s.a. 812 (MGH SS 1:309).

[82] *Annales Xantenses*, s.a. 845 (MGH SrG 12:14); *Annales Fuldenses*, s.a. 877 (MGH SrG 7:89–90) ('sine bello compressit; acceptisque obsidibus nonnullis et muneribus non paucis'); *Chronicon Venetum* (MGH SS 7:22).

(*thesauras*), a promise of future tribute (*censum*), and hostages. Harald of Norway sent Otto II a hostage, but also money, and he promised future payments. Finally, the late tenth-century Anglo-Saxon *Ordinance of the Dunsæte* has the Wentsæte provide *gafol* and *gislas*—tribute and hostages—to the West Saxons.[83]

More telling is the overlap between hostageship and other institutions that create bonds, rather than break them, and here one fact of hostageship in this period—that hostages were often sons—is crucial. The early medieval evidence does not allow a demonstration that the sons in question were youths—the two cases from this period where we can assign ages fairly closely are contradictory—but that this was normally the case may be inferred.[84] One rationale for the appeal of sons as hostages is the desire on the part of the party receiving hostages to have control over an heir to the father's property and power, although this logic would apply equally to a mature son. Another is that the son of the grantor might be thought to offer a greater potential influence on the grantor because of affective ties between parents and children, influence that *might* be stronger in the case of a young son than in the case of an already mature one (as numerous examples of princely rebellions suggest).[85] But there is a third possible rationale for the receiver of hostages, one that stresses the youth of the hostage rather than the family relationship to the grantor. It concerns not the potential influence on the grantor of the young hostage, but potential influences on the hostage himself. The impressionability of the young, their readiness to receive education, offered an opportunity to the receiver of hostages to do more than just influence the grantor. The education of a hostage, young or otherwise, offered the prospect of future benefits. We have already seen this, for example, in the discussion of Christianization. Hostage converts to Christianity might, as with the sons of the Slavic prince Boruth, use their positions of power to contribute to the conversion of their homelands. The possibility of such long-term benefits—longer than the length of detention itself—again lead us to view hostageship, and in particular the hostageship of the young, not just as means of guarantee, but as a practice of political communication. It is not a coincidence that hostageship shares this role with a number of other practices or institutions associated with the young in early medieval society, all of which are related to education, but are directed ultimately at the forging and maintenance of relationships within the framework of family ties.

The first of these is oblation, the practice by which parents dedicated a child to a monastic life, handing the child over to a monastery to be reared. Oblation was

---

[83] Erchempert, *Historia Langobardorum Beneventanorum*, 29 (MGH SrL 245); Fredegar, *Chronica*, cont., 32 (MGH SrM 2:182); *Annales regni Francorum*, s.a. 787 (MGH SrG 6:74); Rimbert, *Vita Anskarii*, 30 (MGH SrG 55:62); *Annales Altahenses maiores*, s.a. 974 (MGH SrG 4:12); *Dunsæte*, 9 (ed. Liebermann, 1:378).

[84] *Annales Altahenses maiores*, s.a. 973 (MGH SrG 4:11) (Boleslaw, around 7); above, p. 64 (Boris and Romanos, in their thirties). See above, p. 33.

[85] There are two issues here: affective ties between parents and their own children, and attitudes toward the young generally. While scholarship has sensibly moved beyond the theory of a post-medieval 'discovery' of childhood, there is little consensus on the subject for the medieval period as a whole; evidence is stronger for the later Middle Ages. See Barbara A. Hanawalt, 'Medievalists and the Study of Childhood', *Speculum*, 77 (2002), 440–60; Amy Livingstone, *Out of Love for My Kin: Aristocratic Family Life in the Lands of the Loire* (Ithaca, 2010), 28–41.

a widespread source of monastic recruitment in the early Middle Ages, when such offerings of children were still considered irrevocable.[86] Of the many parallels between youth hostageship and child oblation, the element of coercion stands out: like young hostages, oblates were, because of a parental act, in a state of lost personal liberty. Indeed, they often shared their monastic homes with noble prisoners and internal exiles;[87] royal support for the principle of monastic stability made many other monks unwilling inmates too, despite the relatively comfortable accommodations. But the parallels also extend to the interest of the grantor and the receiver of the oblate. John Boswell likened the practice to child abandonment: a means for families to dispose of children they could not support—a Christianized version of the ancient practice of exposure of infants.[88] Mayke de Jong's more focused study argued convincingly that this was not at all the case. Oblation, she showed, was not about parents breaking off ties with children, but rather about *establishing* ties: to God in the first instance, but also to particular individuals, to monastic institutions, and to extended spiritual communities. Oblates were one form of currency in the complex early medieval gift economy that linked rulers, religious institutions, and lay society at large. De Jong explicitly rejects a view of oblation as a simple *quid pro quo*, as a reciprocal transaction in which parents traded the oblate for spiritual benefits, focusing instead on the role of oblates in social networks.

Baptismal sponsorship (or godparenthood), while not necessarily involving the physical displacement of a child, operates in a similar fashion. Rooted in the role of witnesses and assistants to adult baptism in the primitive Christian church, sponsorship developed as a part of infant baptism: at first the role of the sponsor was to speak for the infant in the liturgy; soon the sponsor took on responsibilities of religious education of the child, as well.[89] Sponsorship shares with hostageship an association with education of youth and with conversion, and its vocabulary overlaps with that of suretyship: the godparent is fundamentally a guarantor, of the spiritual well-being of the child.[90] But the most interesting parallel lies once again in the way the institution of sponsorship creates lasting social bonds within a family framework, 'establishing a relationship or formalizing one that already existed'.[91] Such bonds were created not only between the sponsor and the baptized, but also between the sponsor and the biological parents of the baptized, as well as their respective biological families. The application of incest prohibitions to these spiritual family members is the most concrete expression of the

---

[86] Mayke de Jong, *In Samuel's Image: Child Oblation in the Early Medieval West* (Leiden, 1996).

[87] De Jong, *In Samuel's Image*, 252–64; Walther Laske, 'Zwangsaufenthalt im frühmittelalterlichen Kloster: Gott und Mensch im Einklang und Widerstreit', *Zeitschrift der Savigny-Stiftung für Rechtsgeschichte*, Kanonistische Abteilung, 64 (1978), 321–30.

[88] John Boswell, *The Kindness of Strangers: The Abandonment of Children in Western Europe from Late Antiquity to the Renaissance* (New York, 1988), esp. 228–55, 296–321.

[89] For what follows, see: Joseph H. Lynch, *Godparents and Kinship in Early Medieval Europe* (Princeton, 1986); Bernhard Jussen, *Spiritual Kinship as Social Practice: Godparenthood and Adoption in the Early Middle Ages*, rev. edn., trans. Pamela Selwyn (Newark, Del., 2000 [1991]).

[90] Jussen, *Spiritual Kinship*, 122–3.

[91] Jussen, *Spiritual Kinship*, 218.

bonds created;[92] the positive aspects of the relationships are harder to see in the sources, but they are certainly present. And as in the case of hostageship, the bonds need not have been created in the context of amicable relations. Thus sponsorship could be used, like hostageship, as an instrument of power or a marker of authority, as in the case of conquered or merely converted pagan rulers.[93] It also served well as an internal political tool, to establish links with powerful bishops in newly inherited territories, or for the 'neutralization of potential opponents'.[94] The lasting relationship created between sponsor and baptizee approximates the relationship that might arise between hostage and hostage-holder, or between oblate and monastery, in that each becomes the focal point of a much wider human and political network.

Sponsorship and oblation grounded social ties in religion. Other institutions associated with youth and education provided secular alternatives. Chief among these was the practice of commendation: parents would hand over a child to a powerful patron, someone with the resources and connections to provide an education, but also possibilities for advancement in the world. Like oblation, commendation entailed obligations, but the locus of education was an aristocratic household or, notably, the royal court. The bonds created between a mentor and his charge (*nutritor* and *nutritus*) lasted well beyond any period of training and, again, implicated wider social and political networks.[95]

The close ties between hostageship and commendation in the early medieval period may be illustrated by the case of William of Septimania. His claim to fame is as the recipient of a book of advice written by his mother, Dhuoda. At the time of her writing (841), William was at the royal court. In the succession struggle after the death of Louis the Pious in 840, William's father had joined the winning side at the last minute, and immediately sent his 14-year-old son to the king. The episode is described as follows in the contemporary sources: 'For I have learned that your father, Bernard, commended you into the hands of the lord-king Charles' (Dhuoda); 'he sent his son William to [the king] with orders to commend himself to [the king], if [the king] was willing to grant to him the honours that he held in Burgundy' (Nithard).[96] Some historians refer to William as a hostage, and, given

---

[92] Lynch, *Godparents*, 219–81; James A. Brundage, *Law, Sex, and Christian Society in Medieval Europe* (Chicago, 1987), 141, 193–4, 437.

[93] Arnold Angenendt, *Kaiserherrschaft und Königstaufe: Kaiser, Könige und Päpste als geistliche Patrone in der abendländischen Missionsgeschichte* (Berlin, 1984); Joseph H. Lynch, *Christianizing Kinship: Ritual Sponsorship in Anglo-Saxon England* (Ithaca, 1998), 205–28. Note the case of a son of Constantine of Scotland, godson and perhaps later hostage to Athelstan of England: William of Malmesbury, *Gesta regum Anglorum*, 2.134 (OMT 1:214); John of Worcester, *Chronicle*, s.a. 934 (OMT 2:390).

[94] Jussen, *Spiritual Kinship*, 145–56, 171–3 (quotation at 172); Lynch, *Godparents*, 74–6.

[95] Matthew Innes, '"A Place of Discipline": Carolingian Courts and Aristocratic Youth', in Catherine Cubitt, ed., *Court Culture in the Early Middle Ages: The Proceedings of the First Alcuin Conference* (Turnhout, 2003), 59–67; De Jong, *In Samuel's Image*, 196–216; Paul Guilhiermoz, *Essai sur l'origine de la noblesse en France au Moyen Âge* (Paris, 1902), 428.

[96] Dhuoda, *Liber manualis*, preface (ed. Thiébaux, 50): 'Audivi enim quod genitor tuus Bernardus in manus domni te commendavit Karoli regis'. Nithard, *Histoire des fils de Louis le Pieux*, 3.2 (ed. Lauer, 82–4): 'filium suum Willelmum ad illum direxit et, si honores, quos idem in Burgundia habuit, eidem donare vellet, ut se illi commendaret praecepit'.

the historical context, this is not an unreasonable claim: the king had good reason to suspect Bernard's loyalty, and the receipt of his son as a hostage would have been an appropriate way to signal and secure that fidelity.[97] If he was a hostage, he was a failed hostage, as his father betrayed the emperor and was executed in 844; William himself later betrayed Charles and was executed in 849.

But the language of the sources refers not to hostageship, but to commendation. Was this 'feudal' commendation, homage in return for a fief? No. The lands in question were William's own, bequeathed to him by his uncle in a testamentary grant, of which the previous king was an executor.[98] The commendation may still have involved homage, but note that Dhuoda says that Bernard commended William to the king, not that William commended himself.[99] This distinction, combined with William's age, the status of the royal court as a centre of aristocratic training, and the very subject matter of his mother's text, suggests that education, protection, and political connections were among the goals of the transaction. This conflation of hostageship and commendation is apparent, too, in the ninth- or tenth-century Latin poem *Waltharius*, wherein the hero is granted as a hostage to Attila, who taught him 'every skill, but especially those useful in the game of war' (an echo of Aetius among the Visigoths).[100]

In anthropological terms, oblation and commendation for educational purposes are both varieties of fosterage: a functional, rather than legal, displacement of the natural parents (as opposed to adoption, which has more direct implications for inheritance and lineage).[101] Fosterage outside of the contexts of oblation and commendation is hardly documented in the medieval Frankish and Mediterranean worlds, but it does seem to have existed: a Visigothic law established a payment for the rearing of children, for example.[102] It is in the Celtic and Scandinavian worlds that the practice is best attested, and with many variations, and although much of the source material for these societies comes from later periods, it is generally accepted (although not without significant caveats) as reflective of early medieval practice. Here, too, parallels to hostageship are clear and, given increasing integration of these regions into wider European political life, relevant to our analysis.

Icelandic society employed a variety of different fosterage arrangements, revealed in both legal sources (the *Grágás*) and saga literature: one in which the foster-parents were of lower status than the biological parents; one in which the families were of equal rank; one in which children of poor parents were fostered by kin; and one in which the foster-parent was a member of the same household (such as a

---

[97] Dhuoda, *Liber manualis*, preface (trans. Neel, 6); Suzanne Fonay Wemple, *Women in Frankish Society: Marriage and the Cloister, 500 to 900* (Philadelphia, 1985), 99; Clarissa W. Atkinson, *The Oldest Vocation: Christian Motherhood in the Middle Ages* (Ithaca, 1991), 96; Elisabeth M. C. Van Houts, 'The State of Research: Women in Medieval History and Literature', *Journal of Medieval History*, 20 (1994), 284.

[98] Dhuoda, *Liber manualis*, 8.15 (ed. Thiébaux, 206). Cf. *HGL* 2:273–4.

[99] On the semantic range of *commendatio* in this period, see Niermeyer, *Lexicon*, s.v.

[100] *Waltharius*, 89–115, 598–600, etc. (MGH Poetae Latini medii aevi 6.1:28–9, 48, etc.), here 101–2: 'sed et artibus imbuit illos/Praesertimque iocis belli sub tempore habendis'. Cf. above, pp. 64–5.

[101] See generally Mireille Corbier, ed., *Adoption et fosterage* (Paris, 1999).

[102] *Lex Visigothorum*, 4.4.3 (MGH Leges nationum Germanicarum 1:194).

servant).[103] Irish law recognized two types of fosterage, for 'affection' and for a fee; contracts of the latter sort are the subject of detailed regulation in a dedicated legal tract, the *Cáin Íarraith*.[104] The legal evidence for Wales is extremely thin, but historical, hagiographical, and legendary sources—where criticism of the conflicts engendered by fostering appears alongside praise for the strength of the bonds created—reveal a similar range of practices.[105]

As in the case of hostageship, the social meaning and symbolic value of a given fosterage transaction would depend not only on the status of the parties, but also the particular circumstances. The act of fostering a child of higher status might be seen as humiliating—'it is said that he is the inferior who fosters another's child', held a Norse proverb—or as a cause for celebration because of the prestigious association.[106] The relation could be inverted, as when a higher-status individual offered to foster the child of a lower-status individual as 'a mild ritualized humiliation, a formalized act of deference' in the context of a dispute settlement. The obligation of kin in Icelandic society to support poorer relatives might also result in a higher-status parent fostering a lower-status child.[107] A foster-child could be forced on a party as a reprisal for an economic transaction gone bad, but fostering for a fee might be a valuable source of income.[108]

Once again, as in the cases of oblation, sponsorship, and commendation, there is a strong institutional similarity between fosterage and youth hostageship.[109] And once again, one of the principal similarities is in the creation of bonds that transcend the particular transaction.[110] In Irish law, foster-children had an obligation to care for their aged foster-parents, while the father was required to avenge the death of his foster-child: he had a right to a portion of any composition payment, even after the end of the term of fosterage; a separate payment was due to

---

[103] William Ian Miller, *Bloodtaking and Peacemaking: Feud, Law, and Society in Saga Iceland* (Chicago, 1990), 122–4, 171–4. Dagobert's youth in the household of Arnulf of Metz might be considered an example of downward fostering: *Gesta Dagoberti I. Regis Francorum*, 2 (MGH SrM 2:401).

[104] Kathleen Mulchrone, 'The Rights and Duties of Women with Regard to the Education of Their Children', in Rudolf Thurneysen et al., eds., *Studies in Early Irish Law* (Dublin, 1936), 187–205; François Kerlouegan, 'Essai sur la mise en nourriture et l'éducation dans les pays celtiques d'après le témoignage des textes hagiographiques latins', *Études celtiques*, 12 (1968–9), 101–46; Fergus Kelly, *A Guide to Early Irish Law* (Dublin, 1988), 86–90; T. M. Charles-Edwards, *Early Irish and Welsh Kinship* (Oxford, 1993), 78–82.

[105] Kerlouegan, 'Essai', 116–18; Smith, 'Fosterage', 3–4, 18–19; Charles-Edwards, *Kinship*, 78–82; Peter Parkes, 'Celtic Fosterage: Adoptive Kinship and Clientage in Northwestern Europe', *Comparative Studies in Society and History*, 48 (2006), 359–95.

[106] *Harðar Saga*, 9 (ed. Vilmundarson and Vilhjálmsson, 23; trans. Kellogg, 200), cited by Jussen, *Spiritual Kinship*, 190; similarly, *Laxdæla Saga*, 27 (ed. Sveinsson, 75), cited by Miller, *Bloodtaking*, 172; Smith, 'Fosterage', 1, 32–3.

[107] Miller, *Bloodtaking*, 123, 172.

[108] Miller, *Bloodtaking*, 172; Kelly, *Guide*, 90; cf. Smith, 'Fosterage', 32.

[109] Miller, *Bloodtaking*, 172; Kerlouegan, 'Essai', 128–30; Stephen S. Evans, *The Lords of Battle: Image and Reality in the Comitatus in Dark Age Britain* (Woodbridge, 1997), 117–20; Smith, 'Fosterage', 13; J. A. Watt, 'Gaelic Polity and Cultural Identity', in Art Cosgrove, ed., *A New History of Ireland*, vol. 2: *Medieval Ireland, 1169–1534* (Oxford, 1987), 320. The latter two locate the *origin* of fosterage in hostageship.

[110] Kelly, *Guide*, 89; Smith, 'Fosterage', 22.

foster-brothers.[111] Icelandic law and saga record a similar integration of foster-children into feuding practices.[112] And one of the few Welsh legal texts on fosterage grants a portion of the inheritance of a villein foster-father to his freeman foster-child. Links created between the natural and the foster-parents were as important, if not more so in some cases.[113] I have already noted the potential role of fosterage in the settlement of disputes. Serial fosterage of high-status children among lower-status families also contributed to the articulation of lordship, integrating both families in networks of protection and prestige.[114]

The early medieval sources thus present a cluster of institutions, centred around the exchange of children, concerned with various aspects of child-rearing and education on the one hand, but also—often more importantly—with the formation of social bonds and networks. It is, of course, easier to distinguish among these various institutions in theory than in practice.[115] Just as hostageship overlaps in particular ways with oblation, sponsorship, commendation, and fosterage, these latter institutions overlap with one another: godparents might serve as foster-parents or as *nutritores* (as perhaps in the case of William of Septimania's uncle); a fosterage apparently designed to provide legal training looks very much like commendation for educational purposes; lay children might receive an education side by side with oblates.[116] Other similar social practices have not been considered here. Some (such as wet-nursing and blood-brotherhood) are further manifestations of 'fictive' kinship,[117] while others pertain to 'real' kinship. Adoption, for example, is closely intertwined with sponsorship,[118] and the inheritance right of the Welsh free foster-son involves legal consequences usually associated with adoption. Marriage is perhaps even more important.[119] As has been observed for the Icelandic context, the choice of marriage or fosterage as the nexus of an alliance might depend on simple issues of supply and demand of women and children.[120] To all these institutions we may add those with a more clearly 'political' aspect that might still involve exchange of children: oaths, vassalage, confraternities, and a wide range of treaties and alliances—what Joseph Lynch has called, in

---

[111] Kelly, *Guide*, 89–90; Kerlouegan, 'Essai', 113.

[112] Miller, *Bloodtaking*, 171–2.

[113] Smith, 'Fosterage', 3–4, 18–19, 24–8. Cf. anthropological literature on *compadrazgo*: Hugo G. Nutini and Betty Bell, *Ritual Kinship*, 2 vols. (Princeton, 1980–4), 1:405–28.

[114] Kelly, *Guide*, 90; Miller, *Bloodtaking*, 172.

[115] Smith, 'Fosterage', 18.

[116] Dhuoda, *Liber manualis*, 8.15 (ed. Thiébaux, 206); Miller, *Bloodtaking*, 124; De Jong, *In Samuel's Image*, 232–45; cf. Kerlouegan, 'Essai', 133–44.

[117] Miller, *Bloodtaking*, 173–4; for the related institution of wet-nursing, Smith, 'Fosterage', 5–6, and Valerie A. Fildes, *Wet-Nursing: A History from Antiquity to the Present* (Oxford, 1988), esp. 26–48. See also John Boswell, *Same-Sex Unions in Premodern Europe* (New York, 1994); Elizabeth A. R. Brown, Claudia Rapp, and Brent D. Shaw, 'Ritual Brotherhood in Ancient and Medieval Europe: A Symposium', *Traditio*, 52 (1997), 261–381.

[118] Jussen, *Spiritual Kinship*.

[119] Below, p. 84.

[120] Miller, *Bloodtaking*, 124.

the early medieval context, 'the luxuriant array of Frankish institutions meant to create solidarity'.[121]

Any given act in which a young person was transferred from one household to another, therefore, had a multitude of potential meanings and connotations, whatever the apparent legal or ritual framework. The choice by parties of any framework (or by contemporary authors of any particular term) emphasized a particular aspect of the transfer of the child. Godparenthood highlighted a concern with spiritual welfare; fosterage, with physical welfare and basic education; commendation, with more advanced training; adoption, with inheritance and lineage; vassalage with protection and service; and so forth.[122] In this context, what was hostageship about? Ultimately, guarantee. We only find sources referring to youths as hostages where there is an agreement to be guaranteed. This may be a negotiated agreement among equals with explicit terms, or a forced submission with an agreement (again forced) of certain behaviour, but the agreement is always there. Precisely because of the similarities between hostageship and oblation, fosterage, sponsorship, and commendation, the use of youths as hostages increased the potential benefits of the agreement to both parties, even in cases where the strict terms of the agreement were violated. It is this characteristic of hostageship that helps to explain the continued use of hostages to secure open-ended commitments such as submission, where their success as guarantors per se seems inconsistent at best. Above all, however, the broader institutional context just reviewed demonstrates that in the early Middle Ages, hostageship rested on familial relationships, real and fictive. It did so because such relationships underlay early medieval political life.

---

[121] Lynch, *Godparents*, 178; Margaret Wielers, *Zwischenstaatliche Beziehungsformen im frühen Mittelalter (Pax, Foedus, Amicitia, Fraternitas)* (Munich, 1959); Ludwig Buisson, 'Formen normannischer Staatsbildung (9. bis 11. Jahrhundert)', in *Studien zum mittelalterlichen Lehenswesen* (Sigmaringen, 1960; repr. 1972), 95–184; Epp, *Amicitia*; Charles-Edwards, 'Alliances'.
[122] Smith, 'Fosterage', 17; Jussen, *Spiritual Kinship*, 220; Charles-Edwards, *Kinship*, 341–2.

4

Hostages in the Later Middle Ages:
Representation, Finance,
and the Laws of War

If the evidence for the use of hostages is somewhat uneven for the early Middle Ages, from the eleventh century on they can hardly be avoided. While there is substantial continuity with early medieval forms of hostageship, however, the increase in evidence is matched by an increase in variety, and the beginning of the period witnesses several major shifts in the practice of hostageship that point to fundamental changes in the nature of the institution. Whereas early medieval hostageship operated in a political world defined by real and fictive family connections, from the eleventh century hostageship evolved in tandem with the politics of a new age. For whatever the pace of change in the years around the millennium, it is undeniable that the medieval world was becoming a very different place by 1200: a world of fiefs and vassals, of towns and guilds, of territorial and bureaucratic kingship, of a revived learned law and practical application of it in the world of trade and commerce. This new society might easily have rejected the use of hostages as outmoded or inappropriate. The increased sophistication of various forms of personal and real surety that accompanied the spread of written contracts in trade and commerce certainly offered parties other options for guarantees, options that remained much more common for most types of transactions than hostageship. Nonetheless, hostageship not only persisted; it proliferated in new contexts.

Hostages for submission—the most frequent variety in the early medieval sources—remain common. In the eleventh century, it was not just William of Normandy's conquest of England that saw widespread grants of hostages,[1] but also Robert Guiscard's in Italy[2] and Emperor Henry III's in the east—descriptions of

---

[1] Above, pp. 25–6. William and hostages before the Conquest: William of Jumièges, *Gesta Normannorum ducum*, 7.7, 8, 13 (OMT 2:122, 124, 160); William of Poitiers, *Gesta Guillelmi*, 1.10, 14, 41, 46, 2.12 (OMT 12, 20, 68, 76, 120); Eadmer, *Historia novorum in Anglia* (RS 81:5–6); Kenneth E. Cutler, 'The Godwinist Hostages: The Case for 1051', *Annuale medievale*, 12 (1972), 70–7.

[2] William of Apulia, *La geste de Robert Guiscard*, 3.340, 647, 648, 4.206 (ed. Mathieu, 182, 200, 201, 214); Comnena, *Alexiade*, 1.16.2 (ed. Leib, 1:57); Lupus Protospatarius, *Annales*, s.aa. 1065, 1083 (MGH SS 5:59, 61); Bernold of Konstanz, *Chronicon*, s.a. 1084 (MGH SrG ns 14:442); Malaterra, *De rebus gestis Rogerii*, 1.17 (RIS² 5.1:18); Amatus of Montecassino, *Storia de' Normanni*, 4.2, 4, 5.27 (ed. De Bartholomeis, 181–2, 186, 254).

the latter echoing Charlemagne's conquests two and a half centuries before.³ Those echoes continue into the thirteenth century, in the submission of the Baltic lands, and hostages served as a useful tool for the English in controlling Gascony.⁴ Hostages also continued to be used for simple safe passage: they were, for example, exchanged for the mutual security of Henry IV and Paschal II during the latter's entry into Rome in 1111 for his coronation; granted to representatives from Avignon to parley with the Albigensian crusaders in 1226; provided to John IV of Brittany to appear before Charles IV of France to do homage in 1381; and offered by the French to Gregory XII during attempts to resolve the Great Schism in 1408.⁵ As earlier, we find hostages guaranteeing specific short-term actions: the exchange of King Stephen and the empress Matilda during the English civil war in 1140; the surrender of castles by the English chancellor William Longchamp after his deposition and excommunication in 1191; the destruction of the walls of Toulouse under the terms of the Treaty of Paris in 1229; or the return of properties seized from the archbishop of Trier in 1371.⁶

The social and cultural functions of hostages explored in the previous chapter continue into this later period as well. Relatives, particularly sons, are still most common among the sureties handed over, even by kings and emperors,⁷ and the line between hostageship and voluntary residence at the lord's court remains difficult to draw.⁸ Hostages continue to be associated with conversion, particularly in the east; in 1255, for example, the prince of Bohemia and duke of Brandenburg received hostages from the Prussians after overseeing a mass baptism and before handing the territory over to the Teutonic Knights, while Louis of Hungary granted hostages to the Lithuanians when entering their country to negotiate their conversion in 1351.⁹ And as in the early Middle Ages, hostages may be found as vectors

³ Hermannus Contractus, *Chronicon*, s.aa. 1039, 1041, 1044 (MGH SS 5:123, 124); *Annales Altahenses maiores*, s.aa. 1041, 1043 (MGH SrG 4:24, 27, 33).
⁴ Henry of Livonia, *Chronicon Livoniae*, 2.5, 4.4, 5.1, 9.9, 13, 10.14, 14.11, 18.7, 19.8, 20.6, 23.9, 24.1, 30.5 (MGH SrG 31:10, 14, 15, 30, 32, 44, 85, 121, 133, 138, 165, 170, 220); *Les registres de Grégoire IX*, 1:482–3, 1201–9 (nos. 761–2, 2287) [Potthast 8865, 8861, —]; *Rôles gascons*, 1:94, 115, 219, 254, 370, Sup:3, 44, 52–3, 54, etc. (nos. 694, 867, 1642, 1988, 2812, 4329, 4592, 4654, 4672, etc.).
⁵ Table 4.1.
⁶ William of Malmesbury, *Historia novella*, 57 (OMT 106); *HGL* 8:892–3 (no. 271.2; cf. Toulouse, Archives municipales, AA5, fols. 45v–46r [no. 5]); Roger of Wendover, *Flores historiarum*, s.a. 1191 (RS 84.1:205–6); *Chronicon Moguntinum*, s.a. 1371 (MGH SrG 20:26–7).
⁷ Above, pp. 31–3.
⁸ e.g. Theodore Evergates, *The Aristocracy in the County of Champagne, 1100–1300* (Philadelphia, 2007), 152–3; Galíndez de Carvajal, *Crónica de Enrique IV*, 10 (ed. Torres Fontes, 91); Georges Duby, ed., *A History of Private Life: Revelations of the Medieval World*, trans. Arthur Goldhammer (Cambridge, Mass., 1993 [1985]), 152. In literature: *De ortu Waluuanii nepotis Arturi*, 3–5 (ed. Day, 2): 'eorum filios partim loco obsidum, partim honestate morum militarique erudiendos disciplina, sua in curia detinebat'. Contemporary Persian–Mongol relations: Thomas T. Allsen, *Culture and Conquest in Mongol Eurasia* (Cambridge, 2004), 73–4.
⁹ *Annales Otakariani*, s.a. 1255 (MGH SS 9:182); *Chronicon Dubnicense*, 169 (ed. Florianus, 160–2). See also *Preußisches Urkundenbuch*, 1.1:100–2 (no. 134) [*Les registres de Grégoire IX*, 3:223 (no. 5139); Potthast 10866]; Helmold, *Cronica Slavorum*, 2.109 (MGH SrG 32:214). Hostages also figured in the conversion of Iceland (e.g. Snorri Sturluson, *Heimskringla*, Óláf Tryggvasonar, 103 [ed. Linder and Haggson, 209]) and in various projects for the conversion of Emperor John V to Latin Christianity (John W. Barker, *Manuel II Palaeologus (1391–1425): A Study in Late Byzantine Statesmanship* [New Brunswick, 1969], 4–8; Oskar Halecki, *Un empereur de Byzance à Rome* [Warsaw, 1930], 33–4, 62, 135, 192).

Table 4.1 Hostages for Safe Passage, 1000–1500

Date	From	To	Notes	Source
1013	Henry II, emp.	Boleslaw I, d. Poland	refused	Thietmar of Merseburg, *Chronicon*, 6.91 (MGH SrG ns 9:383)
1051	Edward, k. England	Godwin, Harold	refused	*ASC* (E), s.a.
1073	Henry IV, emp.	rebels	proposed	Lambert of Hersfeld, *Annales*, s.a. (MGH SrG 38:162)
1082	Henry IV, emp.	Gregory VII, pope	proposed	Henry IV, *Briefe*, 17 (ed. Erdmann, 24–6)
1091	Alexius I Comnenus, emp.	Cumans		Comnena, *Alexiade*, 8.6.4 (ed. Leib, 2:146)
1092	John Ducas	Tzachas, em. Smyrna	exchanged	Comnena, *Alexiade*, 9.1.6 (ed. Leib, 2:160)
1093	William II, k. England	Malcolm III, k. Scotland		*ASC*, s.a.
1093	William II, k. England	Robert of Mowbray	refused	*ASC*, s.a.
1095	Vladimir of Kiev	Polovicians		*Russian Primary Chronicle*, s.a. 6603 (trans. Cross, 180)
1097	Alexius I Comnenus, emp.	Godfrey de Bouillon		William of Tyre, *Chronicon*, 2.11–12 (CCCM 63:174–6)
1098	Alexius I Comnenus, emp.	Godfrey de Bouillon		William of Tyre, *Chronicon*, 2.11–12 (CCCM 63:174–6)
1103	Malik Ghazi	Bohemond, pr. Antioch, Richard of Salerno		Orderic Vitalis, *Historia ecclesiastica*, 10.24 (OMT 5:377)
1108	Alexius I Comnenus, emp.	Bohemond, pr. Antioch		Comnena, *Alexiade*, 13.9.1, 8 (ed. Leib, 3:117, 120)
1127	Ranulf, c. Alife	Ugo *infans*	rejected	Falco of Benevento, *Chronicon Beneventanum*, s.a. (ed. D'Angelo, 96–8)
1186	Henry II, k. England	Roland of Galloway		Roger of Howden, *Gesta Henrici II et Ricardi I* (RS 49.1:348)
1226	Albigensian Crusaders	representatives of Avignon		Roger of Wendover, *Flores historiarum*, s.a. (RS 84.2:313–14)
1354	John II, k. France	Charles II k. Navarre		Froissart 1.654 (SHF 7:224–5)
1408	French	Gregory XII, pope		Monstrelet 1.44 (1:318)
1416	Henry V, k. England	John II, d. Burgundy		Monstrelet 1.161 (3:162–3)
1420	Naples	Louis III, k. Naples		Monstrelet 1.228 (3:413–14)
1424	Charles VII, k. France	Arthur de Richemont		Gruel, *Chronique d'Arthur de Richemont*, 24 (SHF 34)
1429	Sigismund, k. Hungary	Procop		*Urkundliche Beiträge zur Geschichte des Hussitenkrieges*, 2:22 (no. 574)
1467	Louis XI, k. France	Louis, c. Saint-Pol		Gaguin, *Les croniques de France* (trans. Desrey, fol. 182r)
1495	Charles VIII, k. France	pr. Taranto		Gaguin, *Les croniques de France* (trans. Desrey, fol. 213r)

of cultural diplomacy and cultural transmission more generally. Duncan of Scotland, for example, a hostage at the English court from 1072 to 1087 when he was knighted at the accession of a new king, seized the Scottish throne in 1094 with English support—support that was resented by those who quickly deposed him, insisting that his successor not introduce further Normans and English into the land. Richard II of England's knighting of his hostage Alfonso of Villena in 1390 was likely a similar attempt to create a future diplomatic ally.[10] The hostageship of the Nasrid prince Abu'l-Hasan 'Ali and his substantial retinue at Arévalo from 1454 may have made the region a conduit of intellectual currents between mudéjars and the non-Iberian Islamic world.[11] There was, in short, substantial continuity in hostageship practices between the early and later Middle Ages.

It is the changes, however, that are more striking. One major change from the eleventh century on is a marked increase in the absolute number of hostages found in the sources. This may be due to the overall increase in the amount of evidence available: the explosion of surviving narrative and diplomatic sources is well known, and the volume of the latter in particular renders perilous any statements about the *relative* weight of hostages as against other forms of surety, real or personal. But within this evidence, the types of transactions guaranteed by hostages also diversify rapidly beyond the familiar categories of submission, truces, and safe passage.

Hostages are now often found much more regularly guaranteeing the fidelity not of ongoing or vanquished foes, but rather of putative friends and subordinates. This made the most sense in cases of natural enemies or reluctant allies found acting in concert, such as Fulk of Anjou and Mu'in al-Din in 1140; the king of Portugal and the forces of the Second Crusade at Lisbon; rebellious English nobles plotting with the French prince Louis in 1216, or again with Charles VI in 1406; or John of Castile and Abū Naṣr Sa'd of Granada in 1454.[12] In a striking case, the queen of Aragon hired Muslim archers in 1359 on the condition that their wives and children be held as guarantees.[13] Similarly, on two occasions in 1096, at Oedenburg and Nish, the leaders of the First Crusade granted hostages to guarantee the good behaviour of the army en route; Isaac II Angelos repeated the request when faced with Frederic Barbarossa a century later (although ultimately it was the Byzantines who granted hostages to the Franks for their safe passage).[14] In a transaction among Muslims, the

---

[10] Adam J. Kosto, 'L'otage, comme vecteur d'échange culturel du IVe au XVe siècle', in *Les prisonniers*, 171–81. Alfonso: below, n. 119; James L. Gillespie, 'Richard II's Knights: Chivalry and Patronage', *Journal of Medieval History*, 13 (1987), 150.

[11] L. P. Harvey, *Muslims in Spain, 1500–1614* (Chicago, 2006), 110–11.

[12] Fulk: William of Tyre, *Chronicon*, 15.7–8 (CCCM 63A:684–5); Ibn al-Qalānisī, *The Damascus Chronicle* (trans. Gibb, 259). Castile: Galíndez de Carvajal, *Crónica de Enrique IV*, 10 (ed. Torres Fontes, 91). Louis: Roger of Wendover, *Flores historiarum*, s.a. 1216 (RS 84.2:173); Guillaume le Breton, *Gesta Philippi Augusti*, 214 (SHF 1:305); *Foedera*, 1.1:148. Charles VI: Monstrelet 1.26 (1:130–1) (proposal). Lisbon: *De expugnatione Lyxbonensi* (ed. David, 84, 112, 124). See also Roger of Howden, *Gesta Henrici II et Ricardi I* (RS 49.1:350).

[13] ACA, Registres 1569:29–30 (10 Nov. 1359); ed. John Boswell, *The Royal Treasure: Muslim Communities under the Crown of Aragon in the Fourteenth Century* (New Haven, 1977), 183.

[14] William of Tyre, *Chronicon*, 1.19, 2.3 (CCCM 63:144, 164–5); Albert of Aachen, *Historia Ierosolimitana* 1.9, 2.4–7 (OMT 18–20, 64–72); *Historia peregrinorum* (MGH SrG ns 5:140, 150, 152). Cf. Comnena, *Alexiade*, 9.1.6 (ed. Leib, 2:160).

emir of Aleppo granted a hostage to the atabeg of Mosul to guarantee that he would remain neutral in the latter's conflict with Aleppo's ally, Tancred.[15]

Hostages also now regularly secured the support of one's 'own' men. In England, Robert of Gloucester and Henry III each required hostages from barons to guarantee their fidelity, as did Robert of Capua in Benevento in 1132 and Blanche of Champagne in 1218. The practice is even enshrined in the eleventh-century Norman *Consuetudines et iusticie*: 'If the lord of Normandy wants to have as a hostage for keeping faith ('obsidem de portanda fide') the son or brother or nephew of one of his barons (who is not a knight), no one may contradict him'.[16]

Particularly in the eleventh and twelfth centuries, hostages specifically secured the loyalty of subordinates responsible for the control of castles. In this case, we can tie the extension of hostageship quite clearly to a new political context, namely the increase of castle-building from the eleventh century onward and the corresponding transformation in structures of power through which they were governed.[17] The *Conventum Hugonis*, an early eleventh-century account of conflicts surrounding the castles of William V of Aquitaine, vividly depicts the role and importance of such guarantees. Duke William, Count Fulk of Anjou, and Hugh Chiliarchus, the vassal of both of them, were disputing the possession of the castle of Gençay, a castle of Fulk that Hugh had just destroyed and rebuilt:

> Hugh asked the count [William] for advice. The count said to him, 'If he [Fulk] wants to give you guarantees (*fidutias*) that your enemies will not have the castle, you cannot keep it; if not, however, keep it, as he will have no claim against you'. Hugh asked Fulk to give him hostages (*hostaticos*); he gave him none, but said, 'I will make my request to the count and give hostages to him; let him make a grant to you from among his own men'. At that point, the negotiation turned angry.

Earlier in the account, the count is shown holding and refusing to return hostages that Hugh had provided for the castle of Civray.[18]

---

[15] Albert of Aachen, *Historia Ierosolimitana*, 11.39 (OMT 812).

[16] *Consuetudines et iusticie*, 5 (ed. Haskins, 282). Gloucester: William of Malmesbury, *Historia novella*, 3.73–4 (OMT 124); Robert of Torigni, *Chronica*, s.a. 1142 (RS 82.4:143). Henry III: Roger of Wendover, *Flores historiarum*, s.a. 1233 (RS 84.3:52); *Close Rolls... 1231–1234*, 312–13. Robert of Capua: Falco of Benevento, *Chronicon Beneventaum*, s.a. 1132 (ed. D'Angelo, 126). Blanche of Champagne: *Thesaurus novus anecdotorum*, 1:865–6. Similarly, MGH Const. 2:49–50 (no. 40); above, p. 48. On England in this period generally, Robert Bartlett, *England under the Norman and Angevin Kings, 1075–1225* (Oxford, 2000), 49–51.

[17] Briefly, Thomas N. Bisson, *The Crisis of the Twelfth Century: Power, Lordship, and the Origins of European Government* (Princeton, 2009), 41–2.

[18] *Conventum inter Guillelmum Aquitanorum comitem et Hugonem Chiliarchum* (ed. Martindale, 545–6): 'Requisivitque Ugo comiti consilium. Comes vero dixit ei: "Si fidutias vult dare tibi, ut inimici tui castrum non habeant, non poteris eum tenere. Sin autem tene eum quia non poterit te accusare". Ugo vero interrogavit hostaticos ut daret ei Fulco; et nullum dedit ei, sed dixit: "Ego requiram Comiti et ad illum dabo hostaticos et ipse det tibi de suos". Versusque est placitus in ira.' The distinction between hostages and other forms of guarantee in this text is confusing at first glance, but nonetheless clear. With respect to Civray, *ostatici* are clearly true hostages (*in captionem, absolutos*). In the negotiation surrounding Gençay, Hugh asks for hostages (*hostatici*), but William offers only pledges (*fidutias*); Hugh asks in turn for the guardian of the tower of Melle, who is to turn over the tower to him in case of default—he is not a true hostage, but nor is he referred to as one. Later (p. 547), Hugh accepts his fief from the count *in hostaticum*—not referring to a person, the term is used metaphorically.

The structures of power in Aquitaine around 1030 were famously confused, but castle hostages persist in much more stable situations. Frederic Barbarossa held hostages from the castellans of Salzburg during his intervention in the episcopal election in 1169 and threatened to turn them over to a new bishop in 1171,[19] while John of England received the sons of Roger de Lacy and William d'Albini (among many others) as a condition of letting them keep control of their fortifications. John's agreement with Roger of Montbegon specified that if Roger failed to serve faithfully, he would recover his hostages only after returning control of the castle.[20]

FEMALE HOSTAGES

This diversification of uses of hostageship is not particularly significant in itself. There are, however, a number of specific changes that point to a fundamental transformation of the institution. One of the most significant indicators of this change is the appearance of women as hostages. Whereas the Greeks were known to receive female hostages, the Romans rarely did so, Cloelia notwithstanding.[21] This pattern continued into the Late Antique period, despite Tacitus's observation that it was a Germanic custom.[22] Few secure examples date from between the fourth and seventh centuries, and only one involved a daughter rather than a wife or sister.[23] Leaving aside Hildegund in the *Waltharius* tradition,[24] the eighth to the tenth centuries offer only two possible cases of female hostages: the mother of Stephen of Naples in 821 and the daughter or daughters of Julian of Ceuta mentioned in the highly problematic accounts of the Islamic conquest of Spain.[25] The near absence of women, and all the more so of daughters, reflects strongly the kinship framework of early

---

[19] *Salzburger Briefsammlung*, 8 (MGH Briefe der deutschen Kaiserzeit 6:161–3).

[20] Roger of Howden, *Chronica*, s.aa. 1199, 1201 (RS 51.4:91–2, 161); *Rotuli de oblatis*, 275.

[21] Walker, 'Hostages', 28–35; André Aymard, 'Les otages barbares au début de l'Empire', *Journal of Roman Studies*, 51 (1961), 136–42.

[22] Tacitus, *Germ.* 8; Reinhold Bruder, *Die germanische Frau im Lichte der Runeninschriften und der antiken Historiographie* (Berlin, 1974), 145–51.

[23] Eunap. fr. 18.6; *Passio SS. Acepsimae episcopi, Ioseph presbyteri et Aeithalae diaconi*, 30 (ed. Delahaye, 498, 524, 539, 551–2); Sozom., *Hist. eccl.* 2.13; Paulinus of Pella, *Eucharisticos* (SC 209:379–80); Procop. *Vand.* 4.27.25; Paul the Deacon, *Historia Langobardorum*, 5.7–8 (MGH SrL 147–8); and possibly *Vita S. Hermenegildi* (*Acta sanctorum*, Aprilis II 135). Unfulfilled proposal: Malchus fr. 20.1.212–15. See Kosto, 'Late Antiquity'.

[24] *Waltharius*, 93–5 (MGH Poetae Latini medii aevi 6.1:28).

[25] Erchempert, *Historia Langobardorum Beneventanorum*, 10 (MGH SrL 238); Ibn 'Abd al-Hakam, *Conquête de l'Afrique du Nord et de l'Espagne* (trans. Gateau, 87); Pseudo-Isidore, *Crónica* (ed. Benito Vidal, 51); Ann Christys, ' "How Can I Trust You, Since You Are a Christian and I Am a Moor?": The Multiple Identities of the Chronicle of Pseudo-Isidore', in Richard Corradini et al., eds., *Texts and Identities in the Early Middle Ages* (Vienna, 2006), 359–72. There is also an unfulfilled proposal for the hostageship of the children ('natos omnes cum natabus') of Charles of Lorraine, a. 991: Richer, *Historiae*, 4.49 (MGH SS 38:262). The eighth-century Islamic jurist Shaybani mentions female hostages (al-Sarakhsi, *Le grand livre de la conduite de l'État*, 163.3508–10 [trans. Hamidullah, 3:287–8]), although the only example I have come across is *Chronicle of Zuqnīn*, 4, s.aa. 749–50 (trans. Harrak, 189). Later Irish folklore notes a mother employed as a *gíall*-hostage: *Rennes Dindṡenchas*, 18 (trans. Stokes, 311, 313).

medieval hostageship. Within this framework, daughters were not granted as hostages; they were granted as wives. For example, as part of the treaty that brought Boris and Romanos as hostages to Constantinople, a marriage was planned between two Bulgarian princesses and two imperial princes.[26] The relationship between hostageship and marriage is even expressed explicitly. As part of the reconciliation between Conrad of Franconia and Erchanger of Swabia in 913, the latter granted his sister in marriage to the king. The king accepted her, in the words of the Alamannic Annals, '*like* a hostage of peace' (*tamquam obsidem pacis*).[27]

The marriage of daughters as a parallel to male hostageship continued after the millennium. In the 1160s, Diarmait of Leinster granted his son to Ruadri of Connacht, expecting a marriage to Ruadri's daughter in return—just one example of the overlapping hostage and marriage market that characterized the fragmented politics of twelfth-century Ireland.[28] An unfulfilled version of the treaty for the release of Charles of Blois named his sons *and a daughter* as hostages, but also foresaw the marriage of Charles's eldest son to the daughter of Edward I.[29] Similarly, at the same time that René of Anjou granted hostages for a temporary release from captivity, he betrothed his 4-year-old daughter to the son of his captor, with the stipulation that the father would maintain custody of the girl until she was of age.[30] In a case from early thirteenth-century Champagne, noble parents tried to ensure that their under-age daughter, Alix of Grandpré, who had been handed over to the father of her prospective husband, could not be treated as a hostage by inserting a clause into the marriage contract calling for her return if the proposed union did not in fact take place.[31] A preliminary version of the Treaty of Bayonne offers perhaps the most striking example that the parallel between hostage and child bride was understood: the king of Castile was to hand over his second son as a hostage *at the same time* (*in eodem tempore tunc*) as the duke of Lancaster handed over his daughter to be betrothed to the elder son.[32] The characterizations by modern scholars of various brides as hostages, while imprecise, are not unreasonable.[33]

---

[26] Leo the Deacon, *Historiae*, 2.5 (CSHB 79).

[27] *Annales Alamannici*, s.a. (MGH SS 1:56); cf. Jer., *Ep.* 79.2 (*velut obside*).

[28] Gerald of Wales, *Expugnatio Hibernica*, 1.10 (RS 21.5:244).

[29] Robert of Avesbury, *De gestis mirabilibus regis Edwardi Tertii*, s.a. 1356 (RS 93:418).

[30] Lecoy, *René*, 1:104.

[31] Ambroise Firmin Didot, *Études sur la vie et les travaux de Jean Sire de Joinville*, vol. 1 (Paris, 1870), 191–3; Evergates, *Aristocracy*, 117. Margaret of Austria was kept for two years after breakdown of a marriage agreement in 1482: Ghislaine de Boom, *Marguerite d'Autriche-Savoie et la Pré-Renaissance* (Paris, 1935), 12–23.

[32] *The Treaty of Bayonne*, 10 (Trancoso I, art. 8).

[33] e.g. Evergates, *Aristocracy*, 352 n. 8, although the treaty does not refer to the girl as a hostage: *Recueil...Philippe Auguste*, 2:236 (no. 678). See also Annette P. Parks, 'Living Pledges: A Study of Hostageship in the High Middle Ages, 1050–1300', PhD dissertation, Emory University, 2000; Carol Neuman de Vegvar, 'Images of Women in Anglo-Saxon Art: I. Hostages: Women in the "Titus" Scene on the Franks Casket', *Old English Newsletter*, 24 (1990), 44–5. Brides as hostages in Rome: Allen, *Hostages*, 184–8. A similar analogy may be made to wardship, or female captivity generally: Gwen Seabourne, 'Eleanor of Brittany and Her Treatment by King John and Henry III', *Nottingham Medieval Studies*, 51 (2007), 91; Annette Parks, 'Rescuing the Maidens from the Tower: Recovering the Stories of Two Female Political Hostages', in Belle S. Tuten and Tracey L. Billado, eds., *Feud, Violence, and Practice: Essays in Medieval Studies in Honor of Stephen D. White* (Aldershot, 2010), 279–91.

What does change from the eleventh century, however, is that women, and most often daughters, regularly serve as and are acknowledged as hostages per se (see Table 4.2).[34] The poet Jean Regnier, who knew of such matters first-hand from his own captivity and ransoming in the early fifteenth century, claimed that although it was 'contrary to God and to reason, to hold a woman in prison':

> ... these days it is the custom
> in the kingdom of France,
> since many prisoners would die
> if their wives did not free them
> to go join their comrades.[35]

Twelfth-century Iberian *fueros* banned the use of daughters or indeed any women as hostages, although the fact that the codes go on to explain that this was because of a fear of sexual contact with Muslims means that it is perhaps risky in this case to read a normative prohibition as good evidence that the practice in question was current.[36] On the other hand, the presence of the 15-year-old daughter of Baldwin II of Jerusalem among the hostages held by Muslims for that king's ransom did not arouse negative notice, despite the story's wide diffusion.[37] Furthermore, the danger of violation was just as present for female hostages granted to Christians: Eudo of Brittany complained that Henry II of England had impregnated his 'virgin daughter', held as a hostage, and Stephen, count of Mortain, was accused of handing over a female hostage to pimps.[38] Nor was the only danger sexual: Henry I of England permitted the mutilation of two female hostages in revenge for the mutilation of a male hostage who had been received in exchange, Henry II mutilated Welsh boys and girls together (although differently), and Frederic II was said to have had a female hostage burned alive.[39] Even in the first two of those cases, however, male and female hostages are present in the same transaction. Sometimes daughters and wives are granted alone, but they are granted in the company of male hostages often enough that their use cannot be viewed as a last resort. In most cases of female hostages, gender does not seem to have been a pressing issue.

[34] Colleen Slater, ' "So Hard Was It to Release Princes Whom Fortuna Had Put in Her Chains" ': Queens and Female Rulers as Hostage- and Captive-Takers and Holders', *Medieval Feminist Forum*, 45 (2009), 12–40, and ' "Virile Strength in a Feminine Breast" ': Women, Hostageship, Captivity, and Society in the Anglo-French World, *c.*1000–*c.*1300', PhD dissertation, Cornell University, 2009, address the converse phenomenon.

[35] Regnier, *Livre de la prison*, 4625–31 (ed. Droz, 162): 'maintenant l'on tient l'usance/Parmy le royaulme de France,/Car plusieurs prisonniers mourroient/Se femme ne les delivroient/Pour aller leurs amys chercher'; below, p. 119. See André Bossuat, 'Les prisonniers de Beauvais et la rançon du poète Jean Regnier, bailli d'Auxerre', in *Mélanges d'histoire du Moyen Âge dédié à la mémoire de Louis Halphen* (Paris, 1951), 31 n.; Bouton, *Miroir des dames* (ed. Beauvois, 16).

[36] *El fuero de Teruel*, 453–4 (ed. Gorosch, 286–7); *Fuero de Cuenca*, 10.39 (ed. Ureña y Smenjaud, 294–7). The same-sex advances by a Muslim ruler toward his Christian hostage apparent in *Passio S. Pelagii*, 7 (ed. Rodríguez Fernández, 66–8) echo a late Roman trope: Aur. Vict. *Caes.* 39.46, 41.24.

[37] The hostageship of Walter of Beirut's mother (below, p. 116) was much less well known.

[38] John of Salisbury, *Letters*, 279 (OMT 2:602); Orderic Vitalis, *Historia ecclesiastica*, 12.8 (OMT 6:207). Rape of hostages in Roman sources: Allen, *Hostages*, 188–94.

[39] Orderic Vitalis, *Historia ecclesiastica*, 12.10 (OMT 6:210–12); Roger of Howden, *Chronica* (RS 51.1:240); Salimbene de Adam, *Chronica*, s.a. 1240 (CCCM 125:261); also *Historia Selebiensis monasterii*, 2.13 (ed. Fowler, [38]).

Table 4.2 Female Hostages

(For evidence before 1000, see above, p. 83)

Date	Grantor	Grantee	Female(s)	Other(s)	Notes
1002[i]	English	Danes	Gunnhild		fictional?
1038[ii]	Pandulf IV, pr. Benevento	Conrad II, emp.	daughter	son or grandson	
c.1050[iii]	k. Alans	Constantine IX, emp.	daughter		
1071[iv]	Argyritzos, lord of Bari	Robert Guiscard	daughter		
1096[v]	Godfrey de Bouillon	Coloman, k. Hungary	Godechilde (s.-i.-l.)	brother, family, etc.	
1098[vi]	Balduc of Samosata	Baldwin of Boulogne	wife	children	proposal only
1118[vii]	Alençon	Stephen, c. Mortain	wife		
1119[viii]	Eustace of Breteuil	Ralph Harenc	daughters		exchange for son of Ralph
1124[ix]	Baldwin II, k. Jerusalem	Timurtash	Iveta (daughter)	others	
1142[x]	Joscelin II, c. Edessa	John II Comnenus, emp.	Isabella (daughter)		
c.1142[xi]	?	?	wife		

[i] William of Malmesbury, *Gesta regum Anglorum*, 2.177 (OMT 1:300).

[ii] *Chronica monasterii Casinensis*, 2.63 (MGH SS 34:292); cf. *Annales Altahenses maiores*, s.a. (MGH SrG 4:22).

[iii] Psellos, *Chronographie*, 6.145, 151–5 (ed. Renauld, 2.41, 47).

[iv] Amatus of Montecassino, *Storia de' Normanni*, 5.27 (ed. De Bartholmaeis, 254).

[v] William of Tyre, *Chronicon*, 2.3 (CCCM 63:164–65); Albert of Aachen, *Historia Ierosolimitana*, 2.4–7 (OMT 64–72).

[vi] Albert of Aachen, *Historia Ierosolimitana*, 3.24, 5.22 (OMT 176, 364).

[vii] Orderic Vitalis, *Historia ecclesiastica*, 12.8 (OMT 6:207).

[viii] Orderic Vitalis, *Historia ecclesiastica*, 12.10 (OMT 6:210–12).

[ix] William of Tyre, *Chronicon*, 13.15–16 (CCCM 63:603–6), etc.

[x] William of Tyre, *Chronicon*, 15.19 (CCCM 63A:701).

[xi] *Historia Selebiensis monasterii*, 2.13 (ed. Fowler, [38]–[39]).

				sons of others	
1165[xii]	Eochaidh Mac Duinnsleibhe	Muirchertach Mac Lochlainn	daughter		
1165[xiii]	Welsh	Henry II, k. England	daughters	sons	
1168[xiv]	Barisone II of Arborea	Genoese	wife	nephew	
1168[xv]	Eudo, d. Brittany	Henry II, k. England	daughter		
1182[xvi]	Isaac Comnenus of Cyprus	Bohemond III, pr. Antioch	daughter		
1191[xvii]	Isaac Comnenus of Cyprus	Richard I, k. England	daughter	son	
1196[xviii]	Constance, d. Brittany	Ranulf, e. Chester	Emma, daughter of André II de Vitré		proposal only
s.12[xix]	Walter of Beirut		mother		
1200[xx]	Eylas *Longus*	John, k. England	daughter		
1200[xxi]	William of *Albeidston*	John, k. England	daughter		
1203[xxii]	Savaric de Mauléon	John, k. England	Alix de Ré (mother) / Belle-Assez de Chantemerle (wife)		

[xii] *Annals of the Four Masters*, s.a. (trans. O'Donovan, 2:1155).

[xiii] Roger of Howden, *Chronica*, s.a. (RS 51.1:240).

[xiv] *Codice diplomatico della Repubblica di Genova*, 84–6, 87–8 (nos. 34, 35, 37).

[xv] John of Salisbury, *Letters*, 279 (OMT 2:602).

[xvi] Roger of Howden, *Chronica*, s.a. 1180 (RS 51.2:203–4).

[xvii] *L'Estoire de Eracles empereur*, 25.24 (*RHC* Occ. 2:166).

[xviii] Pierre Le Baud, *Histoire de Bretagne* ..., ed. Pierre D'Hozier (Paris, 1638), 1:202, 2:31–2, 35; Arthur Bertrand de Broussillon, *La maison de Laval*, vol. 5 (Paris, 1903), 11 (no. 3200).

[xix] *Lignages d'Outremer*, 296 (ed. Nielen, 74–5).

[xx] *Rotuli de oblatis*, 274.

[xxi] *Rotuli de oblatis*, 274.

[xxii] *Histoire des ducs de Normandie et des rois de Angleterre* (ed. Michel, 101).

(continued)

Table 4.2 Continued

Date	Grantor	Grantee	Female(s)	Other(s)	Notes
1207[xxiii]	Amph' Till'	John, k. England	daughters	brother, son	
1209[xxiv]	William I, k. Scotland	John, k. England	daughters (2)		
1212[xxv]	Alice Peche	John, k. England	daughter	etc.	
1213[xxvi]	Renaud of Dammartin, c. Boulogne	John, k. England	wife, daughter of c. Chiny	etc.	daughter or son
1213[xxvii]	Richard of Clare	John, k. England	Matilda (daughter)		
1213[xxviii]	Mabel of Clare	John, k. England	daughter	son	
1213[xxix]	Robert de Vaux	John, k. England	Alice (mother) Grecia (sister)	sons, nephew	
1214[xxx]	William fitz Sawall	John, k. England	Gilia (daughter)		
1215[xxxi]	Eustace Monach	John, k. England	daughter		
1215[xxxii]	Walter de Lacy	John, k. England	daughter	or son	
1216[xxxiii]	Gilbert fitz Reinfrey	John, k. England	various daughters of others	etc.	as replacement for son

[xxiii] Foedera, 1.1:98.

[xxiv] Roger of Wendover, Flores historiarum (RS 57.2:50). .

[xxv] Rotuli litterarum patentium, 101b.

[xxvi] Rotuli chartarum, 186.

[xxvii] Rotuli chartarum, 197a; Rotuli litterarum patentium, 101b.

[xxviii] Rotuli de oblatis, 478.

[xxix] Rotuli de oblatis, 478.

[xxx] Rotuli chartarum, 192a.

[xxxi] Rotuli litterarum patentium, 144a.

[xxxii] Rotuli de oblatis, 562–64.

[xxxiii] Rotuli de oblatis, 570–1; Rotuli chartarum, 221b.

1216[xxxiv]	Simon fitz Walter	John, k. England	Matilda (daughter)		until replaced with son
1216[xxxv]	William of Bayeux	John, k. England	Beatrice (eldest daughter)		
1216[xxxvi]	William fitz Roscelin	John, k. England	Alice (granddaughter)		
1216[xxxvii]	Ralph de Crubmell	John, k. England	(eldest daughter)		
1216[xxxviii]	Hugh Rufus	John, k. England	Isabella (daughter)	nephew	as replacement for son
1216[xxxix]	William de Lacy	John, k. England	daughter	or son	
1216[xl]	Nicholas Poinz	Henry III, k. England	Cecilia, granddaughter		
1217[xli]	Ranulf fitz Robert	Henry III, k. England	daughters		
1217[xlii]	William *de Albaniaco*	Henry III, k. England	Agatha Trussebut, wife		replaced by son
1217[xliii]	William of Avranches	Henry III, k. England	Matilda, daughter		
1220[xliv]	Roger Le Manaunt	Falk' de Breauté	daughter		
1220[xlv]	castellans of Ireland	Henry III, k. England	daughters	or sons, or other relatives	
1226[xlvi]	Hugh O'Conor	English	daughter	son, and others	

[xxxiv] *Rotuli de oblatis*, 571.

[xxxv] *Rotuli de oblatis*, 580.

[xxxvi] *Rotuli de oblatis*, 589.

[xxxvii] *Rotuli de oblatis*, 581.

[xxxviii] *Rotuli de oblatis*, 587–8.

[xxxix] *Rotuli de oblatis*, 601–3.

[xl] *Patent Rolls...1216–1225*, 108.

[xli] *Patent Rolls...1216–1225*, 118.

[xlii] *Patent Rolls...1216–1225*, 45, 47, 62, 66.

[xliii] *Patent Rolls...1216–1225*, 158.

[xliv] *Curia regis Rolls...4 and 5 Henry III*, 226.

[xlv] *Patent Rolls...1216–1225*, 264.

[xlvi] *Annals of Clonmacnoise*, s.a. (trans. Mageoghagan, 231); *Annals of the Four Masters*, s.a. 1227 (trans. O'Donovan, 3:245).

(continued)

Table 4.2 Continued

Date	Grantor	Grantee	Female(s)	Other(s)	Notes
1239[xlvii]	Alberic de Romano (and Azzo II of Este)	Frederic II, emp.	daughter	son of Azzo	
1239[xlviii]	Paul Traversario	Frederic II, emp.	Aica (daughter)		
1261[xlix]	William of Villehardouin, pr. Morea	Michael VIII Paleologus, emp.	Jadre (sister of grand constable)		
			Marguerite (daughter of protostrator)		
1294[l]	Guy, c. Flanders	Philip IV, k. France	daughter		
1297[li]	Robert the Bruce	Edward I, k. England	Margery (daughter)		
s.13[lii]	John Haraldsson, e. Caithness and Orkney	William I, k. Scotland	daughter		
1320[liii]	Richard Aldred, Richard Barry, Nicholas Byndlowrys	Scots	wives	children	
1338c[liv]	Arnaud de Durfort		wife	son and men	
1340[lv]	?	Peter IV, k. Aragon	women	children and community leaders	

[xlvii] Rolandino of Padua, *Chronica*, 4.11 (MGH SS 19:72); *Annales S. Iustinae Patavini*, s.a. (MGH SS 19:157).

[xlviii] Salimbene de Adam, *Cronica*, s.a. 1240, 1260 (CCCM 125:261, 560).

[xlix] *Chronicle of Morea*, 4494–512, 7301–743 (ed. Schmitt, 299, 474–503).

[l] *Annales Gandenses*, s.a. 1298 (ed. Johnstone, 8); Joseph M. B. C. Kervyn de Lettenhove, *Histoire de Flandre*, vol. 2: *Époque communale* (Brussels, 1847), 566.

[li] *Documents and Records Illustrating the History of Scotland*, 1:199–200 (no. 199).

[lii] John of Fordun, *Chronica gentis Scotorum*, Gesta annalia, 28 (ed. Skene 279).

[liii] *Foedera*, 2.1:437; London, National Archives, SC 8/89/4438.

[liv] London, National Archives, SC 8/35/1732.

[lv] ACA, Registres 1377:67v–68r (1340).

			wives	children
1359[lvi]	Eleanor, q. Aragon	Muslim archers		
1366[lvii]	Peter, k. Castile	Edward, pr. Aquitaine	three daughters	
1375[lviii]	Henry II, k. Castile	Bertrand Du Guesclin	daughter of Pedro Fernández de Villefas	sons of Juan Ramírez de Arellano and Gómez García de Talamanca
1390[lix]	Nerio	Venetians	Francesca (daughter)	
1404[lx]	Suleiman Celebi	Manuel II, emp.	Fatima Khatun (sister)	brother
1431[lxi]	Alexander MacDonald, lord of the Isles	James I, k. Scotland	mother	
1431[lxii]	Robert de Mailly	French	lady of Blangy (daughter of Colart de Mailly)	
1433[lxiii]	Jean Regnier		wife	son
1437[lxiv]	Gilbert de Frenay	viscount of Frenay	Marguerite de Monnay (wife)	
1439[lxv]	Thomas Óg Maguire	Donnall Maguire	wife?	son
1479[lxvi]	Juan de Lara	Abrahén de Mora	Ana (daughter), Beatriz (niece)	

[lvi] ACA, Registres 1569:19–20 (10 Nov. 1359).

[lvii] Foedera, 3.2:799.

[lviii] Diago Hernando, 'Un noble' (below, p. 122, n. 161), 548, 549 n. 102.

[lix] 'Documents concernant divers pays de l'Orient Latin', 98–102 (no. 3).

[lx] Ducas, Historia byzantina, 18 (CSHB 78–9); see Barker, Manuel II , 253 n. 88.

[lxi] Regnier, Livre de la prison, 4597–630 (ed. Droz, 161–2); see Bossuat, 'Beauvais', 31 n. 4.

[lxii] Regnier, Livre de la prison, 4343–8, 4579–84 (ed. Droz, 153, 161).

[lxiii] Livre des Miracles de Sainte-Catherine-de-Fierbois, 118 (ed. Chauvin, 72–3).

[lxiv] Annals of Ulster, s.a. (trans. Hennessy and MacCarthy, 3:143).

[lxv] Bower, Scotichronicon, 16.16 (ed. Watt, 8:262).

[lxvi] Mata Carriazo, 'Los moros de Granada' (below, p. 120, n. 149), 283, 285.

The parallel to marriage practices perhaps made female hostages more acceptable. Even if there were no practical difference between handing over women as
hostages and handing them over as brides (and there were differences: a wife
handed over as a hostage could not be used for a marriage alliance, for example),
the change in vocabulary alone demands explanation. This is all the more true
because the framework for hostageship in the early Middle Ages, as argued above,
was the family. The use of women as hostages points not so much to a change in
the role of women as to a change in the nature of hostageship itself: away from the
early medieval kinship framework to a more de-individualized and bureaucratized
framework itself embedded in entirely new social and political structures.[40] We can
trace this process by examining three further areas in which hostageship changes
from the eleventh and twelfth centuries forward: the nature of hostages for submission, the development of the laws of war, and the use of hostages for financial
transactions.

HOSTAGES AS REPRESENTATIVES

As noted, hostages for submission continued to be one of the most common forms
after the eleventh century, but the way in which such hostages could be selected
underwent a significant shift. To introduce this change (for which further evidence
will be discussed in Chapter 6, below), I consider in detail three sets of hostage
transactions: hostages granted to Philip Augustus in Flanders in 1213; hostages
granted to Frederic Barbarossa by Italian towns during his twelfth-century campaigns; and hostages granted to the French by the Flemish in the fourteenth century. In all three, the victors no longer simply demand an individual son of the
ruler of a defeated group. Instead, they ask for many more hostages, enumerated in
telling ways.

In 1213, following the defection of Ferdinand of Flanders to the English camp
and the loss of the French fleet at Damme, the French king invaded Flanders and
demanded hostages.[41] Like the Carolingians 400 years before, the French made a
careful record of the guarantees. The names of 159 hostages are recorded in the
royal register: 40 from Bruges, 9 from Oudenbourg, 6 from Audenaarde, 18 from
Ypres, 52 from Ghent, and 12 (or 34) from Douai. Again like the Carolingian
Indiculus obsidum, the list records—at least in the case of Ghent—where the hostages were held: Arras, Hesdin, and Douai. And like the *Indiculus obsidum*, the
1213 hostage list was composed at some point after the initial grant and recording

---

[40] The possibility of broader changes in the role of women as sureties generally in this period merits
further investigation, starting from the prohibition and exceptions in Roman law: D. 2.8.8.1, 16.1;
C. 4.29, 8.27.11; Nov. 134.8.

[41] *Les registres de Philippe Auguste*, 1:558–61 (Miscellanea 12); Gaston G. Dept, *Les influences
anglaise et française dans le comté de Flandre au début du XIIIme siècle* (Ghent, 1928), 186–92, 198–201.
I follow Baldwin's solution of the list of names rather than Dept's. The original, Paris, Archives nationales, JJ 7, fols. 87v–88r, is, like the *Indiculus obsidum*, a bifolium blank on one side. It is not clear from
the layout if a list of twenty-four absent hostages is part of the list of hostages from Douai; see Dept,
Les influences, 199.

of the names of hostages, because the list notes hostages who fled ('Isti se sub-traxerunt dolose') or who were not present for other reasons when the census was taken ('Isti duo non venerunt', 'Iste est absens sed causa nescitur', 'Iste est in mer-catura'[!]). Next to one hostage listed as absent it is noted that he eventually came back: 'Iste tamen se obtulit in recessu nostro'. The 1213 list departs from the *In-diculus*, though, in the identification of the hostages. Whereas the *Indiculus obsi-dum* distinguished among three large Saxon subgroups, here the division is explicitly geographical, with the number of hostages from each town providing a good indicator of its relative importance in Philip's attempt to control the region. Furthermore, where the Carolingian hostages were all sons—presumably of Saxon leaders—only thirty-three of the Flemish hostages are so identified, and in those cases it is because another distinguishing name or cognomen is lacking; there are only nine single names on the list, and 'frater N.' is used to identify two other single-name hostages. Thirteen of the Ghent hostages given as guarantees for par-ticular individuals—not always fathers—are indicated in a different way: 'Radulfus Strie *pro Galtero patre suo*', 'Henricus Wisse *pro Henrico Clerico*', 'Terricus Squelpe *pro Wellebart*', and so forth. Finally, at least one of the 'sons' had served as an éche-vin five years earlier. In fact, thirteen of the eighteen Ypres hostages had served or would later serve as échevins, and all before 1220.[42] These hostages were not se-lected as a way of using family bonds to keep powerful fathers in line. They were selected in their own right, as representatives of the towns. Philip's later promise to Douai that he would return their hostages as soon as he had completed a fortress there is as good a sign as any of the value of such hostages in maintaining control. Meanwhile his proposals to Ghent, Bruges, and perhaps Ypres to sell their towns-men back to them (thus effectively changing their status to prisoners) shows these hostages were not the focus of long-term relationships, but rather instruments of the practical exercise of immediate power. The same thing appears to have hap-pened at Douai, which complained to the royal inquest of 1247 that after Bou-vines Philip had refused to return twenty hostages until the town paid 60,000 l.[43]

A half-century before these events, hostages were already a regular feature of the German emperor Frederic I Barbarossa's diplomatic and military activity in Italy, from his first campaign of 1158 and the Diet of Roncaglia in that same year to his defeat at the hands of the Lombard League at Legnano in 1176 (Table 4.3). One of the first acts of the offensive was the mission of Bishop Daniel of Prague, who is said to have sought oaths and hostages from Brescia, Mantua, Verona, Cremona, Pavia, Parma, Piacenza, Reggio, Modena, and Bologna, with other emissaries visit-ing other towns.[44] Frederic's hostages guaranteed a variety of undertakings made by

[42] Dept, *Les influences*, 200–1.

[43] *Recueil... Philippe Auguste*, 3:442–3, 497–8 (nos. 1304, 1351, 1352); Guillaume le Breton, *Gesta Philippi Augusti*, 170, *Philippidos*, 9.551–6 (SHF 1:252, 2:271); *RHF* 24:256–7 (no. 30). It is not certain that these last are the same individuals named in the 1213 list. The king also demanded twenty additional young *hostagios*, whom he used to extort additional sums. Many of the other complaints were for simple imprisonment against ransom. See Gérard Sivery, 'L'enquête de 1247 et les dommages de guerre en Tournaisis, en Flandre gallicante et en Artois', *Revue du Nord*, 59 (1977), 7–18.

[44] Vincent of Prague, *Annales*, s.a. 1158 (MGH SS 17:675). Similarly: Morena, *Historia*, s.a. 1158 (MGH SrG ns 7:62); RI 4.2.2:607.

Table 4.3 Hostages of Frederic I in Italy, 1158–1179

RI 4.2.2	Date	Town(s)	Hostages	Notes
563	1158	Brescia	60	
590	1158	Ferrara	40	
581	1158	Milan	300	
607	1158	Milan		
		Pavia		
		Cremona		
		Piacenza		
776	1159	Crema		
1020, etc.	1162	Milan	400	
1078	1162	Piacenza	500	
1362	<1164	Treviso		
1596	1164	Brescia	60	
1626	1167	Bologna	100	
1656	1167	Milan	300	
1666	1167	Ancona		initial offer rejected
1674	<1167	Genoa		
1695	1167	Rome	280	
2019	1173	Bologna		
2508	1177	Treviso		hostages not mentioned in the original treaty (MGH DD F I 3:206–8 no. 689])
2522	1179	?		

allies and enemies alike: promises of fidelity, payment of fines, and performance of specific actions such as the razing of fortifications. Frederic's practice of housing these hostages in neighbouring, rival towns, rather than bringing them back to Italy, worked initially, allowing him to play towns off against one another, but foundered once the towns were able to present a united front.[45] The sources concerning Milan and Piacenza demonstrate clearly that the emperor, like Philip Augustus, thought of the hostages not in terms of individuals defined by their family ties, but rather of representatives of groups. In his case, however, the groups were not only geographical, but also explicitly social.

Following the siege and capitulation of Milan in 1158, the city promised the delivery of 300 hostages. These were to be taken from all three orders of the town—the *capitanei*, the *vavassores*, and the *populares*—and selected by a committee made up of the archbishop of Milan and three Milanese consuls on the one hand, and two supporters of the emperor on the other.[46] In 1162, after a second siege and capitulation, Frederic again required hostages. The sources conflict as to events, but again identity is an issue. Frederic's own letter reporting the event states that 'they gave us 400 from among the best and the greatest (*meliores et maiores*) of the city'.[47] This passage disguises what was

---

[45] Peter Munz, *Frederick Barbarossa: A Study in Medieval Politics* (Ithaca, 1969), esp. 279 n. 1.

[46] MGH DD F I 2:9 (no. 224).

[47] MGH DD F I 2:192 (no. 351): 'quattuor centum obsides meliores et maiores de civitate nobis dederunt'.

apparently a complicated ritual of surrender, with consuls, flagbearers, knights, and the entire population of the city appearing before the emperor at various times over the course of a week to plead for mercy. At one point the emperor requested that 'all the consuls, exconsuls, *maiores*, knights, jurists, and judges' be retained as hostages. Other passages suggest that the bulk of the hostages were from the knightly order. Whatever the truth, the concern for the social distinctions is patent.[48] Finally, in 1167, Count Heinrich of Diez, acting for the emperor, delivered 100 Milanese hostages to Pavia, 50 from among the burghers (*burgenses*) and 50 from among the *forenses*—most likely a reference to individuals from other towns resident in the city. Shortly thereafter, upon hearing of possibly treacherous negotiations, he received another 200 hostages from Milan, this time from the burghers alone, and then, after another brief period, another 100 from the knights (*milites*).[49]

Piacenza provides even stronger evidence for this pattern. Piacenza definitely presented hostages to the emperor in 1158 and 1162; hostages from the town were still in imperial hands as late as 1167, when a consular oath included a promise to recover them.[50] The terms of the treaty of 1162 were guaranteed by a grant of 500 hostages to be determined by the emperor (*per suam electionem*), who would serve three-month terms in groups of 70, also to be determined by the emperor. If one of the individuals selected by the emperor refused to serve as a hostage, the town was to attempt to compel that service; if they failed, he was to be exiled from the city and bishopric, his goods forfeit to the fisc, and Frederic would choose a replacement. Three contemporary lists of hostages survive; while they cannot be definitively linked to the 1162 treaty, they offer further details of how such an agreement was carried out. Each of the lists contains around one hundred hostages. They are identified in various ways, most commonly: as a simple name (*Bernardus de Cavazola*); as the named son of a named individual (*Gislenzonus filius Agadi*); as an unnamed son of a named individual (*filius Azonis de Matulo*); as one of the unnamed sons of a named individual (*unus filiorum Malvasleti*); or as a named individual *or* his son (*Rozo Daiberti vel filius*). Other relatives—brothers, grandsons, or nephews—occasionally substitute for sons in these various combinations.[51] The optional category (so-and-so *or* a relative) predominates, showing Frederic's concern with the service of members of particular families, rather than given individuals or individuals of a certain age. The emperor was, not surprisingly, interested in holding hostages from influential families. Still, the numbers of

[48] F. Güterbock, 'Le lettere del notaio imperiale Burcardo intorno alla politica del Barbarossa nello scisma ed alla distruzione di Milano', *Bullettino dell'Istituto storico italiano per il Medio Evo e Archivio Muratoriano*, 61 (1949), 64 [RIS 6:918] ('Iussit igitur dominus imperator, omnes consules et exconsulares, maiores et milites, legistas et iudices in obsidatu teneri'); RI 4.2.2:1027ff.

[49] *Gesta Federici I. imperatoris in Lombardia* (MGH SrG 27:60–1); RI 4.2.2:1646, 1656.

[50] 1158: Vincent of Prague, *Annales*, s.a. (MGH SS 17:675); Morena, *Historia* (MGH SrG 7:62); De' Mussi, *Chronicon Placentinum*, s.a. (RIS 16:453); Codagnello, *Annales Placentini*, s.a. (MGH SrG 23:6). 1162: MGH DD F I 2:212–14 (no. 362). 1167: Cesare Vignati, *Storia diplomatica della Lega Lombarda con XXV documenti inediti* (Milan, 1866), 182–5; Vicenzo Boselli, *Delle storie piacentine* (Piacenza, 1793; repr. Bologna, 1976), 320–2.

[51] Ferdinand Güterbock, 'Alla vigilia della Lega Lombarda', *Archivio storico italiano*, 95.2 (1937), 181–5.

hostages involved suggest that the hostages also came from less distinguished groups. In a population of perhaps fifteen thousand,[52] 500 hostages taken from different families would have reached well beyond elite circles. Furthermore, the fact that hostages could be replaced and rotated reveals that Frederic's focus was not on particular families, but on representatives of certain sectors of the town's social structure, across classes.

For a third type of distribution of hostages, we may return to the county of Flanders in the wake of rebellions there against the French crown and its local allies in the late thirteenth and early fourteenth centuries.[53] Towns granted hostages on at least two occasions: following uprisings during the governorship of Jacques de Châtillon (1300–2), and following the Battle of Cassel (1328). Once again, detailed lists of hostages have been preserved, and in each of these episodes, in addition to *geographical* and *social* categorization we find *professional* distinctions.

Châtillon received and sent to Tournai a large group of hostages from the town of Bruges after he forced an end to the conflict in that town between the patriciate and the people in July 1301; as part of the capitulation agreement, the leaders of the revolt were exiled, fortifications around the town were dismantled, and the town's liberties forfeited.[54] These hostages, then, were guarantors of the submission and continued peacefulness of the town. Courtrai also provided hostages at some point to Châtillon, although the circumstances of this grant are unknown. These events are known from two lists—the one for Courtrai is incomplete—and a brief entry in the royal accounts.[55] A quarter-century later, after the defeat of the Flemish peasants and townsmen at Cassel in 1328, Philip VI of France and Louis I of Flanders demanded hostages from Ypres and Bruges. The episode, particularly as concerns Bruges, is recorded in an extensive collection of documents, including royal and comital correspondence and a set of nine interrelated lists. The most remarkable survivals are a 'declaration' issued by the count detailing the terms of hostageship of the men of Bruges, and account books from 1338 to 1341 showing their length of detention and the amounts they were paid for their 'service' to the town.[56] The letter from the royal commissioners to the town of Bruges listing the hostages requested describes them as 'for the good behaviour and the good peace

---

[52] Pierre Racine, 'Plaisance du Xème à la fin du XIIIème siècle: Essai d'historie urbaine', PhD thesis, Université de Paris–I, 1977, 2:676, offers an estimate of 15,000 to 20,000 for *c.*1200.

[53] William TeBrake, *A Plague of Insurrection: Popular Politics and Peasant Revolt in Flanders, 1323–1328* (Philadelphia, 1993); David Nicholas, *Medieval Flanders* (London, 1992), 186–216. The following analysis could be extended to later episodes in this region, such as the hostages claimed by Louis de Mâle from Ghent in 1348: Le Muisit, *Chronique* (SHF 209–11); *Cartulaire...Artevelde*, 133–7, 139 (nos. H15, H21), etc.; *De rekeningen der stad Gent*, 3.1:467–78, etc. Cf. the hostages demanded by Louis de Mâle in 1382 (Froissart 2.283 [10:241]), as well as hostages in Ghent from Dendermonde and Bruges in that same year (*Cartulaire...Artevelde*, 348–53 [no. N108]).

[54] *Annales Gandenses*, s.a. (ed. Johnstone, 15–16).

[55] 'Le registre de la "Loi" de Tournai, de 1302 et listes des otages de Bruges (1301) et de Courtrai', 485–500; *Les journaux du trésor de Philippe IV*, 827 (no. 5713).

[56] Ypres: Maurice Vandermaesen, 'Brugse en Ieprse gijzelaars voor koning en graaf, 1328–1329: Een administratief dossier', *Handelingen van het Genootschap voor geschiedenis gesticht onder de benaming 'Société d'émulation' te Brugge*, 130 (1993), 124–7. The hostages from Ypres must be distinguished from a separate group of exiles. No list of the hostages survives, although the names of some are known from the town registers. Bruges: Ghent, Rijksarchief, 1/1/1115, 1115*, 1116, 1117, 1118, 1431,

of the town'—as in 1301, then, these hostages were not guarantors of a specific financial undertaking.[57]

The Flemish hostage lists are striking in the first instance for their length. The royal letter just cited refers to 500 hostages, though only 494 names appear; the account of 1338–41 lists 499 royal hostages, in addition to another 314 for the count. The 1301 document names 468 individuals. These numbers, while impressive in the historical context of hostage lists, pale in comparison to the length of the confiscation inventory drawn up following the Battle of Cassel, which catalogues the property of 3,185 slain peasant rebels.[58] The most interesting thing about the lists is not their extent, but once again their organization. What is new in the fourteenth century is distribution of hostages by *profession*, that is, by craft guilds. The 1301 list, for example, begins with the rubric 'These are the hostages from the town of Bruges' ('Che sont li hostage delle vile de Bruges').[59] There follows a list of 28 individuals and the rubric *XXVIII bourgeois*. Next come 16 *brasseurs delle chervoise et du mies* (brewers), 100 *tysserans* (weavers), 37 *foulons* (fullers), 19 *tondeurs* (shearers), and so on through twenty-eight subdivisions, some of which include more than one group (for example, *carpentiers, machons et couvreurs* [carpenters, masons, and roofers]). The most complete of the 1328 lists presents the 494 names in thirty-three divisions, beginning with *poorters* (i.e. citizens), and continuing with the various craft guilds. Shorter lists from the 1328 dossier include subsets of these divisions.

The rationale behind the organization of these lists is not difficult to explain. The craft guilds were naturally the heart of the urban opposition, both in 1301 and in 1328. At the Battle of Courtrai in 1302, for example, guildsmen formed roughly four-fifths of a Bruges militia of around 3,000 men, and five of the hostages from the guilds in 1301 served as constables of this force.[60] Although their interests were

---

1/4/428, 618, 619 (lists); Bruges, Stadsarchief, 272/5 ('Rekening van den Ghiselghelde') (register); Ghent, Rijksarchief, 1/1/1446 (declaration); 1/1/1450, 1451, 1452, 1/4/614, 615, 620, 628, 630 (related documents). As at Ypres, not all of the lists are of hostages. Editions and commentary: Vandermaesen, 'Brugse en Ieprse gijzelaars', 141–2 (no. 1); *Codex diplomaticus Flandriae*, 1:405–17 (nos. 180–4); Henri Stein, 'Les conséquences de la bataille de Cassel pour la ville de Bruges et la mort de Guillaume de Deken, son ancien bourgmestre', *Compte rendu des séances de la Commission royale d'histoire ou recueil de ses bulletins*, 68 (1899), 647–64; D. Van den Auweele, 'De Brugse gijzelaarslijsten van 1301, 1305 en 1328: Een komparatieve analyse', *Handelingen van het Genootschap voor geschiedenis gesticht onder de benaming 'Société d'émulation' te Brugge*, 110 (1973), 105–67 (misdates many of the lists); Maurice Vandermaesen, 'De rekening der Brugse gijzelaars, 1328–9/1338–41', *Handelingen van het Genootschap voor geschiedenis gesticht onder de benaming 'Société d'émulation' te Brugge*, 115 (1978), 1–16; 'L'enquête de Bruges après la bataille de Cassel'. The towns of Mude and Houke also offered hostages: Ghent, Rijksarchief, 1/1/1444, 1445.

[57] Stein, 'Les conséquences', 653: 'pour le boin estat et la bone pais de le ville'. Similarly, Bruges, Stadsarchief, 99/325 (20 Dec. 1328): 'Comme pour oster les rebellions et les malefices... et aussi pour ceuls du pais mettre en pais et en transquillite, pour contrainde les rebelles de venir a vraye obeissence, et les contredisans punir, en maniere deue selonc rayson et justice'.

[58] *Le soulèvement de la Flandre maritime*, 1–162. Cf. 'Les confiscations dans la Châtellanie du Franc de Bruges'.

[59] The rubric ends 'de qui estoient en prison', suggesting perhaps that the hostages had been selected from among those already held, as in the case of Brétigny (above, p. 12).

[60] J. F. Verbruggen, *The Battle of the Golden Spurs (Courtrai, 11 July 1302): A Contribution to the History of Flanders' War of Liberation, 1297–1305*, ed. Kelly DeVries, trans. David Richard Ferguson (Woodbridge, 2002 [1952]), 152–62.

not always or precisely aligned with those of the peasants in the quarter-century between Courtrai and Cassel, the guildsmen had taken on increasing power in many of the towns, especially after 1302.[61] While the support of the urban patriciates might be divided, the guilds were not. From the royal point of view, if not from that of the count, the towns and peasants alike were the problem. The fidelity of the towns was in large measure determined by the fidelity of the guilds. The finely articulated power structures of the early fourteenth-century Flemish town demanded equally fine distinctions in requests for hostages: hence the divisions not only by class (*poorter* as against guildsman), but by profession.

Other such lists survive,[62] but hints of this sort of distribution of hostages appear elsewhere in less well documented cases. For example, the surrender agreement at Senlis in 1418 called for six hostages drawn from the three classes of the town (*ex triplici statu urbis*): two nobles, two burghers, and two religious.[63] At Melun in 1420, the English demanded 'twelve noble men from among the most noble after the captains, and six burghers of the town'; at Crotoy in 1423, it was a knight, three squires, and three burghers, identified as such.[64] The English at Caen in 1450 turned over twelve of their compatriots, two Norman knights, and four burghers; at Fronsac in 1451, it was six *gens de guerre* and twelve inhabitants of the town. Flemish rebels offered the duke of Burgundy in 1467 fifty hostages: thirty-two for Liège, six for Tongres, six for Saint-Trond, and six for Hasselt.[65] The episodes of royal ransom to be examined in Chapter 6, below, offer further evidence for the patterns shown here.

In all of these cases, towns are the key, either because of their geographical distribution, or because of their internal social and political make-up.[66] It was in the eleventh century that the political role of towns grew hand in hand with their increasing economic power, and urban autonomy was established through the spread of consulates, communes, and charters of liberties. In the twelfth century, rulers had to include towns in the constitution of the earliest representative assemblies. Italy and Flanders were among the most precocious regions of urban development, so it is not surprising that when Frederic Barbarossa and Philip Augustus were engaged in pacification of those regions in the twelfth and early thirteenth centuries, they could not simply receive as a hostage the son of a local count. The earliest merchant guilds also appear in the eleventh century and played key roles in the development of urban autonomy. By the thirteenth, the spread of craft guilds and the growth of their own economic power led to diversification of structures of

---

[61] TeBrake, *Plague*, 34; Nicholas, *Medieval Flanders*, 201–3.

[62] e.g. London, National Archives, E 101/5/18/16 (ed. John Griffiths, 'The Revolt of Madog ap Llywelyn, 1294–5', *Transactions/Trafodion* [Caernarvonshire Historical Society], 16 [1955], 24); 'Nouvelles preuves de l'histoire de Chypre', 80–4 (no. 14); *Régestes de la cité de Liège*, 4:197–200 (no. 997); and the royal cases below, Chapter 6.

[63] Pintoin, *Chronique du religieux de Saint-Denys*, 38 (ed. Bellaguet, 6:194). Cf. Monstrelet 1.186 (3:252–3).

[64] Monstrelet 1.231, 2.12 (4:12–13, 169): 'douze nobles hommes des plus notables après les capitaines, et six bourgois de la ville'.

[65] Chartier, *Chronique de Charles VII*, 227, 247 (ed. Vallet de Viriville, 2:221, 275); Du Clercq, *Mémoires*, 5.64 (ed. Reiffenberg, 4:288–9).

[66] David Nicholas, *The Growth of the Medieval City: From Late Antiquity to the Early Fourteenth Century* (London, 1997).

power within towns. By the time of the Battle of Cassel, then, Philip VI could not even content himself with any hostages from the towns: their identity was tied not just to family and to location, but to profession.

Hostage lists thus offer urban historians a valuable new approach to their subject, a way to understand the organization of power within towns, and the power of towns within larger polities. For the history of hostageship, such lists demonstrate clearly a break with the early Middle Ages: in some situations a hostage was less an individual to be cultivated or a means to take advantage of the affective bonds of family than he was an interchangeable representative of a group. The logic of hostageship was resting on very different foundations.

HOSTAGES AND THE LAWS OF WAR

The earliest formal examination of the medieval laws of war is Giovanni da Legnano's treatise on civil and canon law entitled *Tractatus de bello, de represaliis et de duello* of around 1360, which was adapted by Honoré Bonet in the 1380s for a vernacular audience as *L'arbre de batailles*, which in turn was a principal source for Christine de Pisan's *Livre des fais d'armes et de chevallerie* of around 1410. Works on chivalry, such as Ramon Llull's *Libre qui es de l'ordre de cavalleria* (1279–83) and Geoffrey de Charny's *Livre de chevalerie* (*c.*1350), show from another perspective what was considered licit and illicit in the context of military conflicts. But these works are all very late, on the one hand, and—like the surviving Roman law on which some of them draw—eccentric rather than systematic in their coverage. Furthermore, none of them represents a formal codification. The customs and practice of warfare in the Middle Ages are instead best reconstructed from the study of practice, supplemented by rare passages of positive law and records of court cases. Such an approach allows for a consideration of the laws—or more properly, customs—across the entire period instead of just at its end. The Hundred Years War has normally been seen as the principal catalyst for formalization and institutionalization of such customs, although the process is already visible from the eleventh century, in the Crusades and the Norman conquest of England.[67] This process of institutionalization provides the context for a second set of changes in medieval hostageship, which was central to two new customs of war: conditional respite and ransoming.

A. Conditional Respite

The story of William Marshal is an example of the integration of hostages into practices of surrender during siege warfare. In particular, William was given to guarantee a conditional surrender: if a relief force did not arrive within a certain period, the garrison would capitulate, and it would not use the intervening truce

---

[67] M. H. Keen, *The Laws of War in the Late Middle Ages* (London, 1965); Matthew Strickland, *War and Chivalry: The Conduct and Perception of War in England and Normandy, 1066–1217* (Cambridge, 1996), esp. 31–54.

to its military advantage by reinforcing defences. Although there are three examples of this particular custom from sixth-century Italy,[68] it is otherwise unattested in the early Middle Ages, while evidence for the use of hostages during siege warfare in other ways is sparse during that period.[69] By the time of siege of Newbury in 1152, however, conditional surrender guaranteed by hostages[70] had become common, as had other customs that relied on hostages to smooth the tricky business of negotiating an end to a siege. Through the early twelfth century, the picture remains unclear, but by the second third of the century it is fair to speak of a recognized custom of surrender involving hostages, if not a *lex deditionis*.[71]

The rare eleventh-century and early twelfth-century evidence for the use of hostages during sieges suggests a very unstable practice that only prefigures the later norm. In 1086, one party of the occupants of the fortified monastery of Saint-Trond handed over hostages to their besieger, Henry, bishop of Liège, with the understanding that he would raise the siege without harm to the inhabitants or their goods, and that they would cease their rebellion. An ill-timed appearance of forces from the neighbouring town of Brustem led to the collapse of the truce, and the episcopal troops attacked the town. The chronicler notes that this was done 'in violation of the faith under which the bishop had received our hostages, and at the very hour they had come before him'.[72] The complaint of the chronicler focuses on the violation of the surrender agreement that the bishop was bound to respect because he had accepted the hostages. Still, the hostages were granted here not only to secure the mechanics of surrender but also to guarantee the continued submission of the town—the commitment of the grantors of the hostages was that they would cease their rebellion. Furthermore, the circumstances—the attack from Brustem and the division within Saint-Trond itself—may explain the violation of the agreement. This is hardly a clear case of a surrender agreement. A near-contemporary episode from the First Crusade shows why besiegers thought they needed hostages to secure a surrender agreement, but at the same time that recourse to them was not yet standard. Albert of Aachen, describing Baldwin of Boulogne's

[68] Procop. *Goth.* 7.12.13–15, 37.17–18, 39.25–7; Agathias, *Historiae*, 1.12–13, 18.5 (CFHB 2:24–7, 33).

[69] Erchempert, *Historia Langobardorum Beneventanorum*, 10 (MGH SrL 238); *Annales Vedastini*, s.aa. 885, 894, 899 (MGH SrG 12:58, 74, 81); *Annales de Saint-Bertin*, s.a. 873 (SHF 194); Richer, *Historiae*, 2.45 (MGH SS 38:130–1); Flodoard, *Historia Remensis ecclesiae*, 4.22 (MGH SS 36:414); Flodoard, *Annales*, s.aa. 932, 943, 945, 958 (CTH 39:54, 89, 97, 145); *Russian Primary Chronicle*, s.a. 6505 (trans. Cross, 123). Cf. Kosto, 'Late Antiquity'.

[70] Conditional surrender without guarantees was also possible: e.g. Robert of Torigni, *Chronica*, s.a. 1173 (RS 82.4:258). See Strickland, *War and Chivalry*, 208–18.

[71] For the later history, see Keen, *The Laws of War*, 128–31. The phrase itself is quite rare, and never used to refer to the conclusion of siege using hostages: Baldric of Dol, *Historia Jerosolymitana*, 1.26 (*RHC* Occ. 4:29), a. 1097; *Chronica de gestis consulum Andegavorum* (CTH 48:53), a. 1026; Gunther the Poet, *Ligurinus*, 6.118–19 (MGH SrG 63:335), a. 1157. See also Bernard S. Bachrach, *Fulk Nerra, the Neo-Roman Consul, 987–1040* (Berkeley, 1993), 305 n. 83, and for later examples, Blondel, *De reductione Normanniae*, 3.2, 4.2, 16/100, 171, 226 (RS 32:95, 162, 208). Cf. Pintoin, *Chronique du religieux de Saint-Denys*, 38 (ed. Bellaguet, 6:194–7) (*bellorum jura*); Laurent de Liège, *Gesta episcoporum Virdunensium*, 13 (MGH SS 10:499) (*iure gentium*).

[72] Raoul of Saint-Trond, *Chronique de l'abbaye de Saint-Trond*, 3.7–8 (ed. De Borman, 1:42): 'Postposita igitur fide, qua episcopus obsides nostros susceperat, eadem hora qua ante eum venerant'.

near capture at Amacha in 1098, has one of his advisors urge him not to enter the fortress—which Balas was offering to surrender precisely in order to trap him—without hostages for his safety. The wisdom of this advice was proven by the fact that the men who went in without him were in fact ambushed.[73]

At Amacha, then, hostages were proposed to avoid deception. At Głogów in 1109, in contrast, hostages were granted as a cover for deception, and on both sides. Thus while the siege of Głogów confirms the continued instability of the practice of conditional respite at the start of the twelfth century, it simultaneously offers evidence for the development of norms, for the deceit relies precisely on the expectation that norms will be adhered to. Besieging the city, Emperor Henry V accepted hostages for a five-day truce, during which time the besieged were to try to get their ruler, Duke Bolesław III of Poland, to make peace; the emperor promised that whether or not the legation was successful, the hostages would be returned. This was, the Gallus Anonymous reports frankly, a ruse: 'The emperor received the hostages on oath because he thought that they would enable him to take the town, despite the perjury that it would involve. The inhabitants of Głogów, meanwhile, handed over the hostages to buy time to fortify certain parts of the town's defences that had deteriorated.' When Bolesław received the legation and heard of the grant of hostages, he was furious, in part because he saw through the emperor's ploy: he threatened to crucify the townsmen if they surrendered because of the hostages (*propter ipsos*) and argued that it was better for citizens and hostages alike to die by the sword than to live in servitude. The townsmen went back to the emperor with their report of Bolesław's response, naively requesting the return of the hostages. The emperor told them that he would return the hostages only if they handed over the castle, threatening to kill both them and the hostages if they refused, which they did. The emperor tied the hostages to his siege engines, hoping that fidelity to their children and friends would lead the townsmen to surrender; this gambit also failed, and the bloody battle began.[74] Deceit aside, both the emperor and the townsmen (if not Bolesław) expected the other side to adhere to the agreement because of the guarantee of hostages: the emperor thought that the townsmen would be moved by affective ties, while the townsmen thought that the emperor would be swayed by the threat of perjury.

Four years later, at the opposite end of Europe, Queen Urraca of Castile concluded a successful conditional surrender agreement involving hostages, at Burgos. Having intercepted the forces of Alfonso I of Aragon on their way to relieve the town, she undertook negotiations with the garrison. They gave hostages and promised that if Alfonso failed to come to their aid within fifteen days, they would hand over the castle; the queen, in turn, was to let them go unharmed. Alfonso did not succeed, and Urraca took Burgos without a fight.[75] Note here again that although

[73] Albert of Aachen, *Historia Ierosolimitana*, 5.19 (OMT 362), although its value for customs in the late eleventh century is questionable.

[74] Gallus Anonymous, *Cronica et gesta ducum sive principum Polonorum*, 3.6–8 (ed. Maleczyńsky, 134–6): 'Ob hoc utique cesar obsides cum iuramento recepit, quia per eos civitatem, licet cum periurio, consequi se reputavit. Ob hoc etiam Glogouienses illos obsides posuerunt, quia loca civitatis interim vetustate consumpta munierunt.'

[75] *Historia Compostellana*, 1.87 (CCCM 70:141–2).

only the garrison grants hostages, the queen's acceptance of them binds her to the agreement, as well. The degree to which this episode of conditional surrender represents a development from earlier practices is not clear. Hostages had been used occasionally in siege negotiations, but a time limit is seen only at Głogów, and the tying of the truce to the possible arrival of a relief force is entirely new. The latter element may be connected to the increasingly explicit contractual nature of obligations between lords and men: for a garrison to surrender without a fight would be treasonous, but it could do so with permission or if the lord could be seen to have violated his obligation to defend his man.[76]

On the other hand, the custom of truces to appeal for relief may be linked to Iberia itself, as two other early examples also come from that region; as the parties granted time to appeal for aid are in both cases Muslim lords, the development of Christian vassalic obligations is unlikely to have been a cause. Ali ibn Yusuf, castellan of Oreja, requested a one-month truce in 1139, promising that if relief forces did not appear, the castle would be handed over. Alfonso VII of León and Castile demanded fifteen noble hostages as a guarantee, and specified the eventual terms of peaceful surrender. One month later, as promised, the garrison surrendered, and Alfonso returned the hostages. The scene was repeated at Tortosa nine years later; the garrison was granted forty days by the Genoese and the count of Barcelona, explicitly so that they might appeal to 'Spain' for aid, and they handed over as a guarantee 100 hostages to the Genoese; at the end of the forty-day period, they promptly surrendered.[77] To these three twelfth-century Iberian cases there can be added just two others from Europe. In 1141, the castle of Bouillon obtained a seven-day respite in hopes of relief—which, in the words of one author, was 'an absolute impossibility'—in exchange for a hostage, and the submission proceeded smoothly.[78] By contrast, at Verneuil in 1178, Louis VII of France violated a three-day truce he had granted to the garrison so that they might appeal to Henry II of England for aid, seizing property, torching the town, and imprisoning the inhabitants.[79]

The likelihood of an Iberian impetus, if not origin, for the practice of conditional respite with hostages is bolstered by the fact that it was not a standard element of Christian–Muslim interactions in the eastern Mediterranean.[80] The sole episode from that region dates from 1192, and its details and outcome are telling. Besieged by Saladin's army, Raoul, patriarch of Jaffa, negotiated a truce until the next day at nones; if at the end of that short period aid had not arrived, the city would be handed over, along with an indemnity of 10 bezants for each man, 5 for each woman, and 3 for each child. Raoul himself served as a hostage for the agreement,

[76] Strickland, *War and Chivalry*, 212–18, 224–9.

[77] *Chronica Adefonsi imperatoris*, 2.57, 60 (CCCM 71:221–2); Caffaro, *Annales*, s.a. 1148 (MGH SS 18:39).

[78] *Triumphus Sancti Lamberti de castro Bollonio*, 19–20 (MGH SS 20:510) ('omnino tunc erat impossibile'); Renier of Saint-Laurent de Liège, *Triumphale Bulonicum*, 4 (MGH SS 20:590).

[79] Roger of Howden, *Gesta Henrici II et Ricardi I* (RS 49.1:50). I can find no independent verification of the claim by the Minstrel of Reims that a hostage was granted for the conditional surrender of Gisors in 1193 (*Récits d'un ménestrel de Reims*, 106–8 [SHF 56–8]).

[80] Kosto, 'Crusades', 12–14.

along with several other barons. In this case, the alleged relief actually arrived—but too late. The most detailed account reports that Richard I's forces appeared to find that the garrison had been induced to begin the surrender early and that Saladin's troops had killed the messengers bearing the indemnity payment. This tale may be designed precisely to build a case that the besiegers had violated the agreement; alternatively, Saladin may have advanced the timetable because he had intelligence of Richard's approach. Furthermore, the recent massacre at Acre may have contributed to the apparent false dealing. In any case it is clear that a surrender agreement collapsed. The hostages remained in Saladin's hands and were sent as captives to Damascus. Sicard of Cremona (no fan of Richard) criticized the king for not arranging for the release of the patriarch during subsequent negotiations.[81]

If conditional respite was rare during the Crusades, hostages were employed in other sorts of twelfth-century siege negotiations between Christians and Muslims. The most specific agreement was at the siege of Lisbon in 1147, where the garrison handed over five hostages to guarantee that they would not interfere with the Crusaders' siege engines or undertake any repairs to their fortifications during the night; the hostages also (and uniquely) seem to have had the power to renegotiate the terms of surrender.[82] At Tyre in 1124, the two sides *exchanged* hostages to smooth the safe transfer of the town, while at Ascalon in 1153 it was only the besieged who provided guarantees for the surrender of the town; each account highlights the carefully negotiated nature of the transaction.[83] At Acre in 1191, the garrison commander al-Mashtub delivered hostages to Philip II of France as a guarantee that he would return to the besieged town after being allowed to cross enemy lines to consult with Saladin.[84] In contrast to the debacle at Jaffa, all of these agreements were successful.[85]

In the eleventh and twelfth centuries, then, a distinct practice of conditional respite can be seen emerging from the general use of hostages during sieges. Of four successful outcomes, three are from Iberia, and all involved longer truces (forty, thirty, fifteen, seven days) than the three failed transactions (five, three, two days). While conditional respite was not common in the Crusades—only one case has come to light—evidence from those conflicts dominates other uses of hostages during sieges (five of the six cases, including Lisbon). This is meagre evidence, to be sure, but sufficient to show that the practice of conditional respite with hostages was a twelfth-century development and one associated with Europe rather than the eastern Mediterranean. In Iberia, it may even have been an established norm, and the splintered twelfth-century political map there makes the region a good candidate for the origin of the practice.

[81] Sicard of Cremona, *Cronica* (CCCM 125:26–7); *Itinerarium peregrinorum et gesta regis Ricardi*, 6.13–15 (RS 38.1:400–9). Sicard claims that the patriarch was the only hostage.

[82] *De expugnatione Lyxbonensi* (ed. David, 164–72).

[83] Fulcher of Chartres, *Historia Hierosolymitana*, 3.34.2 (ed. Hagenmayer, 734–5); William of Tyre, *Chronicon*, 17.30 (CCCM 63A:803).

[84] Roger of Howden, *Gesta Henrici II et Ricardi I* (RS 49.2:174–5); Sicard of Cremona, *Cronica* (CCCM 125:23).

[85] See also Choniates, *Historia*, Isaac Angelos II (CFHB 11.1:399), where the mechanics are unclear.

In the thirteenth to the fifteenth centuries, hostages continued to be used for simple[86] and delayed[87] surrender agreements without mention of the possibility of a relief force. In some cases it is difficult to determine whether the hostages are guaranteeing the mechanics of the surrender or simply the future good behaviour of the conquered. Yet it is clear that conditional respite with hostages—hostages who would be returned upon surrender—had by this point become firmly entrenched as a custom of war; conversely, conditional respite without mention of hostages is much rarer.[88] It is the English conflicts with the French and the Scots that provide the best evidence.[89] New for this period is the occasional diplomatic record of capitulation agreements—from the archives or embedded in narrative sources—which suggest what lies behind the more laconic chronicle accounts.

The earliest such record is the capitulation treaty of Rouen in 1204. Philip II granted a thirty-day truce for John of England either to make peace with the king or 'remove the said king of France from the place in which he is'—the document is dated *ante Rothomagum*—before the town submits. Named knights and burghers are recorded as having sworn oaths; all the others are to do so before the following Sunday, by which time hostages are also to be given: three named nephews and sons of the knights, hostages from all the other knights who control strongholds, and forty hostages from the burghers, 'sons and close heirs from our families, to be chosen by the king himself'. If the surrender terms—addressed in great detail in the treaty—are fulfilled, the hostages will be returned.[90] The agreement offered the same terms, *mutatis mutandis*, to the other two towns holding out against Philip, Arques and Verneuil. Rouen ultimately capitulated on the twenty-fourth day. Roger of Wendover reports that in 1203 the Norman towns had generally agreed to a one-year truce guaranteed by hostages; the terms were likely similar, if less specific.[91]

Two hundred and fifteen years later, Rouen capitulated again, this time to an English king, Henry V. The treaty, dated 13 January 1419, called for the surrender of the town at noon on 19 January. Most of the treaty's roughly two dozen articles concern the specific terms. Deep within the document, however, appears the

[86] Jaume I, *Llibre dels feits*, 87 (ed. Soldevila, 1:182); Froissart 1.214–15 (3:57–8); Monstrelet 1.47, 231, 2.22 (1:373–87, 4:12–13, 204–5).

[87] *Cartes de poblament medievals valencianes*, 362–3 (no. 177); Pulgar, *Crónica de los señores reyes católicos Don Fernando y Doña Isabel*, 3.133 (ed. Rosell, 510); Monstrelet 1.261, 2.267 (4:93–5, 6:55); *Chronique de la Pucelle*, 22, 54 (ed. Vallet de Viriville, 242, 309–10); Chartier, *Chronique de Charles VII*, 212, 226 (ed. Vallet de Viriville, 2:178–9, 213–14). Cf. Du Clercq, *Mémoires*, 1.19 (ed. Reiffenberg, 1:345–7), where a delay is uncertain.

[88] Although this appears to have been more common earlier (above, p. 100, n. 70), the only examples I have identified for the period of the Hundred Years War (there are surely others) are the sieges of La Roche-sur-Yon in 1369 and Thouars in 1373 (Froissart 1.630, 712–15 [7:161–2, 8.2:89–101]), Oisy in 1423 (Monstrelet 2.15 [4:179]), and Bordeaux in 1451 (Du Clercq, *Mémoires* 1.42 [ed. Reiffenberg], 1:413–14).

[89] For an early thirteenth-century case from Wales, see *Brut y Tywysogyon*, s.a. 1213 (trans. Jones, 197).

[90] *Layettes*, 1:250–2 (no. 716): 'tam filios quam propinquos heredes de parentela nostra, quales idem rex elegerit'. The other half of the chirograph survives as well: *Recueil…Philippe Auguste*, 2:379–83 (no. 803); cf. Rigord, *Gesta Philippi Augusti*, 142 (SHF 1:160–1).

[91] Roger of Wendover, *Flores historiarum*, s.a. (RS 84.1:319).

acknowledgement that in theory relief might come; if it did come, the besieged were not permitted to render aid to the relief force. The agreement was to be guaranteed by eighty 'notable hostages': twenty knights or squires, and the rest burghers, who were to be maintained at their own expense.[92] A similar record survives from Brest in 1373. The English forces under John, Lord Neville, promised to turn over the town at the end of a month to the French if the duke of Brittany had not by that time arrived 'in peace, or in such force that he might hold the field *en place egal* before the town of Brest'. As a guarantee, twelve hostages were to be granted, who were to be returned to Neville or his representative upon delivery of the town, freed of all obligations.[93] The agreement for Grancey in 1434 only gave the French defenders a week, for which they were to turn over six hostages, including four squires, a priest-canon, and a burgher.[94]

Monstrelet transcribes similar documents for conditional respite at Crotoy in 1423 and Guise in 1424, along with treaties with hostages for simple or delayed surrender (without expectation of relief) at Liège in 1408, Melun in 1420, and Meaux in 1422; Chartier includes the treaty for Fronsac in 1451. Monstrelet's habit, when simply summarizing the terms of a capitulation agreement, of giving the precise date of surrender even when he does not give the date of the agreement itself, gives some confidence that the bulk of the thirteen other conditional respite treaties he describes were written too.[95]

Tartas capitulated to the English on slightly different terms in 1441. Two temporary guardians—one English and one French—took control of the town and custody of the son of the lord of the castle as a hostage. The besieged agreed to submit the town to whichever of the two kings was in a stronger position ('le plus fort et puissant') on 1 May of the following year. Remarkably, the deadline was extended to 24 June as Charles VII was assembling troops. On the appointed day, Charles appeared with 16,000 troops before the town; the English were nowhere to be seen. The temporary guardians delivered the hostage and the keys to the town to the king.[96] The mechanics of this agreement were new (temporary custodians, basis of the decision), but the structure was essentially the same as in other conditional respite agreements. The town granted hostages as a guarantee that it would submit peacefully by a certain date if help did not arrive. Perhaps the greatest novelty is that this time, the help showed up. In another rare case, at Cosne-sur-Loire in 1422, Anglo-Burgundian forces appeared to meet the French, who returned the hostages even before any battle took place.[97]

Because of the very real possibility of relief, the question of timing was key. The puzzling seven-week extension of the truce at Tartas proved decisive. Similarly, as seen above, at Jaffa the garrison's submission a couple of hours early may have prevented its easy relief by Richard. In both cases, however, the original deadline

[92] *Foedera²*, 9:666: 'notabiles obsides'.
[93] Froissart, 8.1:clx–clxiii (ap. 3).
[94] BnF, Coll. Bourgogne 103, fols. 142v–149v.
[95] Table 4.4.
[96] Wavrin, *Recueil des croniques*, 5.16.14–15 (RS 39.4:354–62).
[97] *La geste des nobles françois*, 192 (ed. Vallet de Viriville, 185–6).

Table 4.4 Hostages for Conditional Respite in the Hundred Years War

sa	Site	Besiegers	Besieged	Days	Hostages	Outcome	Source
1346	Angoulême	English	French	30	24	Surrender	Froissart (ed. Kervyn de Lettenhove, 4:307–8)
1345	Montségur	English	French	30	12	Surrender	Froissart 1.225, 227 (3:76–9, 81)
1369	La Roche-sur-Yon	English	French	30	12	Surrender	Froissart 1.630 (7:161–3)
1373	Brest	French	English	30	12	Violation	Froissart 1.735–6 (8.2:141–7); 8.1:clx–clxiii (ap. 3)
1373	Derval	English	French	4	40	Violation	Froissart 1.730, 742 (8.2:134–5, 158–60)
1374	Gascony	French	English		12	Surrender	Froissart 1.751, 753 (8.2:175, 178–9)
1374	Becherel	French	English			Surrender	Froissart 1.752 (8.2:177–8)
1387	Bragança	English	Galicians	9	12	Surrender	Froissart 3.56–7 (ed. Sauvage, 3:173–7)
1415	Harfleur	English	French	3 or 4		Surrender	Monstrelet 1.143 (3:85); Walsingham, Historia anglicana (RS 28.1.1:309)
1418	Senlis	French	Burgundians	4	6	Executions	Monstrelet 1.186 (3:251–3); Pintoin, Chronique du religieux de Saint-Denys, 38 (ed. Bellaguet, 6:194–7); La geste des nobles françois, 158 (ed. Vallet de Viriville, 167)
1419	Rouen	English	French	6	80	Surrender	Foedera², 9:664–7
1421	Dreux	English	French			Surrender	Monstrelet 1.251 (4:69)
1422	Cosne-sur-Loire	French	English			Relief	La geste des nobles françois, 192 (ed. Vallet de Viriville, 185–6); Monstrelet 1.266 (4:106)
1423	Gamaches	English	French			Surrender	Monstrelet 1.262, 264 (4:98, 101)
1423	Compiègne, Rémy, Gournay, Mortemer, La Neuville-en-Hez, Cressonsac	English	French			Surrender	Monstrelet 1.262, 264 (4:98, 101)
1423	Saint-Valéry	English	French			Surrender	Monstrelet 1.264, 2.1 (4:103)

1423	Crotoy	English	French			Surrender	Monstrelet 2.12, 14 (4:166–9, 177); *La geste des nobles françois*, 198 (ed. Vallet de Viriville, 188)
1423	Compiègne	English	French			Surrender	Monstrelet 2.14 (4:176–7)
1424	Ivry	English	French			Surrender	Monstrelet 2.17, 19 (4:186, 189–90); *La geste des nobles françois*, 213 (ed. Vallet de Viriville, 196–7)
1424	Guise	English	French	165	8	Surrender	Monstrelet 2.22, 29 (4:199–205, 229–30)
1425	Le Mans	English	French	8		Surrender	Monstrelet 2.34 (4:247–8)
1427	La Gravelle	English	French			Execution	*Chronique de la Pucelle*, 25 (ed. Vallet de Viriville, 249)
1433	Passy	Burgundians	French	51		Surrender	Monstrelet 2.141, 144 (5:66, 69–70)
1433	Monchas	Burgundians	French	7		Violation	Monstrelet 2.145, 148, 158 (5:72, 76, 94)
1434	Grancey	Burgundians	French			Surrender	BnF, Coll. Bourgogne 103:142v–149v
1441	Tartas	English	French		6	Raised Siege	Monstrelet 2.263, 266 (6:24–5, 52–3); Wavrin, *Recueil des chroniques*, 5.6.14–15 (RS 39.4:354–62)
1449	Harcourt	French	English			Surrender	Escouchy, *Chronique*, 1.34 (SHF 1:197)
1450	Honfleur	French	English			Surrender	Chartier, *Chronique de Charles VII*, 215 (ed. Vallet de Viriville, 2:189)
1450	Saint-Sauveur-Le-Vicomte	French	English	8		Surrender	Chartier *Chronique de Charles VII*, 226 (ed. Vallet de Viriville, 2:213–14)
1450	Caen	French	English	18		Surrender	Chartier, *Chronique de Charles VII*, 227 (ed. Vallet de Viriville, 2:221)
1450	Falaise	French	English	13	12	Surrender	Chartier, *Chronique de Charles VII*, 229 (ed. Vallet de Viriville, 2:226–7)
1451	Fronsac	French	English	18	11	Surrender	Chartier, *Chronique de Charles VII*, 247 (ed. Vallet de Viriville, 275)

was respected, in that it was altered only by agreement. During the conquest of Mallorca in 1230, the Catalan forces accepted an eight-day truce from a band of besieged and distressed Muslim fighters, insisting in negotiations that they surrender as prisoners, rather than be allowed to leave freely. At dawn on the eighth day, the Catalans called on their opponents to surrender as agreed, but received the reply that 'it was not yet terce and we had to wait'. The Catalans agreed and waited until half-terce for the surrender.[98] When Guise surrendered to John of Luxembourg a mere 2 days early in 1425, fully 163 days after the capitulation agreement was subscribed, John's negotiations with the governor merited special mention.[99]

In theory, such agreements worked because of the threat to the hostages if they were violated; as we have seen, however, such threats were only rarely carried out. Hostages were executed on two occasions in the fourteenth century, each of which involved a dispute about the underlying agreement rather than—as in the emblematic case of William Marshal—an outright abandonment of the agreement and, thus, the hostage(s). After Berwick handed over hostages to the English in 1333 to guarantee a promise to submit if they were not relieved, a Scottish army appeared before the town in advance of the deadline, introduced reinforcements and supplies into the town, and then moved away from the town, despoiling its surroundings in view of the English. The English claimed that the departure of the Scottish forces meant that the town had not been relieved and called on it to surrender. The town claimed that the introduction of men and supplies amounted to relief. The English rejected this argument and executed one of the hostages, the son of Alexander Seton, declaring that they would kill two hostages a day until the town relented. This led to a renewal of the surrender agreement, but now with very specific—and, perhaps significantly, written—terms: relief was either by means of battle or by the entry of 200 men-at-arms into the town.[100] The dispute at Derval in 1373, as reported by Froissart, concerned not the definition of relief, but rather who had the right to enter into a capitulation treaty. Robert Knollys, lord of the castle, rejected a conditional respite agreement arranged by his captain Hues Broe and his brothers, claiming that they had no standing to make promises without his consent. The duke of Anjou considered the agreement violated and had the hostages, two knights and two squires, decapitated before the walls.[101]

Senlis in 1418 offers another case of a dispute concerning relief gone bad. The Burgundian garrison had agreed to surrender unless relieved within four days, on 19 April. According to Monstrelet's more detailed pro-Burgundian account, the French commander, learning of an advancing relief force, went to meet it on 17 April. The besieged, noticing the activity, made an attack on the French camp on

---

[98] Jaume I, *Llibre dels feits*, 102–3 (ed. Soldevila, 195–6).
[99] Monstrelet 2.29 (4:229).
[100] *Brut*, 223 (ed. Brie, 281–3); *Gesta Edwardi de Carnarvan*, s.a. 1333 (RS 76.2:112–13); Gray, *Scalacronica* (ed. Stevenson, 162–3); *Chronica monasterii de Mesla*, 14.27 (RS 43.2:368–9); *Foedera*, 2.2:864–5. See Clifford J. Rogers, *War Cruel and Sharp: English Strategy under Edward III, 1327–1360* (Woodbridge, 2000), 63–9.
[101] Froissart 1.742 (8.2:158–9).

the morning of 18 April. The French commander, considering this to be a violation (a view shared by the Saint-Denis chronicler), demanded the surrender of the town according to the agreed terms. The Burgundians argued that the time was not yet up, and the French executed four of the hostages before deciding to withdraw.[102] A different problem emerged at La Gravelle in 1427: when the duke of Bedford arrived to accept the surrender of the fortress on the agreed date, those who had originally made the agreement were absent, leading the town to refuse surrender, and Bedford to execute the hostages.[103] Although at Brest in 1373 hostages are not reported as killed, the conditional respite agreement there also dissolved in confusion, despite a written agreement. An English relief force under Salisbury arrived before Brest in advance of the deadline and sent a herald to the French under Du Guesclin telling them that they were ready 'to fight and to deliver both their hostages and the fortress'. The herald proceeded to get a workout. The French said that the English would have to come to them. The English said that they had come by boat, and that they could advance to the French position only if the French would send them horses; if they did not wish to do so, they should return the hostages, because they 'would have no further cause to hold them'. The French refused, but proposed that the armies should meet at the site where the surrender agreement was first negotiated; they advanced to the site, and told the English that if they didn't appear, they would lose their hostages. The English offered to travel one-third or even half of the distance—but if the French didn't agree, they had to return the hostages, 'because they would have no cause to hold them'. Ultimately the English gave up and entered the town; the French kept the hostages. The final English letter demanding the return of the hostages survives, supporting the substance of Froissart's colourful account.[104] The submission of Gascony to the duke of Anjou in the following year—a rare conditional respite agreement involving not the siege of a single castle, but rather the control of an entire region—was complicated by a dispute over whether an intervening truce had nullified the original agreement. Once again, force prevailed: the French, who had showed up on the appointed day, claimed their prize and returned their hostages.[105]

The desire to avoid such confusion surely explains the detail in agreements such as the one for the capitulation of Guise in 1424: 'in case on the appointed day they are not relieved, and the lords or princes of the party to which Guise adheres, or any others committed or deputed to this task by them, fail to meet us with all our forces in combat, or one of us, or others named by the king, that is between the

---

[102] Monstrelet 1.186 (3:251–3); Pintoin, *Chronique du religieux de Saint-Denys*, 38 (ed. Bellaguet, 6:194–7).

[103] *Chronique de la Pucelle*, 25 (ed. Vallet de Viriville, 249).

[104] Froissart 1.735–6 (8.2:143–7): 'tout prest pour combatre et de delivrer leurs hostages et le chastiel de Brest'; 'se il ne voloient faire l'une pareçon ne l'autre, il renvoiassent leurs ostages, [car] il y estoient tenu'; 'et, se ce ne volés faire, si leur renvoiiés leurs hostages, car il dient que en avant vous n'avés nulle cause dou tenir'. Knollys had violated the original agreement by leaving Brest to go to Derval (8.1:lxxx n. 3, which also gives the text of the letter).

[105] Froissart 1.751–3 (8.2:175, 178–9); see 8.1:cv–cx. An earlier grant of hostages to guarantee the neutrality the abbot of Saint-Sever seems to have been folded into this larger agreement (1.750 [8.2:173–4]).

town of *Sains* and the house of *Fouquausains*, which we have together with those of Guise chosen and decided upon as the place to hold that combat'.[106] At Monchas in 1433, the parties defined relief as the French king's men appearing for battle 'before the castle of Monchas, or in the *pays Santhers* near *Villers-le-Carbonnel*, one league from *Haplaincourt*'.[107] As these passages suggest, what was foreseen was less an actual attempt to render aid to the besieged town than a pitched battle, a trial by combat writ large. At Cosne-sur-Loire in 1422, the duke of Burgundy and the Dauphin, for example, 'promised each other, through their heralds, to appear in force to fight his opposite number in the said combat'.[108] As in medieval warfare generally, pitched battles were exceedingly rare. Normally, one party simply failed to appear at the appointed time and place. Still, the rules were scrupulously followed. Forces that did appear took up position at the appointed place and remained there the entire day. Bedford, on hearing that the French forces were so small compared to his—and thus unlikely to appear—nonetheless sent an underling to Crotoy. And at Bordeaux in 1451, despite the loss of all hope, a herald made a formal appeal for English aid.[109]

In general, this system worked. The disputes described, while dramatic, were few compared to the surrenders that happened on schedule. The few mentions of the fate of hostages for successful submissions suggest that the victors tended to uphold their end of the bargain. At Moissac in 1374, the duke of Anjou 'sent back the hostages that he held at Périgeux to the count of Foix'. Upon receiving the surrender of Gamaches in 1423, the earl of Warwick returned the hostages that had been granted unharmed. In the same year at Crotoy, Raoul Le Bouteiller returned the hostages to the departing governor, as had been detailed in the original agreement. At Guise in the next year, John of Luxembourg 'returned the hostages to the French who were within, who, with good safe conducts, went where they pleased'. In 1450, English hostages were conducted to a village near their town of Saint-Sauveur-le-Vicomte pending the final surrender, at which point they were freed.[110] Hostages had become a routine part of negotiated surrenders.

B. Conditional Release and Ransom

In a single case in the ninth century, and then in several in the tenth, we find hostages granted in exchange for the release of high-ranking individuals who had fallen captive in some manner. The hostages substituted for the captive, allowing

---

[106] Monstrelet 2.22 (4:200): 'en cas qu'à ce jour prins pour ce faire, ne soient souscourus, et que les seigneurs ou princes du parti que ceulx de Guise tiennent, ou aucuns aultres par eulx commis et députez ad ce, ne combateroient nous, l'un de nous, ou aultres commis de par le roy, et toute notre puissance. C'est assavoir entre la ville de Sains et la maison de Fouquausins, où nous avons à ceulx de Guise esleu et advisé ensemble, plait pour tenir ladicte journée.'

[107] Monstrelet 2.145 (5:72): 'devant le chastel de Monchas, ou ès pays de Santhers emprès Villers-le-Carbonnel, à une lieue de Haplaincourt'.

[108] Monstrelet 1.266 (4:106): 'promirent...par la bouche de leurs héraulx, à estre et comparoir chascun à tout sa puissance, l'un contre l'autre, à combatre son adverse partie à ladicte journée'.

[109] Monstrelet 2.14 (4:177); Du Clercq, *Mémoires*, 1.42 (ed. Reiffenberg, 1:413–14).

[110] Froissart 1.751 (8.2:174); Monstrelet 1.264, 2.14, 29 (4:101, 177, 230), Chartier, *Chronique de Charles VII*, 226 (ed. Vallet de Viriville, 2:213–14).

for his freedom, but the fact that they were in custody was a guarantee of the good behaviour of the individual released—and the good behaviour of that individual's army or retainers. Such transactions were in essence submission treaties, long familiar in the case of defeated armies or peoples or towns, narrowed down to an individual who was physically in custody. Like submission agreements, they were indefinite with respect both to length and to the specific behaviours or actions guaranteed.[111] These sorts of grants continued through the central and later Middle Ages, employed by emperors and kings and counts across Europe in dealing with captives both lay and clerical, often taking their captives' sons as guarantees.[112]

Instead of being individualized versions of submission treaties, however, release agreements guaranteed by hostages might also call for the performance of a specific act. In principle this did not place a time limit on the agreement. Thomas de Turberville, for example, captured in Gascony in 1295, was released back to England against the hostageship of his sons on the condition that he spy for the French. Presumably, this situation could have lasted as long as the French were interested, although Thomas was captured and executed as a traitor.[113] Similarly, in 1342, a merchant of Jugon, captured by the forces of Charles of Blois, provided his son as a hostage to guarantee his promise to betray his town; he, too, was discovered and executed.[114] The Byzantine shipowner Symon Musonus was released against the hostageship of his brother and nephew and was soon forced to transport Hungarians on the Third Crusade at a substantial discount; again, the court's control over Symon could have continued indefinitely, if the hostages had not died in custody.[115]

In practice, though, this sort of demand for performance did foresee an end to the hostageship. It might be upon the return of the captive into custody. A letter of Frederic Barbarossa may offer an example of hostages for 'bail' in the modern sense, that is, appearance at trial: he ordered the release of a prisoner 'against hostages or a guarantee of 100 marks, if he does not return on the appointed day', that day being the one on which it would be decided before the bishop of Münster whether or not the prisoner was a ministerial.[116] But less familiar situations are also found. Galbert of Bruges describes the substitution of hostages for a wounded

---

[111] *Annales regni Francorum*, s.a. 826 (MGH SrG 6:171); Flodoard, *Annales*, s.aa. 924, 941, 945 (CTH 39:21, 80–1, 99); Gerbert of Reims, *Briefsammlung*, 122 (MGH Briefe der deutschen Kaiserzeit 2:149); *Chronicon Sancti Petri Vivi* (ed. Bautier and Gilles, 68). For the capture of Louis IV in 945, see: Richer, *Historiae*, 2.48 (MGH SS 38:133); Orderic Vitalis, *Historia ecclesiastica*, 5 (OMT 3:82); William of Jumièges, *Gesta Normannorum ducum*, 4.8 (OMT 1:114).

[112] Table 4.5. The eleventh-century poem *Ecbasis cuiusdam captivi per tropologiam*, 1182–4 (ed. Zeydel, 90) confirms this custom: 'Moris erat...Si prece, si precio laxatur captio capto,/Obside sucepto seu firmo sit sacramento'.

[113] Cotton, *Historia anglicana*, s.a. 1295 (RS 16:304–6); J. G. Edwards, 'The Treason of Thomas Turberville, 1295', in R. W. Hunt et al., eds., *Studies in Medieval History Presented to Frederick Maurice Powicke* (Oxford, 1948), 296–309.

[114] Froissart 1.180 (2:178–80). Cf. Fulcher of Chartres, *Historia Hierosolymitana*, 1.17.5 (ed. Hagenmayer, 232).

[115] 'Nuova serie di documenti sulle relazione di Genova coll'impero Bizantino', 472–3 (no. 16).

[116] MGH DD F I 1:288 (no. 168): 'acceptis obsidibus vel certitudine centum marcarum, si ad constitutam diem non redierit'. Cf. Bernard of Angers, *Liber miraculorum sanctae Fidis*, 1.33 (CTH 21:79).

Table 4.5 Hostages for Release from Captivity, 1000–1500

Date	Captive	Captor	Notes	Source
1011	Dierrich, d. Upper Lorraine	Henry II, emp.	ambiguous	Thietmar of Merseburg, *Chronicon*, 6.52 (MGH SrG ns 9:410)
1014	Miesko, son of Boleslaw I, d. Poland	Ulrich, d. Bohemia	proposal	Thietmar of Merseburg, *Chronicon*, 7.11 (MGH SrG ns 9:410)
1045	Godfrey III, d. Lower Lorraine	Henry III, emp.		Sigibert of Gembloux, *Chronica*, s.a. 1045 (MGH SS 6:358)
c.1060	Eberhard, abp. Trier	Conrad I, c. Luxembourg	ambiguous	*Gesta Treverorum*, cont., 8 (MGH SS 8:182)
1110	Iorwerth ap Bleddyn	Henry I, k. England		*Brut y Tywysogyon*, s.a. (trans. Jones, 65)
1112	rebels	Urraca, q. Castile		*Historia Compostellana*, 1.74 (CCCM 70:115)
1115	Adalbert, abp. Mainz	Henry V, emp.		*Gesta Treverorum*, cont., 19 (MGH SS 8:193)
1129	Waleran of Meulan, Hugh fitz Gervase	Henry I, k. England		*ASC* (E), s.a.
1146	Ranulf, e. Chester	Stephen, k. England		*ASC*, s.a.; cf. *Gesta Stephani*, 94, 101 (OMT 184, 196)
1158	Hyacinth and Henry, papal legates	Frederic and Henry, c. Eppan		Rahewin of Freising, *Gesta Friderici I. imperatoris*, 3.21 (MGH SrG 46:194); cf. Gunther the Poet, *Ligurinus*, 7.96 (MGH SS 63:371)
1173	Ralph de Fougères	Henry II, k. England		Robert of Torigni, *Chronica*, s.a. (RS 82.4:261); William of Newburgh, *Historia rerum Anglicarum*, 2.29 (RS 82.1:176)
1174	rebels	Henry II, k. England		Roger of Howden, *Chronica*, s.a. (RS 51.2:68)
1178	Conrad of Montferrat	Christian, abp. Mainz	ambiguous	Roger of Howden, *Gesta Henrici II et Ricardi I* (RS 49.1:243)
c.1182	Niclotus Burvinus	Cnut VI, k. Denmark		Arnold of Lübeck, *Chronica Slavorum*, 3.4 (MGH SrG 14:76–7)
1194	Henry III, d. Limburg, son Henry	Baldwin IX, c. Flanders		Gislebert of Mons, *Chronique*, 210 (ed. Vanderkindere, 296)

c.1197	Harald Maddadsson, e. Orkney		William I, k. Scotland	John of Fordun, *Chronica gentis Scotorum, Gesta annalia*, 22 (ed. Skene, 275)
1202	Hugh Le Brun	ambiguous	John, k. England	Ralph of Coggeshall, *Chronicon Anglicanum* (RS 66:138); Bertran de Born *lo fils, Quan vei lo temps renovelar* (razo) (ed. Stimming, 146–8)
1203	Adolph III, c. Holstein		Valdemar II, k. Denmark	Arnold of Lübeck, *Chronica Slavorum*, 6.17 (MGH SrG 14:239)
1208	Gwenwynwyn of Powys		John, k. England	*Foedera*, 1.1:101
1267	Giovanni Savelli		Henry of Castile	Malaspina, *Die Chronik*, 4.6 (MGH SS 35:187)
1416	France	proposal	England	*La geste des nobles françois*, 143 (ed. Vallet de Viriville, 158)
1483	Boabdil, sult. Granada		Ferdinand, k. Castile	*Documentos sobre relaciones internacionales de los Reyes Católicos*, 1:333–5 (no. 53)

prisoner until he recovered or died; he returned two weeks later, and the hostages were released. John of England allowed his prisoner Jordan of Bianney to be released two or more times a day to fence, keeping one Oliver de Vaux as a guarantee during his absences.[117] English rebels in 1381 kept the children of the governor of Rochester castle as hostages while he served as their emissary to the king: Froissart has him plead to the king, 'they are holding my children as hostages and will kill them if I do not return'.[118] The earl of Douglas, captured at Shrewsbury in 1403, was released four years later by Henry IV against a written promise and twelve hostages to 'attend to his affairs', with instructions to return by a specific day. His violation of this agreement—his failure, in the words of ambassadorial instructions, to act 'as a trewe prisoner aughte doo, without fraude or mail engin'—caused major complications in Anglo-Scottish relations, and it was only six years later that the hostages were freed in exchange for payment.[119]

A time limit might also be absent because the action that the released captive was to undertake would obviate the need for a return to custody or continued guarantees in the form of hostages. After the Battle of Vlaardingen (1018), at which Godfrey of Lorraine and his men were captured by the count of Holland, the duke was released while his men were kept in chains until such time as he could negotiate an agreement between the count and the emperor.[120] Similarly, Bishop Diego Gelmírez of Santiago was released *ad tempus* to negotiate with his captor, Arias Pérez, during the Iberian conflicts of the early twelfth century, as was Gerard of Montreuil to parley with Geoffrey Plantagenet.[121] In these latter two cases, it is notable that hostages were required simply for release from strict confinement, as presumably the captives were still under the control of victorious forces.

The classic example of an action that would obviate the need for continued guarantees is, of course, ransom.[122] Instead of releasing a prisoner on faith or with guarantees such as hostages, a captor always had the option of the economic exploitation

---

[117] Galbert of Bruges, *De multro*, 117–18 (CCCM 131:163–5); *Rotuli litterarum clausarum*, 1:88b.

[118] Froissart (ed. Kervyn de Lettenhove, 9:396): 'il ont mes enffans en ostages pour moy vers euls et les feroient morir, se je ne retournoie'.

[119] S. B. Chrimes, 'Some Letters of John of Lancaster as Warden of the East Marches towards Scotland', *Speculum*, 14 (1939), 3–27 (esp. nos. 11, 14). The written undertaking, which does not mention hostages, is at *Foedera²*, 8:478. See also the case of René of Anjou, above, p. 29.

[120] Alpert of Metz, *De diversitate temporum*, 2.21 (MGH SS 4:720).

[121] *Historia Compostellana*, 1.60 (CCCM 70:98); Geoffrey of Clairvaux, *Vita et res gesta Sancti Bernardi*, 3.13 (PL 185:329).

[122] On ransoming generally: Adalbert Erler, *Der Loskauf Gefangener: Ein Rechtsproblem seit drei Jahrtausenden* (Berlin, 1978); A. J. Forey, 'The Military Orders and the Ransoming of Captives from Islam (Twelfth to Early Fourteenth Centuries)', *Studia monastica*, 33 (1991), 259–79; Giulio Cipollone, ed., *La liberazione dei 'captivi' tra Cristianità e Islam: Oltre la Crociata e il Ǧihād: Tolleranza e servizio umanitario: Atti del Congresso interdisciplinare di studi storici (Roma, 16–19 settembre 1998) organizzato per l'VIII centenario dell'approvazione della regola dei Trinitari da parte del Papa Innocenzo III il 17 dicembre 1198/15 safar, 595 H* (Vatican City, 2000); Friedman, *Encounter*, 147–61, 187–211, 239–51; James W. Brodman, *Ransoming Captives in Crusader Spain: The Order of Merced on the Christian–Islamic Frontier* (Philadelphia, 1986); Philippe Contamine, 'The Growth of State Control. Practices of War 1300–1800: Ransom and Booty', in Contamine, ed., *War and Competition between States* (Oxford, 2000), 163–93; Jarbel Rodriguez, *Captives and Their Saviors in the Medieval Crown of Aragon* (Washington, DC, 2007); GCA 331–74.

of his captive. Historically, sale as a slave was possible, but more money could often be raised by returning the captive to his home in exchange for ransom. While the practice of ransoming is very ancient—it is attested in the Code of Hammurabi and the Hebrew Bible, for example, and in the earliest Christian literature—and Roman law allowed for the debt-slavery of the redeemed captive to his benefactor until the ransom payment was repaid,[123] the introduction of hostages into the transaction, as sureties for the deferred payment of the ransom, appears to have been a purely medieval development. The few early medieval examples, all after 850, all involved interactions between Christians and non-Christians—Vikings on the one hand and Iberian Muslims on the other.[124] This phenomenon persists, as the spread of the use of hostages for ransom, in contrast to their use for conditional respite, is clearly linked to the Crusades.

The two eleventh-century uses of hostages for ransom that I have identified concern Mediterranean Europe.[125] A Catalan chronicle notes that 'Bishop Eimeric was captured by the Saracens in the church of Sant Vicenç de Roda; he gave his nephew as a hostage and proceeding to Francia, redeemed his nephew, bringing a ransom from there'; this would have been during al-Mansur's raid of 1006.[126] At the end of the century, in 1091, Jonathan of Carinola, defending Sora against Adenulf of Aquino, captured the count, whose release was negotiated by the abbot of Monte Cassino. The count promised to pay 1,000 l. to his captor, turning over his sons as a guarantee.[127] For the next hundred years, though, evidence of hostages for ransom comes principally from the Holy Land.[128] Joscelin of Courtenay and Baldwin of Le Bourg were the first to employ hostages in their negotiations for release. Both were captured at the Battle of Harran in May 1104 and by 1107 were in the hands of different captors. Some of Joscelin's subjects at Turbessel offered themselves as hostages for a promised 20,000 dinars (they later escaped). Joscelin then presented himself as a hostage for 40,000 of the 70,000 dinar ransom for Baldwin. One source reports that Joscelin was freed in recognition of his chivalrous

[123] Ernst Levy, '*Captivus redemptus*', *Classical Philology*, 38 (1943), 159–76; Carolyn Osiek, 'The Ransom of Captives: Evolution of a Tradition', *Harvard Theological Review*, 74 (1981), 365–86.

[124] Thietmar of Merseburg, *Chronicon*, 4.24 (MGH SrG ns 9:158–61); A. El-Hajji, 'The Andalusian Diplomatic Relations with the Vikings during the Umayyad Period (138–366/755–96)', *Hespéris-Tamuda*, 8 (1967), 72; *Passio S. Pelagii* (ed. Rodríguez Fernández, 40), and Jiménez de Rada, *Historia de rebus Hispaniae*, 4.23 (CCCM 72:146); *Crónica Albendense*, 15.12–13 (ed. Gil Fernández, 177–9). Cf. *Annales de Saint-Bertin*, s.a. 860 (SHF 83).

[125] Émile Vanden Bussche, 'Flamands et Danois', *La Flandre*, 11 (1880), 286, claims that when Olaf of Denmark was ransomed for 10,000 marks from Robert of Flanders in 1086, his brother Niels was left as a hostage. Cf. William of Malmesbury, *Gesta regum Anglorum*, 3.261.3 (OMT 1:482).

[126] *Catalunya Carolíngia*, 3.1:18: 'Aimericus episcopus fuit captus a Sarracenis in ecclesia Sancti Vincentii de Rota, qui dedit nepotem suum obsidem pro se et pergens Franciam redemit nepotem suum, inde ferens redemptionem.'

[127] *Chronica monasterii Casinensis*, 4.14 (MGH SS 34:483).

[128] The release agreement for Christian, archbishop of Mainz, in 1179x80 (*Mainzer Urkundenbuch*, 2.2:698–702 [no. 433]), called for *conditional* hostages—a rarity in this context—to guarantee at least in part a financial payment. Other exceptions: *Historia Selebiensis monasterii*, 2.12–14 (ed. Fowler, [38]–[39]), c.1142; the ransom of Guy, bishop of Lescar, following the Battle of Fraga in 1134 (*Chronica Adefonsi imperatoris*, 1.59 [CCCM 71:177]; cf. William of Malmesbury, *El libro De laudibus et miraculis Sanctae Mariae*, 2.1.12 [ed. Canal, 92]). The latter episode, of course, also took place in the context of a Crusade.

behaviour in substituting himself for his lord. In 1124, Baldwin, now king, was captured again and again turned to hostages to guarantee 60,000 of his 80,000-dinar ransom. Other high-profile episodes from the twelfth century involved Bohemond III and Raymond III of Antioch, captured at Artāh in 1164; hostages for the latter transaction are known because Raymond gained their release not by paying, but by besieging the fortress where they were being held, obtaining at the same time the release of hostages for Eustace of Sidon. And sometime in the 1150s, the mother of Walter of Beirut became a hostage to guarantee the balance of his and his brothers' ransom; the dutiful son went to great lengths to free his mother, only to have her die a month after her release.[129] In each of these cases, hostages were granted by Christians to their opponents, but Crusader lords could also be on the receiving end of such transactions: Amaury, king of Jerusalem, received hostages in 1168 for the balance of the ransom of the son and nephew of Shāwar, vizier of Egypt, and Bohemond of Antioch held the son and daughter of Isaac Comnenus of Cyprus from 1182 against the payment of the balance of his ransom. Hostages may at this stage have been reserved, however, for the ransoms of high-profile individuals. When Balian of Ibelin and the patriarch Heraclius offered themselves as hostages for all of the inhabitants of Jerusalem after the fall of that city in 1187, Saladin is said to have replied that he would never accept 2 men in exchange for 11,000.[130]

It is likely that when the custom of granting hostages for ransoms re-emerges in the sources from late twelfth-century Europe, practices from the East played a role in shaping them, although, as in the case of conditional respite, Iberian developments appear important. The late twelfth-century *fueros* of Teruel and Cuenca placed a three-year limit on the time a father could substitute his son as a hostage for his ransom.[131] This custom hints at an extension of substitution to a lower social scale than that found in the early Crusading sources, a hint that is confirmed elsewhere. In 1193, Rainier de Thoard—hardly a household name—sold lands worth 1500 s. to free hostages that had been left for the ransoms of himself and his nephews, captured when troops of Alfonso II of Aragon took the Provençal castle in 1189.[132] And the *hostagii prisonum* mentioned as being freed along with unnamed *prisones* in the treaty between Philip Augustus and Richard I in 1196 were surely less prominent than the captive earl of Leicester, who is specifically named in the agreement.[133]

In fact, the first surviving written ransom agreement involving true hostages concerns an individual, abbreviated *Amph' Till'* in the record, whom historians have been completely unable to identify. In an agreement of 1207 with John of

[129] *Lignages d'Outremer*, 296 (ed. Nielen, 74–5).
[130] Kosto, 'Crusades', 18–21; Roger of Howden, *Chronica*, s.a. 1180 (RS 51.2:203–4); for Baldwin, see below, pp. 166–7.
[131] *El fuero de Teruel*, 453–4 (ed. Gorosch, 286–7); *Fuero de Cuenca*, 10.39 (ed. Ureña y Smenjaud, 294–7).
[132] *Cartulaire... Chalais*, 119 (no. 74); Jean Pierre Papon, *Histoire générale de Provence*, 4 vols. (Paris, 1777–86), 2:597. To gain release in 1251, a rural dean *hostagiavit se* for 60 l., although what this means is not clear: Richer, *Gesta Senoniensis ecclesiae*, 5.11 (MGH SS 25:338).
[133] *Diplomatic Documents*, 16–18 (no. 6); see now 'Le Traité de Gaillon (1196)'. Similarly, Hugh of Poitiers, *Chronicon*, 4.1153 (CCCM 42:541).

England, this figure promised a ransom of 10,000 marks, with 2,000 marks along with ten horses, each worth 30 marks, to be paid before his release; the remaining 7,700 was to be guaranteed by hostages including his brother, his son, and at least two daughters—and he would have to prove to the king that they were in fact his relatives—along with five of his knights who were also in custody. *Amph'* and his remaining knights would be released; he was to return to his own country to find his ransom. If he raised the money by a set date, all the hostages would be released; if he failed and returned, his family would be released, but the five knights would remain in custody, and the down payment of 2,000 marks plus the value of the horses would be repaid to him pro rata based on the number of freed knights he brought along back to prison.[134] The survival of this complex ransom agreement from such an early date involving an unknown figure is certainly tantalizing. As it is, however, hostages to guarantee ransom in this period remain best attested for causes célèbres, such as the negotiations for the release of Richard I himself.[135]

It was only during the Hundred Years War that the practice seems to have become truly widespread. Leaving aside royal captivities (see Chapter 6, below), hostages for ransom played a role in several major negotiations, the earliest of which involved the release of Charles of Blois, nephew of Philip VI. Charles was captured by the English at the Battle of La Roche Derrien in 1347. An agreement for his release was almost sealed in 1353, when his two sons were brought over to France to serve as hostages, and safe conducts were issued to fifteen French barons in 1354 who were described as possible hostages,[136] but a treaty was not finalized until 1356. Charles was to pay 700,000 *écus* on a fixed schedule over five years, with possible reductions for timely payment that could have cut the payments in half. The sons, Jean and Guy, were to serve as hostages, and the treaty refers to additional hostages that might be presented to allow Jean to depart temporarily or that were to be presented if Jean or Guy died or fled.[137] Charles was released; Guy died in 1385, while his brother was finally freed in 1387. Well less than half of the original ransom was paid.[138] What is most interesting about the Blois hostages is that John IV of Brittany manoeuvred to keep them in custody, as they were rival claimants to his control of the duchy.[139] The hostages were not simple guarantees of the payment of the ransom, but diplomatic pawns. The same may be said of the son of John of Foix, count of

[134] *Foedera*, 1.1:96.

[135] Below, Chapter 6. Other cases pre-1350: John of Trokelowe, *Annales*, s.a. 1317 [RS 28.3:101]; Andrew of Wyntoun, *Original Chronicle* (MS Cotton), 8.29, lines 4905–14 (ed. Amours, 6:85); Matthias of Neuenburg, *Chronicon*, 66–8 (MGH SrG ns 4:177–81); *Preußisches Urkundenbuch*, 1.1:100 (no. 133) [*Les Registres de Grégoire IX*, 3:221–2 (no. 5135); Potthast 10859]; and perhaps *Chronicon S. Martini Turonensis*, s.a. 1226 (MGH SS 26:475). For a ransom hostage in a different sort of cause célèbre, see Steven W. Rowan, 'Ulrich Zasius and the Baptism of Jewish Children', *Sixteenth Century Journal*, 6 (1975), 3–25.

[136] Robert of Avesbury, *De gestis mirabilibus regis Edwardi Tertii*, s.a. 1353 (RS 93:418); *Foedera*, 3.1:290–2.

[137] *Foedera*, 3.1:336–7.

[138] Michael Jones, 'The Ransom of Jean de Bretagne, Count of Penthièvre', *Bulletin of the Institute of Historical Research*, 45 (1972), 7–24.

[139] *Anglo-Norman Letters and Petitions*, 325–6 (no. 265); Michael Jones, *Ducal Brittany, 1364–1399: Relations with England and France during the Reign of Duke John IV* (Oxford, 1970), 64.

Candalle. The count had been captured at the Battle of Castillon in 1453, and Charles VII handed him over to Olivier de Coëtivy as a contribution to Coëtivy's own efforts to raise his ransom following his capture by the English in the previous year. Coëtivy released the count against guarantees, including the hostageship of his son, but at the accession of Louis XI the political winds shifted, and Coëtivy was ordered to release him and to turn over his other guarantees.[140]

Hostages were also at the centre of the negotiations for the release of John I, duke of Bourbon, captured at Agincourt and subject to an astronomical and ever-increasing ransom that was never paid. After the English rejected John's offer of his sons Charles and Louis in 1417, Louis was named as a hostage along with six others in a treaty of 1421: upon payment of a first instalment of 60,000 *écus* (out of 100,000 total), the hostages would enter into custody and John would be released to raise the rest. Despite the payment of that sum later in the same year, John was not freed. Similar terms appear in an agreement of 1429, also not fulfilled. Hostages also figured in a treaty of 1433 with the Florentines, to whom John's wife turned for financial assistance: gentlemen and merchants and one of his sons. It was likely the refusal of John's elder son to defect to the English side that scuttled the various agreements with the English, but the very real political danger to hostages may help to explain why the named guarantors never appeared.[141]

The case of Guillaume de Graville, which may have generated the rule—mentioned by Christine de Pisan and exercised with respect to Joan of Arc—that the king of France could purchase from his subjects any prisoner for 10,000 francs, involved hostages as well. Graville was seized at the Battle of Cocherel (1364) by Guy Le Baveux, who set a ransom of 10,000 francs and released him, accepting Graville's two sons as hostages. Charles V acquired the hostages in exchange for lands worth 10,000 francs, and exchanged them in turn for another knight who had been captured by Graville.[142] Here again, hostages are not just simple guarantees; their role as pledges gives them a monetary value, making them subject to sale and exchange in a developing ransom market.

The economic and political aspects of hostages for ransom came together in the notorious affair of the count of Denia, which is also the only non-heraldic case before the English High Court of Chivalry to have left direct documentation.[143] The treatment of the case in that court is the best evidence for the existence of stable legal customs concerning hostages. The Denia ransom arose from the civil war in Castile between Peter the Cruel (with English support) and Henry of Trastámara (with French support). The count was captured by the forces of the Black

---

[140] P. Marchegay, 'La rançon d'Olivier de Coëtivy, seigneur de Taillebourg et sénéchal de Guyenne, 1451–1477', *Bibliothèque de l'École des chartes*, 38 (1877), 5–48, esp. nos. 12, 15, 16. Similarly, the case of the duke of Alençon: *Chronique de la Pucelle*, 26 (ed. Vallet de Viriville, 249–50).

[141] André Leguai, 'Le problème des rançons au XVe siècle: La captivité de Jean Ier, duc de Bourbon', *Cahiers de l'histoire*, 6 (1961), 42–58; Jean-Louis-Alphonse Huillard-Bréholles, 'La rançon du duc de Bourbon Jean Ier (1415–1436)', *Mémoires présentés par divers savants a l'Académie des inscriptions et belles-lettres de l'Institut de France*, 1st ser., vol. 8, part 2 (Paris, 1874), 37–91.

[142] Paris, Archives nationales, JJ 100, fol. 203r–v (no. 465); Contamine, 'Ransom and Booty', 169.

[143] Much of the fifteenth-century evidence comes from disputes heard in other fora, such as Chancery or the Parlement of Paris; see e.g. below, p. 122, n. 166, and p. 128, n. 200.

Prince at Nájera in 1367. The ransom was set at 150,000 *doubles d'or* and guaranteed by pledges and the grant of the count's son, Alfonso of Villena, as a hostage.
A series of negotiations led by 1375 to the transfer of most of the Black Prince's
rights and the hostage himself to the actual captors, two squires named Hawley
and Shakel, with King Edward III retaining a small interest. In 1377, however,
after the accession of Richard II, a third party challenged Hawley and Shakel's
rights to the ransom in the Court of Chivalry. The hostage was ordered to be
seized. Hawley and Shakel tried hiding him, but they were captured and thrown in
the Tower of London. They escaped and fled to Westminster Abbey, but royal
troops broke in, killing Hawley and a sacristan and dragging Shakel back to the
Tower. The violation of sanctuary was an enormous scandal, but Hawley nonetheless spent thirteen months in custody. Freed, he somehow regained control of the
hostage. He then made a deal in 1380 with the king by which he gained letters of
pardon but lost the hostage and a considerable sum of money. Remarkably, the
hostage was still in Shakel's custody in 1390, when Hawley's heir sued him (again
in the Court of Chivalry). The case itself dragged on until 1432, but the hostage
was freed just months after the case began, and Shakel was awarded letters of
marque against the Aragonese crown for some 23,000 l. This was about 80 per cent
of the original ransom, but the figure would also have included considerable debts
run up by his noble hostage during captivity.[144] There is no evidence that Shakel
ever recovered the money. From one perspective, a twenty-three-year hostageship
was for naught, but in the constant bargaining of the prince, Edward III, and
Richard II over the ransom, as well as the seizure of the hostage in 1377 and his
release in 1390, we can see that royal financial and diplomatic concerns lay behind
almost every chapter in this complex story.

As the case of Guillaume de Graville shows, hostageship was not limited to ransom
agreements for kings and counts. Olivier Du Guesclin, brother of the French constable, captured at Cherbourg in 1378, left three hostages in England while he went to
raise his ransom of 25,000 francs.[145] The English lieutenant Eustache d'Aubrichicourt,
captured in 1372, handed over his son to guarantee the balance of 8,000 francs on
his ransom of 12,000 francs.[146] The knight Pierre de Moutiers, captured in 1357,
paid one-third of a 1,500 florin ransom and delivered four hostages for his release
after three weeks in prison.[147] The bailiff of Auxerre and poet Jean Regnier obtained
his release after an eighteen-month captivity in 1432–3 by leaving hostages for the
balance of his ransom.[148] Around 1315, the minor English lord Robert de Raymes

[144] Edouard Perroy, 'Gras profits et rançons pendant la Guerre de Cent Ans: L'affaire du comte de
Denia', in *Mélanges d'histoire du Moyen Âge dédiés à la mémoire de Louis Halphen* (Paris, 1951), 573–
80; A. Rogers, 'Hoton versus Shakell: A Ransom Case in the Court of Chivalry, 1390–5', *Nottingham
Medieval Studies*, 6 (1962), 74–108, 7 (1963), 53–78; London, National Archives, SC 8/18/895,
8/107/5318, 8/199/9909.
[145] *Foedera*, 4:128 is a royal safe conduct. See Chris Given-Wilson, 'The Ransom of Olivier du
Guesclin', *Bulletin of the Institute of Historical Research*, 54 (1981), 22.
[146] Froissart 1.670 (8.2:6).
[147] *GCA* 68–71.
[148] Regnier, *Livre de la prison*, 4343–8, 4579–84, 4762–5, 4770–3 (ed. Droz, 153, 161, 167);
Bossuat, 'Beauvais'.

was released from Scottish custody to raise his ransom of 500 marks; he left his son as a hostage. At about the same time, the Scottish knight John de Stockhaugh left two hostages in English custody to secure his own release.[149] Hostages might also be granted not by the captive himself, but by his (non-hostage) sureties or heirs. The Parlement of Paris in 1365 released Oger de Donjeux from his obligations as guarantor for the ransom of Erard de Dinteville, but only after Oger's squire and servant had spent 600 days in custody and the two horses that had also been handed over died.[150] In 1426, that same court heard the complaint of a man who had left his son as a hostage to help *a friend* raise a ransom.[151] A settlement of a dispute over the sixteen-year-old unfulfilled ransom treaty for Guillaume de Châteauvillain, which had itself involved four hostages, called for the nephew and heir of the captive (now dead) to remain in Paris until 16,000 *écus* had been paid; if he wanted to leave the city, he would have to provide two other hostages.[152]

The so-called 'fourth vow' of the Mercedarians, a religious order founded in the thirteenth century specifically to ransom captives, is said to have called on members to substitute themselves for a prisoner if ransom money was not available. The vow is not attested in the order's statutes before the sixteenth century, and substitution as practice rather than an ideal in the Middle Ages remains a subject of debate. At least one Mercedarian did substitute himself in the fifteenth century: Domingo Navarro spent sixteen months in captivity to obtain the release of two youths from Tarragona.[153] Still the scarcity of evidence for the fourth vow reflects the fact that the use of hostages to guarantee a promised ransom was never the norm. Most ransoms were guaranteed by more routine personal sureties,[154] or the parties were released on their honour.[155] Breaking one's word might lead to having one's arms

[149] London, National Archives, E 101/376/7, fol. 62r; H. H. E. Craster, *A History of Northumberland*, vol. 10: *The Parish of Corbridge* (London, 1914), 346 n. 1; A. King, '"According to the Custom Used in French and Scottish Wars": Prisoners and Casualties on the Scottish Marches in the Fourteenth Century', *Journal of Medieval History*, 28 (2002), 277. Additional examples: *GCA* 317, 349, 361–6; Froissart 3.242–3 (14:200–5); Juan de Mata Carriazo, 'Los moros de Granada en las actas del concejo de Jaén de 1479', in Mata Carriazo, *En la frontera de Granada* (Granada, 2002 [1971]), 278, 283, 285.

[150] *GCA* 329–31.

[151] Bossuat, 'Beauvais', 31 n. 5; similarly, 31 n. 4.

[152] Bossuat, 'Châteauvillain', 11–12, 23, 24, 28–9; the original ransom agreement is BnF, Coll. Bourgogne 99, fol. 263r.

[153] Jerónimo López, 'En torno al cuarto voto mercedario', *Estudios* (Madrid), 12 (1956), 378; cf. Cijar, *Opusculum tantum quinque super commutatione votorum in redemptione* (1491), fol. 17v. See also Brodman, *Ransoming Captives*, 111–13; Joaquín Millán Rubio, 'El voto mercaderio de dar la vida por los cautivos cristianos', in *Los consejos evangelicos en la tradición monástica: XIV Semana de estudios monasticos, Silos, 1973* (Silos, 1975), 113–41. Similarly, Hugues Cocard, *L'Ordre de la Merci en France, 1574–1792: Un ordre voué a la liberation des captifs* (Paris, 2007), 187–8, finds only one example of a French Mercedarian serving as a hostage in period 1574 to 1790. For a similar tradition concerning Paulinus of Nola, see Gregory I, *Dialogues* 3.1.1–8 (SC 260:256–64); Giovanni Santaniello, 'La prigionia di Paolino: Tradizione e storia', in A. Ruggiero, H. Crouzel, and G. Santaniello, *Paolino di Nola: Momenti della sua vita e delle sue opere* (Nola, 1983), 221–49.

[154] Bossuat, 'Beauvais'; Bossuat, 'Les prisonniers de guerre au XVᵉ siècle: La rançon de Jean seigneur de Rodemack', *Annales de l'Est*, 5th ser., 2 (1951), 145–62; Given-Wilson, 'Olivier du Guesclin'; *GCA* 359–74.

[155] *GCA* 307, 331–5, 339. *Pace* Contamine, 'Ransom and Booty', 185, Arthur de Richemont was not released on parole: substantial real and personal sureties guaranteed his return: *Foedera*², 10:8–13; cf. Gruel, *Chronique d'Arthur de Richemont*, 17 (SHF 22).

displayed inverted, or being depicted in painted posters hanging from one's feet, or having one's effigy carried into battle on a lance point.[156] But where noble faith and the threat of dishonour was in doubt, hostages were a ready option.

In the case of ransom as in the case of conditional respite, then, hostages became established as part of the medieval laws and customs of war. Just as hostageship had been adapted and integrated into a new political landscape, featuring newly important actors such as castellans and towns and guilds, so too was it adapted and integrated into a new military landscape. Christian–Muslim conflicts in Iberia and the eastern Mediterranean in the eleventh and twelfth centuries provided an initial impetus for changes in warfare that became routine by the time of the Hundred Years War. Hostageship in warfare was not about the cementing of alliances and relationships, but rather about facilitating short-term undertakings. The diffusion of such practices is part of a broader shift in the nature of hostageship, seen also in the realm of the economy.

FINANCIAL TRANSACTIONS AND
THE DEVELOPMENT OF RULES

The usual conceptual elision of hostages and prisoners makes hostages to guarantee the ransom of prisoners seem unsurprising. But hostages were also granted during wartime where there were no prisoners involved at all, for purely financial transactions. The similarity of these arrangements to ransom treaties during the Hundred Years War is readily apparent. In the wake of the Treaty of Brétigny, John II accused Edward III of extorting *grantz ransons dargent* for the delivery of castles promised under the terms of the agreement (Edward replied that they were merely *paiementz*); hostages guaranteed delayed payments in several of the transactions.[157] When Charles of Orléans arrived in England in 1415 after his capture at Agincourt, his brother, John of Angoulême, had already been there for three years. John was not a prisoner, but rather a hostage, turned over by Charles as a guarantee under the terms of the Treaty of Buzançais. The Armagnac–Burgundian entente in 1412 having transformed English troops under the duke of Clarence from desired support into a major threat, Charles paid for their departure with the promise of 177,000 crowns, with John of Angoulême and several others serving as hostages. John remained in custody for thirty-two years.[158] The Treaty of Guillon of 1360, by which the duke of Burgundy bought a three-year truce from Edward III for 200,000 *moutons*—a quarter on the following 24 June, a half at Christmas, and the remaining quarter at Easter—involved *conditional* hostages (see Chapter 5, below). If a payment were missed, fifteen named nobles and seven named burghers were to present themselves within a month to be taken into custody at Calais or, if the English had lost that town, London. When the Burgundians defaulted, ten hostages

---

[156] Bossuat, 'Châteauvillain', 22; *GCA* 298, 309.
[157] *Some Documents Regarding... Treaty of Brétigny*, 12–13, 15; *GCA* 432–62.
[158] Monstrelet 1.97 (2:303–4).

were in fact handed over.[159] John of Gaunt's campaigns in the 1380s ended in the Treaty of Bayonne, in which John renounced his claims on the Castilian crown in return for the marriage of his daughter to the son of King John I and a payment of 100,000 l. (plus 6,000 l. a year) secured by up to sixty hostages.[160] This agreement echoed the one between Henry II of Castile and Bertrand Du Guesclin, whereby the latter renounced his claims to lordships promised him in exchange for 240,000 *doblas*; as the king was unable to pay the full indemnity immediately, he granted three hostages for the balance.[161] In 1452, negotiating for a truce with the town of Ghent, the duke of Burgundy requested hostages for the reimbursement of the costs of disbanding and re-raising his army, and for garrisoning a series of fortresses during the six weeks in question.[162]

The practice of buying off actual or potential attackers with payment guaranteed by hostages preceded the Hundred Years War; once again, the evidence for the practice dates back to the eleventh century and manifests a considerable geographical range. Notably, most of these agreements were not kept. Conrad II, called in to adjudicate conflicts in southern Italy in 1038, accepted hostages from Capua for half of a payment of 300 l. gold; one of the hostages fled.[163] In 1146, Almería promised attacking Genoese forces 113,000 *morabetinos* in exchange for a truce, paying 25,000 immediately and granting hostages for the payment of the balance within eight days. Even after the commander who had made the agreement fled as the initial monies were being counted, his replacement delivered the hostages, but Almería did not come up with the money and was attacked.[164] The Portuguese town of Faro similarly defaulted on payment to forces of the Second Crusade and saw their forty or so hostages executed.[165] The northern English town of Ripon bought off Scottish raiders in 1318 with a promise of 1,000 marks, 240 paid up front and the rest guaranteed by six hostages; first the wives, and then some of the hostages themselves—whose longsuffering wives had replaced them in custody— complained to Edward III that the town had made no efforts to redeem them. Similar complaints were made in 1317 by a hostage from Durham who had to come up with the last 36 marks owing on an agreement from 1314, and in 1325 by three hostages granted by the Vale of Pickering for a payment of 300 l. in 1323.[166] The *écorcheurs* who terrorized Lorraine in 1437 required hostages for the

[159] *Foedera*, 3.1:473–4, 3.2:633.

[160] *The Treaty of Bayonne*. The safe conduct for the hostages is *Foedera²*, 7:603.

[161] Máximo Diago Hernando, 'Un noble entre tres reinos en la España del siglo XIV: Juan Ramírez de Arellano', *Príncipe de Viana*, 230 (2003), 547–8.

[162] Du Clercq, *Mémoires*, 2.23 (ed. Reiffenberg, 2:58–9); [Amable-Guillaume-Prosper Brugière, baron] de Barante, *Histoire des ducs de Bourgogne de la maison de Valois, 1364–1477*, new edn., ed. M. Gachard, vol. 2 (Brussels, 1838), 104–5.

[163] *Chronica monasterii Casinensis*, 2.63 (MGH SS 34:292); cf. *Annales Altahenses maiores*, s.a. 1038 (MGH SrG 4:22).

[164] Caffaro, *Annales*, s.a. 1146 (MGH SS 18:20–1).

[165] *Annales Elmarenses*, s.a. 1147 (ed. Grierson, 111–12). Cf. Hugh of Poitiers, *Chronicon*, 4.1324–7 (CCCM 42:546).

[166] London, National Archives, SC 8/8/364, 8/70/3459, 8/89/4438; *Foedera*, 2.1:437; *Calendar of Inquisitions Miscellaneous (Chancery)*, 2:111–12, 222 (nos. 452, 891); *Northern Petitions*, 173–4 (no. 128). Also Raoul of Saint-Trond, *Gesta abbatum Trudonensium* (ed. De Borman, 1:292).

unpaid balance of the protection money that they had extorted from various towns, as did the English at Lihons two years later; one of the hostages for the latter died in prison as the money was never paid.[167]

In some cases of submission, hostages guarantee a combination of financial and other undertakings. Thus at Rouen in 1449, Somerset promised a payment to the French king and the resolution of all debts incurred during the English occupation of the town, but also the delivery of several castles and towns; hostages guaranteed all of these undertakings.[168] Hostages granted to Queen Urraca by the town of Compostela after its rebellion in 1117 were for the money promised as a fine and 'for the rest' (*pro ceteris*).[169] And financial transactions involving hostages might follow from military conflicts without being an explicit element of a treaty. After John IV of Brittany captured Olivier de Clisson and then released him against a payment of 100,000 francs and the transfer of a dozen castles, the agreement was subsequently cancelled. The bulk of the money was only returned as part of the negotiations surrounding the Treaty of Tours between John IV and Charles VI in 1392. Nineteen Breton lords gave hostages for the delivery of portions of the 80,000 francs still due.[170]

Hostages thus spread beyond ransom to guarantee other sorts of monetary debt arising from warfare. Yet from the end of the twelfth century we find true hostages handed over for purely financial transactions not undertaken in the context of open warfare. Hostages functioned in this fashion in imperial elections in 1198 and 1257. In the former case, it was Berthold of Zähringen who left his nephews in the hands of the Archbishop of Cologne to guarantee substantial bribes promised to his electors; after he withdrew in favour of Philip of Swabia, he apparently neglected to redeem his nephews.[171] In 1257, John of Avesnes, negotiating on behalf of Richard of Cornwall, offered one of his sons as a hostage (*obses*) to guarantee a payment of 12,000 marks to Ludwig of Bavaria, one-third within three weeks of Christmas and the remainder on the day Richard was elected emperor or Easter, whichever came first. In addition, he himself and five *fideiussores* were to act as conditional hostages, entering custody at Liège upon default. Ludwig's written promise to support Richard has survived and is dated the same day as the promise of payment; there were other elements to the negotiation, namely a marriage alliance and promises concerning Sicily, but the guarantees were tied only to the promised payment. Richard also bought the vote of Conrad, archbishop of Cologne. 'Because the archbishop has and expects to have committed not a small amount of effort and money to the present business', the agreement reads, Richard is to pay him 8,000 marks. One thousand were to be paid immediately; two

---

[167] Monstrelet 2.226, 245 (5:338, 406).

[168] Escouchy, *Chronique*, 1.37 (SHF 1:227–8); Du Clercq, *Mémoires*, 1.35 (ed. Reiffenberg, 1:392); Blondel, *De reductione Normanniae*, 4.25–6/250–1 (RS 32:227–30).

[169] *Historia Compostellana*, 1.116 (CCCM 70:217).

[170] *Mémoires... Bretagne*, 2:586–8; John Bell Henneman, *Olivier de Clisson and Political Society in France under Charles V and Charles VI* (Philadelphia, 1996), 150, 162. See also *Foedera*, 3.2:799–800.

[171] *Chronica regia Coloniensis*, cont. 1, s.a. (MGH SrG 18:163); *Chronicon Urspergensium*, s.a. (MGH SS 23:367).

hostages were named for an additional 2,000, which would be owed even if the election did not come to pass; if Richard was elected (even if he subsequently refused the election), the 2,000 would count toward the total remaining (7,000), for which three additional hostages were named; again the negotiators promised to serve as conditional hostages (*fideiussores*). Richard also paid 8,000 marks to the archbishop of Mainz, who is likely to have insisted on similar guarantees.[172]

Other sorts of business at the highest levels of the European aristocracy also relied on hostages as guarantees. They were an obvious recourse for royal debts, where no higher authority could enforce the transaction. Barisone of Arborea, king of Sardinia, was forced to deliver hostages in 1168 for his debt to the city of Genoa. Baldwin II, Latin emperor of Constantinople, handed over his son, Philip of Courtenay, to guarantee loans from the Ca' Ferro of Venice *c.*1250. Hostages also figured in Magnus IV of Sweden's acquisition of Skåne and Belkinge from Denmark in 1332, and in Edward III of England's financial crisis of 1339–41, which led not only to the pawning of the royal crown, but to the enforced presence of many noble hostages in Ghent and elsewhere.[173] Hostages could also serve as a guarantee when the king was the *creditor*. A royal mandate for the collection of a fine imposed on French Jews in 1322 specifies that the commissioners were to 'take control of their goods, and a certain number of the richest Jews who are pledges (*pleiges*) for the sum due from each seneschaucy'; they were to be allowed to go about their business within their towns during the day, but at night they were to be 'put under safe and secure guard'.[174] In 1264, the English royal court required hostages to guarantee fine payments due from a royalist baron to the younger Simon de Montfort.[175]

But as in the case of hostages for ransoms, these sorts of transactions were not limited to royal or even aristocratic business. A group of prominent citizens of Manresa in Catalonia were bound to remain in nearby Santpedor as hostages for a loan that the town had acquired from a Barcelona moneylender that it used to pay off a debt to Genoese merchants.[176] On an even smaller scale, in the fifteenth

---

[172] MGH Const. 2:479–84 (nos. 376–84); Wykes, *Chronicon* (RS 36.4:113–14). Cf. MGH Const. 5:112–15 (no. 117), a similar deal between Frederic III of Germany and Rainald I of Gueldre in 1314, with *conditional* hostages.

[173] *Codice diplomatico della Repubblica di Genova*, 2:84–6, 87–8 (nos. 34, 35, 37); *Diplomatarium Danicum*, 2.10:369–76 (no. 403); Robert Lee Wolff, 'Mortgage and Redemption of an Emperor's Son: Castile and the Latin Empire of Constantinople', *Speculum*, 29 (1954), 45–84; E. B. Fryde, 'Financial Resources of Edward III in the Netherlands, 1337–40', *Revue belge de philologie et d'histoire*, 45 (1967), 1142–216. See also *Oorkondenboek van Holland en Zeeland tot 1299*, 2:518 (no. 853), and perhaps RI 11.2:8572.

[174] *HGL* 10:616–20 (no. 223): 'ils se tenissent saysi de leurs biens & de certain nombre de personnes Juys des plus riches…qui sont pleiges pour la somme de chacune seneschaucie…ils soyent mis en seure & sauve garde'. Cf. Guillaume de Nangis, *Chronique latine*, cont. 2, s.a. 1321 (SHF 2:35–6); Jean de Saint-Victor, *Memoriale historiarum* (RHF 21:674); and Elizabeth A. R. Brown, 'Philip V, Charles IV, and the Jews of France: The Alleged Expulsion of 1322', *Speculum*, 66 (1991), 315. Cf. below, p. 131, n. 4, and p. 214.

[175] Charles Bémont, *Simon de Montfort, comte de Leicester, sa vie (120?–1265), son rôle politique en France et en Angleterre* (Paris, 1874), 353–5 (no. 38); cf. *Foedera*, 1.1:454; *Calendar of the Patent Rolls…1258–1266*, 420. See J. R. Maddicott, *Simon de Montfort* (Cambridge, 1996), 326, 331.

[176] Manresa, Arxiu històric de la ciutat, AM, I-5 (1353 July 17).

century, the knight Hervé Le Drouais left his son as a hostage for two years as a guarantee for a personal debt,[177] while the records of the English royal court for 1220 note that a local landowner named Roger Le Manaunt had handed over his daughter as a hostage for a personal debt,[178] and Louis IX intervened in 1260 to free the hostage sons of Hugh de Prêles, held by his lord *pro debitis*.[179] Around 1338, Arnaud de Durfort appealed to the king for help in paying debts for which he had left 'his wife, his son, and his men in hostage' in Bayonne, as well as two of his 'companions' in London.[180] A Venetian notarial register of 1360 records the grant in pledge against 300 *aspres* of the 15-year-old son of the debtor, who was to 'stay and remain with [the creditor] in his house, until he repaid the aforementioned money'.[181] These are only a few isolated cases, so the extent of the use of true hostages for low-level monetary debts remains in question; nevertheless, the evidence does prove that the practice was not the sole preserve of emperors, kings, and counts.

In tandem with the spread of hostages for purely financial transactions, we find references to or evidence of rules that reflect a process of institutionalization of hostageship both within and outside the context of the development of the laws of war.[182] This change is reflected first in the descriptions of hostage agreements themselves, whether in narrative records or charters. Already in the eleventh century, we find a substitution clause, likely adapted from general clauses concerning sureties. A clause of the agreement between Walter of Lens and Gerard, bishop of Cambrai, in 1023 held that if Walter's hostage died, he would provide another 'by whom we [Gerard] will be sure concerning his fidelity'.[183] In an agreement with the archbishop of Vienne, the *miles* Hector undertook to provide two *obsides* as a guarantee that he would not commit any offences against the bishop in his lands. Concerning the hostages (*obstadiis*), the agreement specifies that 'if one of them dies or perjures himself, Hector is to replace him with another worth as much as the one who died or perjured himself was worth, and that if both die or perjure themselves, Hector is to provide replacements of similar value'.[184] These particular *obsides/obstadii* might be non-custodial sureties

---

[177] Paris, Archives nationales, X/1a/1480, fol. 358v; Bossuat, 'Beauvais', 32 n. 1.

[178] *Curia regis Rolls... 4 and 5 Henry III*, 226. Paul Brand, 'Aspects of the Law of Debt, 1189–1307', in P. R. Schofield and N. J. Mayhew, eds., *Credit and Debt in Medieval England, c.1180–c.1350* (Oxford, 2002), 29, noted that this was the only case he had found, but see *Rotuli de oblatis*, 478.

[179] *Cartulaire de l'église de Notre-Dame de Paris*, 14 (no. 21); Jean Lebeuf, *Histoire de la ville et de tout le diocèse de Paris*, 5 vols. (Paris, 1883), 5:325.

[180] London, National Archives, SC 8/166/8274.

[181] Charles Verlinden, *L'esclavage dans l'Europe médiévale*, vol. 2: *Italie. Colonies italiennes du Levant. Levant latin. Empire byzantin* (Ghent, 1977), 932.

[182] Given-Wilson, 'Olivier du Guesclin', 28.

[183] *Gesta episcoporum Cameracensium*, 3.43 (MGH SS 7:482): 'talem per quem nos securos de sua fidelitate reddet'. See below, p. 140.

[184] *Cartulaire de l'abbaye de Saint-André-le-Bas de Vienne*, 150–1 (no. 206): 'si unus ex illis moreretur aut se perjuraret, Hector ei emendaret alium qui tantum ei valeret quantum valebat ille qui mortuus fuerat aut perjurus; & si ambo mortui fuissent aut perjuri, emendasset Hector similiter valentes'. Similarly: *Cartulaire de Maguelone*, 1:108 (no. 55); *Urkundenbuch zur Geschichte der... mittelrheinischen Territorien*, 1:670–3 (no. 610); *Cartulaire de l'abbaye de Savigny*, 1:421 (Savigny, no. 804).

rather than hostages, but other, clearer examples are readily available: in eleventh-century documents from the Midi describing some of the earliest conditional hostages,[185] or others concerning true hostages at Piacenza in 1162, Falaise in 1174, Oloron in 1287, or London in 1424, and in the case of Charles of Blois described above.[186] The focus in such clauses was invariably equal worth. The submission treaty of Liège in 1408 calls for the replacement of any hostages who die by the towns from which they came with replacements equal to the originals in number and worth (*suffisance*); at Guise in 1424, the town promised that if any of the named hostages fled or died, they would at all times maintain eight persons as hostages, as sufficient or more so (*aussi souffisans ou plus*).[187] Similarly, Richard of Cornwall's bribe to the archbishop of Cologne for the imperial election of 1257 included a promise to replace a dead or sick hostage with one equally good (*eque bonus*).[188]

Hostages could also be rotated: in 1162, Frederic I released all but 100 of the Milanese hostages at Pavia, and called on them to be replaced each month; in 1329, Philip VI acceded to a request of the aldermen of Ypres that some of their hostages granted in the previous year be replaced; and a clause of a submission treaty at Liège in 1467 called for the hostages to be sent home and replaced upon payment of the first instalment (the agreement also called for replacement in case of death).[189] Milo fitz Bishop paid 40 marks for the privilege of exchanging a hostage held by John of England in 1215x16, while in 1226 Jeanne, countess of Flanders, granted a blanket privilege to the échevins of Ypres allowing the exchange (or release) of hostages held to guarantee truces between inhabitants.[190]

While substitution of this sort, as noted, could apply equally well to non-hostage sureties, another practice did not: payment of hostages for their service. This practice first appears in sources from the twelfth century. Aimo de Brolio served half a year as a hostage for his lord before he was released; in recompense ('quia tantum moram pro eo fecerat'), he received a horse and a plot of land. Likewise, Arnold de Marmande received a generous grant of land from Edward I in 1289, 'especially because he served as a hostage for us in Aragon'; similar grants survive for two other lords.[191] Two references in the English pipe rolls for 1194 to the allowance (*liberatio*) of hostages show payments amounting to precisely a penny per day per hostage. This figure might refer to reimbursement to the custodian for their upkeep, but as an earlier reference in a roll distinguishes between

---

[185] *Cartulaires des abbayes d'Aniane et de Gellone*, 1:217–19 (Aniane, no. 80); *Liber feudorum maior*, 2:305–7 (no. 821); *Cartulaire de Saint-Jean d'Angely*, 1:234–5 (no. 194); see below, pp. 137, 140–2.

[186] Cf. *Foedera*, 1.1:84–5; *The Treaty of Bayonne*, 11, 29, 52 (revisions of art. 8).

[187] Monstrelet 1.47, 2.22 (1:384, 4:204–5).

[188] MGH Const. 2:483 (no. 383).

[189] *Gesta Federici I. imperatoris in Lombardia* (MGH SrG 27:55); *Inventaire...ville d'Ypres*, 2:59 (no. 440); Du Clercq, *Mémoires*, 5.64 (ed. Reiffenberg, 4:288–9). Similarly, *GCA* 427.

[190] *Rotuli de oblatis*, 552; *Inventaire...ville d'Ypres*, 1:36 (no. 38).

[191] *Cartulaire de l'abbaye royale de Notre-Dame de Saintes*, 61 (no. 62); *Foedera*, 1.2:703 ('specialiter quod idem Arnaldus se pro nobis obsidem posuit in Aragonia'), 710.

a payment for hostages' *liberatio* and another for their 'bread' in that year, the daily payment might also represent wages of the hostages themselves.[192] The Norman exchequer rolls from around the same period refer to a heavy payment of 100 l. to settle with (*aequietare*) two Poitevin knights who were hostages at Rouen.[193] Such a sum may more properly be classified as compensation than as a wage, but the line between the two is difficult to draw.[194] In any case, in the fourteenth century, the practice is quite clear: 3 d. a day to the hostages from Bruges handed over following the Battle of Cassel, and 10 sous a day to the Manresan hostages at Santpedor in 1353.[195]

Even more striking than these clauses as evidence for the institutionalization of hostageship, particularly in the context of the laws of war, comes from an agreement entered into by two English squires in 1421. The essence of the agreement was to make them 'brothers-in-arms' (*freres darmes*). Much of the text details how their profits were to be divided, but the agreement begins with clauses concerning capture, ransom, and hostageship. If one of the two were captured, the other was to do what he could ('acquiteroit hors laultre franc & quite') if the ransom were less than 6,000 *saluz dor*. If the ransom exceeded that figure, the free partner agreed to serve as a hostage for eight or nine months so that the captive could raise his own ransom. Expenses incurred in raising the ransom were, however, to be split. If both were captured at the same time, one would remain as a hostage while the other tried to raise the ransom for both. Thus the agreement foresees that, as a matter of course, the free partner would be accepted as a hostage by the captor, or that one of the two would be accepted as a hostage for the other if both were captured at the same time.[196]

This agreement testifies not only to the routine nature of hostages for ransom in warfare, but also, as the case of the count of Denia showed, to the entry of hostage transactions into the realm of formal law. The Denia case focused on the rights of individuals to ransoms and the attendant hostages, but the status and obligations of hostages themselves also required judgment. The English administration

---

[192] *The Great Roll of the Pipe for the Sixth Year of King Richard the First*, 220 (5 hostages for one half-year plus 15 days, or 987 hostage-days = 4 l. 2 s. 3 d., or 987 d., one half-penny short), 230 (1 hostage for 76 days = 6 s. 4 d., or 76 d.). Cf. *The Great Roll of the Pipe for the Twenty-Third Year of the Reign of King Henry the Second*, 61: 'Et in liberatone .iij. obsidum xxxvij. s. Et in pannis eorum hoc anno .vij. s.'

[193] *Magni rotuli scaccarii Normanniæ*, 1:48.

[194] London, National Archives, SC 8/167/8349: one of the hostages for Charles of Salerno sought confirmation of a grant of land made in compensation for his service. Paris, Archives nationales, JJ 100, fol. 50r (no. 100): in 1368, Charles V created a fair at Germigny as compensation to Mathieu de Roye, who would ultimately serve over thirteen years as a hostage for John II (cit. Froissart, 8.1:xcviii n. 3).

[195] Vandermaesen, 'De rekening der Brugse gijzelaars', 15; Manresa, Arxiu històric de la ciutat, AM, I-5 (1353 July 7). Cf. the payment of 2 d. per day provided *by the custodian* at London, National Archives, E 101/376/7, fol. 62 (above, p. 120, n. 149); the same rate is found at C 81/1674A (olim C 47/22/4/9). The wages (*vadia*) in *Accounts of the Constables of Bristol Castle in the Thirteenth and Early Fourteenth Centuries*, 43–4, with xxxi–xxxii, also appear to be maintenance payments provided by the custodian; similarly, Pugh, *Imprisonment*, 315. See also GCA 409–26; Stacey, *Road*, 85, 91–3.

[196] K. B. McFarlane, 'A Business-Partnership in War and Administration, 1421–1445', *English Historical Review*, 78 (1963), 309; cf. GCA 361–6.

in Gascony in 1255 determined that a townsman of Bordeaux serving as a hostage could not be distrained for certain debts, and that as long as he was a hostage, he should be allowed to acquire necessities using his own resources.[197] The captors of Guillaume de Châteauvillain, whose hostages were later captured by the English, argued in court that because they themselves had not freed the hostages, the hostages were obliged to return to custody.[198] The most notorious such case was the affair of Acova in the Crusader principality of Morea. Captured by imperial forces at the Battle of Pélagonia in 1259, William of Villehardouin obtained his release two years later, in part by granting two hostages, including Marguerite de Passavant. Marguerite inherited the lordship of Acova on the death of her uncle, but, as she was in custody, she was unable to appear before the prince to do homage for her inheritance within the required period of a year and a day, and the prince confiscated the lordship. The subsequent dispute turned on an interpretation of the law that called on a vassal to enter into hostageship for the sovereign; the prince argued successfully that this did not excuse her from the time limit.[199] In the following century, by contrast, several of the hostages for the ransom of John II received *lettres d'état* that suspended judicial action against them until one month after their return.[200] The obligations of custodians of hostages were also potential subjects of suits: at least two of the hostages for Brétigny subscribed formal acknowledgements of their good treatment at the hands of the king and renounced any future legal claims arising from their detention.[201]

While the early medieval kinship framework for hostageship persisted, with its applications in cultural diplomacy and utility for the formation of long-term relationships between the grantor and the custodian as well as between the grantor and the hostage, a new sort of hostageship emerged from around the eleventh century. This new hostageship was increasingly formalized, de-individualized, and monetized. Formalized: As part of the emerging institutionalization of the laws of war, but also independently of that process, hostageship becomes subject to detailed written agreements with increasingly specific clauses, agreements that work their way into and are recognized by formal courts. Monetized: Hostages no longer guarantee just behaviour or fidelity, but also—and then only—payment, of ransom or of debts even outside of the context of warfare and imprisonment. De-individualized:[202] In place of specific hostages meant to operate on a single, usually filial bond as a means of exercising pressure, hostages come to represent geographical, social, or professional groups. A creditor can ask for an individual

---

[197] *Rôles gascons*, Sup:54 (no. 4672). London, National Archives, SC 8/141/7026 (*c.*1302) describes Gascon hostages due at court for an unknown reason.

[198] Bossuat, 'Châteauvillain', 24 and n. 2.

[199] *Chronicle of Morea*, 4494–512, 7301–743 (ed. Schmitt, 299, 474–503); cf. *RHC* Lois 1:268–70; *Regesten des Kaiserurkunden des oströmischen Reiches*, 3:76–7 (no. 1895).

[200] *GCA* 400–4; other cases from the Parlement de Paris in which the legal status of hostages is relevant are at 68–70, 329–31, 428–32, 442–55. See also *Recueil...Philippe Auguste*,2:128–9 (no. 580), in which a conditional hostage is required to present himself only after his principal has been found in violation by the royal court; below, p. 155.

[201] *Foedera*, 3.2:772, 773.

[202] See below, p. 132, n. 7.

or his son, and hostages can be rotated and replaced. While hostages might serve as the foundation for a long-term relationship between the custodian and the grantor, the link between the custodian and the hostage is broken. The hostage has become a marker, a pawn. Each of these new characteristics can be seen in the development of the most curious variation on the institution from the eleventh century on: conditional hostageship.

5

Conditional Hostages

In his treatise *Yconomica* (1353x63), the German polymath Konrad von Megenberg advised the wise manager to avoid both usurious loans and hostage agreements:

> For hostageship (*obstagium*) is an undertaking of expenses by certain persons, the payment of which is inflicted upon the debtor of the principal who has failed to meet his deadline for payment, with the following words: 'You grant to me (for example) 20 talents in pennies, on the condition that, if when the deadline arrives I do not pay you, my guarantor (*fideiussor*) will enter the establishment of a trustworthy innkeeper, with his horse, and whatever expenses he incurs will be added to my debts.'[1]

Despite Konrad's advice, agreements along these lines were widespread in the later medieval centuries, particularly in German-speaking lands. Here the pressure exercised by hostageship was not grounded simply in affective ties or a moral sense of obligation but in money: the debtor was burdened by the expenses that his hostages ran up. Thus agreements regulated the places where hostages were to be housed (sometimes even naming particular inns), the number of retainers and horses that they were allowed, and the number and quality of meals. A sixteenth-century formula-book even notes that the landlord was supposed to supply the hostage with money weekly for baths and prostitutes, and new pairs of shoes every month. As a contemporary proverb had it, 'Geiselmahl köstliche Mahl' (a hostage's meal is expensive).[2] One can understand why legislation quickly appeared to rein

---

[1] Konrad von Megenberg, *Yconomica*, 1.4.19 (MGH Staatsschriften des späteren Mittelalters 3.1:350–1): 'Est autem obstagium expensarum a certis personis aggressio, quarum solucio pro pena infligitur principalis sortis debitori negligenti terminum specificatum, verbi gracia: Tu michi accomodas viginti forsitan denariorum talenta tali pacto, quod, si termino veniente non solvero tibi, fideiussor meus cum caballo ingredietur hospicium hospitis honesti, et quicquid expenderit, connumerabitur debitis meis.'

[2] A. Chaisemartin, *Proverbes et maximes du droit germanique* (Paris, 1891), 264–6. Another proverb held that 'Bürgen, soll man würgen' (sureties should be strangled) (262–4). The literature is best approached through: *Handwörterbuch zur deutschen Rechtsgeschichte*, 5 vols. (Berlin, 1971–98), s.v. *Einlager* (H. Kellenbenz); Werner Ogris, 'Die persönlichen Sicherheiten im Spätmittelalter: Versuch eines Überblickes', *Zeitschrift der Savigny-Stiftung für Rechtsgeschichte*, Germanistische Abteilung, 82 (1965), 165–76; *SP* 2:178–90, 318–27, 577–98, 653–72. Significant earlier studies include: Ernst Friedlaender, *Das Einlager: Ein Beitrag zur deutschen Rechtsgeschichte* (Münster, 1868); Charles Le Fort, 'L'otage conventionnel d'après des documents du Moyen Âge', *Revue de législation ancienne et modèrne française et étrangère* (1874), 408–33; Adolf Lechner, *Das Obstagium oder die Giselschaft nach schweizerischen Quellen* (Bern, 1906); Max Rintelen, *Schuldhaft und Einlager im Vollstreckungsverfahren des altniederländischen und sächsischen Rechtes* (Leipzig, 1908); Lutteroth, *Der Geisel*, 130–8; Walliser, *Bürgschaftsrecht*, 282–370. For the formula-book: Friedlaender, *Das Einlager*, 147; Lechner, *Das Obstagium*, 157.

in excessive customs and eventually to abolish the institution altogether.[3] In this form of hostageship, known in German scholarship as the *Einlager*, and in French as the *otage conventionnel*, the identity of the hostage was almost incidental.[4] Influence was rooted in economic pressure, and we are but one step removed from real surety: a purely monetary guarantee.

This form of hostageship also differs from earlier varieties in that it is *conditional*: the hostage *promises* to enter into captivity, and only *after* the violation. In the cases that we have focused on to this point, hostages were handed over immediately upon conclusion of an agreement; their actual captivity is supposed to pressure the granting party not to violate his or her promises. The conditional hostage is still a hostage: a third party whose captivity is supposed to exercise influence on the principal. In conditional hostageship, however, that captivity is at first, and perhaps only, hypothetical. Classical Roman law distinguished between three sorts of real surety, before the differences were collapsed by the compilers of the *Corpus iuris civilis*: *fiducia*, in which ownership and possession of the pledge was transferred from the debtor to the creditor upon formation of the agreement; *pignus*, in which possession alone was transferred; and *hypotheca*, in which neither ownership nor possession was transferred until default.[5] A conditional hostage is analogous to the *hypotheca*. It serves a guaranteeing function in two ways. Before violation of an agreement, it is the possibility of the captivity of the hostage that pressures the principal to adhere to his promises. After a violation, it is the actual captivity of the hostage that pressures the principal to remedy the situation. Conditional hostageship is a more complicated guarantee, in that there are now two promises: the promise of the principal with respect to the main agreement, and the promise of the hostage to enter into captivity in case of default. The guarantee for the first promise is less firm in that the guarantors, the hostages, are subject to a second promise, which may be entirely unsecured.

In this chapter, I trace the early development of this new, monetized and conditional model of hostageship. A form of hostageship in which the identity of the hostage was less important than the debts that he ran up was only possible in an environment that was not only monetized but where creditors had a reasonable expectation of being able to enforce debts through established legal institutions. Hostageship, regularly extra-judicial in earlier periods, has here been subsumed

---

[3] In the Empire, the *Einlager* was abolished by the *Reichspolizeiordnung* of 1577. Earlier legislation: Wolfgang Sellert, 'Geiselnahme und Pfändung als Gegenstand spätmittelalterliche Landfrieden', in Arno Buschmann and Elmar Wadle, eds., *Landfrieden: Anspruch und Wirklichkeit* (Paderborn, 2002), 231–52.

[4] In the similar institution of *garnisaires* (*mangeurs, comestores*), the figure running up the bills was supplied by the creditor or the state: Charles Du Fresne, sieur Du Cange, *Glossarium mediae et infimae latinitatis*, ed. Léopold Favre, 10 vols. (Niort, 1883–7), s.v. *comestores*; Roy L. McCullough, *Coercion, Conversion and Counterinsurgency in Louis XIV's France* (Leiden, 2007), 21–34; Claustre, *Geôles*, 26, 323. Guarantors in some contexts might also be bound *corps et biens*, which might lead to confinement (e.g. Claustre, *Geôles*, 233, 248–9, 264, 274, 300–3, etc.).

[5] Donald E. Phillipson, 'Development of the Roman Law of Debt Security', *Stanford Law Review*, 20 (1968), 1230–48.

into a system of formal laws and procedures. A form of hostageship in which captivity was only hypothetical required similar changes. True hostages are at root an indication of a profound lack of trust, not simply in the individual granting the hostage, but also in the ability of judicial institutions or, more frequently, the grantor's peers (*fideles*, oath-helpers, etc.) to influence his behaviour, whether actively or passively. In contrast, because of the additional promise involved, conditional hostageship can *only* work in an atmosphere of trust, or at least confidence that those other parties will assure the appearance of the hostage when the time comes. Nevertheless, the political relationships on which conditional hostageship draws, and the institutional matrix in which it operates, are the same.

While early medieval Celtic law knew a type of conditional hostage, the *aitire*, it operated in a very different fashion and is difficult to connect to the developments examined here.[6] The changes in hostageship elsewhere are first evident, as in so many others areas of medieval history, in the late tenth and early eleventh centuries. The first hints of a conditional element in hostageship appear at this time in texts concerning the Peace and Truce of God, a movement by lay and ecclesiastical powers to combat aristocratic violence. Clear examples of conditional hostages and the beginnings of the implication of hostages in monetary guarantees date to the mid-eleventh century, before the beginning of the Crusades (which have been proposed as an explanation for the development of the *Einlager*). Over the course of the twelfth century, this new form of hostageship became a regular feature of written 'international' treaties and the fiscal systems of nascent governmental bureaucracies, and even carved out a minor role in lower-order financial transactions. One result of all this, as suggested above, was the 'de-individualization'[7] of hostageship in this peculiar form of personal surety.

PEACE TEXTS

The first possible indications of conditional hostages appear in texts concerned with the Peace of God. In the face of mounting violence, bishops in southern and central Francia, often in concert with local secular rulers, endeavoured at local assemblies to discourage violation of the property and persons of non-combatants: the church and clerics, but also peasants. As local initiatives spread, the project became more ambitious, adding to these prohibitions of particular violent acts at

---

[6] While the *aitire* took an oath to enter into custody upon violation of an agreement, it differs from the conditional hostages examined here in important ways: the *aitire* was ultimately a paying surety, bound to pay the compensation for a violation in addition to a ransom at the end of the period of hostageship (and had a claim against the principal for double expenses); the period of hostageship was fixed; and the *aitire* was appointed not for a specific contract, but for unexpected occurrences arising out of a general agreement. On the other hand, the increased financial pressure on the debtor parallels the *Einlager* system, and relies on similar ties of kin and clientship. See Stacey, *Road*, 82–111.

[7] *SP* 1:58 uses the term *dépersonnaliser*, but as crucially the hostage remains a *person*, de-individualize seems a more precise concept.

all times, prohibitions of all violent acts at particular times (the Truce of God). Ultimately, kings and local rulers saw the utility of the Peace and Truce as an instrument of control and took responsibility for their enforcement. The Peace movement—if it was in fact that—has been placed at the root of many developments in medieval society, notably the Christianization of military activity that led on the one hand to the Crusades and on the other to the development of chivalry. The Peace has also been linked to the process of organization of secular lordships and thus to the origin of 'states' in the high and later medieval period. Because of its timing, it also offers evidence for an increase in violence accompanying the transformation of the social order by means of the extension of aggressive, extortionate lordship.[8]

Of particular interest for the history of hostageship is the question of guarantees for the Peace. From its inception, the Peace was associated with large public gatherings, where armed men would swear oaths in the presence of saints' relics not to violate their promises. By incorporating relics into the process, the bishops were using the only tool they could legitimately use in a fight against military men: religious sanctions. The threat of excommunication or anathema for violation of an oath taken to protect church property and non-combatants—this is all that stood behind the Peace. When the Peace developed from its 'sanctified' into its 'institutionalized' form, enforcement became a matter for the secular authorities. This view is simplified, in that we know that the early Peace was promulgated in concert with local authorities, and in a few cases we can point to 'Peace militias', which took the question of enforcement into their own hands. Nonetheless, the early Peace is generally seen as marshalling religious tools against secular violence.

In light of this, it is surprising to find, in the very first record of a Peace council, the mention of hostages. At Saint-Germain-Laprade (c.980), Bishop Guy pressured the assembled knights and peasants not only to swear to the Peace, but also to give hostages for its maintenance.[9] The acts of the council of Poitiers (c.1000) fill out the picture: the hostages were granted to pressure the lords who were party to the agreement to enforce judgments against malefactors—if a lord failed to keep his people in line, he would lose the hostages that he had granted (and suffer excommunication).[10] In both cases oaths and spiritual sanctions went hand-in-hand with the more concrete guarantee mechanism of hostages. But what were these 'hostages'? As noted, the term 'hostage' (here *obses*) does not necessarily

---

[8] Thomas Head and Richard Landes, eds., *The Peace of God: Social Violence and Religious Response around the Year 1000* (Ithaca, 1992); for revisions, Dominique Barthélemy, *L'an mil et la paix de Dieu: La France chrétienne et féodale, 980–1060* (Paris, 1999).

[9] *Chronique de Saint-Pierre du Puy*, 413 (ed. Chevalier, 152); Christian Laurason-Rosaz, *L'Auvergne et ses marges (Velay, Gévaudan) du VIIIe au XIe siècle: La fin du monde antique?* (Le Puy-en-Velay, 1987), 413–16.

[10] *Sacrorum conciliorum nova et amplissima collectio*, 19:265–8. Thomas N. Bisson, 'The Organized Peace in Southern France and Catalonia, ca. 1140–ca. 1233', *American Historical Review*, 82 (1977), 294, suggested that these hostages 'evidently grew out of the customary practice in judicial (or quasi-judicial) concords by which private wars were ended'. Cf. above, pp. 15–16.

indicate a third-party surety in actual custody; in some cases, it is used in the more general sense of guarantor. The 'hostages' at Saint-Germain-Laprade might have been mere guarantors, but at Poitiers, the grantor of the hostages will forfeit (*perdere*) them in case of a violation. Furthermore, when we look at slightly later Peace texts, from Verdun-sur-Doubs (1019x21) and Vienne (early eleventh century), we find that the oath sworn included a promise not to attack the hostages granted for the peace on their way to or from their places of detention.[11] Clearly, then, there was a tradition in the earliest Peace assemblies of guarantors in custody.

The descriptions of these hostages are, however, puzzling. In an earlier context, the forfeit of a hostage might indicate enslavement, but while bishops certainly still had slaves in this period, and penal slavery continued to be practised, the individuals involved are unlikely to have been in a position to pressure their lords. As we have seen, in the early Middle Ages hostages were frequently sons or close relatives of powerful men; at Le Puy there is no mention of sons or close relatives. Still, it is likely that these were high-status hostages, as they were not included in the blanket protections afforded to non-combatants. Then there is the statement that hostages (presumably those of other lords) are not supposed to be attacked on their way to or from their place of detention. Hostages being attacked *returning from* detention is understandable, but the only way for a hostage to be attacked by a juror *on the way* to his place of detention is if the detention of the hostage was subsequent to the swearing of the oath. If hostages were not handed over at the time of the swearing of the oath, there are two possibilities: hostages granted at the time of the swearing of the oath had a certain grace period before entering detention, or the hostages only had to enter detention *after violation of the agreement*. In the latter case, they would be conditional hostages.

One further element of the terms of guarantee for the Peace is relevant, namely provisions in the councils of Verdun-sur-Doubs, Vienne, Toulouges (1064x6), and Tours (1095x6) that the jurors of the oaths *present themselves* at appointed places and appointed times. This is a form of procedural *Selbstbürgschaft*, rather than hostageship proper. The earliest text is garbled, but seems to indicate that the juror was to present himself in *hostadio*, on command, for a period of fifteen days.[12] The meaning of this is clarified by the Vienne oath: there the juror promises to submit himself as a hostage at four times and places and remain there for three days in case 'a cleric or a monk or a knight wishes to call me to account', presumably for violation of the terms of the Peace.[13] This procedure is stated even more clearly in

[11] Karl Josef von Hefele, *Histoire des conciles d'après les documents originaux*, trans. Henri Leclercq, vol. 4.2 (Paris, 1911), 1409 ('dum in captione loco obsidum venerint, non eos assaliam in eundo vel redeundo'); Georges de Manteyer, 'Les origines de la maison de Savoie en Bourgogne (910–1060): La paix en Viennois (Anse [17 juin?] 1025) et les additions à la Bible de Vienne (ms. Bern. A 9)', *Bulletin de la Société des sciences naturelles et des arts industriels du département de l'Isère*, 4th ser., 7 (1904), 96 ('nec in eundo nec redeundo, nec quamdiu ibi steterint').

[12] Hefele, *Histoire*, 1409.

[13] Manteyer, 'Les origines', 98: 'mitto me in obisdem…si clericus aut monachus aut caballarius uoluerit me ad rationem mittere'. Cf. Hartmut Hoffman, *Gottesfriede und Treuga Dei* (Stuttgart, 1964), 49.

the Tours text. Although much later, it echoes the Vienne oath: 'all barons and provosts of the count shall submit themselves for detention twice a year, at the start of Lent and at the octave of Pentecost, in the new castle and in the town, and they shall be there for three days; and if during that time a complaint is made against them concerning the Peace of God, they shall not depart from there until they have made amends; and if they depart without having made amends, they will have violated the Peace of God'.[14] The text of the council of Toulouges includes an oath of Gausfred II, count of Roussillon (1013–74), to Raimond, bishop of Elne (1064–87), that is similar in content: he pledges himself to the bishop as a hostage ('facio tibi ostaticum'), promising to return to the site of his oath twice a year.[15]

None of this proves that the hostages referred to in the early Peace texts were conditional hostages; nor is it certain that we may use descriptions of hostages in one situation to elucidate mentions of hostages in other cases. Still, all of the necessary elements are present in these texts: an oath to appear at a certain place and time; the custody of hostages subsequent to the formation of the agreement; and the use of high-status hostages who would actively pressure principals to keep agreements, rather than relatives who would do so only passively. With respect to the Peace of God generally, these often overlooked and decidedly non-spiritual guarantees underline the importance of understanding the institution's local and secular contexts.[16] With respect to the history of hostageship, the likelihood that the sureties seen in the early Peace texts are in fact conditional hostages is enhanced by the fact that many of the first documents that offer certain evidence for the institution come from the same period and regions: eleventh-century south and central Francia.

THE EARLIEST CONDITIONAL HOSTAGES

Legal historians who have studied the *Einlager* generally note that the earliest evidence for the institution is found in twelfth- or perhaps eleventh-century documents from Francia, particularly Francia south of the Loire, but they quickly move

---

[14] *RHF* 14:392 (c. 10): 'omnes barones et præpositi Comitis bis in anno, id est ad caput jejunii et ad octabas Pentecostes, se mittant in captione in Castro novo et in civitate, et erunt ibi per tres dies: et si interim factus fuerit clamore de eis de pace Domini, non exibunt inde donec emendaverint; et si sine emendatione exierint, pacem Domini violabunt'.

[15] *Les constitucions de Pau i Treva*, 35 (no. 6). The text (p. 34, c. 15) also refers to a threat of excommunication against *fideiussores vel ostatici*. Cf. [Paul-Emile] Giraud, *Essai historique sur l'abbaye de S. Barnard et sur la ville de Romans: Complément textuel du cartulaire* (Lyon, 1869), 48–9 (no. 158) (a. 1096x1117, principal presents self yearly); *Westschweizer Schiedsurkunden*, 10–13 (no. 7) (a. 1188, hostages present themselves regularly). *Monuments historiques*, 156–8 (no. 249), dated 997, but composed around 1101, has strikingly similar language; for the date, Léon Levillain, 'Études sur l'abbaye de Saint-Denis à l'époque mérovingienne, III, *Privilegium et immunitas* ou Saint-Denis dans l'Église et dans l'État', *Bibliothèque de l'École des chartes*, 87 (1926), 90–4.

[16] e.g. Thomas Head, 'The Development of the Peace of God in Aquitaine (970–1005)', *Speculum*, 74 (1999), 656–86.

on to the more plentiful, later material from further north and east.[17] In doing so, they have overlooked the importance of the meridional context of these documents, misinterpreting the origin of the *Einlager*, and undervaluing the significance of the appearance of the conditional hostage generally.

The two documents cited by most authorities by way of fixing an eleventh-century 'French' origin for the *Einlager* appear in the cartularies of Cluny and Saint-Victor of Marseille; both date from 1096. In the former, the knight Arcardus pledges lands to Cluny in return for 2,000 s. and four mules, so that he might go on Crusade. As a guarantee against exactions against or usurpations of the pledged lands, Arcardus and two guarantors (*fideiussores*) promise that if a wrong has not been amended within forty days of notification, they will hand themselves over for detention (*custodia*) in the castle of Riottier until the wrong is amended (how precisely Arcardus will do this while on Crusade is not addressed).[18] The transaction recorded in the Marseille document was also inspired by the First Crusade. Two brothers, Gaufredus and Guigo, granted a piece of land to the abbey and received a countergift of 160 s. They swore an oath along with three other brothers not to violate the agreement, presumably by infringing on the lands in question. They also named guarantors called 'hostages' (*obsides*). In case of a violation, two named guarantors—they are called *fideiussores* at this point in the text, but probably are the same as the aforementioned *obsides*—promise to enter into the castle of Signes until released by the abbot, prior, or cellarer of the abbey.[19]

To these two documents we may add two more, from the same decade. The first also dates from around 1096, and is again from the Rhône–Saône corridor. In return for cash, Savaric, count of Chalon, pledged to Gautier, bishop of Chalon, the half of the county that he had purchased from his uncle, who was (like Arcardus, Gaufredus, and Guigo) heading off on Crusade. To guarantee that he would abide by his quitclaim of various fiscal rights in the county, Savaric offered twenty *obsides*, who are not named. If compensation had not been made within forty days of a warning, the hostages were to be confined to the town of Chalon: they are 'not to exit from the territory bounded by the walls of the town of Chalon'. In contrast

---

[17] Friedlaender, *Das Einlager*, 14–15; Lechner, *Das Obstagium*, 51–3; Jean-Jacques Leu, *Le cautionnement dans le pays de Vaud (XIIe–XVIe siècle)* (Lausanne, 1958), 60; Ogris, 'Die persönlichen Sicherheiten', 170 n. 158; Walliser, *Bürgschaftsrecht*, 290. Most follow Le Fort, 'L'otage', who focuses on documents from Burgundy. See also Achille Luchaire, *Manuel des institutions françaises: Période des Capétiens directs* (Paris, 1892), 193; Heinrich Mitteis, *Lehnrecht und Staatsgewalt: Untersuchungen zur mittelalterlichen Verfassungsgeschichte* (Weimar, 1933; repr. Darmstadt, 1958), 618 n. 124; Auguste Molinier, 'Étude sur l'administration féodale dans le Languedoc (900–1250)', *HGL* 7:136; Dmitri Starostine, 'Hostage by Agreement and the Language of Dependence in the Eleventh Century: Mutation or Corruption?', in Michael W. Herren, Christopher J. McDonough, and Ross G. Arthur, eds., *Latin Culture in the Eleventh Century: Proceedings of the Third International Conference on Medieval Latin Studies, Cambridge, September 9–12, 1998* (Turnhout, 2002), 965–79. Adam J. Kosto, 'Les otages conditionnels en Languedoc et en Catalogne au XIe siècle', *Annales du Midi*, 118 (2006), 387–403, is an earlier version of this section.

[18] *Recueil… Cluny*, 5:51–3 (no. 3703).

[19] *Cartulaire de l'abbaye de Saint-Victor de Marseille*, 1:167–8 (no. 143).

to the cases at Marseille and Cluny, the hostages had an explicit option: they could pay the compensation themselves or remain in custody until the property seized had been restored. The agreement adds that if one of the hostages dies, another should be substituted quickly.[20] Slightly different terms appear in a transaction concerning the estate of Muron, near the western French abbey of Saint-Jean d'Angely, around 1093. Guilduin de Tonnay and his son Raoul promise to allow the monk Benedict to retain control of the estate until certain monies are repaid to him. As a guarantee that they will not infringe on his rights, they grant eight hostages (*ostacios*), each of whom is bound to pay 100 s. in case of violation. They are to remain in custody until the fines are paid, some in a local castle, others outside. If one dies, he is to be replaced within eight days by another of similar value.[21]

Despite differences, all four cases offer clear examples of the conditional hostage: a promise of detention, in case of default, in a particular place, of a third-party guarantor, until an obligation is discharged. A number of things are worthy of note in these cases. First, the language used to refer to the conditional hostages is inconsistent. The third-party guarantors are referred to as *fideiussores* in the Cluny document and *obsides* or *ostacios* in the Chalon and Saint-Jean d'Angely documents; in the Marseille document, it is not clear if the *fideiussores* are the same as the *obsides*. Second, the *fideiussores* and *obsides* are not guaranteeing a specific pre-existing monetary debt, but rather the performance of satisfaction for a possible violation of the agreement. Third, the relationship between the guarantors and the principal is inconsistent. In the Cluny document, the principal agrees to conditional detention alongside the guarantors; it has been suggested that the same is true in the Marseille case, although the language is very ambiguous.[22] This possibility is not presented by the Chalon and Saint-Jean cases. Similarly, the Cluny and Marseille documents make no specific claim on the *fideiussores* other than their entry into custody; they do not specify that the *fideiussores* (as opposed to Arcardus or the brothers) have a responsibility to amend the damage. In contrast, the Chalon and Saint-Jean agreements, as noted, directly implicate the *obsides* in the payment of a fine. Legal historians have focused on such facts in determining the precise nature of the status and obligations of the hostages. Still, the timing of the creation of the debt in relation to the constitution of the hostage, the presence of the principal alongside the hostage, or the subsequent possibility of financial obligation on the part of the hostage, do not alter the fundamental fact of the conditional detention of a third party because of the debt or obligation of another.

These documents show that the conditional hostage was known in southern and western Francia in the eleventh century, or at least at its very end. Earlier studies of the institution claimed that twelfth-century cases were rare, but dozens have been

---

[20] Gautier of Chalon, *Diplomata*, 1 (*PL* 160:1165–7): 'ambitu murorum urbis Cabilonensis non exibit'.

[21] *Cartulaire de Saint-Jean d'Angely*, 1:234–5 (no. 194).

[22] Le Fort, 'L'otage', 411 n. 6.

accumulated, from regions all over Europe.[23] The 1096 dates of the Cluny and Marseille documents—not to mention the reason behind the grants in question—has suggested a link between the conditional hostage and the Crusades; the Chalon document, if not the one from Saint-Jean d'Angely, also shows such a connection.[24] While the *spread* of the institution may have been facilitated by interregional contacts of the first century of Crusading, the 1096 date alone, so soon after the launch of the First Crusade at Clermont, suggests that its origins must be independent of that movement. It is possible, in fact, to push back the origin of the institution more securely into the eleventh century, and to localize its early development more precisely—in the creatively literate notarial culture of Languedoc and Catalonia. An examination of the meridional context of the earliest conditional hostages also allows us to examine two further questions: the role of economic factors in the origin of the *Einlager*, and the relationship between conditional hostages and true hostages.

The agreements from Marseille and Cluny do *not* specify that the hostages' expenses are to be charged to the debtor. Why, then, are these seen as the first evidence for the *Einlager*? Because the economic aspect of the *Einlager* has been interpreted as a later development of the institution, whose fundamental characteristic is its conditional nature. The *Einlager* began, it is argued, as a noble and knightly institution, and the individuals who served were bound by feodo-vassalic ties to the principals. The pressure exercised on the defaulting principal was not a result of the high cost of maintaining the conditional hostages, nor solely in a moral (and here quasi-legal) obligation to one's men (an obligation found also in the case of true hostages), but in the removal from the principal of military force. When from the thirteenth century on the institution was adopted in other milieux—among townsmen and even peasants—the importance of these elements diminished, and the economic factors came to the fore.[25] Because we do not know who the guarantors were in these three cases—either because they are not named or because they are named but unrecognizable individuals—the argument about feodo-vassalic ties as the rationale for their use is moot. But we can show that the documentary context for these earliest agreements argues against the notion that such ties were the *only* reason behind their use: economic factors were very important in this form of hostageship from the outset, at least in this region.

On a broader level, debates in German legal scholarship about the origin of the *Einlager* are tied up in controversies over the origin of suretyship itself. Older theories saw various forms of personal surety as developments and descendants of the institution of hostageship—the surety was an 'ideal' rather than an actual hostage.

---

[23] Le Fort, 'L'otage', alone cites over twenty from his region of interest; see also *SP* 2:320, 577–9, 588. The earliest twelfth-century document I have located dates from 1108: Achille Luchaire, *Louis VI le Gros: Annales de sa vie et de son règne (1081–1137) avec une introduction historique* (Paris, 1890), 50–1, 332–3 (no. 92).

[24] Friedlaender, *Das Einlager*, 14; followed by Le Fort ('L'otage', 412), *SP* 2:657, etc.

[25] Ogris, 'Die persönliche Sicherheiten', 168–9; *SP* 2:657–60.

The *Einlager* fits perfectly into this genealogy, representing the weakest form of hostageship, one step removed from suretyship that did not involve physical control of the body of the surety. More recent theory, stemming from the work of Franz Beyerle, sees hostageship and other forms of surety as separate; from this point of view, the *Einlager* was a strengthened form of (non-captive) executory suretyship—in which the surety 'executed' the judgment on behalf of the creditor against the property of the debtor—rather than a weakened form of hostageship.[26] Both theories have a problem explaining the sudden reappearance in the realm of private law of an archaic institution that was thought to have disappeared from private law long before. For Lutteroth, the explanation was simple: the *Einlager* developed not from the *private* law hostage, but from the *public* law hostage, which was still (as we have seen) in use; the transition was facilitated by the blurring of public and private in the central Middle Ages. The key development was the introduction of the *conditional* aspect of the grant of the hostage. To secure treaties or recognize submission, hostages were handed over immediately. In the case of the conditional hostage, the guarantor was only handed over upon default.[27] In focusing on certain aspects of these eleventh-century agreements, we find that if Lutteroth was correct in seeing a link to what he thought of as 'public law' agreements, the particular analogy that he developed was incorrect. The conditional hostage was not a weakened version of the true hostage; it developed, rather, out of security agreements involving castles.

A number of agreements, all strikingly involving bishops or abbots, offer *possible* examples of conditional hostages that pre-date the Crusades. Around 1050 the bishop of Limoges and the count of Poitou concluded a pact concerning episcopal elections. The count named two *obsides* to guarantee his responsibility to defend the bishopric; they were to be replaced if they died, but there is no firm indication whether or not they are in custody (the open-ended context of this part of the agreement suggests that they were not). In addition, the count named six hostages to guarantee the terms of the next election. They, too, were to be replaced at death, but if the count failed to do so within fifteen days of being warned, those remaining were to enter the castle of Saint-Étienne and not depart until they were released. The terms are certainly puzzling, and the text appears to be corrupt; nonetheless, this appears to be a case of conditional hostageship.[28] Around 1055, the abbot of Corbie and his advocate reached a settlement concerning the latter's rights. The advocate named seven *obsides*, whose first responsibility was to warn their lord to appear for judgment; if he continued to ignore the summons, the *obsides* were either to pay a fine to the abbot or 'ipsi abbati [...] tradent'. If we supply *eum*,

[26] Franz Beyerle, 'Der Ursprung der Bürgschaft: Ein Deutungsversuch vom germanischen Rechte her', *Zeitschrift der Savigny-Stiftung für Rechtsgeschichte*, Germanistische Abteilung, 47 (1927), 567–645.
[27] Lutteroth, *Der Geisel*, 131.
[28] *Cartulaire du chapitre de Saint-Étienne de Limoges*, 174–6 (no. 181); Michel Aubrun, *L'ancien diocèse de Limoges des origines au milieu du XIᵉ siècle* (Clermont-Ferrand, 1981), 137–8.

their task is to hand over the advocate: the *obsides* are simply influential guarantors. If, on the other hand, we supply *se*, then they are to hand themselves over to the abbot: the *obsides* are conditional hostages.[29]

Perhaps the earliest example comes not from a charter but from a section of a narrative source, the *Deeds of the Bishops of Cambrai*, composed as early as 1025, although parts of this particular section may instead be contemporary with the Limoges and Corbie documents just discussed.[30] The author describes here the conflict between Bishop Gerard and Walter of Lens, the castellan of Cambrai, and relates to a settlement between the two brokered by the local count; the author here is likely reproducing texts of a series of agreements. In one, the count named two of his men as hostages (*obsides*), with the understanding that if Walter violated the agreement, the count would not side with Walter; if summoned, the hostages were to enter into the control of the bishop ('venirent...in potestatem').[31] In another, Walter granted to the bishop twelve hostages (*obsides*), who in case of a violation were to attempt to force him to appear for judgment; if that failed, they were to 'come (*venirent*) to the bishop with their benefices', grant Walter no aid and counsel, and aid the bishop against him.[32] The puzzle here is the meaning of 'venire in potestatem'—whether it means physical or simply moral control. Earlier in the section, Gerard is said to have held the son of Walter as a hostage (*obses*) in his *potestas*, and the language suggests that this refers to physical custody: if Walter dies and his son in still in the bishop's control, the bishop will return him to Walter's knights; if Gerard dies before the son has been returned, the son is to be returned to the father.[33] The specification in the case of Walter's hostages, which speaks of their benefices and does not use the term *potestas*, looks more like moral control, but the author uses the same term (*obses*) to describe them. This is even slimmer evidence, then, for conditional hostageship in the mid-eleventh century, but better proof is available elsewhere.

Four cases from Languedoc and Catalonia from well before 1096 offer clear evidence for the use of conditional hostages. The first, and earliest, is an agreement between the abbot of Aniane and a certain Eneas concerning rights in the abbey's

---

[29] The key word is missing from the earliest surviving version, BnF, ms. lat. 17760, fol. 2r. The best edition, 'Les chartes de l'abbaye de Saint-Pierre de Corbie', 101–16 (no. 9), gives *se*, as do Du Cange, *Glossarium*, s.v. *obses* 1, and *Actes et documents anciens intéressant la Belgique*, 132–4; *Chartes de coutume en Picardie*, 130–1 (no. 2), supplies *eum*. See Walliser, *Bürgschaftsrecht*, 290 n. 28; *SP* 2:308 n. 120, 315 n. 143.

[30] *Gesta episcoporum Cameracensium*, 3.39–47 (MGH SS 7:481–3). For the dating, Theo M. Riches, 'Episcopal Historiography as Archive: Some Reflections on the Autograph of the *Gesta episcoporum Cameracensium* (MS Den Haag KB 75 F 15)', *Jaarboek voor middeleeuwse geschiedenis*, 10 (2007), 7–46, esp. 22. Walter had previously granted hostages (3.2 [MGH SS 7:467]), and the author mentions *obsides* elsewhere (1.98, 101, 115 [MGH SS 7:441, 443, 452]).

[31] *Gesta episcoporum Cameracensium*, 3.45 (MGH SS 7:482).

[32] *Gesta episcoporum Cameracensium*, 3.47 (MGH SS 7:482–3): 'ad episcopum cum beneficiis eorum...venirent'.

[33] *Gesta episcoporum Cameracensium*, 3.43 (MGH SS 7:482). Theo Riches (personal communication) points out that as the author may be copying pre-existing texts composed by others, and at different dates, there is no need for the language to be consistent.

fisheries; it is datable only to the period 1036x60.[34] If Eneas or his men violate the agreement and refuse to submit to judgment within eight days, Eneas is to hand over either 50 s. or his hostage (*obstaticus*), one Petrus Farengus, who is to be held at the abbey. Similarly, if the monks violate the agreement, they are to hand over either 50 s. or their own guarantor, one Petrus Geraldus, who is to appear at Frontignan. The purpose of the pledges and guarantors, which seem to be subject to time limits of one month, is not entirely clear, though it appears to be related to a judicial appearance. The hostages are not to depart without permission, and (in the case of Eneas, at least) a hostage who dies is to be replaced with another of equal value.

A second case, dated *c.*1076, is an agreement between the men of the young Guilhem V of Montpellier and Raimond IV of Toulouse. Raimond promised to protect and not to seize Guilhem's lands. If he failed to keep the agreement, within eight days of a warning, five named hostages ('those who have made *hostaticum*') were to appear at one of four locations to be determined by Guilhem's men: Montpellier, Pézénas, Béziers, or Servian. They were not to leave without permission of Guilhem's men. Again, the precise rationale behind the guarantee is not given.[35]

The third case, from the period 1050x68, comes from the other side of the Pyrenees: an agreement between Guillem Guifré, bishop of Urgell (1041–75), and Ramon Guifré, count of Cerdanya (1035–68), concerning tribute payments, called *parias*, from neighbouring Islamic polities. As a guarantee for his undertakings, Guillem offered five named hostages, each given a value of 1,000 s. If Guillem violates the agreement, the hostages are to present themselves to the count within thirty days 'in the castle of Sant Martí, in the courtyard, and from there they should not depart until the said funds have been given for them'. The text may or may not be interpreted as placing the obligation for payment upon the hostages themselves.[36]

We learn of the fourth, and best-documented case, from the group of texts that record the alliance forged in 1068x70 between the Trencavel family and the counts of Barcelona; this case thus links the neighbouring regions represented in the other three documents.[37] In 1070, Raimond-Bernard Trencavel and his wife Ermengard sold their rights in various Languedocian counties to Ramon Berenguer I of Barcelona (1035–76), his wife Almodis, and their son, Ramon Berenguer (II); this principal transaction is recorded as a sale and quitclaim. A complementary agreement specified terms concerning the abbeys of Montolieu (Valsiger) and Caunes—specifically excepted from the main grant—which the Trencavels held as a fief (*per*

---

[34] *Cartulaires des abbayes d'Aniane et de Gellone*, 1:217–19 (Aniane, no. 80).

[35] *Liber instrumentorum memorialium*, 147–8 (no. 78) [= *HGL* 5:624 (no. 323)]: 'habet factum hostaticum'.

[36] *Liber feudorum maior*, 2:91–2 (no. 586); *Els pergamins*, 3:1276–7 (no. 736) ('in kastrum Sancti Martini, intus in ipso solario, et inde non deseschant usque eis prescriptum avere abeant donatum').

[37] Fredric L. Cheyette, 'The "Sale" of Carcassonne to the Counts of Barcelona (1067–1070) and the Rise of the Trencavels', *Speculum*, 63 (1988), 826–64.

fevum) from the counts of Barcelona. The two documents, dated on consecutive
days, are closely linked, and may represent a single, complex transaction.[38] While
the first does not mention guarantees, other than a standard sanction clause establishing a twofold compensation, the second does, and the guarantees would appear
to refer to the terms of both documents. The viscounts named as hostages ('mittunt in illorum potestate et ostaticum') seven individuals.[39] In case of a violation,
within twenty days of a warning, the hostages are to amend the wrong; how this is
to be done is not specified. If they fail to do so, they are to submit themselves
within ten days to the counts at Carcassonne, Saissac, Laurac, or Razès. The agreement goes on to say that the hostages should not disregard the summons, and that
a dead hostage is to be replaced with one of equal value within ten days of a summons. The hostages are apparently for appearance at a judicial duel: 'And if the said
viscount and viscountess do not wish to amend the wrong, the said hostages shall
make them exculpate themselves by oath and by battle'. If the viscounts fail to
appear at the duel, the hostages remain in the control of the count and countess.[40]

These terms make an earlier reference in the text to hostages puzzling. The
abbeys are to be maintained 'just as they stood on the day when Raimond Stephan
of Servian and Arnaud Guillem of Sauvian entered into hostageship to the count
and countess concerning the aforesaid at Girona'.[41] Raimond Stephan and Arnaud
Guillem are two of the seven hostages named later in the document. This passage
has been used to locate the place of the agreement at Girona, an interpretation that
assumes that the hostages were guarantors for the present agreements, and that a
ritual for the naming of hostages was performed at the time the charters were
drafted. This would be, to be sure, an odd way to note a date in a document in this
region, with its relatively sophisticated documentary practices. The possibility of a
precedent (oral?) agreement must be entertained, one entered into perhaps not
that much before the final agreement. Thus, the sale excluded the abbeys because
of this precedent agreement, but they were then integrated into the overall agreement, and the earlier hostages folded into the hostages for the overall agreement.

This group of cases from Languedoc and Catalonia demonstrates the same characteristics as the trio from 1096: inconsistent language; lack of a pre-existing monetary debt; and the possibility that the hostages are implicated in payments, in
addition to subjection to captivity. The mention of waiting periods, replacement of
dead hostages, and permission to depart finds strong echoes in the records from
1096, particularly the one from Chalon, which includes all three of these provisions. Still, the key elements are consistent: the conditional appearance of third-
party guarantors at a specific place in case of default of agreement.

[38] *Liber feudorum maior*, 2:303–7 (nos. 820, 821) [*HGL* 5:573–9 (nos. 293–4)]; Cheyette, 'Sale',
851–3; Hélène Débax, *La féodalité languedocienne, XIe–XIIe siècles: Serments, hommages et fiefs dans le
Languedoc des Trencavel* (Toulouse, 2003), 64–5, 263 n. 175; Mitteis, *Lehnrecht*, 618 n. 124.
[39] See Cheyette, 'Sale', 844 n. 65.
[40] 'Et iam dicti ostatici tales habeant iam dictum vicecomitem et vicecomitissam, si noluerint
emendare ipsum malum, ut excondigant per sacramentum et per bataliam.'
[41] 'sicut consistebant ipsa die quando Raimundus Stephani de Cerviano et Arnallus Guillelmi de
Salviano miserunt se in ostaticum de iam dictis comite et comitissa et illorum filiorum apud
Gerundam.'

Conditionality, as noted, is the aspect of these agreements that ties them to the history of the *Einlager*, and we can be confident of the presence of conditionality in these four cases because of the mention of particular places of detention: if the guarantors are to appear at such-and-such a place in case of default, then they were not there before the default. In the Trencavel document, therefore, we can distinguish between the *naming* of the hostages—'grant into their power and hostage-ship' ('mittunt in illorum potestate et ostaticum')—and the *appearance* of the hostages for detention—'they shall return into the power of the said count and countess of Barcelona and their son, Ramon, either in the city of Carcassonne, or in the castle of Saissac' ('revertantur in potestatem de iam dictis Barcheonensi comite et comitissa et filio eorum Remundo aut in civitate Carcassona aut in castro de Sexag'). The famously slippery word *potestas* here clearly has two different meanings: in the first case, *potestas* means control but not physical custody (in modern terms, ownership without possession); in the second case it means both.[42] Without the mention of a place of custody, however, the nature of *potestas*—and thus the conditionality of the grant of the hostages—would remain ambiguous.

Consider, for example, an agreement between the counts Ramon Berenguer I of Barcelona and Ermengol III of Urgell (1038–66) from 1062. This was adduced by Lutteroth as a 'borderline' case: a use of hostages that demonstrated the transition from public law hostage to private law *Einlager*. Yet he read this as still a 'true hostage treaty', in that the detention of the hostages was not yet conditional on a violation of the agreement: *potestas* meant physical control.[43] In fact, the key passage that he cites represents a conditional outcome, so whatever *potestas* means there, it is not proof that this is a 'true hostage treaty'. But as in the Trencavel document, there are shades of *potestas*. Five passages refer to guarantors. (1) First, the count of Urgell grants as pledges ('mitto in pignora') a number of his men. (2) and (3) In case of default, the count's men, whom he has granted as pledges ('quos ego ... mitto in pignora'), shall default into the power of the count ('incurrant in potestatem') [twice]. (4) If one of the hostages dies, he is to grant others ('mittam alios homines vel aliam ... in potestatem predicti Reimundi'). (5) If Ermengol fails to appear at a judgment or judicial duel as ordered, the hostages are to come into the power of Ramon ('veniant predicti ostatici in potestate'). When we compare the language of this agreement to the Trencavel document, the Urgell/Cerdanya document, and fourteen other contemporary documents from this region that mention *obsides* or *ostatici* (but with similarly ambiguous language), we begin to see a pattern.[44] The

---

[42] Michel Zimmermann, '"Et je t'empouvoirrai" (*Potestativum te farei*): À propos des relations entre fidélité et pouvoir en Catalogne au XIe siècle', *Médiévales*, 10 (1986), 17–36; Débax, *La féodalité*, 151–2.

[43] *Liber feudorum maior*, 1:146–50 (no. 149); Lutteroth, *Der Geisel*, 131 n. 2, 133; cf. Rintelen, *Schuldhaft*, 136 n. 3.

[44] One exception to this group is the contract for the marriage between Cecilia, daughter of the count of Provence, and Bernard Ato IV, viscount of Carcassone, in 1083: *HGL* 5:682–3 (no. 356); *Layettes*, 1:29 (no. 24). These individuals are hostages for a monetary debt—the dowry—but not assigned monetary values. The language of the document is correspondingly different: the text begins 'Breve memoratorium de ostaticos que dedit', and each of the hostages named is said to 'plevire ... per suam fidem'. See Débax, *La féodalité*, 77 and n. 348.

initial description of the grant of guarantors generally uses the word *mittere*.[45] So, too, does the phrase describing the replacement of a dead hostage.[46] Conditional outcomes in case of violation, however, are phrased differently: *incurrere, venire*, or *revertere*.[47] The key term, therefore, is not the noun *potestas*, but rather the verb. Here *mittere* should be construed not as 'send' but something closer to 'name' or 'appoint'.[48] Detention is a second, separate step.

The problem is that not all of these cases reveal what happens in case of default, and captivity for the guarantors is not the only possible outcome. In each of these additional agreements, the guarantors are assigned a monetary value, presumably a sum to be paid, either by themselves or by the principal, to release them from their obligations as guarantors. There are thus a number of possibilities for the procedure in case of default, where this is not specified clearly in the agreement. First, the hostages (*obsides/ostatici*) may be required to pay without submitting to captivity; here they would simply be 'paying sureties', indistinguishable from sureties designated by a dozen other terms in contemporary documents.[49] For example, the obligation of a set of hostages granted for a judicial proceeding from 1066x92 is simply to 'redeem (*redimere*) themselves for 100 ounces [of gold]'; *redimere* here means not ransom, but simply discharge an obligation.[50] In other cases, though, the combination of detention and payment is clear. It may be, in fact, that the use of the word *obses* or *ostaticus* indicates precisely that the surety is susceptible to detention, and that we should understand conditional detention in all such cases, even when a term such as *incurrere* or *venire* is not used.[51] If this is true, we can claim an additional fourteen cases from between *c.*1035 and 1095 attesting to the use of the conditional hostage. If it is not true, we have at least three additional cases, dating from *c.*1054 to 1062. In either case, taken with the four cases discussed above in which the presence of a conditional hostage is more certain, these documents establish the use of the conditional hostage firmly in the eleventh century and firmly in a meridional context. Whether this is in fact the region and period of origin of the institution is difficult to claim, given the vagaries of documentary survival. Nevertheless, it is a suggestive conglomeration of evidence.

---

[45] *HGL* 5:415–17 (no. 206); *Els pergamins*, 2:700–2, 836–8, 3:1171–2, 1493–4 (nos. 334, 441, 655, 925); *Liber feudorum maior*, 1:141–4, 146–50, 423–5, 2:91–2, 135 ('obsides et federatores'), 305–7 (nos. 146, 147, 149, 403, 586, 627, 821); Jaime Villanueva, *Viage literario a las iglesias de España*, 22 vols. (Madrid, 1803–52), 6:326–7 (ap. 39.1); ACA, Ramon Berenguer II 69, Extrainventari 3154/3204; and a fragment from the Trencavel cartulary (no. 500), cited by Débax, *La féodalité*, 50.

[46] *Liber feudorum maior*, 1:146–50, 423–5, 2:305–7 (nos. 149, 403, 821); *Els pergamins*, 2:1171–2 (no. 655); ACA, Ramon Berenguer II 69.

[47] *Els pergamins*, 2:836–8 (no. 441); *Liber feudorum maior*, 1:146–50, 423–5, 2:91–2, 305–7 (nos. 149, 403, 586, 821).

[48] Niermeyer, *Lexicon*, s.v., 9; Eulalia Rodón Binué, *El lenguaje técnico del feudalismo en el siglo XI en Cataluña (Contribución al estudio del latín medieval)* (Barcelona, 1957), s.v.

[49] Adam J. Kosto, *Making Agreements in Medieval Catalonia: Power, Order, and the Written Word, 1000–1200* (Cambridge, 2001), 125.

[50] *Els pergamins*, 3:1493–4 (no. 925): 'unusquisque de istos hostaticos sibi redimant uncias C'.

[51] e.g. *Els pergamins*, 3:1171–2 (no. 655): 'Et si predictus Gerallus non abet ad eos missum alium bonum ostaticum in loco illius predictus Umbertus, *stet* tantum cum predictis comite et comitissa usque donet ad eos II milia solidos' (my emphasis).

How does this expanded body of eleventh-century evidence fit in with theories about the origin of conditional hostageship and the relationship between conditional hostages and true hostages? On one issue, namely the role of economic factors, there is an immediate conflict.[52] While the documents from Cluny and Marseille do not assign any monetary value or obligation to pay to the conditional hostages, the agreement from Chalon does: the hostages were given the option of paying the compensation themselves, thereby redeeming themselves from detention. On the surface, this is not precisely the same mechanism as is found in the mature *Einlager*, where the monetary cost, and thus the economic pressure on the principal, increased with the passage of time. Still, economic pressure is at play: if the hostages did redeem themselves, they would certainly expect the principal to reimburse them. The same may be said of a Cerdanya/Urgell agreement of 1050x68; each of the five hostages was assigned a value of 1,000 s. and would not be released from the castle of Sant Martí until that amount was paid. Each of the three agreements that does not name a place of confinement but does use the phrase 'incurrere in potestatem' assigns a similar monetary value to the hostages. A Barcelona/Urgell agreement of 1062 simply says that there were ten hostages for (*per*) 1,000 s. apiece, but an agreement with the count of Besalú *c.*1054 specifies that his ten hostages had to redeem themselves (*se redimere*) for 1,000 s. apiece. Hostages for the viscount of Cabrera in 1061 had to redeem themselves (*se redimere*) for 2,000 s. apiece.[53] Monetary values are also assigned in the remaining eleven agreements, those for which detention of the hostages is least certain.

This is not to deny that the political factor—the withdrawal from service of the supporters of the principal—was not an important one; this is much more clear in the earlier agreements than in the three from 1096. The men listed as hostages are often identifiable as important men of the principal; one agreement explicitly refers to them as 'my men'.[54] More tellingly, in an agreement between the count of Barcelona and the viscount of Cabrera in 1061, a hostage had to be replaced not only in case of death, but also if 'he removed himself from the lordship or benefice of the said viscount'.[55] It could be that these ties were simply firmer foundations for the economic pressure: a lord would be more bound to repay his own man than an unconnected third party, who had at this point no legal remedy. The creation of competing moral obligations, however—the hostage would have sworn both to serve his lord and to remain in a position in which it was impossible to do so—would surely weaken the principal's position. And we do find here the large numbers—five, ten—of hostages pointed to as evidence for the intended politico-military impact of

---

[52] Cf. *SP* 2:659, which is more concerned, however, with drawing a line between *executorischer Bürgschaft* and *Zählungsbürgschaft* than in querying the economic pressures involved; the author denied that these could come into play at all among the nobility.

[53] *Liber feudorum maior*, 1:146–50, 423–5 (nos. 149, 403); *Els pergamins*, 2:836–8 (no. 441). *Obsides* are also assigned a monetary value in *HGL* 5:496–503 (no. 251).

[54] *Liber feudorum maior*, 1:149 (no. 149): 'mei homines'. See Cheyette, 'Sale', 844 n. 65.

[55] *Liber feudorum maior*, 1:424 (no. 403): 'se separaverint a senioratico vel beneficio predicti vicecomitis'. Similarly, 'Chartes angevines', 401–2 (no. 10).

violations.[56] That said, the political and military factors were closely tied to economic ones. We are not witnessing the monetization of an institution born in a non-monetized, 'feudal' context. Money played a role in conditional hostageship from the beginning.

The second issue to consider is Lutteroth's contention that the conditional hostage grew out of the 'international law' agreement. Although hostages had disappeared, he argued, from private law transactions at some time in the distant past, hostages were still a part of interactions between 'states'. Because of the political conditions of the central Middle Ages, the interactions of lesser lords took on the character of 'international law'. Both kings and lords granted their vassals as hostages to secure agreements. When international agreements began to employ conditional rather than true hostages, so too did agreements between lesser lords.[57] As with most discussions of this topic, it is difficult to be precise about chronology, but, as I will show below, the earliest examples of royal treaties involving conditional hostages *post-date* the earliest non-royal examples, reversing the supposed direction of influence.[58]

In any case, if Lutteroth is correct, we should expect to find, in eleventh-century agreements from this region, the use of true hostages in similar situations. We do not. In fact, outside of the agreements already mentioned—which, if they do in fact refer to hostages, refer only to the conditional variety—hostages rarely appear. True hostages were known in the region, or at least nearby; as noted in the previous chapter, Iberian town customs dating back to the eleventh century regulate practices of substitution for individuals captured by Islamic lordships.[59] But these are not the sort of high-level treaties that Lutteroth had in mind. Nevertheless, the agreements with conditional hostages are clearly closely related to the larger body of what Lutteroth thought of as 'international law' agreements in this region. All of the agreements discussed above from Languedoc and Catalonia may be classified as *convenientiae*, a flexible type of written agreement that flourished in just this time and place.[60] The agreements secured by conditional hostages share with *convenientiae* generally many characteristics, notably discussions of notification of default, assignment of grace periods within which obligations were to be carried out, procedures for replacement of individuals named in the agreements, and above all the role of *potestas*.[61] *Convenientiae* also employed a wide range of guarantees, and it is here that the parallels to these earliest cases of conditional hostages are most striking.

The passages describing conditional hostages echo, in the first instance, similar passages describing simple pledges of real property. In an agreement from 1049, the counts of Barcelona commended to one Hug Guillem the castle of Fornells. As

[56] Ogris, 'Die persönlichen Sicherheiten', 168.

[57] Lutteroth, *Der Geisel*, 131.

[58] See below, pp. 148–56.

[59] e.g. *Fuero de Cuenca* 10.39 (ed. Ureña y Smenjaud, 294–7); *El fuero de Teruel*, 453–4 (ed. Gorosch, 286–7). See above, p. 116.

[60] Kosto, *Making Agreements*; Débax, *La féodalité*, esp. 111–15.

[61] Kosto, *Making Agreements*, 90–4, 134–7.

a guarantee, Hug pledged ('mittimus in pignus') his allod in the county of Girona, on the condition that if he violated the agreement concerning Fornells, the allod would default to the counts ('incurrat in vestra potestate').[62] Similarly, two moneyers of Barcelona agreed in 1056 that if they violated their agreement with the counts, their properties, movable and immovable, would fall to the counts ('veniat...in potestate').[63] The conditional hostage agreements that involve the payment of fines find parallels in the many cases where paying sureties are named, but with no hint of potential captivity. For example, in 1057, three guarantors (*fideiussores*) were named to hand over 1,000 s. apiece within fifteen days if Ricard Altemir failed to finish construction at a certain castle on time.[64] A clear bridge to the conditional hostage appears when pledges of real property are combined with personal sureties. In 1089, Bernat Guillem de Queralt commended by homage to Berenguer Ramon II (1076–96) three of his men; if Bernat violated the agreement, the men were to enter into the *potestas* of the count along with the castles they controlled.[65] In a more complicated agreement from 1054, Guillem II of Besalú (1052–66) granted the double castle of Finestres to the count of Barcelona ('tradidit et iachivit...in potestatem'), but also pledged the same castles along with their guardian as a guarantee for the wider agreement. He agreed that if that castle guardian were to die, it would be his wife and heirs who would be responsible for handing over the castle. If another castellan had taken over, he would be the guarantor. In the language of the document, both the real sureties (the castles) and the personal sureties (the guardians) were pledges (*pignora*): 'he grants (*mittat*) them as the aforesaid pledges, along with the aforesaid castles'. And in case of a violation of the agreement, both the real and personal sureties would default ('incurrere...in potestatem') to the count of Barcelona: 'the castle of La Guàrdia shall default into the power of the said count, with its castellany, and with Ramon Bernat, who holds it'.[66]

In each of these cases, we should not imagine the personal sureties being thrown into a dungeon because of the violation of the agreement; their role was to deliver the keys to the castles they controlled. It is not difficult, however, to see how in an environment with a wide range of options for surety, both personal and real, scribes ready to formulate new sorts of documents, and structures of power that were complex and fluid, moral and political *potestas* over an individual—readily attested in situations that do not necessarily involve custody[67]—might become actual physical control, or at least the potential of physical control. All we have evidence of

---

[62] *Liber feudorum maior*, 1:453–5 (no. 433).

[63] *Els pergamins*, 2:873–4 (no. 468); cf. 3:1122–3 (no. 618), *Liber feudorum maior*, 1:127–8 (no. 126).

[64] *Liber feudorum maior*, 1:183 (no. 173); generally, Kosto, *Making Agreements*, 127–8.

[65] Albert Benet i Clarà, *La família Gurb-Queralt (956–1276): Senyors de Sallent, Oló, Avinyó, Gurb, Manlleu, Voltregà, Queralt i Santa Coloma de Queralt* (Sallent, 1993), 260–1 (no. 18).

[66] *Els pergamins*, 2:828–32 (no. 437): 'mittat eos vel eum in ipsa pignora supradicta, cum predictos castros...incurrat ipsum castrum de ipsa Guardia, cum sua castellania et cum Remundo Bernardi, qui eum tenet...in potestatem iam dicti comitis Remundi'.

[67] Debax, *La féodalité*, 152 n. 62.

here, after all, is proposals, not actual hostageships. Lutteroth's instinct that the conditional hostage grew out of 'international law' treaties is thus, in a way, correct. The conditional hostage was not, however, a weakened form of hostages that were already present in these agreements. Instead, it was a variation on other forms of surety found there, both real and personal.

While the evidence does not contradict the notion that conditional hostageship came into being in an aristocratic milieu, this does not translate into the absence of money, and thus economic pressures—pressures that according to current theory were only introduced into the institution of the conditional hostage when it was extended to urban and peasant milieux. On the other hand, it is true that the agreements in question are generally not about economic goods per se—the simple loans against real pledges that are recorded in hundreds of surviving *cartae impignorationis* from the region[68]—but about property and power: castles, fidelity, and military aid. The new forms of guarantee seem to suggest that the old ones—oaths, and promises of fidelity—were now insufficient. The appearance of the conditional hostage at this point in time and in this region is thus parallel to the spread of true hostages in the same changed eleventh-century circumstances: the proliferation of castles and castellans on the one hand, and the general economic resurgence that also led to the growth of the political power of towns.

INTERNATIONAL TREATIES

The notion that the conditional hostage grew out of international law agreements is undermined by the evident chronology. The comital documents from Catalonia and Languedoc just examined are in a sense public, but decidedly local in impact. Written international treaties survive in substantial numbers only from the beginning of the twelfth century.[69] The first of these come not from Mediterranean Europe, but from the North. Conditional hostages are present in these documents from the start, showing that experimentation with this new form of personal surety was already widespread. A detailed look at the Anglo-Flemish 'Treaty of Dover' of 1101 allows us to examine this experimentation in a context where it directly challenged the true hostage model, which, as we have seen, had long been employed in medieval diplomacy.

The Anglo-Flemish treaty of 1101[70] has attracted interest as the earliest royal example of a 'money-fief', or *fief-rente*,[71] but has not played as prominent a role as

---

[68] Jehan de Malafosse, 'Contribution à l'étude du crédit dans le Midi aux Xe et XIe siècles: Les sûretés réelles', *Annales du Midi*, 63 (1951); Aquilino Iglesia Ferreirós, *La prenda contractual: Desde sus orígines hasta la recepción del Derecho Común* (Santiago de Compostela, 1977). See the exception noted above, p. 143, n. 44.

[69] For this section, Benham, *Peacemaking*, 166–70. While the distinction between 'local' and 'international' is questionable, the involvement in these agreements of a bona fide king, however weak, is relevant because later international law focused on diplomacy between *nations*, magnifying the importance of earlier royal documents.

[70] London, National Archives, E 30/2; *Diplomatic Documents*, 1–4 (no. 1); trans. 'The Anglo-Flemish Treaty of 1101'.

[71] Bryce D. Lyon, *From Fief to Indenture: The Transition from Feudal to Non-Feudal Contract in Western Europe* (Cambridge, Mass., 1957), 33–4, 201; C. Warren Hollister, *The Military Organization of Norman England* (Oxford, 1965), 186–9; Reynolds, *Fiefs*, 163–4.

it might have in the history of treaty-making generally.[72] Although we have texts for several early medieval treaties (most are known only from mentions in chronicles),[73] few approach it in length and detail—and much of the detail is given over to the guarantee clauses, which include hostages. The treaty was made by Henry I of England (1100–35) as he was solidifying his position against the expected invasion of his brother, Robert Curthose, duke of Normandy (1087–1106).[74] In the treaty, Count Robert II of Flanders (1093–1111) swears an oath promising to protect King Henry and to defend England against all men, saving his allegiance to Philip I of France (1060–1108). If Philip plans to invade England, Robert is to try to dissuade him; if he fails and must accompany Philip, he promises to bring only enough knights to fulfil his commitment to his lord. He must, within forty days of Henry's request, have ready a force of 1,000 knights to send to England. If the threat to England is from a quarter other than France, or if one of Henry's own barons revolts, Robert himself is to accompany the Flemish troops. Additional clauses specify Robert's similar commitments to Henry in Normandy and Maine; for the latter he had to supply only 500 knights. The agreement details at length logistical issues, times of service, responsibility for maintenance in various locations, the multiple issues arising from the potential for conflicting obligations, and numerous exceptions involving Eustace III, count of Boulogne. An especially noteworthy passage of the treaty foresees multiple invocations of its terms: if Robert supplies more than the required number of knights for a given expedition, the surplus will be subtracted from the total required at the next summons. In return for all of this, King Henry promises (but does not swear) to protect Robert (though *not* his lands), and to pay 500 l. a year for his services, to be paid in three instalments.

The reasoning behind the treaty is fairly straightforward. Henry was not concerned so much with an invasion by the king of France, but rather an invasion by his brother, the duke of Normandy, and possible Norse, Danish, and even English allies.[75] In gaining a promise of aid from Robert, and especially a promise that enemies of the English king could not take refuge in Flanders—a favourite destination in the past for English rebels—Henry essentially neutralized a potential opponent. Although Robert might have pushed for a number of additional concessions, the only thing he got out of the agreement was money. It is not entirely

[72] Although see François Louis Ganshof, *The Middle Ages: A History of International Relations*, trans. Rémy Inglis Hall (New York, 1970 [1968]), 139–40; George Peddy Cuttino, *English Medieval Diplomacy* (Bloomington, 1985), 3–5.

[73] *Politische Verträge des frühen Mittelalters*. See François Louis Ganshof, 'Les traités des rois mérovingiens', *Tijdschrift voor Rechtsgeschiedenis*, 32 (1964), 163–92, esp. 168, 182–7; Ganshof, 'The Treaties of the Carolingians', *Medieval and Renaissance Studies*, 3 (1967), 23–52, esp. 23, 36–9; Patrick Wormald, *The Making of English Law: King Alfred to the Twelfth Century*, vol. 1: *Legislation and Its Limits* (Oxford, 1999), 285 n. 100; and above, pp. 55–7, 61–2; Kershaw, *Peaceful Kings*, 26–8.

[74] C. Warren Hollister, *Henry I* (New Haven, 2001), 134–42.

[75] François Louis Ganshof, Raoul Van Caenegem, and Adriaan Verhulst, 'Note sur le premier traité anglo-flamand de Douvres', *Revue du Nord*, 40 (1958), 249–50; Renée Nip, 'The Political Relations between England and Flanders (1066–1128)', *Anglo-Norman Studies*, 21 (1998), 160.

clear why money was so pressing a need for the Flemish count at this point. He had just returned a hero from the Crusade, was well established in his county, and was at peace with his main rival, Philip of France. His only major initiative involved expanding his territory into Cambrai at the expense of the German emperor,[76] but if this were his goal in entering the treaty, we might expect to find some reference to it. The passages concerning Normandy are odd, given that Henry did not at that point control Normandy, and it could not have been in Robert's interest to have Henry do so. They may be viewed as royal propaganda—as Henry acting as though he were in control of Normandy—but it is equally possible that the text of the treaty copies an earlier document, from a time when England and Normandy were not in open conflict.[77]

The 1101 treaty stands in the middle of a series of similar Anglo-Flemish agreements from the eleventh and twelfth centuries. The only other surviving texts date from 1110, when Henry and Robert renewed their agreement on similar terms, though with notably different guarantees; 1163, when the parties were Henry II of England (1154–89) and Thierry of Flanders (1128–68), whose agreement also drew heavily on the text of the 1101 document; and 1197, when it was Richard I of England (1189–99) and Baldwin IX of Flanders (1195–1206).[78] References in other sources indicate that treaties may have been in effect at various points during the reigns of the first five post-Conquest kings of England.[79] Despite all of these agreements, however, Flemish policy toward England ranged from neutrality to outright hostility, depending on the relationship between England and Normandy at any given moment. The only hint that these treaties were ever invoked positively—that the count of Flanders lent military support to the king of England—comes in a tangential passage of a grant of Robert II to the abbey of Hesdin, probably in 1094 during William Rufus's campaign against Robert Curthose in Normandy.[80] As noted, however, the negative clauses, prohibiting counts of Flanders from aiding and harbouring enemies of the English, were probably more important and may have influenced Flemish actions at key moments: Robert II did not intervene, for example, during Henry's Norman campaigns of 1105–6.[81] It is clear that the Flemish counts actively violated the terms of the treaty on a number of occasions, normally by aiding the king of France in operations against England or Normandy. But without records of payment it is impossible to know if the

[76] Nip, 'Political Relations', 159–60.

[77] Nip, 'Political Relations', 161; Frank Barlow, *William Rufus* (Berkeley, 1983), 325–6.

[78] London, National Archives, E 30/1, 3; *Diplomatic Documents*, 5–14, 18–20 (nos. 2, 3, 7); see below, p. 155, n. 103.

[79] William of Malmesbury, *Gesta regum Anglorum*, 5.403 (OMT 1:728–30); Eadmer, *Historia novorum in Anglia* (RS 81:39); *Liber monasterii de Hyda* (RS 45:320); Orderic Vitalis, *Historia ecclesiastica*, 12.45 (OMT 6:378); Galbert of Bruges, *De multro*, 122 (CCCM 131:169); Roger of Howden, *Gesta Henrici II et Ricardi I* (RS 49.1:246–7). Lyon, *From Fief to Indenture*, 35 and n. 89, lists references in the Pipe Rolls. See generally, Nip, 'Political Relations'.

[80] *Actes des comtes de Flandre*, 58–9 (no. 18); *Calendar of Documents Preserved in France*, 481 (no. 1325).

[81] Hollister, *Henry I*, 135.

agreement was in fact in force in any given year. The *effectiveness* of the guarantee clauses is thus outside the realm of investigation. This does not, however, diminish the interest of their content.

The guarantee clauses of the 1101 treaty are remarkable for their detail. The few texts of early medieval treaties that have survived—and it is probably the case that few were written down—do not have particularly complex guarantee clauses. The Treaty of Andelot of 587, for example, simply states that the violator of the agreement forfeits all benefits granted to him by the agreement, while the treaties among the Carolingians were fortified principally by oaths and maledictions. The Anglo-Saxon examples have been transmitted in the form of law codes rather than diplomas. Perhaps for that very reason, guarantees are not addressed: a sanction clause was a natural part of a diploma, but not of a legal text.[82] As we move into the eleventh century, detailed agreements do start to appear: a treaty from *c.*1020 between the counts of Barcelona and Urgell, in Catalonia, whose intricate guarantee clauses call for pledges of real property, various layers of personal sureties, and settlement of disputes through judicial battle, is a notable example.[83] But if the 1101 treaty is not the first of its kind in Europe, it is among the first.

The treaty introduces guarantors called 'hostages' (*obsides*).[84] Following the end of the substantive clauses addressing Robert's obligations we read that 'concerning the maintenance of these agreements' ('de istis conventionibus atendendis'), Robert has granted to Henry twelve hostages, each for 100 marks. The agreement goes on to describe their responsibilities in detail.[85] There follow the substantive clauses concerning Henry's obligations, and a similar list of hostages granted by Henry; eleven are named, the first for 200 marks, the remaining ten for 100 marks. Rather than detail the responsibilities of these hostages, the agreement simply states that they are identical to those of the Flemish hostages. A final clause binds the hostages on both sides not to flee a summons to fulfil their responsibilities and to protect the summoners (*summonitores*) from harm.[86]

If the treaty is violated by the count, the function of the hostage-guarantors develops in three stages. First they have 120 days to persuade their lord to make amends. If they fail, a monetary fine of 1,200 marks comes into effect; each of the guarantors is to pay his share of the fine, again within 120 days. If he fails to do so, he is to present himself for confinement in the Tower of London or another suitable place; the king is not to demand from guarantors thus confined more than

[82] Gregory of Tours, *Historiae*, 9.20 (MGH SrM 1.1:434–9); *Alfred and Guthrum, Edward and Guthrum, II Æthelred, Dunsæte* (ed. Liebermann, 1:126–8, 128–35, 220–7, 374–9).

[83] *Liber feudorum maior*, 1:158–64 (no. 157); Kosto, *Making Agreements*, 26–9.

[84] Emily Zack Tabuteau, *Transfers of Property in Eleventh-Century Norman Law* (Chapel Hill, 1988), 165, 363 (n. 192); also 361 (n. 176).

[85] If Robert is not able to accompany the knights, six of the hostages are to do so, or at least two of them along with four other barons of the count who will be of equal use to the king; this is not properly part of the gurarantee.

[86] There does not seem to be any significance to Robert fitz Hamon's higher value. Henry only presented eleven hostages; for the value of the fine to be equal, one of them would have to be for 200 marks. In the 1110 agreement, Henry also offered one fewer hostage, suggesting that the disparity of interest is in numbers rather than in value: a king could not be seen to participate in such an act with the count on precisely equal terms.

their designated share. The agreement also stipulates that if one of the guarantors dies, breaks fealty with Robert, or leaves his land, he is to be replaced with one of equal value upon demand. If money sent by the guarantors is lost en route in England, the guarantors will be freed; if the money is lost at sea, the guarantors are given an extra forty days to replace it. While Henry's hostages are said to be subject to the same terms, the agreement does not state where they would be held. These are recognizably conditional hostages of the sort found in the eleventh-century agreements from Catalonia and Languedoc examined above.

As in those earlier cases, the guarantors here are *not* assuming the responsibility of their lord to fulfil the terms of the treaty. If Robert fails to provide the required number of knights, it is not up to the guarantors to do so. Given that Henry's obligations were limited to payment of 500 marks, we might interpret the 1,200 marks for which the guarantors were responsible as a fulfilment of his obligations. It is more likely, however, that this was conceived of as a fine.[87] What the guarantors *are* doing may be broken down into three elements: active persuasion of the principal; passive persuasion, brought about by their potential and possibly their actual detention; and involvement in the payment of a fine. Active persuasion is clear: they are supposed to attempt to convince the principal to amend the violation of the treaty. Passive persuasion is more complex: the idea here is that the principal will be reluctant to violate the terms of the treaty knowing that this might lead to the confinement of his men. Partly this is a question of honour: a lord—a good lord, anyway—would feel an obligation to prevent the detention of his men. It is also a question of power: the lord would be reluctant to be deprived of individuals who were in a strong position to lend him military support. The involvement of the guarantors in the payment of a fine is more ambiguous, as it may be that they are not the ultimate source of payment; the second 120 days would allow them time to pressure the lord into paying, and any hostage who did pay in the first instance would have a strong moral claim to reimbursement by his lord. In legal terms, then, these guarantors conflate three distinct types of personal surety. In their responsibility to persuade the principal to amend a violation, they are influencing guarantors. In their implication in the payment of a fine, they are amending guarantors. And in their potential confinement, designed to pressure the lord into adherence to the treaty, they are hostages.[88]

If the fundamental responsibility of the hostages, then, was to influence, were they in a position to do so? The hostages for the count of Flanders certainly were: Robert III of Béthune; Baldric of Cohem; Robert II, castellan of Bruges; Froulf, castellan of Bergues; Amaury II of Ninove, the constable; Alard II of Eine and Oudenburg, butler; Roger II, castellan of Lille; Osto of Thérouanne, butler; Baldwin, castellan of Saint-Omer; Hugo III Havet of Aubigny-en-Artois; Gerard, castellan of Cassel; and Theinard, castellan of Bourbourg.[89] This group included four

---

[87] See Tabuteau, *Transfers*, 363 n. 192.

[88] For these categories, see above, p. 7.

[89] Ernest Warlop, *The Flemish Nobility before 1300*, 2 vols. in 4 parts (Kortrijk, 1975–6), 1:169–70, 2:623, 653, 664, 702, 721–2, 730, 781, 940, 1017, 1111, 1149 (nos. 15.5, 20.7, 21.3, 31.1, 40.5, 45.5, 64.3, 130.4, 155.4, 192.5, 205.5).

peers of Flanders (the lords of Béthune, Eine, Lille, and Aubigny), six castellans (Bruges, Bergues, Lille, Saint-Omer, Cassel, and Bourbourg), and three current or future comital officers (the constable and two butlers).[90] The only figure who does not fall into one of these categories is Baldric of Cohem, who is not attested elsewhere. The castellans, but also the peers, constituted the military infrastructure of the county. In addition to being capable of leading the comital host in his absence (as required by the terms of the treaty[91]), therefore, their absence would be most sorely felt. They were, too, most likely to be in a position to contribute to the fine.

Henry's hostages were not as thoroughly prominent. They included three leading members of the great magnate families (Gilbert fitz Richard of Clare; Stephen of Richmond, 'count of Brittany'; Arnulf of Montgomery, earl of Pembroke) and two major *curiales* (Robert fitz Hamon and Hamo the Steward)—enough to convince the count of Flanders that pressure would be brought to bear on the king and that, if necessary, the 1,200 mark fine could be covered. The rest of the group, however, were relatively insignificant players: William of Courcy appears occasionally as a royal steward, but much less frequently than Hamo; Miles Crispin, Roger de Nonant, Hugh Maminot, Hugh de Beauchamp, and Mannassel Arsic were neither major landowners nor prominent figures in Henry's (or his predecessor William II's) court.[92] They appear to have been added to the list simply because they were current members of the king's entourage: Hugh Maminot, Hugh de Beauchamp, Roger de Nonant, and Miles Crispin appear together, along with Robert fitz Hamon and Hamo (the Steward), as subscribers on a confirmation charter to Tewkesbury Abbey in October 1100.[93] Their absence in the case of hostageship would only have put a small dent in Henry's military capabilities. Here the lists of hostages reveal the power differential between the two rulers; Henry did not have to be seen to risk as much to gain what he wanted.

Hostages were, as we have seen, a common feature of early medieval treaties, but the 1101 Anglo-Flemish treaty is the first major international agreement to employ *conditional* hostages. The 1110 treaty, although it copied much of the text of the 1101 document, turned away from this particular guarantee mechanism.[94] The guarantors there were still called 'hostages' (*obsides*), but they had very different functions. The ultimate incentive to keep to the agreement has changed from a monetary fine to the arbitration of a designated authority. If Count Robert departs

---

[90] Warlop, *Flemish Nobility*, 1:450 n. 171.

[91] Above, p. 151, n. 85.

[92] C. Warren Hollister, 'Magnates and "Curiales" in Early Norman England', *Viator*, 4 (1973), 115–22; Charlotte A. Newman, *The Anglo-Norman Nobility in the Reign of Henry I: The Second Generation* (Philadelphia, 1988); Judith A. Green, *The Aristocracy of Norman England* (Cambridge, 1997); Hollister, *Henry I*.

[93] *Regesta regum Anglo-Normannorum*, 2:3 (no. 497). Additional citations for the minor figures in acts of William II and Henry I: Roger de Nonant, nos. 319, 377, 398, 486, 544, 626, 633, 735a; Hugh Maminot, nos. 1077, 1990; Manassell Arsic, nos. 639, 944, 950; William of Courcy, nos. 544, 699, 700, 702, 813, 816, 828, 958–9, 966–7, 970, 1000; Miles Crispin, nos. 313, 454, 455, 496, 674n, 813; Hugh de Beauchamp, nos. 370, 419, 446, 477, 659.

[94] London, National Archives, E 30/1; *Diplomatic Documents*, 5–8 (no. 2).

from the terms of the treaty, Henry may summon him to Boulogne where it will be judged by Count Eustace which of the two has broken the agreement. The violator will have forty days to make amends; if he does not, he will forfeit the agreement, and the other party will be freed from his commitments. If Eustace of Boulogne is dead or has lost favour with the king, the judgment will take place at Eu. If Robert summons Henry, the judgment will take place at Dover. The guarantors here are, once again, required actively to persuade their lord to abide by the treaty, but they do not risk detention. They simply promise to testify against their lord at the arbitration.

The 1163 treaty between Henry II and Thierry returned for its guarantee clauses not to the 1110 document, but to its 1101 predecessor, calling for conditional hostages. If we had only the 1163 text, we might argue that this was a simple case of archaism: the scribe copied from the older rather than the more recent text terms that were essentially meaningless. Later in the century, however, conditional hostages are still there. In 1166, the count of Nevers named four *obsides* who promised to serve as hostages at Sens if he broke his promises to the count of Blois.[95] In 1173 as part of a proposed marriage alliance with Henry II, some fifty of the men of Count Humbert of Maurienne promised to 'hand themselves over as hostages to the lord king in his land, wherever he wishes, and remain in his captivity' in case of default.[96] The Treaty of Sahagún of 1170 saw Alfonso VIII of Castile and Alfons I of Barcelona name three nobles each as *obsides* who were to enter into custody if the terms were not kept.[97] The guarantees of the agreement of 1179 by which the imperial chancellor was freed from captivity at the hands of Conrad of Montferrat similarly saw powerful lords on both sides promising to enter into custody.[98]

It was Richard I of England, Baldwin IX of Flanders, and Philip II Augustus of France (1180–1223) who made such clauses standard in the last decade of the twelfth century. Richard and Tancred of Sicily named sureties for their agreement of 1190 who swore an oath to place themselves in the custody of the other party if their lord should violate the treaty.[99] As part of the Treaty of Messina in 1191, Philip named *fideiussores et obsides* who promised, in case of default, to deliver themselves and their fiefs into the hands of Richard.[100] In 1193, with Richard in captivity, royal agents wrote up a treaty with Philip in which four named lords as well as others to be designated by Philip were to swear to enter into royal custody

[95] Hugh of Poitiers, *Chronicon*, 4.2659–97 (CCCM 42:580–1).

[96] *Recueil... Henri II*, 2:1–4 (no. 455) [*Foedera*, 1.1:28–9]: 'reddent se obsides domino regi in terra sua, ubicunque voluerit, et tamdiu in sua captione morabuntur'. See Christopher Holdsworth, 'Peacemaking in the Twelfth Century', *Anglo-Norman Studies*, 19 (1996), 13.

[97] Julio González, *El Reino de Castilla en la época de Alfonso VIII*, 3 vols. (Madrid, 1960), 2:239–41 (no. 139).

[98] *Mainzer Urkundenbuch*, 2.2:698–702 (no. 433); cf. Roger of Howden, *Gesta Henrici II et Ricardi I* (RS 49.1:243).

[99] Roger of Howden, *Chronica* (RS 51.3:61–5); Roger of Howden, *Gesta Henrici II et Ricardi I* (RS 49.2:133–6): 'ego ponam me in captione... ponent se in captione'.

[100] *Diplomatic Documents*, 14–16 (no. 5) [*Recueil... Philippe Auguste*, 1:464–6 (no. 376); *Foedera*, 1.1:54].

in Paris in case of violation.[101] In 1196, Baldwin similarly promised Philip to force a total of 100 men, to be chosen by the French from three different territories, to swear to submit themselves into custody in Paris should the count break his word.[102] In a treaty of 1197 between Richard and Baldwin, fifty-six men of the king and thirty-four men of the count swore to deliver themselves for detention within one month in case of a violation of the agreement by their lord.[103] In 1198, Philip received promises of hostages from the counts of Boulogne and Champagne, with interesting provisions: the hostages for the count of Champagne were permitted to leave their place of detention on parole during the day, as long as they returned at night; the hostage for the count of Boulogne was to submit himself immediately if the violation were clear, but otherwise only after a judgment in the royal court.[104] In the very next year, the count of Boulogne switched sides and entered into an agreement with the new English king, John (1199–1216); both parties stated that their guarantors would enter into custody in case of default.[105] Rigord suggests that hostages were on the table at the discussions leading to the five-year truce between Richard and Philip in 1199, but that Richard avoided their inclusion by deception.[106] In 1200 at Le Goulet, John and Philip offered their vassals as conditional hostages (*ostagii*).[107]

Even from before 1163, there are agreements concerning the internal political affairs of the English kingdom that resort to the use of conditional hostages, particularly from the reign of Stephen (1135–54). The clearest example is the agreement from the early 1140s between Robert of Gloucester and Miles of Hereford. Each offered *obsides per fidem et per sacramenta* who, if their principal violated the treaty, were first to demand that he make amends and then, if he had not done so within forty days, hand themselves over to the other earl 'either to retain them in his service until he releases them, or punish them with a lawful ransom, in such a way that they not lose any land'. This agreement also includes a true hostage: Miles's son, Mahel.[108]

Why did the 1110 Anglo-Flemish agreement reject the novelty of the conditional hostage to try something different? An obvious solution is that the terms did

---

[101] Roger of Howden, *Chronica* (RS 51.3:217–20).

[102] *Die Register Innocenz' III.*, 1:194–7 (no. 1.130) [Potthast 153].

[103] *Diplomatic Documents*, 18–20 (no. 7); cf. Ralph of Diceto, *Ymagines historiarum* (RS 68.2:152–3). These are perhaps the *obsides* referred to by the chroniclers: William of Newburgh, *Historia rerum Anglicarum*, 5.32 (RS 82.2:496); Roger of Wendover, *Flores historiarum*, s.a. (RS 84.1:270); Roger of Howden, *Chronica* (RS 51.4:20).

[104] *Recueil...Philippe Auguste*, 2:128–30 (no. 580–1); Henri Malo, *Un grand feudataire: Renaud de Dammartin et la coalition de Bouvines: Contribution a l'étude du règne de Philippe-Auguste* (Paris, 1898), 258–9 (nos. 35–6); *Documents relatifs au comté de Champagne*, 1:467–8 (ap. 3, nos. 3–4).

[105] Malo, *Dammartin*, 259–60 (no. 37).

[106] Rigord, *Gesta Philippi Augusti*, 125 (SHF 1:144).

[107] *Diplomatic Documents*, 20–3 (no. 9) [*Recueil...Philippe Auguste*, 2:178–85 (no. 633); *Foedera*, 1.1:79–80].

[108] R. H. C. Davis, 'Treaty between William Earl of Gloucester and Roger Earl of Hereford', in *A Medieval Miscellany for Doris May Stenton* (London, 1962), 145–6 (no. 2): 'uel ad illos retinendum in suo seruitio donec illos quietos clamaret, uel ad illos ponendum ad legalem redempcionem ita ne terram perderet'. Renewal of 1147x50 is 144–5 (no. 1).

not work, but, as I have argued, the effectiveness of the treaties is not susceptible to proof—or even convincing argument—one way or the other. Even if we could show that the 1110 agreement turned away from conditional hostages because of the failure of the 1101 pact, we would then need to explain why the 1163 agreement returned to that institution as a means of guarantee. We may speculate, however, that the 1110 agreement turned to a different model not because of the failure of the older one, but because of the existence of plausible alternatives. Just as the 1101 agreement is one of the earliest examples of the use of the conditional hostage in an international treaty, the 1110 agreement represents one of the earliest to include an arbitration clause, a device that remained common in such pacts. To cite just two examples, arbitration commissions were established by treaties between the counts of Flanders and Holland in 1167, and between Louis VII of France (1137–80) and Henry II in 1180.[109] We can also identify other forms of guarantee, some closely tied to conditional hostageship. The conditional hostages of the Treaty of Messina promised to turn themselves over along with their lands, but more powerful lords, who did not wish to risk detention, might simply offer to hold their lands from the wronged party. Henry, count of Champagne did this, as a guarantee that Louis VII would adhere to the terms of an agreement that the count had negotiated in Louis's name. In the renewal of the Hereford–Gloucester treaty, entered into between the sons of the original parties between 1147 and 1150, the guarantors (*obsides*) did not promise to submit to detention, but simply to withdraw service from their lords. All of these variations were proposed in a world, as seen in Chapter 4, where true hostages were still common in these sorts of high-level political interactions.

These various guarantees drew on ties of fidelity between lords and their men, threatening loss of money, revenue, military support, legal support, moral support, and honour. With this as a common denominator, negotiators and drafters of diplomatic agreements experimented in the course of the twelfth century with a variety of guarantee mechanisms, of which conditional hostageship was only one. This experimentation was encouraged and made possible by the fact that more and more agreements of this sort were being put to parchment, which allowed for the construction of (and lasting memory of) more complex conditions. Two points deserve note. The first is that while the evidence disproves the theory of the growth of the conditional hostage out of international agreements, we see here—if slightly later—the same sort of personal surety mechanisms seen in eleventh-century documents from Catalonia and Languedoc. The second is that, again, even at the highest levels of international politics, monetary incentives were at work. When it came to guarantees, the world of fiefs and vassals was also a world of pounds and marks.

[109] *De oorkonden der graven van Vlaanderen*, 2.1:424–7 (no. 269); *Recueil... Henri II*, 2:128–9 (no. 550). Arbitration: Ganshof, *Middle Ages*, 152–3; Michel de Taube, 'Les origines de l'arbitrage international: Antiquité et Moyen Âge', *Recueil des cours* (Académie de droit international), 42 (1932), 1–115; Siegried Frey, *Das öffentlich-rechtliche Schiedsgericht in Oberitalien im XII. und XIII. Jahrhundert: Beitrag zur Geschichte völkerrechtlicher Institutionen* (Lucerne, 1928).

HOSTAGES FOR MONETARY DEBTS

Ultimately the conditional hostage did not win out as the preferred guarantee mechanism in international treaties or even regional political agreements; arbitration was more successful, and, as we have seen, true hostages continued to be used in certain situations. Conditional hostages do still appear in such agreements, however, particularly where financial terms such as ransoms are involved.[110] The standard narrative of the *Einlager* opposes a feudal to a monetary model with a development from the former to the latter as the institution spread from the noble context of its origin to the mercantile context of the later Middle Ages. We have seen that even in the earliest evidence and at the highest social levels, a monetary *incentive* was often integrated into conditional hostageship. It is also possible to show, however, that from early on, and at the highest social levels, money was not just an incentive, but also an *object* of agreements. Just as military needs drove the development of finance in the later Middle Ages, so too in the twelfth century the scale of aristocratic expenditure could call forth new mechanisms. And there was not even a need to borrow from merchant practices; the model of castle-holding agreements was ready at hand.

Once again, the rich meridional sources clarify the story, particularly those concerning the operations of the house of Barcelona in its Provençal holdings in the second half of the twelfth century. Conditional hostages to guarantee control of castles, as seen in the eleventh-century documents discussed above, were still known, as was the overlap of hostages and paying guarantors. Consider, for example, settlements between the counts of Barcelona/Provence and the Baux family during the latter's revolt between 1145 and 1162, which centred principally on the disposition of the castle of Trinquetaille.[111] The first two major settlements between the parties each involved a grant of conditional hostages. In 1150, over thirty partisans of the Baux swore that if the Baux in any way infringed upon the agreement, and in particular if Hugh de Baux refused to hand over the castle of Trinquetaille, they would within ten days appear wherever they were ordered and remain there until the Baux made amends.[112] In 1156, to secure a similar submission, the guarantee mechanisms were increased. Thirty-eight supporters of the Baux swore that if the agreement were violated and the castle not returned, they would enter into hostageship (*ostaticum*) on the island of Vallabrègues, not to depart until the castle was turned over. If the Baux failed to do so, some of the hostages were to pay fines: four promised 10,000 s. apiece, and another fourteen promised 1,000 s.

---

[110] e.g. the ransom treaty of René of Anjou involved conditional hostages for 400,000 *écus*: Lecoy, *René*, 2:224–33 (no. 10). The undertaking of the twenty-two guarantors is BnF, Coll. Lorraine 238, no. 31. See also above, p. 8, n. 23 (a. 1295), and pp. 121–2.

[111] Edwin Smyrl, 'La famille des Baux', *Cahiers du Centre d'études des sociétés méditerranéennes*, 2 (1968), 31–44; Jean-Pierre Poly, *La Provence et la société féodale: Contribution à l'étude des structures dites féodales dans le Midi* (Paris, 1976), 336–40.

[112] Smyrl, 'Baux', 85 (no. 12), cf. 39; Gérard Giordanengo, *Le droit féodal dans les pays de droit écrit: L'exemple de la Provence et du Dauphiné, XIIe–début XIVe siècle* (Rome, 1988), 58.

apiece. Eight *fideiussores* pledged 2,500 s. apiece to guarantee performance by the hostages.[113]

At the same time that Ramon Berenguer IV (1131–62) was forcing the Baux to get their allies to stand surety as conditional hostages, however, he was pressuring his own allies to stand surety for him, to secure the loans he required to carry out his trans-Pyrenean adventures.[114] In January 1156, he recognized the first of what would prove to be a long series of debts to the Montpellier financier Guilhem Leteric: 4,700 *morabetins*, due at Easter. Ten of the count's barons swore that, if the count failed to pay the debt by Easter, they would deliver themselves to Montpellier as hostages (*per hostaticum*), to remain there until the debt was paid. Two others subscribed as *manulevatores et persolutores atque pacgatores*—the last two terms suggesting that they, and they alone, were promising to pay the debt if the hostage-guarantees failed to work.[115] The hostages are still from the upper aristocracy: the list begins with the seneschal, Guillem Ramon II,[116] and includes representatives of many of the great castellan families (Castellvell, Llers, Monells, etc.). Furthermore, the procedures are similar to those seen in the guarantees for castle holding. Here we see, however, the use of these means of guarantee for a purely monetary debt.

Subsequent new loans and consolidations of old loans over the next quarter-century exhibit similar guarantee mechanisms. In 1159, the count recognized a second debt to Guilhem Mainard, another Provençal financier: 2,500 *morabetins* in addition to the 3,200 he had incurred to the same creditor at an earlier date. The count pledged revenues from the comital domain according to a specific schedule, but if the payments were not made, seven hostages (*ostatici*) were to deliver themselves into custody, just as they had agreed to do to guarantee the earlier debt.[117] The hostages included some of the same individuals named in the debt to Guilhem Leteric in 1156. By 1160, the total owed to Guilhem Leteric had risen to 6,700 *morabetins*, and ten hostages (*ostaticos et tenedors*)—five of whom were named in 1156—were promising to enter into custody immediately, remaining there until the debt was paid or paying it themselves; a long list of *manlevatores* promised to pay, but without presenting themselves for confinement.[118] In February 1162, the count recognized yet another debt to Guilhem Leteric, this time of 6,000 *morabetins*, and added additional guarantors to those named in 1160. Three very high-ranking figures—Trencavel, viscount of Béziers; Ermessenda, viscountess of Narbonne; and Guilhem of Montpellier—are named as *obsides*, but only the three other hostages (*obsides*) named undertake to present themselves at Montpellier in

---

[113] Smyrl, 'Baux', 94–7 (no. 17.1–3).

[114] *Fiscal Accounts*, 1:23–86.

[115] ACA, Ramon Berenguer IV 296 [*Colección de documentos*, 4:228–30 (no. 86)].

[116] John Shideler, *A Medieval Catalan Noble Family: The Montcadas, 1000–1230* (Berkeley, 1983), 104–5.

[117] ACA, Ramon Berenguer, apéndix 6 [*Fiscal Accounts*, 2:47–9 (no. 8); *Colección de documentos*, 4:277–9 (no. 111)].

[118] ACA, Ramon Berenguer, apéndix 8, sense data 15 [*Colección de documentos*, 4:300–4, 357–60 (nos. 121, 149)].

case of default: again, these are conditional hostages. The count also pledged specific revenues toward payment of the debt; those revenues in turn were backed by the guarantees of three bishops, two abbots, the seneschal, and others.[119]

Ramon Berenguer IV's son, Alfons I (1162–96), continued these dealings with the financiers of Montpellier, and his barons, too, regularly stood as conditional hostages for his undertakings. In 1166, Guilhem of Montpellier, acting as royal procurator, acknowledged a debt of 2,500 *morabetins* to Guilhem Leteric; among other guarantees, the bishops of Vic, Barcelona, and Zaragoza promised to pay the debt or to deliver themselves on demand as hostages in Montpellier.[120] An account of 1171 reveals that Alfons owed to Guilhem of Montpellier 24,000 *morabetins*; Alfons offered sixteen additional hostages, who were to deliver themselves to Perpignan on Guilhem's demand, whence they were not allowed to depart without permission until the debt was paid.[121] Finally, an undated document notes a debt of Alfons to Guilhem Leteric of 22,600 s., in addition to 1,600 *morabetins* owed previously and the 6,000 *morabetins* debt—as yet unpaid—of his father (presumably the debt of 1162). Guilhem Leteric may have been losing patience by this point, as Alfons promised that he would head straight back to Barcelona from Montpellier and not leave there until the debt was paid. In addition, Gui Guerreiat, uncle(?) of the lord of Montpellier, promised to deliver to Montpellier seven hostages, including the king's brother and the sons of six major barons, if the debt were not paid on time; Gui himself would serve as a hostage at Villeneuve; and nine additional barons, including the count of Foix, promised to appear at Montpellier, one of whom was to serve as Guilhem's bodyguard during his comings and goings.[122] As the debts increased, so too did the status of the individuals who had to promise to enter into custody as hostages.

The use of hostages by the counts of Barcelona in their financial dealings was not limited to the securing of loans from Montpellier. Around 1170, Alfons I entered into a complex agreement with the merchant Trepelezinus to finance a voyage to Constantinople, perhaps related to an embassy proposing a marriage alliance. Alfons promised that if Trepelezinus were not paid his due by Christmas, six barons, including Ramon de Montcada, were to serve as hostages ('tenebunt ostaticum')

---

[119] ACA, Ramon Berenguer, apéndix 9, apéndix 9 duplicat [*Fiscal Accounts*, 2:58–63 (no. 13); *Colección de documentos*, 4:305–8 (no. 122)]. The list of hostages appended to apéndix 9 duplicat is identical to the lists in apéndix 8 and sense data 15; the names of the *manulevatores* and other guarantors are the same, although their order of appearance and function is different.

[120] ACA, Alfons I 48. Cf. 49 (3,000 *morabetins* owed by Guerau de Iorba), 55 (1,500 *morabetins* owed by Alfons).

[121] ACA, Alfons I 105 [*Fiscal Accounts*, 2:78–81 (no. 23)]; twenty hostages are promised, but only sixteen are named.

[122] ACA, Alfons I, extrainventari 3627 [*Alfonso II... Documentos*, 863–5 (ap.[6]61). In 1172, Guilhem (VII?) of Montpellier had recognized a debt to Guilhem Leteric of 5,000 s. [ACA, Alfons I 124]; in 1173, 1174, and 1176, Guilhem VIII of Montpellier acted as a (paying) guarantor and then a co-debtor for debts of 6,000 s., and then 14,100 s., and then 22,100 s., owed by his uncle to Guilhem Leteric [ACA, Alfons I 162, 171, 207, 207 duplicat]. These are further indications of the complex network of debt that had developed around Guilhem Leteric. No hostages are involved in these transactions.

at Marseille until the debt was fulfilled.[123] The 1153 treaty by which the Genoese sold to Ramon Berenguer IV their rights in Tortosa called on the count to provide five hostages, from among the sons of barons from eight different lineages, until the total amount of the purchase was paid.[124] And, as seen in the earliest cases discussed, as in the case of hostages generally, the use of conditional hostages appears from early on for transactions well below the level of royal finance.[125] By the third quarter of the twelfth century, then, the conditional hostage for a monetary debt was an established western Mediterranean institution.

Promises of conditional hostageship were, of course, contractual tactics. Were the terms ever enforced? The transactions of the house of Barcelona, for example, reflect a complex process of loan, partial repayment, consolidation, and refinancing; obviously, simple payment of debts on schedule was a rarity. Did the hostages named to guarantee adherence to schedule ever deliver themselves as required? There are indications that they did. The account of 1171 mentioned above notes that the money owed is 'in addition to the debt of the Aragonese hostages who are at Montpellier'.[126] This phrase shows that hostages were in custody to pressure payment of a previous debt to Guilhem VII. This same account reveals another aspect of the institution, namely that the expenses of the upkeep of the hostages were being charged to Alfons.[127] Later, in 1173, in an account with the merchants of Montpellier, he noted that he owed them for the 'expense and transport of hostages'.[128]

In these years, then, we see not only some of the earliest uses of the conditional hostage, and the earliest uses of the conditional hostage for monetary debts, but also the origin of the custom that would develop into the true force behind the late medieval *Einlager*: a mechanism that made the basis of a guarantee mediated through physical control of an individual not honour, but money.

A disjunction between normative texts and documents of practice is characteristic of early medieval legal history—in Mediterranean Europe, at least, before the return in tandem of the notariate and Roman law. It is not surprising, therefore, that the few mentions of hostageship that have been identified in twelfth-century municipal codes do not correspond to the conditional hostages whose origin I have

---

[123] ACA, Alfons I, extrainventari 2621 [*Alfonso II... Documentos*, 871–2 (ap. 63)]. See Kosto, *Making Agreements*, 131, and works cited there, now with Maria Teresa Ferrer i Mallol and Daniel Durán i Duelt, 'Una ambaixada catalana a Constantinoble i el matrimoni de la princesa Eudòxia', *Anuario de estudios medievales*, 30 (2000), 963–78.

[124] ACA, Ramon Berenguer IV 266 quadruplicat, 266 quintuplicat [*Colección de documentos*, 4:214–16 (no. 78.2)]; see Kosto, *Making Agreements*, 132. The exact status of the hostages is not clear.

[125] Above, pp. 124–5; Giraud, *Essai historique*, 48 (no. 158) (a. 1096x1117, yearly render amounting to 24 s. plus grain); *Cartulaire de Béziers (Livre noir)*, 199 (no. 146) (a. 1134, 50 s.).

[126] ACA, Alfons I 105 [*Fiscal Accounts*, 2:79 (no. 23)]: 'excepto debito hostaticorum Aragonensium qui sunt apud Montem pessulanum'.

[127] Similarly, ACA, Ramon Berenguer IV 297, 316 [*Colección de documentos*, 4:230–2, 247–9 (nos. 87, 96)]. Cf. above, p. 37.

[128] ACA, Alfons I 140 [*Fiscal Accounts*, 2:83 (no. 25)]: 'expensam et conductam hostaticorum'. Later examples of enforcement: *Foedera*, 1.2:513–14, 555 (a. 1274); *GCA* 329–31 (a. 1365). *GCA* 456–67 describes a suit against conditional hostages who failed to appear.

traced in this chapter.[129] By the thirteenth century, however, legislation was widespread throughout Europe, with not only towns but everyone from the Cistercian General Chapter to the Hapsburg emperor trying to control the institution, and collections of customs such as that of Philippe de Beaumanoir and the *Sachsenspiegel* taking note.[130] Even when we cannot point to formal legislation, the existence of norms is evident: an agreement brokered by the abbots of Sankt-Gallen and Reichenau in 1259, for example, refers to the 'custom of the land concerning hostageship observed to this point'.[131] Conditional hostageship died out quickly in some regions and more slowly in others, lasting into the nineteenth century in some parts of Switzerland. In its evolved form, it was very different from true hostageship as practised in the later Middle Ages.[132] But in the eleventh and twelfth centuries, the development of true and conditional hostageship went hand-in-hand.

This is a pivotal moment in the history of guarantees in medieval Europe. The conditional hostage—I will hand over a body *if* the agreement fails—replaces in certain situations the earlier use of true hostages, hostages physically handed over at the conclusion of an agreement. The question, then, is why in some cases parties in the eleventh and twelfth centuries have essentially become more trusting of their adversaries, willing—in crude terms—to let them hold on to the collateral that they have pledged. There are a number of obvious directions in which one might look: increasing confidence in the ability of some outside party to enforce the agreement, for example, although it is precisely in international agreements that there is no such outside party (and the eleventh century, at least, is hardly known for its political stability); or the fact agreements of this type are now being written down, which allows for a greater complexity of terms; or the fact that the clerks who were doing the writing at this time were starting to think in new ways about the law.[133] Most important may be what we saw in the last chapter, namely the

---

[129] Two passages from the municipal statutes of Arles of the late twelfth century indicate that it is the debtor who is subject to *hostagia*—a form of *Selbstbürgschaft* rather than the form of hostageship under consideration here: Le Fort, 'L'otage', 412 n. 9; Charles Giraud, *Essai sur l'histoire du droit français au Moyen Âge*, 2 vols. (Paris, 1846), 2:189–90, 227–8. The same is true of three passages from a collection of statutes concerning Aix (a. 1234x45), although one of these does also allow for the possibility of the *fideiussor* serving as a hostage: *Recueil... Provence*, 2:477–8, 481; cf. 339 (Raimond Bérenger V, no. 389, art. 10, 22–3; cf. no. 250, art. 7–8) [Giraud, *Essai*, 2:20, 23–4]; similarly, *Statuto del comune di Perugia del 1279*, 481 (ed. Caprioli et al., 1:429). *HGL* 8:463–5 (no. 103), a consular decree of 1200 from Toulouse, seems to refer to true rather than conditional hostages. Iberian codes seem to refer only to true hostageship connected to ransoming of captives: above, p. 116; cf. *Siete Partidas*, 5.13.3 (ed. Ungut Alamano and Polo, s.p.). Systematic searches of meridional municipal codes and Iberian *fueros* would be useful. See also below, pp. 168–9, 214.

[130] MGH Const. 3:119–20 (no. 124); *Statuta capitulorum generalium ordinis Cisterciensis*, a. 1275, c. 10 (ed. Canivez, 3:141); Beaumanoir, *Coutumes de Beauvaisis*, 43.1341 (CTH 30:185); *Sachsenspiegel*, Landrecht, 2.11.3 (MGH Fontes iuris Germanici antiqui, ns 1.1:136).

[131] *Chartularium Sangallense*, 4:437–9 (no. 1609): 'consuetudinem terre super obstagiis hactenus observatam'. Similarly, *SP* 2:493 n. 24.

[132] See below, pp. 219–20.

[133] Susan Reynolds, 'The Emergence of Professional Law in the Long Twelfth Century', *Law and History Review*, 21 (2003), 347–66.

development of what Matthew Strickland has called a 'common currency of chivalric conduct' in the course of conflicts: the nascent laws of war.[134] Despite these
changes, however, it is worth reiterating that a shift from actual to conditional
hostages keeps the guarantee in the realm of personal surety. Despite the new
bureaucracies for which some of these agreements offer evidence, and despite the
increasing role of finance in government—particularly visible in the Anglo-Norman
and Aragonese realms—and despite the ultimate development in the *Einlager* of a
fully de-individualized form of personal surety, power still depended upon actual
or potential physical control of a person.

[134] Matthew Strickland, *War and Chivalry: The Conduct and Perception of War in England and
Normandy, 1066–1217* (Cambridge, 1996), 46.

6

The King's Ransom

The capture of the French king, John II, at Poitiers in 1356 was shocking, but comprehensible. In the fourteenth century, kings still led their armies in battle, at least on occasion, and on occasion they were killed or taken. John's voluntary return to England in 1363, however, confounded his advisors and chroniclers alike. He had been released in 1360 as part of the Treaty of Brétigny, against a promise of a ransom of 3,000,000 écus over a six-year period, 600,000 immediately, with the rest guaranteed by eighty-three hostages. Half of these were prominent nobles, including two of the king's sons, his brother, and his cousin; those who were already prisoners had their status changed by the treaty.[1] By 1363, the ransom payments were overdue, the hostages were clamouring for a release that should have come months earlier, and one of the hostages—the duke of Anjou, the king's second son—had violated his parole. Even if John's purpose was more to forestall the resumption of war than to remedy his son's unchivalrous conduct by re-entering English captivity, it was in large measure the fate of the hostages for his ransom that prompted his surprising voyage to England.[2]

John of France had distinguished company in the role of captured king ransomed against hostages. Hostages for ransom were not only a royal affair, but the best-known cases of hostages for ransom are royal, and they were some of the great events of the later Middle Ages: Baldwin, king of Jerusalem, in Palestine; Richard the Lionheart in Germany; Louis IX in Egypt; Charles of Salerno in Aragon; and John II of France, and David II and James I of Scotland in England. Because these episodes involve kings, they are remarkably well documented; they allow an unprecedented reconstruction of—admittedly exceptional—examples of hostageship.[3] Previous commentators have tended to focus on the captivity itself and the

---

[1] *Les grands traités de la Guerre de Cent Ans*, 2 (CTH 7:33–68). The clauses concerning the hostages are nos. 14–17 (pp. 47–52).

[2] For the chivalry interpretation, see e.g. Barbara W. Tuchman, *A Distant Mirror: The Calamitous Fourteenth Century* (New York, 1978), 213–14. Raymond Cazelles, *Société politique, noblesse et couronne sous Jean le Bon et Charles V* (Geneva, 1982), 447–8, observes that the safe conduct granted to John II on 10 December 1363 was not only for his coming to England, but also for his *return* to France, but this may have just been standard safe conduct formula. More suggestive is the fact that the safe conduct not only had a terminus (12 May 1364), but that it was later extended (to 13 April 1365); see *Foedera*, 3.2:718.

[3] Carl Pfaff, 'Der gefangene König', *Basler Zeitschrift für Geschichte und Altertumskunde*, 71 (1971), 9–35, is the only general study of the subject. René of Anjou, like Charles of Salerno, became king during his captivity; see above, p. 29. Other cases of captured kings involving hostages include: García Íñiguez of Navarre, a. 859 (A. El-Hajji, 'The Andalusian Diplomatic Relations with the Vikings

negotiations for release, rather than the aftermath. Meanwhile those who have investigated the aftermath tend to be most interested in the financial aspects, for the proverbial 'king's ransom' was often responsible for significant fiscal innovations in countries unfortunate enough to suffer its burdens.[4] The case of John of France is an exception in this regard, in part because of the parties involved, and in part because of the notoriety of the affair of the duke of Anjou. Already in the mid-eighteenth century, the editors of Rapin's *History of England* were tracing the fates of individual hostages, and the work of subsequent generations of historians has made this the best-studied episode of hostageship in the Middle Ages.[5] A brief survey of the case will serve to introduce the problems to be addressed in the present chapter.

The Brétigny treaty was the result of four years of negotiations aimed at the release of the king. The idea of a ransom guaranteed by hostages was already on the table in 1358, when a draft treaty was drawn up, and reappeared in the Treaty of London of 1359.[6] The treaties list the names of all of the noble hostages appointed at each stage of the negotiations. Those who ultimately served appear in a wide variety of later records, most as routine as obligatory letters and safe conducts, but some as curious as the pained correspondence between John's successor and a reluctant replacement hostage.[7] Because of the high status of many of the noble

during the Umayyad Period [138–366/755–796]', *Hespéris-Tamuda*, 8 [1967], 72; above, p. 115, n. 124); Louis IV of France, a. 945 (above, pp. 32, 34); William I of Scotland, a. 1174 (above, p. 17); Valdemar II of Denmark, a. 1223 (*Diplomatarium Danicum*, 1.6:21–38, 58–64, 148–52 [nos. 16, 17, 42, 109]); Maximilian I, then king of the Romans, a. 1488 (Molinet, *Chroniques*, 182–4 [ed. Buchon, 3:306–56]). James of Cyprus was a hostage-turned-prisoner in Genoa when he became king (Luis de Góngora Alcasar e Pempicileón, *Real grandeza de la serenissima República de Genova*, trans. Carolo Speroni [Genoa, 1669], 104; 'Nouvelles preuves de l'histoire de Chypre', 80–4 [no. 14]) and was released against the hostageship of his son, Janus (Machairas, *Chronikon Kyprou* [ed. Miller and Sathas], 343 [ἀμάχιν]; Amadi, *Chronique* [ed. Mas Latrie], 1:492 [*hostagio*]; cf. the text of the treaty, which makes no mention of this fact: Góngora Alcasar e Pempicileón, *Real grandeza*, 116–37); Janus in turn became king, was captured in 1426, and was ransomed, perhaps with a hostage (noted only by Sālih ibn Yahyā, *Histoire de Beyrouth*, ap. [ed. Cheiko, 358]). Hostages were proposed for the release of Louis XI at Peronne in 1468 (below, p. 200). Barisone of Arborea's status as both a king and a prisoner is ambiguous (above, p. 124). Benham, *Peacemaking*, addresses the cases of Valdemar II and Richard I, but at present the only detailed study of the former is C. Paludan-Müller, *Studier til Danmarks Historie i det 13de Aarhundrede*, vol. 1: *Underhandlingerne om Kong Valdemar den Andens Fangenskab. Grevskabet Nørrehalland* (Copenhagen, 1869).

[4] Nick Barratt, 'The English Revenue of Richard I', *English Historical Review*, 116 (2001), 635–56; John Bell Henneman, *Royal Taxation in Fourteenth-Century France: The Captivity and Ransom of John II, 1356–1370* (Philadelphia, 1976).

[5] Paul Rapin de Thoyras, *The History of England*, trans. N. Tindal, 3rd edn., 4 vols. in 5 (London, 1743–7), 1:429–41; Jonathan Sumption, *The Hundred Years War*, vol. 2: *Trial by Fire* (London, 1999), 496–500.

[6] R. Delachenal, *Histoire de Charles V*, 5 vols. (Paris, 1909–31), 2:402–11; *Les grands traités de la Guerre de Cent Ans*, 1 (CTH 7:1–32); John Le Patourel, 'The Treaty of Brétigny, 1360', *Transactions of the Royal Historical Society*, 5th ser., 10 (1960), 19–39; Clifford J. Rogers, 'The Anglo-French Peace Negotiations of 1354–1360 Reconsidered', in J. S. Bothwell, ed., *The Age of Edward III* (Rochester, NY, 2001), 193–213.

[7] *Foedera*, 3.1:487–3.2:864, *passim*; *Original Documents Relating to the Hostages of John*, 40–5; GCA 398–407; Juliette Turlan, 'Prisonniers et otages des pays de Loire pendant la Guerre de Cent Ans (1337–1369) d'après les registres du Parlement', *Mémoires de l'Academie des sciences et arts de Touraine*, 4 (1991), 23–32.

hostages, we know something of the conditions of their captivity: Froissart describes them as 'hunting and hawking freely' and travelling 'around the country visiting ladies and lords as they pleased'.[8] The hostages from the towns are anonymous in the treaties themselves, but many have left traces in other documents, both royal and municipal: not many names, but plentiful evidence of the measures undertaken to raise funds to support them.[9]

The availability of a series of detailed lists of hostages enables a fuller analysis of the political context of John's release. The hostages in the 1357 draft treaty are almost entirely members of the 'party of Navarre', at that point royal opponents. In fact, the draft shows five who were not members of that group replaced by five others who were. John, it has been argued, was trying to use the negotiations over hostages to get his internal enemies out of the country. On the 1360 list, under changed circumstances, two of the six reappeared. A geographical analysis of the lists yields different information about the political circumstances. Of the twenty towns that furnished hostages, all but Lyon and Toulouse were in the north, thirteen of them north of the Seine, and most associated with reformist tendencies in Paris. The hostage lists thus also reflect the greatly reduced scope of royal power at this juncture.[10]

The treaty itself ultimately collapsed. The ransom was supposed to be paid off completely by 1366, but half was still due in 1369 when war resumed and payments stopped entirely.[11] By that point, too, few of the noble hostages remained in England. Some died during the plague of 1361–2. Others purchased their freedom (without thereby reducing the king's ransom debt), followed in the footsteps of the duke of Anjou and violated their parole, or simply escaped.[12] Some of the hostages of the towns remained, although one report has many of them dying in a London plague of 1363.[13] John himself was long dead, having succumbed to illness soon after his arrival in England in 1364. As in many other cases from the medieval period, as simple guarantees John's hostages were failures.

The exceptionally rich documentation associated with the ransom of John II allows us to: (1) trace the evolution of the treaty, in which changes in the clauses

[8] Froissart 1.488 (6:56): 'Et li signeur aloient cachier et voler à leur volenté et yaus esbatre et deduire sus le pays et veoir les dames et les signeurs ensi comme il leur plaisoit'; cf. Orville, *La chronique du bon duc Loys de Bourbon* 1 (SHF 4–5); Sumption, *Hundred Years War*, 496.

[9] *Original Documents Relating to the Hostages of John*, 13 n., 52–5 (Lyon); *GCA* 407–32; *Recueil des monuments inédits de l'histoire du tiers état*, 1:614–19, 826–7 (nos. 248–9, 320) (Amiens); *Mandements et actes divers de Charles V*, 153–4, 155 (nos. 311, 315) (Douai); Henneman, *Royal Taxation*, 219 nn. 84 (Paris), 86 (Châlons-sur-Marne); L. Carolus-Barré, 'Recherches sur les otages de Beauvais et de Compiègne', *Mémoires de la Société académique d'archéologie, sciences et arts du département de l'Oise*, 25 (1926), 165–91; L. de Lauwereyns de Roosendaele, *Les otages de Saint-Omer, 1360–1371: Épisode de la Paix de Brétigny* (Saint-Omer, 1879). Toulouse, Archives Municipales, AA 35/117 (royal order to provide hostages), 45/54 (administrative order regulating local contributions to hostages' expenses).

[10] Cazelles, *Société politique*, 379–83; Henneman, *Royal Taxation*, 85, 87.

[11] *The Ransom of John II* is the most detailed account.

[12] *Original Documents Relating to the Hostages of John*, 10–12; Rapin de Thoyras, *History*, 1:441.

[13] *Chronique des quatre premiers Valois* (SHF 130–1); London, National Archives, SC 8/297/14835 ('qun des ditz hostages appellé William de Essars esteant en leur garde morust... de la maladie del pestilence'). *Original Documents Relating to the Hostages of John*, 52–3, shows that hostages from Lyon were in London in 1371.

concerning hostages show the importance of this issue to the negotiators; (2) analyse the numerical, social, and geographical strength and distribution of the hostages, which contributes to understanding of the political context of the transaction
and the political networks underlying royal power; (3) follow the fate of the hostages after they are granted, including their parole, death, replacement, or outright
release; (4) understand how changing circumstances alter the role of the hostages
after their initial grant; and (5) examine the outcome of the agreement for which
the hostages served, unsuccessfully, as guarantors.

None of the other episodes of hostages for a royal ransom to be studied here is
as richly endowed in terms of volume of evidence, but each nevertheless offers
more than almost all of the cases examined in earlier chapters. It is possible, therefore, to address many, if not all, of the issues that arise in the case of John II in a
series of transactions over a 350-year period. Hostages granted to secure royal ransoms synthesize the developments studied in the previous two chapters. They are
true, rather than conditional hostages, as well as hostages whose identity remains
important, but they share the *Einlager*'s focus on financial obligations. Furthermore, hostages for royal ransoms are strongly implicated in the overall formalization of practices of hostageship in the later medieval period. Finally, viewed over
time, hostages for royal ransom illustrate the development of new social and political rationales for hostageship that transcend the family connections that underlay
the institution in the early Middle Ages.

CAPTIVE CRUSADER KINGS: BALDWIN II OF JERUSALEM (1123) AND LOUIS IX OF FRANCE (1250)

I have argued that the Crusades are not responsible for the introduction of hostages
for ransom into Western Europe. They may, however, be responsible for the practice
of the use of hostages for *royal* ransom, for the first recorded case involves Baldwin
II, the second Latin king of Jerusalem (1118–31). Baldwin was actually captured
and ransomed twice, first in May 1104 at the Battle of Harran when he was simply
count of Edessa, then, as king, in 1123. While ransoming of captives became common practice during the Crusades, the use of hostages was limited to high-profile
cases. As Baldwin's example shows, though, high-profile did not just mean royal,
and the use of hostages for kings was simply a variation on an elite practice.[14]

The first ransom and release of Baldwin is closely tied to that of his fellow captive from Harran, Joscelin of Courtenay. In 1107, three years after his capture by
the emir Sukman, Baldwin was being held in Mosul by Djawālī; Joscelin had
passed to Sukman's brother, Ilghazi, at the former's death in 1105. Ilghazi released
Joscelin in return for promises of 20,000 dinars and military aid. According to one
account, Joscelin's subjects at Turbessel presented themselves as hostages for the

---

[14] Kosto, 'Crusades', 17–21; above, pp. 114–21.

sum and later escaped. Now free, Joscelin went to attempt to free Baldwin. Joscelin presented 30,000 of the 70,000 dinars requested and offered himself as a hostage for the remaining sum if Baldwin were released. The Muslim lord who brokered the deal kept Joscelin at his castle, sent the down payment to Djawālī, and may have sent his own hostage to Djawālī for the balance. The chronicles disagree as to subsequent events: Baldwin was released, but Joscelin was either freed in exchange for additional hostages or simply granted his freedom in recognition of his chivalrous behaviour, not least in taking the place of Baldwin.[15]

When Balak of Aleppo captured Baldwin in 1123, he imprisoned the king in Khartpert, once again with Joscelin of Courtenay, who had been taken prisoner in the previous year. With the help of Armenian allies, Baldwin and Joscelin managed to gain control of the fortress that was their prison. Baldwin remained while Joscelin slipped away to find help. Before Joscelin could mobilize a relief force, however, Balak retook the fortress and transferred the king to Harran. At Balak's death in May 1124, the royal captive passed to the Artukid ruler Timurtash, who set about negotiating ransom terms, which were agreed upon at the end of the following month: the cession of five towns held by the Franks; military aid; and a payment of 80,000 dinars, 20,000 in advance, and 60,000 guaranteed by hostages to be held at Shayzar. The hostages included the king's 4-year-old daughter, Iveta; Joscelin's 11-year-old son and heir; and ten other noble youths. Meanwhile, the emir of Shayzar, who was brokering the agreement, sent members of his family as hostages to Timurtash at Aleppo as a further guarantee of the ransom. This time, Baldwin did not honour the terms of his release. First he refused to hand over the required towns; then he met with the rebel against whom he was supposed to provide military aid. Timurtash may have executed two other prisoners (not among the hostages) in retaliation. In 1125, the emir of Shayzar turned over the hostages for Baldwin's ransom to a new custodian, Āk Sunkur al-Bursukī. Baldwin defeated al-Bursukī in the Battle of 'Azaz, collected the balance due on his ransom from the spoils, paid it, and the hostages were freed.[16]

Two elements of these transactions stand out. The first is the practice of partial payment: the hostages do not guarantee the entire ransom, but are only accepted along with a down payment, 30,000 of 70,000 dinars in the first ransom of Baldwin, 20,000 of 80,000 in the second. In 1107, the 30,000 may be all that Ilghazi received; in the second, the transaction seems to have been ultimately successful, with the entire ransom paid, despite Baldwin's betrayal. Partial payment becomes

[15] Michael the Syrian, *Chronique*, 15.10 (trans. Chabot, 3:195–6); *Anonymous Syriac Chronicle* (trans. Tritton, 80–1); Ibn al-Athīr, *Chronicle* (trans. Richards, 1:138); Bar Hebraeus, *Chronography* (trans. Budge, 1:242); Fulcher of Chartres, *Historia Hierosolymitana*, 2.28.1 (ed. Hagenmeyer, 477–9); William of Tyre, *Chronicon*, 11.8 (CCCM 63:506–7); Steven Runciman, *History of the Crusades*, 3 vols. (Cambridge, 1951–4), 2:107–11.

[16] Matthew of Edessa, *Chronique*, 236, 241, 247 (trans. Dulaurier, 212–13, 309–10, 318); Ibn al-'Adīm, *Chronique d'Alep* (trans. *RHC* Or. 3:637, 644, 651); Usāma ibn Munqidh, *Memoirs* (trans. Hitti, 133); Fulcher of Chartres, *Historia Hierosolymitana*, 3.38.1–2, 39.6, 44.2 (ed. Hagenmeyer, 750–1, 755–6, 770–1); Orderic Vitalis, *Historia ecclesiastica*, 11.26 (OMT 6:126); William of Tyre, *Chronicon*, 12.19, 13.15–16 (CCCM 63:569–70, 603–6); Michael the Syrian, *Chronique*, 15.13 (trans. Chabot, 3:211); Runciman, *History*, 2:161–5.

the standard in royal ransoms with hostages. The second striking element is the role of 'subjects' in replacing or supplementing family members or noble youths as hostages: Joscelin's men at Turbessel for their lord and then Joscelin himself for Baldwin. This became a legal norm in the Crusader States. The compilation known as the *Livre au roi* (*c.*1200) cites the obligation of the liegemen of the king of Jerusalem to serve as hostages for the king's debts; the first case discussed is that of ransom if the king should fall into the hands of the 'Turks' and the required sum could not be raised immediately.[17] I know of no case where this principle was in fact invoked, but the issue was not completely academic. The king associated with the compilation—Amaury II (1197–1205)—was twice captured and ransomed before he assumed the throne. The compiler of the *Livre* could also look to the examples of Guy of Lusignan, the only other king of Jerusalem to fall captive, seized at Hattin in 1187 and released without ransom the following year, or the various princes of Antioch: Bohemond I (1099–1111), captured in 1100 and ransomed in 1103; Raynald of Châtillon (1153–60), captured in 1160 and ransomed in 1176; and Bohemond III (1163–1201), captured in 1164 and ransomed in 1165.[18] But of these, only the ransom of Bohemond III employed hostages.

The notion of vassalic obligation for the king's ransom was current in European legal circles around this time. The lawyer-pope Innocent III referred to the principle for rhetorical purposes in a letter of 1199, written to urge the kings of England and France to go to the same Amalric's aid in the Latin Kingdom: if vassals who refused to offer not only their possessions but their bodies to ransom their captive lord were worthy of punishment for treason, what could the kings expect if they ignored the fate of their master, Christ, ejected from his land by the Saracens and crucified 'like a captive'?[19] The specific obligation not only to provide money for the king's ransom, but also to serve as a hostage, appears to derive from two distinct currents of customary law. One is the inclusion of ransom in the short list of occasions on which a lord might demand extraordinary levies or 'aids'. As enshrined in Magna Carta (1215) cc. 12 and 15, for example, a lord was permitted to demand an aid for the marriage of an eldest daughter, for the knighting of an eldest son, and for his ransom; aids for the lord going on Crusade and even for his purchase of property are attested. The earliest mentions of these rules appear in northern and western France in the late eleventh century; the ransom aid tends to drop out over the course of the thirteenth century, but was still very much current around 1200.[20] A second strand comes from family law and seems prompted if not by the Crusades themselves, then by increased contact and conflict with Islam. The late twelfth-century *fueros* of Teruel and Cuenca, municipal codes from northern Iberia, placed a three-year limit on the time a father could substitute his son as a

---

[17] *Le livre au roi*, 7–8 (ed. Greilshammer, 151–6). Similarly, John of Ibelin, *Le livre des assises*, 175, 216 (ed. Edbury, 441–2, 559–62). See Joshua Prawer, *Crusader Institutions* (Oxford, 1980), 458.

[18] Runciman, *History*, 1:321–2, 2:32–3, 38–9, 357–8, 369–70, 405–6, 408. See also the case of Janus (John II) of Cyprus, above, p. 164, n. 3.

[19] *Die Register Innocenz' III.*, 2:459–62 (no. 2.241) [Potthast 924] ('quasi captivo detento'); Prawer, *Crusader Institutions*, 459.

[20] Reynolds, *Fiefs*, 154, 312–14, 364–6.

hostage for his ransom (the use of daughters was prohibited).[21] Meanwhile, *Lo codi*, a mid-twelfth-century treatise on Roman law composed originally in Provençal, included failure to redeem a parent or child 'among the Saracens' as one of several grounds for disinheritance. *Lo codi* and its immediate sources are closely intertwined with the earliest traces of legislation from the Crusader states, which call for the disinheritance of children who refuse to ransom a parent, if they have the means to do so, or to substitute for a parent so that he or she can raise a ransom.[22] Thus, in the hands of the compiler of the *Livre au roi*, the idea of responsibility for the ransom of a lord, linked to vassalic relationships, merged with the idea of a familial obligation for ransom that sometimes involved or required hostageship. The result was a custom about hostages for royal ransoms of the kings of Jerusalem that was never used, but that had a future elsewhere.

Before returning to Western Europe, we must consider the other great royal ransom episode of the Crusades, namely the capture and release of Saint Louis following the Battle of Mansura in 1250. It is an ambiguous case, but one that demonstrates the persistence of the elite ransoming traditions developed in the twelfth century. After Louis's army managed to turn victory into defeat by pursuing Egyptian forces into the town of Mansura, the king and thousands of his men were taken captive.[23] The king refused to surrender castles in the Latin Kingdom under any circumstances, and refused to acknowledge a monetary ransom for himself: 'it was not appropriate', writes Joinville, 'for him to barter himself for money'. He did agree, though, to a payment of 500,000 l. for the freedom of the captives and the surrender of Damietta in return for his own freedom. The sultan, impressed with the king's refusal to haggle over money, reduced the payment by 100,000 l.[24] After the sultan was overthrown, the terms were renewed and clarified: the king and the barons would be released only after the surrender of Damietta, at which point the king would deliver 200,000 l. before being allowed to embark, and the remaining 200,000 l. upon reaching Acre; the common captives had apparently been killed or transferred to Cairo.[25] Damietta was surrendered on Ascension Day, and the king and the barons released, with the exception of the count of Poitiers, the king's brother, whom 'they kept in prison (*en prison*) until the king paid the 200,000 l. of ransom due before he left the river'. After a delay of about a day, during which Joinville himself plundered the Templar treasure to come up with the last of the payment, the count was released.[26] Only a small number of the common prisoners were later released, and the balance of the ransom was not paid.

---

[21] *El fuero de Teruel*, 453–4 (ed. Gorosch, 286–7); *Fuero de Cuenca*, 10.39 (ed. Ureña y Smenjaud, 294–7).

[22] *Lo codi in der lateinischen Übersetzung des Ricardus Pisanus*, 3.17, 19 (ed. Fitting, 50–1); *Livre des assises de la cour des bourgeois*, 234–5 (ed. Kausler, 266–70). See Prawer, *Crusader Institutions*, 430–68. The tradition on inheritance ultimately goes back to Nov. 115.3.13 and 115.4.7.

[23] The narrative is best followed in Runciman, *History*, 3:261–74.

[24] Joinville, *Vie de Saint Louis*, 342–3 (ed. Monfrin, 346).

[25] Joinville, *Vie de Saint Louis*, 358–9 (ed. Monfrin, 354).

[26] Joinville, *Vie de Saint Louis*, 368–89 (ed. Monfrin, 360–72). Cf. William of Tyre, *Chronicon*, Rothelin cont., 67–8 (*RHC* Occ. 2:616–20). See also Friedman, *Encounter*, 96–9, 153.

The count of Poitiers here clearly acts as a type of hostage: he is retained to guarantee payment of a promised sum, and, as a close relative of the debtor, he is perfectly suited to the role. He was, of course, initially a prisoner of war, captured along with the king, so unless we are willing to argue that the 200,000 l. was simply his own ransom and that the other magnates had been released free of charge, we must acknowledge that the count's status had changed from prisoner to hostage—the same thing as would happen in the Brétigny treaty a century later. Nevertheless, if we follow Joinville's argument, Poitiers was not a hostage for the king's ransom, in that the king refused to be traded for money. The king's ransom was quit with the surrender of Damietta, and the 200,000 l. was, under the revised agreement, the ransom for the nobles released along with him. Furthermore, Joinville does not employ here the language of pledge: the count is retained 'in prison'.

What portion of the gains applied to which prisoners probably mattered less to the Egyptians than to Joinville, with his hagiographic designs, but an earlier passage places the guarantees of the final treaty in a fuller context and suggests that Poitiers would have been seen as a true hostage. After the Battle of Mansura (8 February), but before the capture of the king (6 April), the king attempted negotiations with the sultan for the surrender of Damietta. Joinville reports:

> They asked the king's council what surety they would give for the recovery of Damietta. The king's council offered that they might detain one of the brothers of the king until they recovered Damietta, either the count of Anjou or the count of Poitiers. The Saracens said that they would do nothing of the sort unless they left them the body of the king himself as a pledge (*en gage*). To which my lord the good knight Geoffroy de Sergines responded that he would sooner have the Saracens kill and imprison them all than be blamed for leaving the king in pledge (*en gage*).

The negotiations collapsed—a fact that took on increasing importance after the capture of the king.[27] Thus a month before the final agreement, the count of Poitiers had been proposed as a true hostage, to be granted voluntarily by the French to guarantee the surrender of Damietta. Given the continuous nature of diplomatic negotiations and the way the details of treaties evolve over time, this proposal would have coloured understandings of the count's position as he awaited the payment of the ransom.

---

[27] Joinville, *Vie de Saint Louis*, 302 (ed. Monfrin, 324): 'Il demanderent au conseil le roy quel seurté il donroient par quoy il reussent Damiete. Le conseil le roy leur offri que il detenissent un des freres le roy tant que il reussent Damiete, ou le conte d'Anjou ou le conte de Poitiers. Les Sarrazins distrent que il n'en feroient riens se en ne leur lessoit le cors le roy en gage. Dont mon seigneur Geoffroi de Sergines, le bon chevalier, dit que il ameroit miex que les Sarrazins les eussent touz mors et pris que ce que il leur feust reprouvé que il eussent lessié le roy en gage.' Other accounts of these negotiations do not mention the request for a guarantee: al-Makrīzī, *Histoire d'Égypte* (trans. Blochet, 224–5); Ibn Wāsil, *Mufarridj al-kurūb fī akhbār banī Ayyūb*, s.a. 647 (trans. Jackson, 147); Paris, *Chronica majora* (RS 57.5:105–6). *Eventus infortunii transmarini secundum Templariorum mandatum* (RS 57.6:196–7) describes the earlier negotiations after discussing the capture of the king, noting that the peace had been blocked *infeliciter*.

RICHARD I OF ENGLAND (TREATY OF WORMS, 1193)

Louis's saintly image did not suffer from his captivity and ransom. In part this was due to the exertions of Joinville, but the brevity of Louis's imprisonment—one month in the course of a reign of forty-four years—and the fact that the events took place far from his home were more decisive. Richard the Lionheart shared Louis's experience of captivity, but for over a year and in the heart of Europe. Returning from Crusade in December 1192, Richard I was seized by Leopold, duke of Austria, who was still bitter from his treatment at the hands of the king during the siege of Acre. Thirteen months later, in February 1194, the archbishops of Mainz and Cologne, acting on behalf of the emperor, handed over Richard to his mother, Eleanor of Aquitaine.[28] In the interim, Richard was a valuable pawn in a complex and highly public international diplomatic episode involving the duke of Austria, the emperor, the pope, the king of France, and Richard's own lieutenants and rivals back in England. It is thus Richard, and not Louis or Baldwin of Jerusalem, who became the model of the captive king. Grants of hostages played a key role in the agreements that resulted first in Richard's transfer from the duke to the emperor, and then in his ransom and ultimate release. The development of the hostage clauses over the course of the negotiation of the agreements demonstrates that they were a central issue in the negotiations.

The first agreement to emerge from the affair was the Treaty of Würzburg, concluded between Duke Leopold and Emperor Henry VI on 14 February 1193.[29] It is important to note that while the treaty imposed obligations on the English king, he was not technically a party to it, although, as I will demonstrate later, it is clear that his interests were represented during the negotiations. According to the treaty: (1) Leopold was to hand over Richard to Henry; in return Richard was to grant to the emperor 100,000 marks, half of which was to be given to Leopold. Leopold's half was officially to serve as a dowry for Richard's niece, Eleanor of Brittany, who was to marry one of Leopold's sons. The money was to be handed over in two stages, half by the date of the marriage, which was set for September 1193, and the other half by the following February. At each date, the emperor promised to hand over Leopold's half of the money. (2) The emperor was to hand over to the duke 200 hostages to guarantee that if the emperor should die with Richard still in his possession, the royal prisoner would be returned to the duke, or to one of his sons if the duke had died. (3) Richard was to supply the duke with 50 fully-stocked galleys, 200 knights, 100 crossbowmen, and his own presence in service of the emperor's Sicilian campaign. (4) As a guarantee of his obligations (in clauses 1 and 3), Richard was to grant to the emperor 200 hostages of the

[28] John Gillingham, *Richard I* (New Haven, 1999), 222–53; Gillingham, 'The Kidnapped King: Richard I in Germany, 1192–1194', *German Historical Institute London Bulletin*, 30 (2008), 5–34; Ulrike Kessler, *Richard I. Löwenherz: König, Kreuzritter, Abenteurer* (Graz, 1995), 248–306. The details of the release are given by Roger of Howden, *Chronica* (RS 51.3:233).
[29] Ansbert, *Historia de expeditione Friderici imperatoris* (MGH SrG ns 5:103–5). Also MGH Const. 1:502–4 (no. 354); *Urkundenbuch zur Geschichte der Babenberger*, 4.1:120–2 (no. 88); RI 4.3:280.

emperor's choosing, excluding the sons of his sister and the son of his brother. (5) The custodians to whom these hostages were to be distributed were to swear that if the emperor were to die, they would release the hostages. (6) The emperor promised Leopold that if Richard fulfilled all of his obligations, he would retain the hostages until Richard had acquired for Leopold from the pope papal absolution (for seizing a Crusader). (7) If Richard failed to fulfil his promises, the hostages were to be at the sole disposal of the emperor; the duke would have no say in their fate. The emperor was to have ten of his nobles, chosen by the duke, swear that if Richard fulfilled his promises, the hostages would be released. (8) The emperor would detain the king until he released from captivity the deposed lord of Cyprus and his daughter; if they had been released against payment of a ransom, the king was to be retained until the ransom had been fully repaid. (9) If Richard failed within a year to hand over either the money or the hostages, and the emperor did not offer to hand over the prisoner to the duke, the duke would have the right to require control of the prisoner, along with fifty of the hostages granted by the emperor (clause 2)—youths, not knights—with the rest being released. (10) If the king were to die in the emperor's custody, the 200 hostages of the emperor were to be released, *unless* the emperor had already collected some of the money without handing over the duke's half, in which case the hostages would be released only once the duke received the money. (11) If all of the terms of the agreement were fulfilled, the emperor was to maintain peace with the king.

The core of the agreement was thus a ransom: in exchange for his liberation and a promise of subsequent peaceful relations, Richard would have to supply 100,000 marks and military support for the emperor's Sicilian campaign. In addition, he had to supply a niece for a marriage alliance, release two royal prisoners of his own, and obtain a papal pardon for the duke. Seven of the eleven clauses, however, address guarantees for the agreement, namely the disposition of hostages. There are two sets of hostages proposed: 200 to be granted by Richard to the emperor, as a guarantee that he would provide the money, military resources, and the papal pardon for Leopold; and another 200 to be granted by the emperor to the duke as a guarantee that the duke would receive his portion of the ransom, or that the duke (or his heirs) would get possession of the prisoner if the emperor were to die or if Richard failed to raise the ransom. In the latter case, the duke would be able to compensate for his loss by ransoming the fifty young imperial hostages who would become his prisoners. The attention lavished on the disposition of the duke's imperial hostages testifies to the tension between him and the emperor. But this tension does not explain all of the terms.

Although on its face the treaty is an agreement between the duke and the emperor, and indeed is so described in the protocol ('Hęc est forma conventionis sive tractatus habiti inter domnum Heinricum Romanorum imperatorem et Liupoldum ducem Austrię'), its various clauses—particularly the ones concerning hostages—only make sense in the context of a trilateral undertaking.[30] Consider,

---

[30] *Pace* Gillingham, *Richard I*, 235.

for example, the provisions in case of the emperor's death. If the king were to be in imperial custody, he would revert to the duke (clause 2); if, however, the king had been released against hostages, those hostages were to be released (clause 5). The only possible beneficiary of the release of the hostages is Richard, not the duke or the emperor. Consider, too, what was to happen in case of fulfilment of the terms or default. Leopold was to have no say in how the emperor responded against the English hostages in case of Richard's default (clause 6). Leopold's recourse was rather against the imperial hostages (clauses 9, 10). If Richard fulfilled the terms, however, their release was to be guaranteed by the oaths of ten of the emperor's men *selected by the duke*. Who benefits here? Leopold clearly does not trust the emperor, and would be unlikely to name guarantors for his agreement who would not enforce its terms. But, as noted, Leopold has no direct interest in the fate of the hostages. Thus the only possible beneficiary here is Richard. The clause may be an outcome of the (separate) negotiations between Richard and Leopold. Finally, the last clause (11) establishes peace between the emperor and the king, while Leopold was probably in a stronger position if the king and the emperor were in conflict. Thus what has been interpreted as an agreement imposed on Richard conceals agreements between Richard and Leopold, on the one hand, and between Richard and Henry on the other. As Leopold's overlord, Henry was in a position to press Leopold on the terms of his negotiations with Richard; Leopold's possession of the body put him in a perfect position to press Henry on the terms of his negotiations with Richard. The reported intervention of Savaric, bishop of Bath, and perhaps Hubert Walter in the discussions leading to the treaty are a final proof that Richard's position was not as weak as it appeared.[31] At this point, he appears to have played an extremely poor hand brilliantly.

The Würzburg agreement was altered by the course of events. A 'show trial' at Speyer on 22 March was meant to provide the pretext for the payment of the ransom; Richard was not, after all, a legitimate prisoner of war, but a captive Crusader. Richard's eloquence forced the emperor to withdraw the various charges, grant him the kiss of peace, and promise to reconcile Richard and the king of France. A new agreement was reached on 25 March. The 100,000 marks would now be considered the emperor's fee ('quasi pro mercede') for his services as negotiator; the emperor promised Richard that if he failed in his duties, he would release the king without payment. Richard would also supply 50 galleys and 200 knights for one year of service (presumably on the Sicilian campaign), reducing the requirements of the Würzburg agreement in terms of both personnel (the 100 crossbowmen and Richard himself are no longer included) and length of service (no longer open-ended).[32] Presumably the rest of the terms of the treaty remained set, for Richard wrote to England to obtain hostages.[33] Further negotiations in March altered the timetable of payment and release: in the Würzburg treaty, Richard would be released against the hostages, while the first payment of 50,000 marks

---

[31] Roger of Howden, *Chronica* (RS 51.3:197). For Walter, see Gillingham, *Richard I*, 238.
[32] Roger of Howden, *Chronica* (RS 51.3:199, 205).
[33] Roger of Howden, *Chronica* (RS 51.3:206).

would be due in September 1193. In a letter of 19 April to England, Richard noted
that he would not be released until 70,000 marks had been supplied, along with
hostages for the remainder; the letter suggests that the selection of the hostages
would be negotiated between the king and the emperor, rather than simply at the
will of the emperor as was stated in the Würzburg agreement.[34] The sources remain
silent on Duke Leopold and his claim to 50,000 marks of the ransom.

The third and final version of the agreement for Richard's release was completed on 29 June at Worms, after vigorous diplomatic activity on Richard's part
to settle the emperor's conflict with his barons and to block a pact between the
emperor and Philip II of France.[35] The king would grant to the emperor 100,000
marks, along with an additional 50,000 marks for his Sicilian campaign. Eleanor
of Brittany was named as the subject of the marriage alliance with the ducal
house of Austria. Richard would be released as soon as 100,000 marks had
crossed into imperial territory; hostages were to be granted to secure the remaining 50,000 marks, due both to the emperor and to the duke of Austria: sixty
hostages to the emperor for 30,000 marks, and seven hostages to the duke for
20,000 marks. If the king kept an unspecified promise to the emperor concerning Henry of Saxony, however, he would be quit: he would not have to supply
the 50,000 marks and the hostages, while the emperor would pay the 20,000 due
to the duke.[36] In a side agreement (and thus not a condition for the king's release),
the lord of Cyprus and his daughter were to be released and the latter turned over
to the duke of Austria. The money was raised by the autumn of 1193; further
diplomatic manoeuvring on the part of Henry VI, Philip II, and John of England kept Richard in captivity until 4 February 1194, when hostages were presented and he was released.

In contrast to the Treaty of Würzburg, the Treaty of Worms was explicitly
between Richard and Henry ('Hæc est forma compositionis inter dominum
imperatorem, semper Augustum, et dominum Ricardum, illustrem regem Angliæ');
here it is Leopold's interests that play a supporting role. While the terms of the
Würzburg agreement had not been entirely transformed, Leopold was now in a
weaker position. No longer able to demand hostages from the emperor himself, he
had to settle for seven English hostages for a royal payment which could be abro-
gated by the emperor; in that case, his only claim on the money would be an imperial promise to make a substitute payment. Finally, the imperial promise to retain
hostages to guarantee a papal absolution for Leopold was dropped.

Over the course of a year, then, the negotiators of these three agreements haggled over and altered the overall number of hostages, their identities, who would
select them, the obligations for which they were granted, the individuals to whom
they were granted, and the mechanics of their delivery and release. Perhaps because
of the centrality of the issue to the negotiations, the hostages came to take on more

[34] Roger of Howden, *Chronica* (RS 51.3:209).
[35] Roger of Howden, *Chronica* (RS 51.3:215–16); RI 4.3:305.
[36] Gillingham, *Richard I*, 244 n. 75.

significance to contemporaries than the simple texts of the treaties might suggest. Although in the final treaty the hostages guarantee only the payment of the outstanding ransom money, in various narrative accounts they play a larger role. For Ansbert, the hostages were 'not only for the money, but also for the other articles of the treaty'; for Gislebert of Mons, they were 'for the promises and friendships made between them'; and for Roger of Howden, who transmits the full text of the treaty and thus knew its terms perfectly well, they were 'for the rest of the money for his ransom, and for keeping peace with the emperor and his empire'.[37] Again, we see the hostages doing something more than simply guaranteeing the payments for which they were granted.

Despite the level of detail available about the guarantees for the treaty of Würzburg, the identities of only ten of the sixty-seven hostages are known for certain, and that short list must be cobbled together from diverse sources.[38] Roger of Howden mentions only Walter of Coutances, the archbishop of Rouen; Savaric, bishop of Bath; and Baldwin Wake. We learn later from the same source that Baldwin of Béthune was one of the hostages held by the duke of Austria.[39] Ansbert names only a son (probably Ferdinand) of King Sancho of Navarre and a son of Henry the Lion, the former duke of Saxony. The *Stederburg Annals* claim that it is two sons of the Lion: Otto and William. Ralph of Diceto names, in addition to the archbishop of Rouen, William Longchamp, the chancellor and bishop of Ely. Gislebert of Mons relates that a 4-year-old son of Roger de Tosny, destined as a hostage, was seized in transit by his kinsman, the count of Hainault, who let the emperor know that he would be holding on to this particular pledge.[40] The poet Ulrich von Zatzikhoven claims in his *Lanzelet* that he learned the story from a *welsches buoch* brought to Germany by one of the hostages for Richard, one Hugh de Morville.[41] A letter from Henry VI to Richard has been interpreted to mean that Robert of Thurnham was another hostage, though this is not certain.[42] Other possible hos-

---

[37] Roger of Howden, *Chronica* (RS 51.3:233): 'de residuo pecuniæ redemptionis suæ, et de pace servanda imperatori et imperio suo, et omni terræ suæ dominationis'. Ansbert, *Historia de expeditione Friderici imperatoris* (MGH SrG ns 5:107): 'Qui obsides non solum pro pecunia, verum etiam pro reliquis articulis conventionis solvendis servabantur'. Gislebert of Mons, *Chronique*, 198 (ed. Vanderkindere, 284): 'pro promissis et amiciciis inter eos firmandis'. Cf. William of Newburgh, *Historia rerum Anglicarum*, 4.41 (RS 82.1:404); Gerhard of Steterburg, *Annales Stederburgenses*, s.a. 1194 (MGH SS 16:229); Ralph of Diceto, *Ymagines historiarum* (RS 68.2:113); Roger of Howden, *Chronica* (RS 51.3:275), referring just to the hostages granted to Duke Leopold.

[38] See Gillingham, *Richard I*, 248 n. 94; Lionel Landon, *The Itinerary of King Richard I* (London, 1935), 82–3, 98. The hostages are mentioned, but not named, at *The Great Roll of the Pipe for the Sixth Year of King Richard the First*, 243.

[39] Roger of Howden, *Chronica* (RS 51.3:233, 275).

[40] Ansbert, *Historia de expeditione Friderici imperatoris* (MGH SrG ns 5:107); Gerhard of Steterburg, *Annales Stederburgenses*, s.a. 1194 (MGH SS 16:229); Ralph of Diceto, *Ymagines historiarum* (RS 68.2:113, 115); Gislebert of Mons, *Chronique*, 198 (ed. Vanderkindere, 284). It is possible that Walter of Rouen and some others were not original hostages, but additional hostages, added after the failure of Richard to produce the full amount due at his release; Kessler, *Richard I.*, 301.

[41] Ulrich von Zatzikhoven, *Lanzelet*, 9324–41 (ed. Hahn, 218).

[42] Ralph of Diceto, *Ymagines historiarum* (RS 68.2:118); *The Great Roll of the Pipe for the Sixth Year of King Richard the First*, 212; *The Great Roll of the Pipe for the Seventh Year of King Richard the First*, 2 (which also mentions Baldwin Wake).

tages include five individuals named in a pipe roll entry alongside Otto; the payment was for 'passage', perhaps to Germany, perhaps to serve as hostages, but perhaps simply as his retainers.[43] Finally, there is the case of Robert of Nunant, who refused when Richard requested that he serve as a hostage on the grounds that he was the man of John; the king had him thrown in prison.[44]

These names indicate a rather miscellaneous group: ecclesiastical magnates, sons of secular princes, simple knights, and children of simple knights. The impression is confirmed by the general descriptions of the hostages in contemporary chronicles, which mention both nobles and sons of nobles, and in the Würzburg version of the agreement. The hostages are first referred to there as from among the best men (*meliores*) in the lands under Richard's control, but the king's nephews were explicitly exempted from service. Otto and William, two nephews known to have served, were 16 and 9 years old respectively in 1193; Arthur of Brittany, likely the other nephew referred to, was 6. Finally, in clause 9 of that treaty, Duke Leopold was given a claim on fifty hostages who were 'youths and not knights' ('qui pueri sint et non milites'), which suggests that both categories were to be included in the overall group.

The hostages guaranteed payments totalling 50,000 marks to the emperor and the duke. The full amount was never paid, but the debts were in fact discharged. In the summer following Richard's release, Pope Celestine III excommunicated Duke Leopold for his seizure of Richard. Leopold may have threatened to kill the hostages, and in any case sent one of them, Baldwin of Béthune, to demand that Richard fulfil his obligations. By the end of the year, the duke suffered a fatal riding accident and on his deathbed enjoined his son and heir to forgive the ransom and release the hostages.[45] Then, in 1195, the emperor forgave Richard 17,000 marks, presumably the balance remaining from the portion of the ransom due to him.[46] Thus political developments altered the role of the guarantors. Leopold was forced to give up his guarantees, while Henry VI did so voluntarily.

The parallels of this episode to the case of the Treaty of Brétigny some 170 years later are striking: an evolving treaty, in which the disposition of the hostages was a crucial part of the negotiations; a substantial number of hostages reflecting a significantly more complex basis for royal power than just family ties; the development of the political role of the hostages even after the initial grant, reflecting functions beyond simple service as guarantees; and the ultimate failure of the hostages to ensure the payment for which they had been originally granted. Richard was, as noted, a key figure in the popularization of conditional hostages in 'international treaties'. He provided a model for the use of true hostages as well, and ought to be recognized as a key figure in the history of European diplomacy.

---

[43] *The Great Roll of the Pipe for the Fifth Year of the Reign of King Richard the First*, 166–7: Henry de Berenvall, Hugh Ésturmy, Alexander Arsic, Alard the Fleming, and Robert de Dive.

[44] Roger of Howden, *Chronica* (RS 51.3:233).

[45] *Urkundenbuch zur Geschichte der Babenberger*, 4:223–38 (nos. 927, 935, 937, 941, 945).

[46] Roger of Howden, *Chronica* (RS 51.3:304).

CHARLES II OF NAPLES (TREATY OF CANFRANC, 1288)

The prize captive brought home by the Aragonese admiral Roger de Llúria from his victory off Naples in June 1284 was none other than the heir to the throne of Naples, Charles of Salerno. The death of his father, Charles I of Anjou, in March 1285 inflated the value of the prisoner enormously, and the pace of the complex international negotiations for his release accelerated. The treaties of Cefalù (October 1285) and Oloron-Sainte-Marie (25 July 1287), both directed toward this end, were never fulfilled, because of papal opposition in the first instance and French royal opposition in the second. Charles was ultimately released as part of the Treaty of Canfranc (27 October 1288), concluded between Charles, Alfonso III of Aragon, and Edward I of England.[47] Here, as in the case of Richard I, records of a series of treaties have survived; in addition, however, we can draw on extensive lists of hostages and other ancillary documentation to show how the final treaty was carried out.

As in the treaties for Richard I, the guarantees of the agreements of Cefalù, Oloron-Sainte-Marie, and Canfranc were more complex and detailed than the principal terms, and in all three, hostages played a key role. Cefalù established the basic framework.[48] As a guarantee of the terms of the agreement in general, Charles was to hand over to Alfonso as hostages three of his sons (but not the eldest, Charles Martel), along with other French, English, and Provençal nobles; he also was to provide a certain sum of money. If within two years the terms of the treaty had not been met—and in particular, if Charles had failed to secure papal and French royal approval—the money would be forfeit, Charles would return to his Aragonese prison, and all the hostages would be freed.

At Oloron two years later, these guarantee provisions had become more complex.[49] Charles again was to present three sons: his second and third sons (Louis, the future bishop of Toulouse and saint,[50] and Robert, the future king of Naples) before his release, and the eldest, Charles Martel, within the ten months following; his fifth son, Raimond Berengar, would serve as a hostage for the appearance of the eldest. As in the Cefalù agreement, additional hostages appear: sixty first-born sons of men of Provence, half before Charles's release, half within three months. In case of a violation or failure of the treaty, all sixty-three of the hostages were forfeit to

---

[47] Steven Runciman, *The Sicilian Vespers: A History of the Mediterranean World in the Later Thirteenth Century* (Cambridge, 1958), 247–66; Andreas Kiesewetter, *Die Anfänge der Regierung König Karls II. von Anjou: Das Königreich Neapel, die Grafschaft Provence und der Mittelmeerraum zu Ausgang des 13. Jahrhunderts* (Husum, 1999), 160–99, who cites most of the documents in the following notes. Adam J. Kosto, 'Hostages and the Habit of Representation in Thirteenth-Century Occitania', in Robert F. Berkhofer, Alan Cooper, and Adam J. Kosto, eds., *The Experience of Power in Medieval Europe, 950–1350* (Aldershot, 2005), 181–91, is an earlier version of this section.

[48] Bartholomeo de Neocastro, *Historia Sicula*, 99 (RIS² 13.3:79); *Les registres d'Honorius IV*, 566–8 (no. 814) [Potthast 22581].

[49] *Foedera*, 1.2:677–8; cf. 1:681–3 [*Les registres de Nicolas IV*, 1:109–13 (nos. 560–1); Potthast —].

[50] Louis's status as a hostage was remembered in two hymns: *Analecta hymnica medii aevi*, 4:186–7 (no. 344), 22:169 (no. 286).

Alfonso (although they could not be physically harmed); in the case of Charles's premature death, they were not forfeit, but would remain in Alfonso's control until the conclusion of a peace. Individuals were not as important as families: if an individual had no son, either he could serve himself, or a relative approved by the Aragonese king could serve in his stead. This conclusion is strengthened by additional guarantee clauses designed to transfer the lordship of Provence to Alfonso if Charles failed to arrange a peace or return to prison on schedule. One of the clauses called for the castellans of all of Charles's castles in Provence to do homage to Alfonso before Charles's release, promising to observe the agreement. If one of the castellans were to die, he could only be replaced by a close relative of one of the sixty hostages.

The Oloron treaty failed in part because these extensive guarantees were seen as insufficient. The terms of the Canfranc treaty were thus even more intricate; this is particularly true with respect to the hostage clauses.[51] In advance of his release, Charles was to present Louis and Robert as hostages; within three months, he was to deliver Raimond Berengar (once again to be replaced by Charles Martel within ten months) and the sixty Provençal hostages. As a guarantee of the post-release obligations, Edward I was to provide seventy-six English hostages; if Edward himself had to return to England, he was to provide an additional four hostages. If one or more of the Provençal hostages did not appear or fell ill, an English hostage would be retained in his stead. If Raimond Berengar were to die before being handed over, only fifteen of the English hostages would be retained until Charles's fourth son, Philip, took his place. The English hostages were not to be held responsible for the actions of the town of Marseille; if Charles was unable to obtain for Alfonso an oath of support from the syndics of Marseille, he was to deliver an additional twenty hostages from that town. The mechanics of the exchanges of the Provençal for the English hostages and of Charles Martel for Raimond Berengar were determined and were to be guaranteed by oaths. The conditions under which the English hostages were to be held were spelled out in considerable detail.

Ultimately, then, the release of Charles of Salerno required 159 hostages: Charles's sons (Louis, Robert, and Raimond Berengar; Charles Martel never appeared), 76 'English', 60 from Provence generally, and 20 from Marseille. The attention given in the negotiations to the matter of the selection of the hostages carried over into the execution of the terms. Procurators for Canfranc were sent on 19 October 1288 to choose hostages, that is, eight days before the agreement was finalized. On the day of the agreement, another procurator was sent to receive oaths from the English hostages that they would not flee. Robert and Louis were handed over, and Charles was freed, on the 29th. Edward delivered the English hostages in mid-November.[52] In mid-December, Gaston of Béarn reiterated in

---

[51] *Foedera*, 1.2:687–8. At one point, Alfonso proposed that he himself grant hostages to Edward in advance of the delivery of the hostages for Charles's release: Georges Digard, *Philippe le Bel et le Saint-Siège de 1285 à 1304*, 2 vols. (Paris, 1936), 2:231–4 (no. 5.1).

[52] 'Documenti sulla prigionia di Carlo II d'Angiò', 2:541–2 (no. 47); *Foedera*, 1.2:692, 693.

writing his status and obligations as a hostage.[53] When the delivery of Raimond Berengar was delayed, Alfonso proposed an extension of the deadline in return for sixteen additional Provençal hostages.[54] Alfonso appointed procurators to receive the Provençal hostages on 24 February, they were delivered on 4 March, and the English hostages were released by 9 March.[55] The princes and the Provençal hostages remained in custody for seven more years, finally freed by the Peace of Anagni in 1295.

The Angevin princes named in the treaties themselves were obviously the principal concern of the parties, but an intense interest in the identity of the lesser hostages is evident at each stage of the negotiations—interest that offers further evidence for the representational basis for hostageship explored in Chapter 4. In the first place, there was a concern with the social status of the hostages. The Treaty of Cefalù called for French, English, and Provençal nobles (*nobiles*), which is the status of hostages seen in all earlier royal ransom agreements. But the Provençal hostages were described in the Oloron treaty as the 'first-born sons of barons and magnates, knights, citizens, [and] burghers of Provence', who were to be selected by the Aragonese king.[56] Alfonso also had a right to approve replacements and to determine the fifteen of that number who would remain in the case of Raimund Berengar's death. The English hostages for Canfranc were to include 'thirty-six nobles and barons...and forty good and fully acceptable burghers, or others equivalent to them',[57] the four hostages in case of Edward's departure were to be barons (*barones*), and the twenty hostages from Marseille were to be from among the town's best men (*meliores*). Alfonso thus endeavoured to obtain hostages from at least three distinct ranks: princes; nobles or barons; and citizens or burghers.

An examination of the lists of hostages that have survived, however, reveals a second distributional principle in the selection, namely a geographical concern. The English hostages appear at length in three documents. The first two are documents subsidiary to the Treaty of Canfranc, dated on the day of the treaty. One is Edward's acknowledgement of his obligations to Alfonso under the treaty; it includes a list of the four hostages for his own absence, a list of the seventy-six hostages for the appearance of the Provençal hostages, and a list of substitutions. The other is Alfonso's acknowledgement of the receipt of the hostages, repeating with only minor discrepancies the names of the four, the seventy-six, and the substitutions.[58] The third is an English royal account dated 3 December 1288

[53] Isidoro Carini, *Gli archivi e le bibliotheche di Spagna in rapporto alla storia d'Italia in generale e di Sicilia in particolare*, 2 vols. (Palermo, 1884–97), 2:230–1 (no. 276).

[54] Kiesewetter, *Regierung*, 195.

[55] *Actes de la famille Porcelet*, 420–1, 422–4 (nos. 487, 489); Historical Manuscripts Commission, *Report on Manuscripts in Various Collections*, vol. 1 (London, 1901), 253; Jean Paul Trabut-Cussac, *L'administration anglaise en Gascogne sous Henry III et Edouard I de 1254 à 1307* (Geneva, 1972), 92 and n. 282.

[56] *Foedera*, 1.2:677: 'primogenitos baronum & magnatum, militum, civium, burg' Provinciæ'.

[57] *Foedera*, 1.2:687: 'quadraginta burgenses bonos & benè sufficientes; seu alias personas æquivalentes'.

[58] *Foedera*, 1.2:689–90.

recording disbursements for travel expenses incurred by the hostages, who were apparently held at Zaragoza and Lérida. Although the account lists only sixty names, all of these appear on the treaty documents as well.[59]

The organization of the lists in the treaty documents is not readily apparent, save for the placement of the most distinguished hostage—Gaston of Béarn—at the head of the list. The account documents, however, identify many of the hostages as citizens or burghers of particular towns, others as knights (*milites*), and others with the title lord (*dominus*). Collation of the lists reveals their logic: the required thirty-six barons and nobles come first, followed by eight pages (*domicelli hospicio regis*) and thirty-two burghers, in contiguous groups of from three to eight individuals, from the towns of Bordeaux, La Réole, Bazas, Bayonne, Dax, and Saint-Sever—the majority of the main towns of English-controlled Gascony.

The list of Provençal hostages, which comes from a (lost) notarial register, includes seventy-seven names, beginning with Raimond Berengar. Immediately following are twenty hostages identifiable as the sons of the most prominent noble families in the region, including the Baux, Fos, and Porcelet—the barons, magnates, and knights of the treaties. Then come groups of between one and four hostages identified as from each of eighteen different towns: Sisteron, Forcalquier, Apt, Arles, Aix, *Villemari*, Hyères, Toulon, Brignoles, Saint-Maximin, Castellane, Tarascon, Drauguignan, Grasse, Reillanne, Martigues, Digne, and one whose name is missing. These are the burghers and citizens. Finally come twenty hostages from Marseille.[60]

In both cases, then, Alfonso was interested not just in the *social* distribution of his hostages, but in their *geographical* distribution. The Gascon towns parallel, but do not duplicate, those required to swear oaths and/or provide funds under the terms of the treaty: Bordeaux, Bayonne, Dax, Bazas, Lectoure, Condom, Marmande, and La Réole were to deliver to Alfonso written guarantees.[61] Nevertheless, the sites are well distributed throughout the area of English control (Map 6.1). No similar enumeration survives for the Provençal towns, but the procurators' brief was comprehensive: 'to receive in our name...the written undertakings of the syndics of all of the cities, villages, castles, and all other places in the county of Provence'.[62] In fact, the seventeen towns named in the list—eighteen, including Marseille—are spread over a wide area of the region (Map 6.2).

This fine articulation of the selection of hostages according to two different criteria reflects an increased awareness on the part of the negotiators of the foundations of

[59] London, National Archives, E 101/308/10 (ed. Trabut-Cussac, *L'administration anglaise*, 91 n. 280). Gaston of Béarn is listed as 'cum sua comitiva', which may account for some of the missing names.

[60] Antoine de Ruffi, *Histoire de la ville de Marseille...*, 2nd edn., ed. Louis-Antoine de Ruffi (Marseille, 1696), 1:151–3; reg. *Actes de la famille Porcelet*, 422 (no. 488).

[61] *Foedera*, 1.2:688, 693; examples at 1:697–700. See also London, National Archives, E 36/275, fols. 204r–211v, esp. 204r–v (Bordeaux), 206v–207 (Marmande), 208v–209v (Agen), 209v–210v (Lectoure), 210v–211v (Condom); Trabut-Cussac, *L'administration*, 91.

[62] *Actes de la famille Porcelet*, 420 (no. 487): 'ad recipiendum nomine nostro...instrumenta sindicatuum omnium civitatum, villarum, castrorum ac locorum omnium comitatus Provincie'. Aragonese towns, which were enumerated, made similar promises: *Foedera*, 1.2:692–3, 698–704.

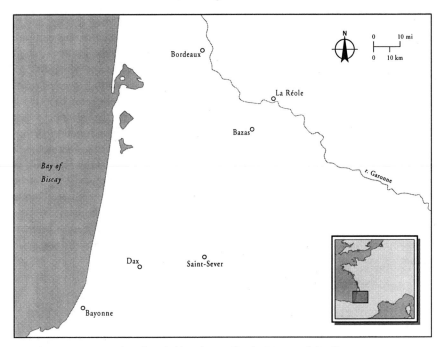

Map 6.1. Towns Providing 'English' Hostages for the Treaty of Canfranc.

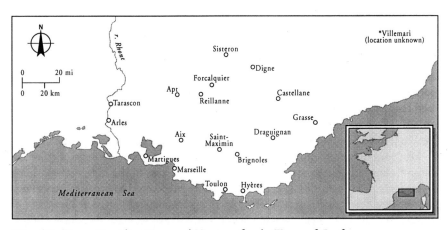

Map 6.2. Towns Providing Provençal Hostages for the Treaty of Canfranc.

royal power. The extension of the pool of hostages beyond the military elite and the introduction of an explicit geographical element corresponds well to contemporary changes in the political life of the French kingdom, notably the rise in the thirteenth century of representative institutions. The various hostages were not—like the proc- urators sent to Alfonso III to receive the oaths from the Gascon and Provençal towns, and the syndics who proffered them—true 'representatives', in the sense of individu- als possessed of formal delegated authority. But if we focus on the selection process that brought the hostages together, rather than their particular function or legal standing, the parallels to representative status are clear. In Occitania, by the time of the Treaty of Canfranc, control of those historically designated as the powerful, the nobles, was no longer sufficient, as the hostages demanded by Alfonso III in Gascony and Provence confirm. The key to securing the agreement lay in the physical posses- sion not only of the princes, but also of nobles and burghers distributed across each region. The numbers of individuals involved indicate that even the most powerful from among these categories of persons—the most influential nobles and the richest citizens—were insufficient guarantees.

DAVID II OF SCOTLAND (TREATY OF BERWICK, 1357)

As the Treaty of Canfranc and its aftermath show, well before the Hundred Years War, complex hostage transactions had been integrated into practices surrounding royal ransoms. In addition to the case of John II of France, the period of the Anglo- French war offers two other royal ransoms featuring hostages, both in England, and both involving kings of Scotland. The first was that of David II, captured by the English forces of Edward III at the Battle of Neville's Cross on 17 October 1346. With neither the English puppet, Edward Balliol, nor the heir-presumptive, Robert Stewart ('the Steward'), particularly invested in his return, and with the Scottish estates strongly opposed to the terms presented by the English, the king spent the next eleven years in custody. He was finally freed in exchange for a prom- ised ransom on 5 October 1357 by the Treaty of Berwick. Once again voluminous records allow us to follow the negotiations that ultimately led to his release, the evolving role of hostages in securing his ransom, and their ultimate fate.[63]

Hostages first enter into the story not as guarantees for payment of the royal ransom, but rather as guarantees for conditional release of the king himself. From November 1351 to April 1352, David was allowed to travel to Scotland to attempt to convince the Scots to accept terms of an agreement negotiated at Newcastle in the summer of 1351—an agreement that would have secured his release without ransom and hostages, but with the introduction of the English royal house into the line of succession for the Scottish throne.[64] As security for his return, he offered

---

[63] Michael A. Penman, *David II, 1329–71* (East Linton, 2004), 124ff.; 'A Question about the Suc- cession', 5–20; E. W. M. Balfour-Melville, *Edward III and David II* (London, 1954), 14–22.

[64] A. A. M. Duncan, '*Honi soit qui mal y pense*: David II and Edward III, 1346–52', *Scottish His- torical Review*, 67 (1988), 113–41.

seven noble hostages, the sons and/or heirs of prominent Scottish lords.[65] John Murray of Bothwell, whose brother and heir was on the list, ended up going in his brother's stead and dying in custody.[66] The king's attempt failed, but the transaction set two precedents for hostage dealings between David and Edward III. First, we see here the use of sons and/or heirs of leading magnates and supporters.[67] Second, we see that proposed hostages were not always the ones who went.

With the more ambitious settlement of 1351–2 having failed, the parties set their sights on a more limited agreement that would result in a simple truce and the release of the king in return for the payment of a ransom. This was proposed in a draft treaty dated 13 July 1354 that called for a ransom payment of 90,000 marks (60,000 l.), to be paid over a period of nine years, with a truce lasting until the ransom was fully paid. As with the cases of Richard I and Charles of Salerno, the guarantees were a central issue: close to half of the text of this treaty concerns the hostages.[68]

Twenty initial hostages are named, sons, and mostly heirs, of Scottish lords. The hostages are to be held and treated courteously, with reasonable expenses charged to their grantors. Two of the lords named—Patrick Dunbar, the earl of March, and Robert Erskine—were the two lay negotiators on the Scottish side named at the start of the treaty. March, at least, took advantage of his role to secure special treatment for his son and heir: he was to be released after payment of the first instalment of 10,000 marks and housed with Ralph de Neville, an undertaking that was to be guaranteed separately in writing by the king and the prince to March, and by the issuance of a special royal commission to Neville. March's son was to be replaced by the son and heir of the Steward until the payment of the second instalment; the Steward's heir would in turn be replaced by the Steward's second son, if alive, or by another of his sons along with the son and heir of Hay, the constable, 'or another as sufficient'. This last pair of hostages was to be replaced (a time is not specified) by the son and heir of the earl of Ross, 'if he is of an age to travel', or by Ross's brother.[69]

These last few lines reveal that the concern of the English negotiators was not the number of hostages, but rather their value. Indeed, the treaty continues with a number of clauses on this subject. First comes the vague order that 'on account of the weakness (*feblesse*) of the aforesaid hostages', David and the Scottish lords were to undertake in writing and by oath to work to find 'the best hostages, sons of the most sufficient lords that they can find in the land of Scotland, to place in hostage in exchange for those who are of lesser value (*maindre value*)'. There follows the puzzling statement that 'hostages should be delivered according to the quantity of payment, but hostages that remain should be as sufficient as those who are delivered, with the exception of the son of the Steward of Scotland and the son of the

[65] *Rotuli Scotiæ*, 1:743–4 (order to receive hostages; safe conduct; renewal); Bower, *Scotichronicon*, 14.15 (ed. Watt, 7:321); *Foedera*, 3.1:241–2; Duncan, '*Honi soit*', 133–4, 141 n. Cf. Penman, *David II*, 169.

[66] Penman, *David II*, 160, 169, 179, 248; James Balfour Paul, ed., *The Scots Peerage*, vol. 2 (Edinburgh, 1905), 129.

[67] Penman, *David II*, 169, reads the distribution of hostages as an indicator of political strength, suggesting that the fact that two of the seven were supporters of the Steward, while five were supporters of the king, shows that 'the Steward was back on top'.

[68] *Foedera*, 3.1:281–2.

[69] 'ou un autre auxi seuffissant...s'il soit d'age pur travailler.'

earl of March'.[70] After clauses unrelated to hostages, the treaty returns to the subject. If any of the payments are not made on time, the king is supposed to re-enter captivity within three weeks of default, at which time the hostages will be released; when the arrears are paid, the king is to be freed and the hostages returned. Alternatively, instead of returning himself, the king may send two from among four leading nobles who are to remain with the hostages as reinforcements (*en afforcement de les hostages*). Finally, the hostages are to be held only against the ransom or against their expenses. The king of England, the prince of Wales, and other English nobles were to undertake, by oath and in writing, to deliver the hostages as required.

This treaty was duly confirmed by Edward III and by the prince of Wales on 5 October, with the English constable (William, earl of Northampton), Henry, duke of Lancaster, and Richard, earl of Arundel, empowered to swear on behalf of the king and the prince. Orders were given for David's release and the receipt of the hostages, conservators of the truce were appointed, and safe conducts were issued for the hostages. Edward even issued the promised commission to Neville to release March's son in a year's time.[71] The plan was still in place on 12 November, when an indenture repeated the terms of the agreement and ordered parties to be present at Berwick on the Sunday after Saint Hilary (19 January 1355) to finalize the transaction.[72] But something went wrong between December and January—most likely the plan was sabotaged by the Steward[73]—and the king was not released.

Negotiations resumed in 1356, and most details seem to have been worked out by mid-August of the following year, when Edward III issued a flurry of commissions, indemnities, and safe conducts.[74] Notable among these are a royal commission to his negotiators that highlights the issue of hostages, and two documents related to the hostages that do not specify names. The first is a safe conduct for twenty hostages—sons of certain nobles, and others from Scotland—along with forty retainers, horses, and equipment, to last for ten years (in contrast, a separate safe conduct does name three nobles who were to join the regular hostages). Similarly, no names are given in the second document, a promise that neither the hostages nor the additional nobles will be detained outside the terms of the treaty unless they violate the law in some way after their arrival. This suggests that the identity, if not the number, of the hostages had not yet been settled.[75]

---

[70] '&, pur la feblesse des hostages susditz...de purchacier les meillours hostages, filz & heirs des seignurs apperantz des plus seuffissantz q'il pourront trover en la terre d'Escoce, de mettre en hostage, en eschange de ceaux qui sont de maindre value...les hostages soient delivrez selonc la quantite du paiement: issint, toutefoiz, que les hostages qui demouront, soient auxi seuffissantz come ceaux qui serront delivrez; forpris le filz au seneschall d'Escoce, & le filz au count de la Marche.' See below, p. 192, n. 106.

[71] *Foedera*, 3.1:285–9; *Rotuli Scotiæ*, 1:768–73.

[72] *Foedera*, 3.1:291. The supposed reconfirmation by Edward III and the prince of Wales on 5 December (*Foedera*, 3.1:293) never took place; see James Campbell, 'England, Scotland and the Hundred Years War in the Fourteenth Century', in J. R. Hale, J. R. L. Highfield, and B. Smalley, eds., *Europe in the Late Middle Ages* (Evanston, 1965), 198 n. 3.

[73] Duncan, '*Honi soit*', 134.

[74] *Foedera*, 3.1:364–8.

[75] *Foedera*, 3.1:365 (commission), 366 (safe conduct for hostages), 367 (safe conduct for superhostages).

The final agreement was enshrined in the Treaty of Berwick, concluded on 3 October 1357, ratified by David and the Scottish nobles and commons on 5 October, and re-ratified at Scone on 6 November.[76] The principal change in the core terms of the treaty from the failed 1354 agreement was simply an increase of the ransom by 10,000 marks, with the consequent extension of the term of payment by one year. In terms of detail, however, the major changes were in the guarantee mechanisms, which were strengthened in a number of ways. An intricate web of oaths and ecclesiastical censures is responsible for most of the new language, but the greatest change was the addition of another layer of personal sureties to the twenty hostages from the 1354 draft. The earlier treaty recognized the *feblesse* of some of the hostages, and remedied it with a royal promise to replace them when possible with better ones; similarly, the king would be allowed to remain free in case of default if he sent two of four named barons *en afforcement de les hostages*. The promise to exchange better hostages for weaker ones remains in the 1357 treaty, but there the supernumerary barons have become the true remedy for the *feblesse*; they have become 'super-hostages'[77] to be rotated into service alongside the regular hostages. Immediately following the list of twenty hostages, the 1357 treaty reads: 'It is agreed, on account of the weakness (*feblesse*) of these hostages, that to back them up (*en afforcement de eux*) concerning the release of the king of Scotland, three of the lords listed below [eight names are given]...shall enter into hostageship for him'. They are to remain until replaced by others from that same list, with at least three in hostageship as long as the full ransom remained unpaid. The treaty and ancillary documents do distinguish between the hostages (*hostages*) and the super-hostages (*afforcementz*), but they have essentially the same status: they are, as the treaty says, to enter into hostageship.[78]

The 1357 treaty also strengthened the guarantee mechanisms in case of default. In the 1354 draft, if the king returned, the hostages were to be released, although if he substituted the two barons, the hostages were to remain. In the final treaty both the hostages and the super-hostages are to remain even while the king has re-entered captivity (the king is again allowed to substitute barons—two from a list of three—for his own presence).[79] The hostages and super-hostages have also become guarantors of the truce: if the Scots seize an English castle or town and refuse to return it, with payment of damages, the hostages are to remain in custody

[76] *Foedera*, 3.1:372–4 [*Rotuli Scotiæ*, 1:811–14] (treaty), 374–6 (ratification by David), 376–7 (ratification by nobles), 377–8 (ratification by commons), 382 (6 November ratification). See also Andrew of Wyntoun, *Original Chronicle* (MS Cotton), 8.38, lines 6899–916 (ed. Amours, 6:232–3).
[77] Ranald Nicholson, *Scotland: The Later Middle Ages* (Edinburgh, 1974), 163; 'A Question about the Succession', 9.
[78] *Foedera*, 3.1:373: 'est acorde, pour la feblesse de ditz hostages, q'en afforcement de eux, sur la deliverance du dit Roi d'Escoce, qe trois de seygneurs de souz escripts; cest assavoir...entreront pour luy en hostage'.
[79] *Foedera*, 3.1:373. Duncan ('A Question about the Succession', 7) suggests that 'none of these was truly a hostage, for he was not penalised if the Scots defaulted'. It is true that they were not subject to a monetary penalty, but they were kept in detention: they were not paying sureties, but they were sureties nonetheless.

until the town is returned—possibly extending the length of hostageship beyond the planned ten-year term. And the new treaty specifies that if any of the royal sureties should die in English custody, they are to be replaced by others 'as sufficient...so that the number of hostages, as of the super-hostages and others mentioned above, shall always remain complete'.[80] Finally, a clause from the 1354 treaty enjoining the king and nobles to return any escaped hostages 'without delay' has been strengthened to include a firm three-week time limit.

In contrast to the first two agreements for the release of Charles of Salerno, there is little to suggest that the 1354 agreement was scuttled because of English concerns about the sufficiency of the guarantees. As noted, it is more likely that it was Scottish opposition that was responsible for the failure. Why, then, were the principal changes in the 1357 treaty a strengthening of the guarantees, and the hostage clauses in particular? A. A. M. Duncan has argued convincingly that the 1354 and 1357 agreements were fall-back positions for Edward III, who had his eye on a political settlement that would at least put a Plantagenet on the Scottish throne, if not unite the two kingdoms. But perhaps by 1357 the fiscal pressures of the French war were beginning to weigh more heavily, and the English were thus that much more concerned to get the ransom money. After 1360 and the Treaty of Brétigny, the situation would be completely different.

Four lists of hostages for David II have survived: those named for David's 1351–2 release; those named in the 1354 draft; those named in the 1357 final treaty; and those named in a document ancillary to the 1357 treaty that lists not only hostages but also their guardians.[81] What becomes clear is that the lists of hostages reflect as much the political needs and circumstances of the Scots as the desire for guarantees on the part of the English king. Scottish nobles may be identified in this period as royalists or as partisans of Robert Stewart, a grandson of David II's father and since 1318 the heir presumptive (Edward Balliol's Scottish support after 1346 was negligible). Unlike the Treaty of Canfranc, in which the 'creditor' was allowed to select the hostages, here their identities were subject to negotiation. Changes in the relative weight of supporters of one or the other parties on a list may thus be indicative of shifts in political power.

The hostages granted safe conducts for David's release in 1351–2 were: John, son and heir of the Steward; John Dunbar, son of the earl of March; John, son of the earl of Sutherland; Thomas, grandson of the earl of Wigtown; James Lindsay, son of David Lindsay; Hugh, son of the earl of Ross; and Thomas Murray, brother of John Murray of Bothwell. We cannot be certain that these are the hostages who actually went; safe conducts were issued prospectively and not necessarily accepted, and John Murray ended up going in his brother's stead. Of this list, Sutherland, Wigtown, and Lindsay are clearly associated with David's camp, and Murray with the Steward's, while Ross and March were certainly reaping the benefits of David's

---

[80] 'q'autres auxi suffisantz soient mis, de temps en temps, en lieu des mortz, si q' le nombre, sibien des hostages, come des afforcementz, & autres susditz, soit tous jours plein.'

[81] The edition of the ancillary list in *Rotuli Scotiæ* (1:814) is more complete than the one in *Foedera*, 3.1:366–7.

captivity. Thus a failure to return would have hurt David's supporters and opponents equally.[82] This does not present too much of a problem from the English perspective, in that the Stewart party was even more of an opponent than the royalist party; it does, however, show that David's influence, despite his absence and the Steward's grip on the government, remained sufficient to force his adversary's hand.

The balance of the 1354 list is very different. The draft treaty named the sons and/or heirs of the earls of Sutherland, March, and Wigtown, as well as of William Cunningham, William More, David Graham, Robert Erskine, Thomas Somerville, John Danielston, Thomas Bisset, Andrew de Valence, Adam Fullarton, John Stewart of Darnley, Roger Kirkpatrick, John Kennedy, John Barclay, John Gray, David Wemyss, William Hay of Locherworth, and William Livingston. This is a resolutely royalist group.[83] Sutherland was the king's brother-in-law, whose son (the hostage) would soon replace the Steward—in David's mind at least—as the heir presumptive; Wigtown was a father figure of sorts to the king, and owed his earldom to David's grant; Cunningham, who fought beside the king at Neville's Cross, would likewise be granted an earldom by him in 1358; Livingston is one of the most frequent witnesses of David's early charters; More, Kirkpatrick, and Graham were all captured at Neville's Cross; Bisset visited the king in his captivity; Barclay and Wemyss had been granted lands and offices in the 1340s. Kennedy, Somerville, de Valence, Gray, and Stewart have left few traces before 1354, but are recognizably royalist thereafter. Only Danielston (the Steward's guardian of Dumbarton castle), and perhaps Erskine and March, can be counted among the Steward's men, although Erskine had been ousted by Stewart as chamberlain in April, and both March and Erskine played a role in the negotiations for David's release.[84] Notably, March's son's spot in the group of hostages is to be filled by the Steward's sons, then by the constable's, then by Ross's; while the constable's status is uncertain at this point, Ross was definitely in league with the Steward. If most of the spots on the hostage roster are taken by royalists, in contrast, all of the reinforcements in case of default were major royal opponents: the Steward, Thomas Murray, Lord Douglas, and John, lord of the Isles.

Only two changes were made in the families represented in the core list of twenty hostages in the 1357 list:[85] the March heir was removed, and the Stewart heir (who was slated to replace him after a year in the 1354 draft) promoted to the position of original hostage; similarly the Ross heir was moved from the replacement list to the slot occupied by the heir of Adam Fullarton; the constable's heirs are no longer mentioned. Dunbar was by 1357 recognizably royalist; Fullarton

---

[82] Penman, *David II, passim*.
[83] Penman, *David II*, 179.
[84] Penman, *David II, passim*.
[85] Individuals may have changed, but as the heirs are not named in the 1354 document, such shifts are hidden. One individual named in the 1354 document, William Livingston, has been replaced in 1357 by his son and heir, Patrick. The ancillary list corresponds in most particulars to the text of the treaty, save for two apparent scribal errors (the heir of the earl of Wigtown is Thomas, not John; and the lord of Danielston is John, not Robert).

always had been. Thus two royalists on the hostage list were replaced by two opponents. The list of reinforcements, now required from the beginning rather than just in case of default, is again mostly composed of royal opponents: the Steward, Ross, Angus, Douglas, and Thomas Murray, alongside Sutherland and March. The list of three barons from whom two may be sent in the king's stead should he default is entirely made up of his opponents: the Steward, Douglas, and Thomas Murray.

The first payment was made on time in June 1358.[86] David was allowed to delay the second payment until December 1359, but missed that deadline and paid only half of the amount due, which does not seem to have been credited toward the balance. The third full payment was made on time in 1360.[87] But then payments stop. When the agreement was renegotiated in 1365, 80,000 marks were thus still due on the original debt. The new agreement raised the debt to 100,000 l., payable over the length of a twenty-five-year truce (at 4,000 l. per year), unless David wished to return to the original terms and a shorter truce after four years. This renegotiation made no mention of hostages or other guarantees.[88] In a second renegotiation in July 1369, the remainder of the ransom was stated to be 56,000 marks, meaning that the 1357 figure of 100,000 marks was now the basis, with 20,000 subtracted for payments in 1358 and 1360—with the partial payment of 5,000 marks in 1359 still ignored—as well as an additional 24,000 marks, which would correspond to four yearly payments under the 1365 treaty (in February of 1366, 1367, 1368, and 1369[89]); the sum was to be paid off over the course of a fourteen-year truce at 4,000 marks per year.[90] This agreement, too, made no mention of hostages or other guarantees. Ransom payments under this third agreement were in fact kept up for a while, with regular payments of 4,000 marks made each year from 1370 to 1377—that is, continuing after David's death in 1371, but ceasing immediately after Edward's death. In the end, 24,000 of the original 100,000 marks remained unpaid.[91]

The continuing balance on the ransom meant that the hostages should have been kept, and the fact that from at least December 1359 to the renegotiation of 1365 David was in violation of the terms of the treaty meant that default clauses—some involving hostages—should have been invoked. These failures—and their implications—were acknowledged by the Scots, as revealed by a briefing paper prepared in advance of negotiations in 1364. One of the reasons given in favour of accepting the English proposal (i.e. the succession of Edward III or his heir to the Scottish throne) was that the English will not 'allow any hostages for the captives,

[86] This is shown by the fact that John Stewart is replaced by his brother, as called for by the treaty: *Rotuli Scotiæ*, 1:828.

[87] *The Exchequer Rolls of Scotland*, 2:55; *Rotuli Scotiæ*, 1:845–6; Penman, *David II*, 241.

[88] *Foedera*, 3.2:766; Penman, *David II*, 335–7.

[89] Campbell, 'England', 202; *Foedera*, 3.2:856; *The Exchequer Rolls of Scotland*, 2:225, 264, 291, 305.

[90] *Foedera*, 3.2:877; Nicholson, *Scotland*, 173.

[91] That payments were made may be inferred from the difference between the balances in 1369 (56,000) and 1377 (24,000): 32,000 marks, or eight payments of 4,000 marks each, starting in 1370 and ending in 1377. Direct evidence for the payments is spotty: *The Exchequer Rolls of Scotland*, 2:344, 355, 363; *Rotuli Scotiæ*, 1:944–5. See Penman, *David II*, 401; Nicholson, *Scotland*, 194.

because we have behaved improperly concerning our hostages last given to them for the king'.[92]

If all went as planned, and the hostage terms of the 1357 agreement were followed, we should find twenty regular hostages and three reinforcements perpetually in custody from 1357 on, along with two of the three hostages in case of default in custody at some point in 1359–60 and then from 1361 to 1366, when regular payments resumed on a new schedule. In addition, we should find the first son of the Steward replaced in 1358, and the second son replaced in 1360, after the second full payment.

The fate of the hostages may be traced only partially. We can begin with the ancillary list from 1357, which records the hostages actually handed over on the day the treaty was finalized. Eighteen of the twenty hostages named in the treaty appear to have been delivered as planned. Because William Ross was ill, he was held back; the king and nobles had to promise to deliver him—or, if he died, the subsequent heir—before Christmas. Similarly, Thomas Bisset arranged for a delay until All Saints (1 November) for the delivery of his son. Assuming that Ross and Bisset were ultimately delivered, the fate of the original twenty original hostages is as shown in Table 6.1.[93] In short, ten of the twenty hostages are attested *as hostages in England* after the conclusion of the treaty, but only four for certain after 1360, and one after 1363.

The agreement also called for the presence of three super-hostages from a list of eight. Here we have more complete evidence—not surprising, given the status of the individuals involved. One was the earl of Angus. On Easter Day 1357, Edward granted to the earl, identified as one of the hostages for David Bruce, safe passage to return to Scotland to consult with the king; he was to be back in London by 16 February 1358.[94] This was followed by a series of additional safe conducts and extensions granted over the next two years.[95] Then on 15 March 1360 he was declared in violation of his parole; despite Edward's monitory letter, he never returned.[96]

A second was Thomas Murray. Like Angus, he was named as a hostage in letters of safe conduct allowing him to return to Scotland on 8 May and 8 December 1358,[97] as well as in letters granted to twelve of his knights to come to London (4 July 1359) and in two others granted to Murray's retainers so that they might return to Scotland for 'money and other things necessary for the maintenance of Thomas' (10 November 1359, 16 April 1360).[98] According to the chronicler

---

[92] 'A Question about the Succession', 30 (c.14): 'nec aliquos obsides pro captiuis admitterent, eo quod de obsidibus nostris vltimo eis pro rege datis nos indebite habuimus'.

[93] Penman, *David II*, 213–14; Campbell, 'England', 202 n. 1.

[94] *Rotuli Scotiæ*, 1:818.

[95] *Rotuli Scotiæ*, 1:821, 832, 834, 840.

[96] *Rotuli Scotiæ*, 1:847; cf. *The Acts of David II*, 262–3 (no. 233).

[97] *Rotuli Scotiæ*, 1:821, 832; a safe conduct for some of his *homines et familiares* was also granted on 8 December.

[98] *Rotuli Scotiæ*, 1:838, 843, 847 ('pro pecunia et aliis necessariis pro sustentatione ipsius Thome').

Table 6.1 Original Hostages for the Treaty of Berwick, 1357

1. John Stewart of Kyle, son of the Steward	1358 replaced by (*Rotuli Scotiæ*, 1:828, 24 June 1358)
brother	1360 replaced by (*Rotuli Scotiæ*, 1:849, 13 June 1360)
brother	
2. Thomas, grandson of e. Wigtown	1358 transferred to sheriff of Northumberland perhaps for release (*Rotuli Scotiæ*, 1:831–2)
3. Reginald, son of William More of Abercorn	" "
4. John, son of Andrew de Valence	" "
5. Gilbert, son of John Kennedy of Dunure	" "
6. John, son of John Barclay	" "
7. David, son of David Wemyss	" "
8. John, son of earl of Sutherland	1361 dies at London (see below, p. 191)
9. John, son of John Gray of Broxmouth	1362 transfer order to Newcastle (*Foedera*, 3.2:650)
10. Thomas, son of William Hay of Locherworth	1362 transfer order to Newcastle (*Foedera*, 3.2:650) 20 June 1363 order repeated (*Foedera*, 3.2:706 [*Calendar of Documents Relating to Scotland*, 4:81]: 'Præcipimus tibi, firmiter injungentes') 1369 safe conduct to Rome (*Rotuli Scotiæ*, 1:930, 16 May 1369)
11. Patrick, son of David Graham	1362 expenses paid to father? (*The Exchequer Rolls of Scotland*, 2:117)
12. Robert, son of John Danielston	1362 expenses paid to father (*The Exchequer Rolls of Scotland*, 2:116: 'pro expensis filii sui, obsidis in Anglia')
13. William, son of Thomas Bisset	1363 back in Scotland? (*Rotuli Scotiæ*, 1:876–7, 8 December 1363: safe conduct for, among others, *Wills Byset de Scot*')
14. Thomas, son of Robert Erskine	1366 back in Scotland? (*Rotuli Scotiæ*, 1:905, 13 October 1366: safe conduct, for, among others, *Thomas de Erskyne de Scot*')
15. Robert, son of William Cunningham	not mentioned
16. Patrick, son of William Livingston	"
17. William, son of Thomas Somerville	"
18. Robert, son of John Stewart of Darnley	"
19. Humphrey, son of Roger Kirkpatrick	"
20. William, son of earl of Ross	"

Bower, Thomas was one of at least two Scottish hostages who succumbed to the plague in London in the autumn of 1361.[99]

The third super-hostage was William, earl of Sutherland, whose son John was also one of the regular hostages until his death in the same plague. The ancillary list from 1357 notes that John was sent in the company of his father to be housed by the chancellor.[100] He is named as a hostage in a safe conduct of 26 October 1358, lasting until 2 February 1359, and another of 1 April 1359 granted to one of his retainers to return to Scotland to conduct the earl's business.[101] William himself was again granted three more leaves, each time extended, between 1362 and 1364; he may never have returned from the last, as there is no further evidence for his presence in England, and he is thought to have been killed in Scotland in 1370.[102]

Angus, Murray, and Sutherland are the only super-hostages who certainly served in that role. Four of the others on the list—the Steward, Douglas, March, and Ross—are referred to together in a safe conduct granted on 6 June 1358 so that they might 'enter as hostages in the place of other Scottish nobles'.[103] But this came in advance of the first payment, which was made on time, and David was certainly in no position in 1358 to force the departure of the Steward. There is no evidence of any of these men ever serving as hostages, even after the default. And since the Steward and Douglas were two of the three from this list who were supposed to substitute for David in case of default, it is likely that that particular clause was not invoked. As for the last figure on the list of super-hostages, the earl of Mar, a safe conduct was granted to his retainers in 1364 to go to Scotland to acquire '100 cattle and foodstuffs for his maintenance', but he is nowhere described as a hostage.[104] Nevertheless, it does appear that three of the eight—Murray, Sutherland, and Angus—did serve as hostages in the early years of the agreement, even if they were regularly released on parole.

The evidence concerning the super-hostages corresponds well to the evidence concerning the regular hostages. The presence of many hostages and super-hostages in England in 1360–1 suggests that the basic guarantees were followed in the first few years of the treaty, even if the default clause was not. Indeed in 1359, the issue of the hostages was raised in a proposed treaty between the Scots and the French. The Scots would promise to attack the English if the French would pay the remaining ransom, thereby releasing the hostages.[105] What happened after 1360 is less

[99] Bower, *Scotichronicon*, 14.25 (ed. Watt, 7:322). See also Andrew of Wyntoun, *Original Chronicle*, 8.40, lines 7127–32 (ed. Amours, 6:249).

[100] *Rotuli Scotiæ*, 1:814.

[101] *Foedera*, 3.1:409; *Rotuli Scotiæ*, 1:837.

[102] *Foedera*, 3.2:635, 709 [*Rotuli Scotiæ*, 1:864]; *Rotuli Scotiæ*, 1:863, 889; *The Exchequer Rolls of Scotland*, 2:113, 142, 166; Penman, *David II*, 280, 409.

[103] *Rotuli Scotiæ*, 1:826: 'se in obsides...loco aliorum nobilium obsidum de Scotia...intraturi'.

[104] *Rotuli Scotiæ*, 1:889: 'pro centum bobus et aliis victualibus...pro sustenatione sua'.

[105] Penman, *David II*, 230–1; Delachenal, *Histoire de Charles V*, 2:103–5; Michael Penman and David Tanner, 'An Unpublished Act of David II, 1359', *Scottish Historical Review*, 83 (2004), 59–69. Cf. Penman, *David II*, 213, 230.

clear. The Treaty of Brétigny certainly changed the priorities of the English king, and the details of the guarantees may have been overlooked in an effort to reach a broader settlement. It has been suggested that hostages were gradually released as the payments were made, but the evidence for the first few years does not support this, and the evidence for the period after 1360–1 is far too scanty to be useful.[106]

What is reasonably clear, though, is that by the time of David II, hostages were being used politically not only by the creditor, who depleted the strength of the debtor to pressure adherence to the agreement, but also by the debtor, who was able to use hostage assignments to get rid of his opponents. David had to suffer the extended absence and even loss of figures such as William and John Sutherland, but he was also able to remove Murray and Douglas from the scene at key times, to keep one of the sons of the Steward out of play, and to use the possibility of an invocation of the default clause or of rotation as a super-hostage as a threat against figures such as the Steward himself. This was possible in part because of the increasingly streamlined bureaucratic procedures for the assignment, movement, exchange, and return of hostages that allowed the debtor—in this case David—to manipulate the list as circumstances demanded.

JAMES I OF SCOTLAND (TREATY OF LONDON, 1424)

The captivity and ransom of David II were echoed three-quarters of a century later in the early reign of James I.[107] David's efforts to keep the Steward off the throne ultimately failed, and at the king's death his rival succeeded as Robert II (1371–90). This first king of the Stewart line was succeeded by his eldest son, Robert III (1390–1406), who in 1406 decided to send his 12-year-old son and heir, James, to France for safety. He did so fearing the hand of his brother, the duke of Albany, who at the old king's death would become both regent for James and the next in line to the throne—a dangerous pair of offices. The boat carrying the heir was seized by pirates, who handed over their prize to the English king. Robert III died of grief two weeks later, and Henry IV of England now held captive the Scottish king.

As in the case of David II, the political situation was not particularly auspicious for a quick end to the captivity. The duke of Albany, whose own son was also a captive in English hands, was in no hurry to have James return, nor was Henry IV eager to give up his prize. Negotiations for release of the king—along with Albany's son, Murdoch, and a third noble captive, Archibald Douglas—began

---

[106] Campbell, 'England', 202; Penman, *David II*, 179, 188, 213. This may have been envisaged in the 1354 draft, which called for hostages to be 'released according to the amount of the payment' (above, p. 184, n. 70), but this clause is notably absent from the final treaty. A similar mechanism was eventually included in an agreement supplementary to the Treaty of Brétigny, a fact that may have inspired the speculation on this point. See *Foedera*, 3.1:538.

[107] E. W. M. Balfour-Melville, *James I, King of Scots, 1406–1437* (London, 1936), which pays uncommon attention to the hostages; Michael Brown, *James I* (Edinburgh, 1994).

immediately.[108] Douglas arranged for his release in exchange for twelve hostages in 1407; Murdoch was freed in an exchange for a captive English noble in 1416.[109] The first serious move toward the king's release came only after Murdoch's release, when Henry V agreed in principle to release James against hostages to guarantee a 100,000 mark fine in case of violation, but nothing came of the plan; a second proposed release against hostages, in 1421, also failed.[110]

It took the deaths of both Albany (1420) and Henry V (1422) to pave the way for James's freedom. The first indication of terms appears in instructions given to the English negotiators in July 1423: a ransom secured by hostages, a truce leading to a peace agreement, and a marriage alliance. A preliminary draft of 10 September fixed the ransom at 40,000 l., payable over six years, but as the Scottish ambassadors could not at that point provide names of hostages, negotiations on that matter were postponed: James was to appear at Durham on 1 March to arrange with his nobles for some of them to enter into custody.[111] The treaty concluded on 4 December is solely concerned with the ransom and the hostages. James's appearance at Durham was moved up to 9 February to allow him the rest of the month to arrange his hostages, who were to be handed over by 31 March at the latest. The terms were spelled out in great detail: The hostages were to be those contained in a schedule attached to the treaty, or others equivalent in wealth and income; the ambassadors would have to swear to their identities. The Scots would be allowed to substitute hostages of equal value to obtain the release of those held. The hostages had to swear to remain in custody until the ransom was fully paid. Any lord on the list who sent his heir in his stead as a hostage had to supply letters of obligation vouching for the son's behaviour, promising to return the son if he fled custody, and—notably—undertaking not to disinherit the son; a model letter was annexed to the treaty.[112] The hostages were to be maintained at their own expense. Any hostage who died had to be replaced within three months by one or more equivalent in value.[113] The annexed list of hostages included twenty-one names, and here what was meant by value is made explicit, as each of the hostages has a monetary figure assigned, representing annual income and totalling 16,500 marks.[114] Eleven of the twenty-one were allowed to substitute an heir.[115]

The final version of the agreement was sealed on 28 March. The list of hostages had in the meantime changed, with nine hostages worth a total of 5,500 marks replaced with fifteen others worth the same amount.[116] The treaty produced an explosion of surviving ancillary documentation, much of it concerning

[108] Nicholson, *Scotland*, 230.
[109] Douglas: Nicholson, *Scotland*, 230; William Fraser, *The Douglas Book*, 4 vols. (Edinburgh, 1885), 3:46–7; *Rotuli Scotiæ*, 2:181–3, 186. Murdoch: Balfour-Melville, *James I*, 61–6; *Rotuli Scotiæ*, 2:187 (proposed hostages in 1408).
[110] *Foedera*², 9:417; Brown, *James I*, 23.
[111] *Foedera*², 10:294–5, 299–300.
[112] *Foedera*², 10:306–7.
[113] *Foedera*², 10:302–5. See Balfour-Melville, *James I*, 98–9.
[114] *Foedera*², 10:327.
[115] *Foedera*², 10:307–8.
[116] *Foedera*², 10:327–8. Cf. Balfour-Melville, *James I*, 103; Nicholson, *Scotland*, 285.

the hostages:[117] a collective oath of the hostages;[118] four of the seven promised letters obligatory of fathers who were sending their sons;[119] various orders effecting the transfers of the hostages to certain castles and ultimately of twenty-two to the Tower of London;[120] a request from the hostages for and orders to grant safe conducts for various retainers to join them in London;[121] and safe conducts.[122] James returned to Scotland with his new English wife in April 1424 to begin his independent reign.

The original treaty called for the rotation of hostages from time to time, and this happened first one year into the treaty. At least sixteen hostages were moved from London and Knaresborough beginning during the spring and summer of 1425.[123] Eleven were ultimately granted licences to depart and were exchanged for eleven others at Durham in August. Three of the replacements had been in the initial offer of hostages from the previous year; one was the son of one of the released lords.[124] A second exchange was arranged in 1427, although this was complicated by the death from plague of several of the hostages in London, who had not been replaced as promised, and disputes over matching released hostages to substitutes of equal value. In the end, fourteen hostages were exchanged for fifteen others, this time with hostages carefully matched to their substitutes; the earl of Crawford was replaced by two hostages, each of the others by one. But because the dead hostages had not been replaced, the total number in custody dropped to twenty. Of the original hostages, only one remained, while only four of those granted in the first exchange were kept on.[125] The Scots began to press for another rotation in 1430,[126] but it did not come to pass until 1432, when fifteen hostages were replaced by eighteen newcomers. Again, substitutions were effected on an individual basis to ensure that the new arrivals were of sufficient value, and the dead hostages remained unreplaced.[127] This transaction still left one of the

[117] *Foedera²*, 10:325–6, which must be misdated, records the transfer to the royal treasurer of a dossier of documents concerning James's release. See in addition to the documents cited below *Calendar of Documents Relating to Scotland*, 5:984–5, 987.

[118] *Foedera²*, 10:333–4.

[119] *Foedera²*, 10:334–5. Cf. Balfour-Melville, *James I*, 103 n. 4.

[120] *Foedera²*, 10:335–7. Balfour-Melville, *James I*, 103, adduces additional unpublished texts that I have not had the opportunity to consult; see also 127.

[121] *Foedera²*, 10:337–8.

[122] *Foedera²*, 10:340; *Rotuli Scotia*, 2:248–9, 252; *Calendar of Documents Relating to Scotland*, 4.195–6, 198–9 (nos. 961, 970). See also Balfour-Melville, *James I*, 127.

[123] Balfour-Melville, *James I*, 127; *Foedera²*, 10:345 (Robert Erskine and James Dunbar from Knaresborough to the sheriff of York; fourteen others from Henry Lounde to the sheriff of York), 346–7 (order to sheriff of York to receive these hostages).

[124] *Foedera²*, 10:348–9. March, Montgomery, and Hay had been on the original hostage schedule; Robert of Lisle was replaced by his son, George. See also *Foedera²*, 10:351, 364–5 (safe conducts).

[125] Transfer orders: *Foedera²*, 10:369–70, 373, 375–6; *Registrum honoris de Morton*, 1:xlii. Licences to depart: *Foedera²*, 10:372, 381–2. See also *Calendar of Documents Relating to Scotland*, 4:206–8 (nos. 1005, 1009–11, 1013); Balfour-Melville, *James I*, 143, 146–50; *Foedera²*, 10:416 (later transfer of hostages); 460–1 (request for expenses); 471, 497, 522–3 (safe conducts for retainers); *Rotuli Scotia*, 2:270, 273, 274, 275, 276, 280 (safe conducts).

[126] *Rotuli Scotia*, 2:269; *Foedera²*, 10:482–3; Balfour-Melville, *James I*, 182–3.

[127] *Foedera²*, 10:509–14, 521–2; *Rotuli Scotia*, 2:276–9; *Calendar of Documents Relating to Scotland*, 4:218 (no. 1057); Balfour-Melville, *James I*, 201–3.

original hostages from 1424, one from the first rotation in 1425, and four from the second rotation of 1427, raising the total number of hostages to twenty-four. This was to be the last wholesale rotation. While the average period of custody of the hostages released by 1427 was around three years, the twenty-four who remained were much less fortunate. As many as eight may have died in custody; another five disappear from the records after the 1432 rotation, one after 1435, one after 1438, and two after 1444. Of the seven whom we know were released, five had to wait until after 1444 for their freedom. Malise, earl of Menteith, only gained his freedom after twenty-six years, in 1453.[128] James had been assassinated sixteen years earlier.

Once again, as simple guarantee mechanisms, the hostages failed to work. The original debt of 40,000 l.—in six yearly instalments of 10,000 marks, with the sixth instalment likely to be forgiven as the dowry of James's new wife[129]—was in arrears almost from the beginning, and, despite formidable taxation, a papal dona-tion, and evidence that plenty of money was raised and often ready for payment, only 9,500 marks were ever delivered.[130] This does not mean that the hostage trans-action was a sham. The attention paid by the English to the details of the hostage-ships is evidence enough that they took it seriously, but they were not the only ones. The Scottish parliament acceded to taxation demands with payment in mind, and the risk to the hostages was acknowledged by Charles VII of France when entering a military alliance with James in 1428.[131] James didn't pay the ransom because he didn't have to; England was not about to attack Scotland over 40,000 l., and in any case her forces were well occupied in France.[132] Not paying the ran-som meant leaving hostages in custody, of course, but this does not appear to have been a problem for James. Rather, like David II before him, he may have used the situation to his advantage.

In this case, too, we can see a disconnect between the perceptions of 'value' of the hostages on the two sides of the transaction. The English were notably con-cerned with yearly income as a measure of value: the figures were listed on the initial schedule; the substitutions for the initial grant were different in number, but had an identical total income; the English ambassadors in 1424 were specifically instructed to see to it that the hostages were 'of the requisite wealth';[133] fathers who sent their sons were required to promise not to disinherit them; three hostages brought north for the first exchange in 1425 may have been kept back because the substitutes were of insufficient wealth;[134] hostages offered by the Scots in 1427

---

[128] Balfour-Melville, *James I*, 293–93 (ap. D). Menteith: Balfour-Melville, *James I*, 150; Nicholson, *Scotland*, 368; *Calendar of Documents Relating to Scotland*, 4:256 (no. 1259). Safe conducts for serv-ants of hostages following 1432: *Foedera²*, 10:537, 590, 712. Exchange of Alan Cathcart for his son: *Foedera²*, 11:117. See also *Calendar of Documents Relating to Scotland*, 5:294 (no. 1022).

[129] *Foedera²*, 10:322–3.

[130] Balfour-Melville, *James I*, 110, 126–7, 146–7, 182–3, 258–9; Nicholson, *Scotland*, 244, 282–4.

[131] Nicholson, *Scotland*, 289.

[132] Brown, *James I*, 109.

[133] Balfour-Melville, *James I*, 101.

[134] Balfour-Melville, *James I*, 128; *Foedera²*, 10:349.

were certainly rejected, which contributed to the delays in that exchange;[135] and in the second and third exchanges, hostages were matched one-for-one (or in a few cases one-to-two) to their substitutes, which would have made controlling for wealth a simpler matter. The income of the hostages bore no relationship to the amount of the debt, nor did it have to, as the hostages were explicitly *not* paying sureties. The towns were: as part of the 1425 treaty, Dundee, Aberdeen, Edinburgh, and Perth each undertook through letters of obligation to pay the entire ransom, should James default.[136] From the English perspective, then, income was simply an indicator of status and presumably ability to exercise political pressure. Titles were of no concern, for titles were not necessarily an index of wealth. The original schedule named six earls, the marshal, and the constable, but none of these was the wealthiest on the list: that honour belonged to Duncan Campbell of Argyll and James Douglas of Dalkeith. The first set of actual hostages included only two of those six earls, and while the son of the earl of March was replaced at one point by the earl of Sutherland, the earl of Crawford could be replaced by the son of the sheriff of Angus and a simple knight.[137]

The English may have been correct in their analysis that wealth was a better indicator of political power than office, but it did them little good, for their hostages failed to exercise the desired influence. Why? Allies and opponents break down less easily here than in the case of David II, but like his predecessor James was able to use the fact of hostageship to his own advantage in dealing with the Scottish nobility.[138] The nobility had run the country during the king's long captivity, and the simple fact of his return meant a loss of their power. James was, in the early years of his personal rule at least, a master at manipulating his magnates and playing lineages off against each other.[139] Hostageship was a convenient tool for his machinations.

The enforced departure of a substantial number of nobles on James's return from captivity has been seen as contributing to his success in establishing his independent power. The differences in the hostage lists of the draft treaty of December 1423 and the final version of March 1424 show the king at work. The initial list, negotiated principally by the magnates, had spared the Douglas, Mar, and Albany families, and had weighed heavily upon their rivals, such as the earls of March and Angus. The nine hostages struck from the list once the king gained the upper hand in the negotiations included March and Angus, two of the king's nephews, and a number of other figures who would prove to be influential royal allies. One was a simple pawn: James used Malcolm Fleming as an intermediary in the discussions that led to the arrest of Walter Stewart—and of Fleming himself. Another, John Kennedy of Dunure, was a nephew whom the king wished to favour in a dispute internal to that family.[140] Later, Malise Graham's long hostageship served the twin

---

[135] Balfour-Melville, *James I*, 146.
[136] *Foedera²*, 10:324–5.
[137] *Foedera²*, 10:381.
[138] Nicholson, *Scotland*, 291.
[139] This is the central thesis of Brown, *James I*.
[140] Brown, *James I*, 42–3, 46–7, 128. See also Nicholson, *Scotland*, 288.

goals of weakening the Graham family while gaining the support of the earl of Atholl.[141] This is not to deny that James would have preferred some of the hostages to stay in Scotland. Three of the hostages in the first exchange, for example, played a role in the condemnation of the duke of Albany. Yet Balfour-Melville surmises that it was precisely James's need to have them on hand that led to the delay in delivering them for the exchange: James had to give up his men, but because of the way the process worked, he could do it on his own schedule.[142] In the end, James's manipulation of his hostages may have contributed to his undoing: his assassins were led by the head of the Graham family and abetted by the earl of Atholl, whose own son had died as a hostage in London some three years earlier. Their violent action is further evidence that his policy was working.

The case of James I demonstrates how much the balance of power between debtor (captive) and creditor (captor) had shifted in royal ransom transactions since the twelfth century. The simple fact of the participation of the debtor in the choice of hostages was itself a novelty, first explicitly stated in the second ransom treaty for Richard I, and evident in the French proposals concerning the count of Poitiers before the capture of Louis IX. Respect for the status of a royal negotiating partner, even one in captivity, may have played a role. But the shift was principally a result of the number of individuals now involved; with dozens or even hundreds of hostages required, there would never be enough royal sons or close relatives available. Although princes might head the lists of hostages, others were included, and because the relative value of these others might not be as obvious to the creditor, an opening was created for the debtor to exercise more control over the proceedings. The increased complexity of diplomacy, with multiple drafts of written treaties and supplementary documentation for various parts of the agreements, presented numerous opportunities for bargaining and manipulation.

It was not only royal diplomacy that had become more complex. The political environment itself in which high-level negotiations played themselves out involved more segments of society. The hostage lists for Charles of Salerno and John II, for example, reflect the rising importance of the towns to royal power and the increasingly territorial articulation of that power. Like the increase in the numbers of hostages, the expansion of the pool of possible hostages also presented opportunities to both creditor and debtor. Guarantees for high-stakes agreements such as those for royal ransoms could be more finely tailored to fit the realities of power and the exigencies of international diplomacy.

Perhaps for this reason, hostages for royal ransom offer a middle ground between the hostageship of the early Middle Ages, in which identity was essential, and the developing de-individualized model of later medieval hostageship, which reached its extreme in the institution of the *Einlager*. In their dealings with the Scots and French, the English did care more about the income, value, or 'sufficiency' of hostages than about who precisely they were; this is why substitutions and rotations

[141] Balfour-Melville, *James I*, 149–50; Nicholson, *Scotland*, 320–1; Brown, *James I*, 86–7.
[142] Balfour-Melville, *James I*, 128.

were permitted and expected. And Alfonso III and Edward III probably cared little exactly which men various towns offered as hostages, as long as hostages were delivered. Yet the creditors in these cases were not ignoring entirely the question of identity. Money served not as an end in itself, as in a transaction involving an *Ein-lager*, but rather as a marker of identity. In English eyes, the wealthy were more likely to be individuals who could exercise influence. Similarly, citizenship in a town served as a marker of political power: the fate of citizens of a given town would be more or less relevant to the debtor's power. To the debtors granting the hostages, however, identity per se remained important; it is what allowed them to use hostageship to their own ends, to manipulate magnate politics. Just as in the early Middle Ages, where certain cross-cultural hostage transactions clearly meant different things to the two parties involved, here too a differential understanding of the import of the hostages themselves was what made agreements possible.

Hostages were no more likely to work as simple guarantees in royal ransom transactions than they were in less high-profile agreements. Baldwin of Jerusalem did fulfil his obligation, even though he was in a position not to, but the ransoms of Louis IX, Richard I, Charles II, David II, and James I were never entirely paid off. Their failure is perhaps easier to understand. In some cases the ransom demands were unrealistically high, while the political situations that engendered the agreements were almost guaranteed to change more quickly than such sums could be raised. Still, these partial failures did little to deter royal negotiators from turning to hostages. They, like their non-royal contemporaries and their early medieval predecessors, saw hostageship as more than a simple guarantee, and they continued to find physical control of individuals essential to the workings of political life.

7

Hostageship Interpreted, from the Middle Ages to the Age of Terrorism

The preceding chapters have developed a composite picture of hostageship, explaining how it operated in various situations, how the broader institutional context extended its possible social and political roles, and how it changed over time. The medieval hostage, designated by the Latin term *obses* or vernacular terms such as *ostage* or *gisl*, was a third-party guarantor of an agreement, actually or potentially subject to loss of liberty, and given rather than taken. Sources consistently distinguish such figures from captives or prisoners of war. These terms occasionally refer to non-custodial sureties—always more common—such as guarantors who promised to pay the principal's debt themselves, or to persuade or force the principal to pay, but this is normally evident from context. The putative force of hostageship as a form of surety lay in the threat to the life of the hostage in case of default; ties of blood magnified the threat, hence the prevalence of sons as hostages. In practice, however, execution or even mutilation of hostages is strikingly rare throughout the Middle Ages and often not directly related to violation of the underlying agreement. Furthermore, treatment of hostages before or after a default depended more on social rank and particular circumstance than on legal status. And the range of possible hostages extends well beyond sons of the grantors. Medieval hostageship is thus best studied by examining its changing contexts, rather than its rate of success as a guarantee or adherence to a theoretical model.

In the early Middle Ages, hostageship was an element of the mechanics of diplomacy and warfare, but the ways in which hostages implicated individuals beyond the grantor and the receiver reveal how the institution was embedded in the structures of kinship and practices of alliance characteristic of elite political society in that period. Hostages served as guarantees, but their symbolic and communicative roles often predominated. From the eleventh and twelfth centuries, hostageship diversifies, with more people, and more kinds of people, giving and receiving hostages for a wider variety of purposes. Female hostages appear, as do conditional hostages and hostages representing newly powerful segments of society. Uses of hostageship only rarely apparent in the early medieval sources become common: conditional release and ransom transactions or conditional respite agreements, but also guarantees for monetary debts unconnected to warfare. This diffusion of hostageship is further evident in its formalization: the development of norms and even laws governing the institution. Hostages continue to appear most commonly among the highest elites, and cases involving the ransom of kings offer the most

detail; nevertheless, the extension of the institution into the realm of simple monetary transactions means that hostages may be found at much less exalted levels of
society. Most striking is the fact that hostageship persists as a form of guarantee
despite the spread of a legal and financial culture that would seem to have made it
superfluous. In this way, hostages may be considered a characteristic aspect of
medieval political life.

This study, then, has offered a framework for the modern historian to understand a medieval practice. Little has been said, however, about how hostageship
was understood by medieval contemporaries—information normally concealed
behind the language of the sources. Limited evidence does survive that allows us to
see that various aspects of hostageship were the subject of debate. Much of this
evidence deals with situations when hostages were *not* used, either because requests
were refused or were not made in the first place—when the question of how hostages functioned as guarantees was bypassed. Indeed, when we hear their voices,
contemporaries seemed concerned less with the mechanics of agreement than with
issues of behaviour and status. The sources often offer conflicting views, but we can
detect a strain of disapproval of hostageship in many of these sources—a strain that
clearly runs counter to the widespread and even increasing use of hostages in the
Middle Ages. Such views thus had little apparent impact when first voiced, but
they were in the end quite significant for the later history of the institution.

MEDIEVAL VIEWS OF HOSTAGESHIP

Serving as a hostage, whether as a volunteer or not, could be viewed as honourable,
whether because of the perceived danger of service, or the obligation to one's lord.
In Ammianus's account of the Battle of Adrianople, Ricomer volunteers to serve as
a hostage for Fritigern's safe passage, 'thinking it a great deed and one fitting for a
brave man'.[1] The Saint-Denis chronicler instead focused on the selfless nature of
the unfortunate hostages for the capitulation of Senlis in 1418: they 'offered themselves freely, impassioned by a desire for the peace and concord of the town', and
the author goes on to praise their 'true and heartfelt fidelity'.[2] Of course these
descriptions might mask internal doubts. Commynes's (largely discredited) account
of Louis XI and Charles the Bold at Peronne in 1468 acknowledges this possibility:
'Those whom the king named as hostages offered themselves enthusiastically, at
least in public—I do not know if they said the same in private...I doubt it.' Even
if they thought, like Commynes, that the king would abandon them, they could
not abandon their kinsman and lord.[3] Conversely, violating one's duties as part of
a hostage agreement was shameful. The case of Louis of Anjou, whose broken oath

---

[1] Amm. Marc. 31.12.15: 'pulcrum hoc quoque facinus et viro convenire existimans forti'.

[2] Pintoin, *Chronique du religieux de Saint-Denys*, 38 (ed. Bellaguet, 6:194): 'zelo pacis et concordie
rei publice succensi, se obsides libere obtulerunt...sincera et cordialis fidelitas'.

[3] Commynes, *Mémoires*, 2.9 (SHF 1:172): 'Ceulx que le Roy nommoit pour estre ostaiges, se
offroient fort, au moins en public. Je ne scay s'ilz disoient ainsi à part: je me doubte que non.' Peronne:
Richard Vaughan, *Charles the Bold: The Last Valois Duke of Burgundy* (London, 1973), 53–8.

led to the return into captivity of John II of France, offers the clearest proof, which may also be found in the concern evident in the record for the oaths of hostages. Questions of honour also applied to the duties of the debtor to his hostage. Roger of Wendover pointed to Richard I's need to free his hostages as excusing his treatment of John's supporters upon his return to England, behaviour that might otherwise be seen as 'greedier than befit the royal majesty'.[4] More explicit is the complaint of Thomas Muschamp, left as a hostage in Scotland by John de Lilleburn for three weeks to allow the latter to seek his ransom. Abandoned, he appealed to the king: Lilleburn's behaviour was 'Contrarie to the order of Chivellrie' and the source of 'a scandall and infamie to the English nacion'.[5] Honour applied in the case of the creditor, as well: in Saxo's account of the siege of Arkon in 1168, when the Danish army objects to a surrender treaty, their commander says that if they repudiate the treaty the hostages they had received had to be sent back unharmed, lest they be thought to have dealt with 'less than sincere faith' or their good word be besmirched.[6]

As has been seen, scandal hardly stopped debtors from abandoning their hostages, and this helps us to understand the efforts made by individuals to avoid such service.[7] Fear of abandonment and its consequences is never cited explicitly, for this would require a direct insult to one's lord. The arguments of reluctant hostages were more practical or legalistic. Ricomer offered himself as a hostage because the tribune Equitius had refused, citing fear of reprisals for having escaped on a previous occasion from Gothic custody.[8] Jean des Haies argued successfully to the Parlement of Paris in 1361 that he should not have to serve as a hostage for Orléans, on the reasonable grounds that he 'was not a native of the town, nor did his family live there'.[9] Ingerer d'Amboise objected strongly in correspondence with Charles V to the king's order that he be sent to England as a replacement hostage for Guy of Blois in 1366. His principal arguments were that it was unjust for someone to suffer captivity twice as a result of the same battle and that his relationship with Blois did not require such service: he was not Guy's man, and in fact had a long series of complaints against the count. But above all his concerns were financial: a return to England would interfere with his continuing efforts to raise his own ransom.[10] Robert of Nunant had tried the argument from lordship years earlier, when he refused to serve as a hostage for Richard I, claiming that he was John's man. And the *History of William Marshal* has David de la Roche refuse to serve as a hostage

---

[4] Roger of Wendover, *Flores historiarium*, s.a. 1194 (RS 84.1:232): 'avidius quam regiam deceret majestatem'.

[5] A. King, ' "According to the Custom Used in the French and Scottish Wars": Prisoners and Casualties on the Scottish Marches in the Fourteenth Century', *Journal of Medieval History*, 28 (2002), 278.

[6] Saxo Grammaticus, *Gesta Danorum*, 14.39.26–7 (ed. Olrik and Ræder, 1:470–1): 'ne parum sincera fide'.

[7] As well as the efforts of towns. The Lord Edward granted the town of Bergerac the right not to serve as hostages (*Rôles gascons*, 4:12–13 [no. 4378]).

[8] Amm. Marc. 31.12.15.

[9] *GCA* 408–9: 'non est natus de dicta villa nec in ea habet cognationem suam'.

[10] *Original Documents Relating to the Hostages of John*, 40–5.

on the grounds that the Marshal had been a *bad* lord to him (an act of defiance that is described as shameful, if not treasonous).[11] Where expressions of fear are heard, it is in the voices of parents of child hostages. Ammianus tells of the pleas of Ala-mannic leaders, 'fathers of hostages', to Valentinian I not to build fortifications that would surely lead to war, and thus to the death of their sons.[12] Matilda of Braose countered King John's request for her sons in 1209 by stating her concern for their lives, accusing the king of murdering his nephew, Arthur, 'whom he ought to have taken care of honourably'.[13]

I have argued that execution of hostages was a rarity, both because it is rarely attested in the sources and because one would *expect* it to be attested in the sources when it occurred. Even when mentioned, executions did not always engender comment, critical or otherwise: John of Salisbury's discussion of the hanging of a Brescian noble in 1168, for example, is surprisingly dispassionate.[14] In addition, sources are often biased toward one or another view, or take more or less of an interest in emotional detail or even veracity. Guillaume le Breton, assembling jus-tifications for Philip Augustus's designs on England, rounded out his portrait of the monster King John as a murderer not just of his nephew, Arthur, but also 'a great number of children and 183 hostages'. When Albert of Aachen characterized Mawdud's execution of the son of Ridwan as 'wicked and treacherous', he was describing not only a Muslim enemy, but an offence against someone who was in a state of truce with Tancred; the parallel Muslim source passed over the episode without comment. Later the Saint-Denis chronicler lamented movingly the fate of the hostages at Senlis, while Monstrelet offered no comment.[15] Still, discussions of execution offer revealing evidence for contemporary views, which turn out to be very complex.

Froissart suggests a general disapproval of the execution of the hostages at Derval in 1373 by the duke of Anjou, as well as of the retaliatory executions of prisoners by Robert Knollys, despite the fact that Knollys had clearly violated the conditional surrender agreement. Anjou's men tried to convince him not to carry out execu-tions, and the chronicler concluded that 'all things considered, it was a great pity that, because of the judgment of those two, eight gentlemen had to die thus'.[16] This stands in sharp contrast to Henry V's execution of *prisoners* at Montereau in 1420, eleven men captured during the assault on the town whom Henry threat-ened to execute if the town did not capitulate. It was not Henry, but rather the

---

[11] Roger of Howden, *Chronica* (RS 51.3:233); above, p. 176; *History of William Marshal*, 14400–46 (ed. Holden, 2:220–2). Cf. Molinet, *Chroniques*, 181 (ed. Buchon, 3:311).

[12] Amm. Marc. 28.2.6: 'obsidum patres'.

[13] Roger of Wendover, *Flores historiarum*, s.a. 1208 (RS 84.2:48–9): 'quem honorifice custodisse debuerat, turpiter interfecit'.

[14] John of Salisbury, *Letters*, 272 (OMT 2:554–60).

[15] Guillaume le Breton, *Gesta Philippi Augusti*, 171 (SHF 1:253) ('et plurimos parvulos, CLXXXIII obsides suspenderat'); Albert of Aachen, *Historia Ierosolimitana*, 11.39 (OMT 812) ('impie et dolose'); Ibn al-Athīr, *Chronicle* (trans. Richards, 1:156–7); Monstrelet 1.186 (3:251–3); Pintoin, *Chronique du religieux de Saint-Denys*, 38 (ed. Bellaguet, 6:196).

[16] Froissart 1.742 (8.2:159–60): 'tout considéré, ce fu grans pités que, pour l'oppinion d'yaus deus, huit gentil homme furent ensi mort'.

commander of the garrison who was blamed for pointlessly leaving them to their deaths, as he surrendered anyway six days later.[17] In the case of the hostages, whose lives custom should have protected, the stubbornness of both parties was at fault; in the case of the prisoners, whose lives were in fact forfeit, it was only the garrison commander who received criticism—not simply because he let them die, but because he let them die when he should have known that his situation was hopeless.

Two more detailed commentaries come from the very beginning and the very end of our period. The first is Agathias's account of Narses' siege of Lucca in 553.[18] The general and the town had entered into a conditional surrender agreement, with the town promising to submit if not relieved within thirty days and granting hostages as a guarantee. When the town violated the agreement, Narses staged a mock execution of the hostages. Narses then told the town that if it surrendered, the hostages would be 'restored to life'. The town agreed, and Narses revealed that the hostages were not in fact dead. Still the town refused to keep its agreement, but Narses simply released the hostages, who then worked (unsuccessfully) to convince the town to submit. Modern scholars, who hold a dim view of Agathias's talents as a historian, find little to trust in this account.[19] The mock execution, the release of the hostages despite the violation of the agreement, and the support of the hostages for Narses are not implausible, as has been demonstrated throughout this study; but the veracity of the account is less important than the interpretations of hostageship that it presents.

As in the case of William Marshal, we find here advisors arguing for the execution of the hostages. Like Stephen, Narses rejected their advice: 'The general, however, who would never allow anger to cloud his judgment, did not descend to such cruelty as to kill people who had done no wrong, merely as a reprisal for the misdeeds of others.'[20] Of course the townsmen were unaware of this, and when they thought the hostages had been killed, they attacked him as wicked (ἀτάσθαλον) and a murderer. Narses' response was to point out that they were the ones at fault for breaking the treaty. After he freed the hostages, the townsmen 'were marvelling at what he did and quite unable to understand why he did it'. We have just seen the argument that blame lies not with the party that executes the victims but rather with the party that put them in the position of being executed. Agathias seems to agree with this position: Narses would have been perfectly within his rights had he in fact executed the hostages. Of course he did not do so, and his reasoning—that killing innocents for the crimes of others is unfair—is very important. I return to the issue below.

---

[17] Fenin, *Mémoires* (SHF 140–2); Le Fèvre, *Chronique*, 110 (SHF 2:11–12); Monstrelet 1.227 (3:404–6); Chastellain, *Chronique*, 1.50–1 (ed. Kervyn de Lettenhove, 1:145–9); J. H. Wylie and W. T. Waugh, *The Reign of Henry the Fifth*, 3 vols. (Cambridge, 1914–29), 3:209–10.

[18] Agathias, *Historiae*, 1.12–13, 18.5 (CFHB 2:24–7, 33; trans. CFHB 2A:19–21, 26).

[19] M. Ites, 'Zur Bewertung des Agathias', *Byzantinische Zeitschrift*, 26 (1926), 281; Ernst Stein, *Histoire du Bas-Empire*, 2 vols. (Paris, 1949–59), 2:606 n. 2; Averil Cameron, *Agathias* (Oxford, 1970), 51.

[20] Trans. CFHB 2A:19.

Philippe de Commynes's reputation as a historian is not that much better than that of Agathias, although the use of hostages during the conflict between the dukes of Burgundy and the town of Liège in 1466–7 is well corroborated by other sources.[21] His account offers a view of the later medieval noble understanding of hostageship. The Burgundians held fifty hostages from Liège and allied towns, granted in 1466 under the terms of the Treaty of Oleye to guarantee payments of 100,000 florins per year for six years. When open warfare broke out the following year, Charles the Bold would have been within his rights to execute the hostages, but he apparently released them.

Commynes addresses hostages at three stages in his account of the affair. The first is during the original grant of hostages. The Liègeois were supposed to deliver the hostages named in the treaty at eight in the morning; by twelve, they had not been handed over, and the duke needed to decide what to do. In the course of a heated debate, two advisors, among them the lord of Contay, pushed him to take advantage of the fact that the Liègeois were disbanding and attack, a position supported by the troops eager for booty. He chose, however, to follow the advice of the count of Saint-Pol, who argued that 'it would be contrary to his honour and promise to do so, saying that so many men could not agree so soon on a question such as that of the delivery of the hostages, and in such a great number'. Neither argument was particularly strong: the identity of the hostages had been decided in advance, as Commynes himself writes ('named in a roll'), and the Liègeois had in fact violated the agreement. Nonetheless, Commynes praises the duke for this decision.[22]

The Liègeois violated the peace in 1467, as Commynes notes, 'notwithstanding the hostages they had granted the previous year, who were subject to capital punishment if they broke the treaty'. There ensued another debate, this time about the fate of the hostages. Contay was among those urging that they all be killed. It was the argument of the lord of Humbercourt, however, that prevailed:

> that in order to put God on his side in all things and to make it known to everyone that he was neither cruel nor vindictive, he should free all 300 hostages, given that they were granted in good faith and in the hope that the peace would hold; but that they should be told as they left of the grace accorded them by the duke, and encouraged to try to bring this people back to a state of peace; and if they wouldn't accept that, that they at least, given the good turn that had been done for them, would not take up arms against him, nor against their bishop, who was in his company. This argument prevailed, and as they were released the said hostages promised to do the abovementioned things. They were also told that if they engaged in warfare, and were captured, it would cost them their heads; and so they went.

---

[21] e.g. *Régestes de la cité de Liège*, 4:197–200, 202–4 (nos. 997, 999); Du Clercq, *Mémoires*, 5.64 (ed. Reiffenberg, 4:288–9). See Vaughan, *Charles the Bold*, 11–25; Geneviève Xhayet, *Réseaux de pouvoir et solidarités de parti à Liège au Moyen Âge (1250–1468)* (Geneva, 1997), 331.

[22] Commynes, *Mémoires*, 2.1 (SHF 1:118–20): 'ce seroit contre son honneur et promesse de ainsi le faire: disant que tant de gens ne peuvent estre si tost acordez en telle matiere, comme de bailler ostaiges, et en si grant nombre'; 'nommez en ung rolle'.

Commynes clearly approves, and even suggests that Contay's death a year later was tied to the harshness of his advice concerning the 'poor hostages'[23]—another echo of King Stephen's counsellors from the *History of William Marshal*, who likewise argued for execution.[24] He notes, without comment, the fact that some of these freed hostages were among townsmen handed over at the capitulations of Saint-Trond and Tongeren and executed, although later comments suggest that they had violated their promise by participating in the defence of those towns, as had others elsewhere. He contrasts their behaviour to that of a small group of hostages who returned to Liège itself. These orchestrated the capitulation of that town, delivering the keys of the city at the head of 300 townsmen who made the formal submission, and then acting as go-betweens for Humbercourt as he arranged for the actual opening of the city to the Burgundian forces.[25] The behaviour of the hostages, like the behaviour of the Burgundian and French lords, offers an occasion for moralizing. Just as Contay's death was linked to his advice concerning the hostages, the duke's success was tied to his decision not to follow that advice: 'In the judgment of men he received these honours because of the grace and favour which he had shown towards the hostages.' Commynes frames the duke's treatment of the hostages as an act of leniency: it was an example not of the princely virtue of adherence to a promise (as in Saint-Pol's flawed argument), but of how doing a generous thing could have positive results. He writes:

> One should never fail to do good, because just one man, or the meanest of those to whom you have once done good, may by chance do you a good turn or service which will recompense you for all the knavery and ingratitude which others would have done in a similar circumstance. Thus you have seen how the hostages acted, some well and gratefully, the majority badly and ungraciously. Yet five or six alone sufficed to conclude this exploit to the duke of Burgundy's satisfaction.[26]

Once again, although the juridical realities of hostageship are acknowledged, they function more effectively outside the strict letter of agreements. The duke would

---

[23] Commynes, *Mémoires*, 2.2 (SHF 1:122–6): 'nonobstant les ostaiges qu'ilz avoient bailler l'an precedent, en peine capitalle, ou cas qu'ilz rompissent le traicté...que pour mettre Dieu de sa part de tous poinctz et pour donner à congnoistre à tout le monde qu'il n'étoit cruel ne vindicatif, qu'il delivrast tous les trois cens ostaiges: veu encores qu'ilz s'y estoient mis en bonne intention et esperans que la paix se tinst; mais que on leur dict, au despartir, la grace que ledict duc leur faisoit, leur priant qu'ilz taschassent à reduire ce peuple en bonne paix: et au cas qu'ilz ne voulsissent entendre, que au moins eulx, recongnoissans la bonté que on leur faisoit, ne se trouveroient en guerre contre luy, ne contre leur evesque, qui estoit en sa compaignie. Ceste oppinion fut tenue, et feirent les promesses dessusdictes lesdictz ostaiges, en les delivrant. Aussi leur fut dict que si aucun d'eulx se desclaroit en guerre, et fussent prins, qu'il leur cousteroit la teste: et ainsi s'en allerent'; 'ces povres ostagiers'.

[24] *History of William Marshal*, 509–10 (ed. Holden, 1:26).

[25] Commynes, *Mémoires*, 2.3 (SHF 1:133–7).

[26] Commynes, *Mémoires*, 2.3 (SHF 1:138–40; trans. Jones, 128): 'Et, au jugement des hommes, receut tous ces honneurs et biens pour la grace et bonté dont il avoit usé envers les ostaiges...l'on ne se doibt jamais lasser de bien faire. Car ung seul et le moindre de tous ceulx à qui on aura jamais faict bien, fera à l'adventure ung tel service, et aura telle recongnoissance, qu'il recompensera toutes les laschetez et meschansetez que avoient faict tous les aultres en cest endroict. Et ainsi avez vous veu de ces ostaiges, comme il y en eut aucuns bons et recongnoissans, et les aultres et la pluspart, mauvais et ingratz: cinq ou six seullement conduisoient cest œuvre aux fins et intentions du duc de Bourgongne.'

not have been culpable if he killed the hostages, but it is his trust in them—as honourable men rather than as mere pledges—that draws the chronicler's praise.

The complex link between hostageship and honour may also be traced in reactions to the use of hostages as a negotiating tactic or an instrument of power. Being in a position to receive hostages is, from the Roman sources forward, generally seen as a good.[27] Consequently, failure to accept or even to demand hostages in the course of a conflict could be a source of criticism. Charles the Fat was castigated by the Fulda annalist for buying off a Viking invasion instead of taking hostages: 'What was still more of a crime, he did not blush to pay tribute to a man from whom he ought to have taken hostages and exacted tribute, doing this on the advice of evil men and against the custom of his ancestors.'[28] This attack follows the annalist's description of how the emperor exchanged hostages with the Viking leader as part of their peace in 882. The chronicler stresses that both the granting of tribute and the peace with Godfrid generally were undertaken on the advice—once again—of false and treacherous counsellors. Thus it was not only the failure to receive hostages from the Northmen that was viewed as weakness, it was also the exchange, which involved a grant of hostages. Ceolwulf of Mercia's nearly contemporary characterization by the Anglo-Saxon chronicler as a 'foolish king's thegn' for granting hostages to the Vikings represents a similar critique.[29] Lambert of Hersfeld was more explicit: granting hostages, even for safe passage, was 'repugnant to royal majesty'. A good king always received hostages; he never turned them over.[30]

Failure to receive hostages from an enemy was not simply a sign of weakness. Writing to the empress Theophano, Hugh Capet criticized the refusal of Charles of Lorraine to accept a negotiated end to the siege of Laon: 'Wishing to maintain a state of most faithful alliance and holy friendship, we wanted to accept hostages from Charles and lift the siege, according to your will. But Charles, defying the legates and your imperial status, did not agree to this, nor did he release the queen, nor did he accept any hostages from the bishop [of Laon].' Here the refusal to accept hostages is described as obstinate—Hugh says that all this demonstrates Charles's *pertinatia*—and a direct insult to the empress, who was attempting to serve as mediator.[31] Refusal to accept hostages (again, in the context of a negotiated settlement) could also be associated with pride. Liutprand's account of the Battle

[27] The sentiment is shared by Irish sources: *Cert cech ríg co réil*, 5 (trans. O'Donoghue, 261) ('Take hostages from all, so that you may be a keen prince'); *Advice to a Prince*, 3 (trans. O'Donoghue, 51) ('the king who has not hostages in keeping is as ale in a leaky vessel'); and above, p. 38.

[28] *Annales Fuldenses*, s.a. 882 (MGH SrG 7:99; trans. Reuter, 93). Similarly: *Annales Fuldenses*, s.a. 849 (MGH SrG 7:39); Saxo Grammaticus, *Gesta Danorum*, 14.25.2 (ed. Olrik and Ræder, 1:426).

[29] *Annales Fuldenses*, s.a. 882 (MGH SrG 7:98–9); *ASC*, s.a. 874 ('unwisum cyninges þegne'). Cf. Lavelle, 'Use and Abuse', 279; Stephen S. Evans, *The Lords of Battle: Image and Reality in the Comitatus in Dark Age Britain* (Woodbridge, 1997), 117–18.

[30] Lambert of Hersfeld, *Annales*, s.a. 1073 (MGH SrG 38:163): 'abhorrere a maiestate regia'. Cf. Caes. *B Gall.* 1.14.

[31] Gerbert of Reims, *Briefsammlung*, 120 (MGH Briefe der deutschen Kaiserzeit 2:147–8): 'Benivolentiam ac affabilitatem vestram circa nos sentientes, obsides a K. accipere et obsidionem solvere secundum voluntatem vestram voluimus, fidissimam societatem ac sanctam amiciciam conservare cupientes. Porro hic K. legatos et imperium vestrum contempnens nec super his adquiescit nec reginam relinquit nec ab episcopo ullos obsides accipit.' Cf. *The Song of Roland*, 16.239–42 (ed. Brault, 2:16).

of Brenta in 899, which opened the way into Italy for the Magyar forces, relates that Berengar of Friuli turned down an offer of retreat and a promise—secured by their sons as hostages—never to enter Italy. 'But alas', Liutprand writes, 'the Christians, deceived by the swelling of pride', decided to fight.[32]

Despite these arguments associating hostages with power and sensible leadership, there remained a very good reason to reject the use of hostages. Another option was viewed as even better, both in terms of perception and pragmatism, namely trust. Lambert of Hersfeld's comment above describes the furious reaction of Henry IV when he learned that his legates had arranged for an exchange of hostages with Saxon rebels to guarantee safe passage to a peace conference. On his order, the archbishops of Mainz and Cologne appeared at the time and place for the exchange and convinced the Saxons to accept simple pledges of faith. In the following year, Lambert has Archbishop Anno reject Henry IV's request that he hand over six of his knights as a guarantee of his fidelity, arguing that 'no prior king had demanded such a thing of any of his predecessors'.[33] For Anno as for Henry, unsecured promises should have been enough.

Because of this, the rejection of an offer of a hostage could be a good. In Dudo of Saint-Quentin's somewhat confused account of the run-up to the Peace of Visé in 942, William, duke of Normandy, turns down an offer of a hostage from the German king for his and the French king's safety at negotiations. The king's envoy, Cono, had presented himself to William with these words: 'he has ordered me to remain as a hostage wherever you like'. When Cono returns with William (rather than being kept elsewhere as a guarantee), Cono explains to the king, 'Not wanting to keep me as a hostage for your solemn promise, he has come to you.' And when the duke and the king meet, the duke boasts: 'You sent Duke Cono to me, as a sort of pledge and hostage, so that I would come to you. But see how I, not distrusting you, am here with him!' Refusal of hostages is here a form of honourable behaviour. By accepting a hostage from the German king, William would be calling into question his solemn promise and not trusting him. In refusing the hostage offered, William not only honours the king by respecting his word, but also shows that he is himself honourable. This is, for Dudo, all part of an intricate dance: before deciding to send Cono back, William tests him to see if he is being deceitful; the German king, meanwhile, upon learning of the refusal of his hostage, marvels at William's dignity and sense of honour.[34] The offer and refusal of the hostage thus do not themselves establish trust, but they are central to it.[35]

---

[32] Liutprand of Cremona, *Antapodosis*, 2.13 (MGH SrG 41:43): 'Verum heu Christiani superbiae tumore decepti'.

[33] Lambert of Hersfeld, *Annales*, s.aa. 1073, 1074 (MGH SrG 38:163, 196): 'quod nullus regum priorum tale quid ab aliquo precessore suo postulasset'.

[34] Dudo of Saint-Quentin, *De moribus et actis primorum Normanniæ ducum*, 3.51–2 (ed. Lair, 195–7): 'præcipitque me morari pro obside quo mavis positum…Nolens me retinere pro obside, sacrosanctæ fidei tuæ tenore venit ad te…Misisti Cononem ducem ad me, ut venirem ad te, quasi pro pignore et obside. Sed, non tui diffidens, cum eo ego ecce.' See RI 2.1.1:110a; Geoffrey Koziol, *Begging Pardon and Favor: Ritual and Political Order in Early Medieval France* (Ithaca, 1992), 155.

[35] On hostages as a source of *mistrust*, see W. A. P. Martin, 'Traces of International Law in Ancient China', *The International Review*, 14 (1883), 73.

Gerbert of Reims's letter to Archbishop Ekbert of Trier after the victory of Hugh Capet seems to draw on a similar sentiment, praising the return of Verdun to the Empire 'without slaughter and blood, without hostages, and without payment'.[36] Odo of Cluny's depiction of Gerald of Aurillac dismissing a defeated enemy without first receiving hostages or an oath is potentially ambiguous, though given the hagiographical context, the writer probably meant this to be viewed as a merciful action that brought credit on the saint and no shame to his enemy.[37] Commynes's analysis of the events at Liège similarly played on these sentiments. Trust was a virtue.[38]

And not just among enemies. The author of the *History of William Marshal* makes the same point with reference to one's allies. When William was summoned to England by King John in 1207, one of his advisors recommended—presciently, as it turned out—that William demand hostages from his men for their fidelity. William rejected the advice: 'I would not wish just now, even for the price of a hundred marks in silver, that they came to know for certain that you had said such a thing, for it would be recorded to our eternal shame.'[39] The same discourse appears in the conflict between Henry VII of Germany and his father, the emperor Frederic II. For the father, Henry's taking of hostages from the margrave of Baden and the duke of Bavaria was an insult to his honour and evidence of tyranny.[40] A good lord trusted his men.

A practical argument could be made for elevating simple trust over the guarantee of hostages. Cassiodorus, as noted above, argued that hostages were no guarantee of faith in the absence of affections, suggesting that family ties were stronger.[41] Four centuries later, Atto of Vercelli offered a more pointed critique. In his letter to his suffragans concerning a royal request that the bishops grant hostages as proof of their loyalty, he argued that hostages should not be the issue: 'We have seen and heard of many cases in which a promise is broken after hostages have been given, and even some where faith is kept unto death without hostages.' Those who demand hostages are 'stupid, twisted, and not mindful of God'. In short, hostages don't work. Fidelity is all.[42] In context, Atto's theoretical argument against hostages misses the point, grounded as it is in a defence of the liberty of the church from

---

[36] Gerbert of Reims, *Briefsammlung*, 100 (MGH Briefe der deutschen Kaiserzeit 2:129–30): 'sine caede et sanguine, sine obsidibus, sine pecuniis'.

[37] Odo of Cluny, *De vita S. Geraldi comitis*, 1.40 (*PL* 133:667).

[38] Cf. Joseph Shatzmiller, *Shylock Reconsidered: Jews, Moneylending, and Medieval Society* (Berkeley, 1990), 117.

[39] *History of William Marshal*, 13513–22 (ed. Holden, 2:176; trans. 177).

[40] MGH Const. 2:236–8, 431–3 (nos. 193, 322); see Björn Weiler, *Kingship, Rebellion, and Political Culture: England and Germany, c.1215–c.1250* (Basingstoke, 2007), 39–52, 56, 70. Cf. *Annales Marbacenses*, s.a. 1235 (MGH SrG 9:96); Gottfried of Viterbo, *Gesta Heinrici VI.*, cont. Funiacensis et Eberbacensis, s.a. 1235 (MGH SS 22:348); *Annales Wormatienses*, s.a. 1233 (MGH SS 17:43); Weiler, *Kingship*, 57–8.

[41] Cassiodorus, *Variae*, 3.4 (MGH AA 12:80–1); above, p. 45.

[42] Atto of Vercelli, *Epistolae*, 11 (*PL* 134:120–4): 'Multos quoque audivimus et vidimus post datos obsides irritam fecisse sponsionem. Quosdam vero etiam absque datis obsidibus usque ab mortem fidem servasse...stolidis et perversis Deumque non curantium.' Cf. Atto of Vercelli, *Polipticum quod appellatur Perpendiculum*, 3 (ed. Goetz, 15).

secular powers rather than a cool analysis of the political situation of the church in tenth-century northern Italy. Yet the emotional, as opposed to practical, import of the request for hostages comes through: it is an insult to him and to his colleagues. The king should just trust them.

Given the significance of the papacy in medieval society, papal involvement with hostageship, both in practice and in theory, is another important source for contemporary views, if necessarily a particularly elite view. The popes employed hostages throughout the medieval period. As in the evidence just surveyed, their attitude was far from monolithic. Nevertheless, the notion of the superiority of unsecured faith appears clearly, and alongside this positive critique appears a negative one, attacking hostageship on the grounds of individual responsibility and liberty—ideas that were ahead of their time.

We have seen (Chapter 3, above) how the papacy was deeply involved in the hostage politics of the Carolingian–Lombard conflict, as when Hadrian I wrote to Charlemagne encouraging him not to release his hostage Grimoald after the death of the latter's father, Arichis (787).[43] This sort of papal intervention in hostage transactions continued past the Carolingian period. For example, in 1022, Benedict VIII took possession of the son of Waimar of Salerno, who had been handed over as a hostage to the archbishop of Cologne at the siege of Troia. Alexander III and Honorius III ordered parties to release hostages in 1165 and 1220.[44] Gregory IX intervened on at least three occasions to release hostages serving as guarantees in agreements involving ecclesiastics: once for return of property, once for a monetary debt, and once for orthodox behaviour.[45] In other cases, he allowed a bishop who had been released from captivity to use church income to liberate his hostage; directed a town to grant hostages to his delegates to help settle a conflict with another town; and required that hostages be delivered for a noble to be released from captivity.[46]

But medieval popes, like individuals and institutions both religious and secular in the period, also granted and received hostages *directly* as guarantees of agreements. It was in no way frowned upon as too worldly an activity by the eleventh- and twelfth-century reforming popes. Gregory VII demanded hostages from the Roman noble Cincius twice, in 1074 and 1075, and later from the Roman nobility generally in 1084.[47] Paschal II may have received hostages from the Romans in 1108 after putting down their revolt, and three years later hostages, principally for

[43] *Codex Carolinus*, 80, 83, 84 (MGH Epp. 3:611–14, 616–20); above, pp. 61–2.

[44] Hugh of Poitiers, *Chronicon*, 4.1150–61 (CCCM 42:541); *Royal and Other Historical Letters*, vol. 1, ap. 5, no. 10 (RS 27.1:536) [Potthast 6367]. Cf. Romuald of Salerno, *Annales*, s.a. 1022 (MGH SS 17:403).

[45] *Les registres de Grégoire IX*, 1:362–3, 815, 842–3 (nos. 568, 1465, 1523) [Potthast —, —, 9303]. See also above, p. 79, n. 4.

[46] *Preußisches Urkundenbuch*, 1.1:100 (no. 133) [*Les registres de Grégoire IX*, 3:221–2 (no. 5135); Potthast 10859]; *Spicilegium Liberianum*, 1:646 [Potthast 11011]; *Collectio monumentorum*, 1:137–8 (no. 3.14) [Potthast 11058].

[47] Bonizo of Sutri, *Liber ad amicum*, 7 (MGH Libelli de lite imperatorum et pontificum saeculis XI. et XI. conscripti 1:604–5); Bernold of Konstanz, *Chronicon*, s.a. 1084 (MGH SrG ns 14:439–40); H. E. J. Cowdrey, *Pope Gregory VII, 1073–1085* (Oxford, 1998), 227–8, 326. Cf. Henry IV, *Briefe*, 7 (ed. Erdmann, 24–6); Paul of Bernried, *Vita Gregorii VII*, 40 (*PL* 148:58).

safe passage, played an important role in the negotiations between that pope and Henry V,[48] while Innocent III and Honorius III's pacification of southern Francia during the Albigensian Crusades employed hostages.[49] Two sets of hostages were discussed in negotiations between Gregory IX's representatives and Piacenza after the revolt in that town in 1233.[50] And the sources pass over without comment the proposals that Innocent VI accept the son of the Byzantine emperor himself as a hostage in 1355 and 1357.[51]

Popes did reject the use of hostages in various cases, but for complicated reasons that mirror secular concerns. Like kings, popes might view granting hostages as beneath them, as evident in the angry reply of John VIII to Lambert of Spoleto, who had requested hostages from the Roman nobility and entry into the city. The pope's letter does not make clear the precise function of the hostages, whether they were to guarantee Lambert's safety in the city or the city's allegiance to Carloman in the upcoming contest for the imperial crown. What is certain is that Lambert was not about to receive them: 'We do not find anywhere that the sons of Romans—let alone Romans who have remained faithful to the Empire in their minds and, with God's help, in their works—have been given as hostages.... The senate of the Roman flock would sooner choose death than consent in any way to this unheard of and horrible thing.' And Lambert certainly wasn't welcome in the city: 'it is in no way fitting that you come, since, as we have said, we are in no way able, dearest son, to receive you'. This is, of course, papal bluster. If anyone in the city knew about the long history of sons of Roman nobles being given as hostages, they were working in the papal chancery. Still, the pope's reasoning is noteworthy. Hostages are not unacceptable per se, only hostages from Rome; hostages, he argued, were beneath the city's dignity. Furthermore, hostages should not be taken from those who have demonstrated fidelity in other ways, in mind and in deed.[52] A similar rejection of hostages in a particular case, rather than in general, is found in the *Deeds of Innocent III*, whose author wrote that the pope rejected Conrad of Spoleto's offer of submission, which included a promise of hostages, because he thought the alliance would look bad, not because he didn't find the terms useful. The same pope rejected Walter of Palearia's offer of his two nephews as hostages for good behaviour (alongside other guarantees), this time appealing again to the

---

[48] *Liber pontificalis*, Paschalis II (ed. Duschesne, 2:300, 3:148); MGH Const. 1:137–9, 143–4 (nos. 83–5, 94).

[49] *Layettes*, 1:400, 401–2, 415–16, 2:85–6, 87–9 (nos. 1069 [*HGL* 8:643–6 (no. 172)], 1072 [*HGL* 8:847–51 (no. 174)], 1115 [Potthast 4969], 1787, 1789). *Layettes*, 1:402 (no. 1072) specifies that 'obsides juxta voluntatem summi Pontificis et vestram puniantur'.

[50] *Les registres de Grégoire IX*, 1:861–2 (no. 1569) [Potthast —]; *Acta imperii inedita seculi XIII*, 515–16 (no. 638) [*Les registres de Grégoire IX*, 1:983 (no. 1795); Potthast 9404]; see also 208 (no. 340). The town apparently argued that a grant of hostages would be against their statutes.

[51] Above, p. 10. See also *Die Register Innocenz' III.*, 2:459–62 (no. 2.241) [Potthast 924] (above, p. 168); and the Treaty of Rome of 1495 (below, p. 219).

[52] John VIII, *Epistolae*, 63 (MGH Epp. 7:56–7) [JE 3112]: 'Romanorum filios sub isto cęlo non legitur fuisse obsides datos, quanto minus istorum, qui fidelitatem augustalem et mente custodiunt et opere Deo iuvante perficiunt?... Quamvis antea Romani ovilis senatus mortem eligant, quam hanc inauditam et pessimam rem fieri quocumque modo consentiant... nullo modo te venire oportet, quia nullo modo te, sicut diximus, recipere, fili karissime, possumus.' See Arthur Lapôtre, *L'Europe et le Saint-Siège à l'époque carolingienne*, vol. 1: *Le pape Jean VIII (872–882)* (Paris, 1895), 341–2.

superiority of trust: 'Since we expect spontaneous rather than forced adherence, we have not taken care to receive guarantees of this sort at this time, wishing to see if you will follow through voluntarily on what you have promised.'[53]

This complex view of hostages extends to papal intervention in external affairs. Alexander III tried to get certain Lombard lords to return half of the forty hostages they held from the monastery of Nonantola, not because they were objectionable per se, but because, given the status of the institution, they should have been content with a lesser number.[54] Celestine III's order that the duke of Austria free the hostages he held as part of the ransom agreement for Richard I was grounded in the duke's violation of the king's status as a Crusader;[55] similarly, in 1226, Honorius III ordered Heinrich of Schwerin to release hostages held from Valdemar II of Denmark on the grounds (among others) that he had violated his vassalic obligations in extorting them.[56] In 1219, however, that same pope was more than willing to enforce the claims of Henry III of England to hostages held at Merpins by Reginald de Pons.[57] The closest thing to an outright dismissal of hostageship is found in a letter of Paschal II, in his reply to a complaint from the monastery of Savigny, yet here too the rejection is qualified. Archbishop Hugh of Lyon, intervening in a dispute between the monastery and Étienne de Varenne, had excommunicated the abbot and monks and retained procedural hostages that he had received from them. The pope determined that the hostages had been 'seized in error and contrary to the custom of ecclesiastical judgments'.[58] The hostages, as the monastery's cartulary shows, had not in fact been seized, but sought and accepted, from both parties in the dispute, as a guarantee that they would appear on the day agreed for the court hearing and abide by its judgments. What the pope was objecting to was not the use of hostages itself, but rather a procedural error: not that the archbishop retained the hostages but that he took them in the first place.[59] Other evidence from contemporary papal correspondence hints at the use of such procedural hostages in ecclesiastical affairs, although it is not always clear that the *obsides* in question are not simple guarantors.[60]

The most influential papal statements on hostages were two that made their way into the principal collections of medieval canon law, the *Decretum* of Gratian (*c*.1140) and the *Liber extra* of Gregory IX (1234). Their importance lies less in

---

[53] *Gesta Innocenti papae III*, 9 (*PL* 214:xxiv); *Die Register Innocenz' III.*, 6:98–100 (no. 6.71) [Potthast 1923]: 'Quia vero magis spontaneam devotionem requirimus quam coactam, non curavimus ad presens huiusmodi recipere cautiones, probare volentes, si absque compulsione aliqua, quod sermone promittis, opere velis prosequente complere.' See above, p. 47.

[54] Alexander III, *Epistolae et privilegia*, 1198 (*PL* 200:1042) [JL 12542].

[55] *Urkundenbuch zur Geschichte der Babenberger*, 4.1:231–3 (no. 937) [JL 17119].

[56] *Mecklenburgisches Urkundenbuch*, 1:318–21 (nos. 325–9) [Potthast 7584–5, 7593–4].

[57] *Foedera*, 1.1:156 [Potthast 6080]; their exact nature is somewhat obscure.

[58] *Cartulaire de l'abbaye de Savigny*, 1:475 (Savigny, no. 900) [JL 6444a]: 'perperam et contra ecclesiasticorum morem judiciorum, censemus extortos'. See Auguste Bernard, 'Excommunication de l'abbaye de Savigny au XIIe siècle', *Revue du Lyonnais*, ns 6 (1853), 177–90.

[59] *Cartulaire de l'abbaye de Savigny*, 1:479–80 (Savigny, no. 904).

[60] Honorius II, *Epistolae et privilegia*, 8 (*PL* 166:1265–8) [JL 7268]; Urban III, *Epistolae*, 8 (*PL* 202:1343–6) [JL 15481]. *Die Register Innocenz' III.*, 2:37–42 (no. 2.27) [Potthast 647]. See also above, pp. 15–16.

their specific content than in the fact that they were the subject of academic commentary. The first is a letter of Gregory I concerning the defence of Roman territory against the Lombards in 592. Ariulf of Spoleto had sent a letter to Rome claiming that the town of Suana was negotiating its surrender and had granted hostages. The pope forwarded the letter to the *magister militum* Vitalian and the commander Maurisio, ordering them to determine the status of the town and, if it were still faithful to Rome, to accept their own hostages from it.[61] As just seen, popes throughout the Middle Ages turned to hostages in the context of military conflict; Gregory was simply one of the first.

The second statement is a letter of Alexander III (1159–81) to two bishops ordering them to intervene in a dispute. An abbot borrowed 8,000 s. from a local lord, granting some of his monks as 'hostages, who swore concerning the maintenance of the agreement, that if they were to fail to fulfil their roles (*deficere*), other monks would be placed in hostageship in their place'. The abbot also provided as a back-up two other lay guarantors (*fideiussores*), who promised to uphold the agreement. All of these guarantees were apparently of little use, as the pope instructed the bishops to warn the abbot and the monks and the guarantors to carry out the agreement, lest they bar the abbot and monks from their church and place the lands of the laymen under interdict.[62]

The hostages of sixth-century Rome are straightforward examples of hostages granted in the course of a military conflict, here either to guarantee the surrender of the town or its long-term fidelity. The precise role of the monks in the twelfth-century case—true hostages, conditional hostages, or mere guarantors—is not entirely clear: given the time and place, it is most likely that they were conditional hostages. The two papal letters thus treat very different sorts of hostages. Furthermore, neither of the compilers of the collections in which these letters are found were specifically concerned with the issue of hostages. Gratian's interest lies in the question of clerical involvement in military action generally, as he places it in the *causa* (23) devoted to that issue; he is not concerned with the specific issue of hostages.[63] Ramon de Penyafort, who compiled the *Liber extra*, included the letter of Alexander in his title on oaths, prefacing it with a rubric highlighting the fact that the monks were being forced to keep their oaths. The ordinary glosses on these collections, however, do highlight the question of hostages, and in a way that collapses the distinctions between the two cases. In part this is a result of the glossators' and decretalists' knowledge of Roman law, and before examining their ideas we must reintroduce those ancient sources and their medieval commentaries.

Hostages (*obsides*) make five appearances in the *Corpus iuris civilis*, the sixth-century compilation of legislation and commentary on which rested the later medieval study of Roman law. The killing of a hostage was an act of treason, as was

---

[61] C. 23.8.18; Gregory I, *Registrum epistolarum*, 2.33 (MGH Epp. 1:129–30) [JE 1188]. For Gregory's other mention of *obsides*, see 3.62 (MGH Epp. 1:222–4) [JE 1268].

[62] X 2.24.9 [JL 14095]: 'obsides dedit, qui de observanda conventione iuraverunt, ut, si ipsi deficerent, alii monachi loco eorum in obstagio ponerentur'.

[63] Anders Winroth, *The Making of Gratian's Decretum* (Cambridge, 2000), 220, includes this canon in his reconstruction of the 'first recension'.

an act that led to the necessity of granting further hostages to the enemy (D. 48.4.1, 4).[64] Hostages were unable to make a will without permission (D. 28.1.11). Hostages' goods were forfeit to the imperial fisc, unless they had been acting as Roman citizens, in which case they were permitted to transfer their goods to their heirs (D. 49.14.31–2). In the second- and third-century context from which these opinions arise, hostages would have referred to high-status foreigners resident in Rome.[65] Hostages for debt appear only in legislation of Justinian of 556 (Nov. 134.7) banning the practice of creditors accepting the sons of debtors in pledge, under the penalty of a loss of the debt itself, an equal amount of compensation, and corporal punishment; the term *obses*, notably, is not present.[66] The ordinary gloss on these texts, composed by Accursius and completed by around 1230, omits discussion of the killing of a hostage, and he treats the two sorts of hostages differently. He clearly identifies the hostages mentioned in the Digest as arising from conflict, links their legal status to that of captives, and stresses their connection to the emperor and the fisc. The discussion of the novel of 556, in which language of credit and debt is employed, focuses on the status of the children as free, not slave: the only situation in which a father might pledge a child is one in which he would also be allowed to sell the child into slavery.[67]

In striking contrast to the Roman law sources and commentaries, the canonical tradition brings together the two sorts of hostages—and draws on these Roman sources in doing so. The standard glosses on the *Decretum*, by Johannes Teutonicus and Bartholomew of Brescia, and on the *Liber extra*, by Bernard of Parma, coalesced in the 1240s and 1250s, two decades after Accursius finished his work. The gloss on the letter of Gregory the Great, at the mention of *obsides*, begins by stating that the canon shows that 'a free man can be a hostage for the preservation of peace, but not for money'.[68] This position, which conflicts with the evident approval of hostages for money in the *Liber extra* (X 2.24.9), is backed up by reference to the Digest's discussion of both conflict-hostages (D. 28.1.1) *and* debt-hostages (D. 49.14.31). The author focuses, like Accursius in discussing debt-hostages, on the issue of the ability of a free man to be subject to such an obligation, citing another passage of the *Liber extra*, and a passage of Justinian's Code (C. 8.16.6) that had been crucial to Accursius's analysis of debt-hostages in Nov. 134.7. He finesses the clear conflict of his view that free men cannot be bound for monetary obligations with the content of the Alexander III order by appealing, on the one hand, to fine distinctions in Roman law (*ius pignoris* v. *ius retentionis*), and on the other, to the fact that it was done for the good of the church and the pope. The author clearly has trouble, however, with the concept of hostages: free men should not be subject to such treatment.

---

[64] Cf. *Le Assise di Ariano*, 18/12 (ed. Zecchino, 40, 78).

[65] Above, p. 3.

[66] Cf. C. 4.43.2, 4.10.12, 8.16.6.

[67] Glossa ad D. 28.1.11 Obsides, permittitur; glossa ad D. 49.14.31 Divus, captivorum; glossa ad D. 49.14.32 Sed si accepto, eorum; glossa ad Nov. 134.7 Quia vero, parentibus (*Corpus iuris civilis*, s. p.).

[68] Glossa ad C. 23.8.18 obsidesque: (*Corpus juris canonici*, 1:1812) 'Ergo liber homo potest esse obses pro pace seruanda, non pro pecunia'.

The gloss on the Alexander III letter in the *Liber extra* is similar. It opens by asserting that the monks must have been given as hostages voluntarily, 'otherwise they would not be able to be detained: they were hostages as free men'. (Note that the gloss assumes that these are true or conditional hostages, rather than simple guarantors.) It notes the conflict between those sources, including and especially Nov. 134.7, that prohibit hostages and the evident appearance of hostages elsewhere, including the Gregory I letter from the *Decretum*, and the passages from the Digest on their testamentary capability (D. 28.1.11) and fiscal rights to their property (D. 49.14.1). It similarly takes refuge in legal distinctions (there was no obligation, so the hostage was not technically a *pignus*), and ends with another possibility: a free man may not be bound for a monetary debt, but may be so bound for the purposes of peace.[69] Again, the solutions are weak, and the commentator is worried by free men being subject to captivity.

Precisely contemporary French royal legislation on imprisonment for debt hints at a similar concern. Philip Augustus's prohibition in 1219 of seizures for debts to Jews extended to the goods *and persons* of pledges. The language of Louis IX's extension of the principle to all non-royal debts in 1254 is more ambiguous, but the legislation was likely influenced by complaints uncovered in the inquests of 1247–8 concerning imprisonment of third parties, principally the dependants of indebted lords, but in at least one case a personal surety (*fideiussor*). This position was, however, quickly rejected by Louis's successors.[70] Noble prescriptions about the justice of hostageship were completely at odds with the historical reality examined in the preceding chapters. Suggestions that there was something fundamentally wrong with hostageship because a free man should not be punished for someone else's fault had little impact. Nonetheless, these views had a great future.[71]

FROM VITORIA TO NUREMBERG AND BEYOND

Pierino Belli's *De re militari et bello*, one of the earliest of the early modern treatises on the laws of war, devotes its final chapter to the subject of hostages. His survey of *ius commune* thought on hostages (citing Bartolus, Baldus, Panormitanus, and many others) addresses the familiar issues of free will and consent. Distinctions had multiplied. Was it permitted for a hostage to be granted by a king (maybe) or a private person (no, unless he has given an oath, in which case perhaps)? By the pope (yes), a bishop (no), or an abbot (yes)? In a matter of state (yes), or a financial

---

[69] Glossa ad X 2.24.9 <u>obsides dedit</u> (*Corpus juris canonici*, 2:802–3): 'Voluntate illorum, alias detineri non possunt. Sed qualiter liberi homines obsides erunt.'

[70] *Ordonnances*, 1:37 ('capientur corpora eorum', sc. *debitor* or *plegius*), 72 ('detineant, aliquem subditorum'); *RHF* 24:95 (no. 3); Claustre, *Geôles*, 95–103. Links between debates on usury and hostageship merit further investigation.

[71] This only scratches the surface of the rich possibilities in the analysis of *ius commune* sources. For example, Johannes Andreae, *Novella in Decretales*, extends the prohibition on hostages making wills to hostages appointing procurators: glossa ad X 1.38.10 <u>libera</u> (*Corpus iuris canonici*, 2:468).

matter (no, unless it is a matter of state)?[72] With this focus on will and consent, Belli's work may be considered the culmination of the medieval academic discussion of hostageship. Most of his fellow authors at the origin of the law of war tradition, however, took the discussion in a very different direction, a direction strikingly prefigured not in Christian sources, but Islamic ones.

The ninth-century historian al-Balādhurī, referring to an agreement between Mu'āwiya and the emperor Constans in 658, claimed that Muslims did not consider it legal to execute hostages for a violated agreement, citing the eighth-century jurist al-Awzai.[73] The same opinion is found in the work of al-Awzai's contemporary, Shaybani, citing this same historical episode; al-Sarakhsi, in his eleventh-century commentary, adds that killing the hostages is prohibited because they are present under safe conduct, because one cannot kill one person for another's crime, and because an agreement allowing for the execution of hostages is contrary to Islamic law and therefore invalid. Hostages may not be killed or mutilated by Muslims even if the enemy has killed or mutilated Muslim hostages, and the state was bound to pay for the upkeep of hostages even if the enemy failed to do so, as required.[74] The Islamic legal tradition was also highly protective of hostages *granted by* Muslims, holding that Muslims should continue a truce past the agreed deadline if the enemy was refusing to return their hostages.[75] Al-Mawardi (d. 1058), who also cites the episode of 658, adds that in the case of a declaration of war by Muslims, any hostages were to be returned to the enemy.[76] As in the medieval Christian sources, the Muslim jurists thus raise the problem of punishment for another's fault. Their main concern, though, is the treatment of hostages, specifically their execution. This is the question that exercised the Christian writers on the laws of war in early modern Europe.

The new concern is signalled in the work of the Spanish Dominican, Francisco de Vitoria. In his *De iure belli* of 1532, in his only comment on hostages, he states that if hostages are guilty, as if they had borne arms, they may be killed; if not, as in the case of children or women or other innocents, they may not be killed. Note that here their guilt may arise from actions unrelated to their hostageship, such as simple participation in the conflict that preceded the agreement. In his later account, part of his commentary on Aquinas (*c*.1535), his views harden. In scholastic fashion, he presents the two sides of the argument. May hostages be killed if the ruler who has granted them violates the agreement (he cites the recent example of the sons of Francis I, discussed below)? On the one hand, it may be argued that they may be killed if a promise is violated, for that is why they were given in the first place. On the other hand, they are innocent and should not suffer for another's action. Vitoria is now unequivocally in the second camp: they cannot be killed. Furthermore,

---

[72] Belli, *De re militari et bello*, fols. 148v–150v (part 11).

[73] al-Balādhurī, *Origins of the Islamic State*, 2.14 (trans. Hitti and Murgotten, 1:245).

[74] al-Sarakhsi, *Le grand livre de la conduite de l'État*, 163 (trans. Hamidullah, 3:282–305), esp. §§ 3502, 3529, 3537, 3547, 3552 (3:285, 295, 297–8, 301, 303).

[75] al-Sarakhsi, *Le grand livre de la conduite de l'État*, 163 §3513 (trans. Hamidullah, 3:289).

[76] al-Mawardi, *The Ordinances of Government*, 14 (trans. Wahba, 56; trans. Fagnan, 4.5.4, pp. 102–3), which also cites the case from 653.

he argues, the hostage agreement itself is iniquitous.[77] Vitoria's view was cited, and echoed, by Luis de Molina in his *De iustitia et iure* (1593).[78]

Jean Bodin comes to the opposite conclusion in his *Six livres de la république* (1576).[79] He discusses hostages at several points, citing a range of ancient, medieval, and contemporary examples, but his most pertinent arguments appear in his chapter on security for alliances between princes. He notes that although Narses at Lucca and Charles of Burgundy at Liège both spared hostages (he appears to be the first person to connect these two cases), it would have been licit to execute them: 'The clause "hostages are subject to capital punishment" was unknown to the ancients, for it was always permitted to kill hostages, not just if they fled, but also if those who had given hostages broke their word.' If they fled, they themselves were guilty and subject to punishment for that reason, but they could be killed even if they themselves were innocent. Moderns, he says, have introduced such a clause, so that the hostages could not claim ignorance of the law and to counter the argument 'that it seems overly cruel and harsh to suffer for another's offence'.[80]

Bodin also introduces into the discussion over hostages the question of whether the very granting of hostages absolves the grantor from a promise. His leading case is that of Francis I, who promised to return to captivity if he could not get the Estates to ratify the Treaty of Madrid, leaving his two sons as hostages. Bodin finds that it is not the content of the promise—an alienation of sovereignty—that nullifies the promise, but the grant of hostages itself. In this case, as in the medieval case of James of Cyprus, the kings were 'absolved of their promises by their enemies themselves, as they required guarantees and did not trust the oaths of their prisoners'. The same was true of John II of France: he famously did return, but he didn't have to.[81] Bodin does not see faith as superior to hostages, as many of the medieval sources surveyed do. He sees them as mutually exclusive. Hostages do not reinforce faith; they replace it. Bodin's position was quickly (and convincingly) refuted by Balthazar de Ayala in his *De iure et officiis bellicis et disciplina militari* of 1582. As hostages are accessories to principal obligations, and as an accessory cannot be said to exist in the absence of the principal obligation, there is no way that the former can be said to invalidate the latter. Francis was in the wrong; John was right.[82]

---

[77] Vitoria, *De Indis et de iure belli relectiones*, 2.43 (ed. Nys and Wright, 291), *Comentarios a la Secunda secundae de Santo Tomás*, 40.1.20 (ed. Beltrán de Heredia, 2:287).

[78] Molina, *De justitia et jure*, 1:466 (1.2.120).

[79] The following editions are cited: *De republica libri sex*, 3rd edn. (Frankfurt, 1594); *Les six livres de la republique* (Lyon, 1579).

[80] 1.6, 9, 10, 2.3, 4.1, 5.6, 6.5. '*Ut obsides in pœnam capitalem accipiantur*, veteribus ignota fuit, quia semper iure licuit obsides non modo fugientes necare, verumetiam si ii qui obsidibus cauerant, fidem fefellissent...alienam culpam luere nimis crudele & acerbum videretur' (5.6, p. 965). The passage is absent in the French edition. In the French (though not the Latin), he takes aim at Commynes: 'qu'il pouuoit iustement faire mourir, quoy que die Philippe de Comines' (p. 579). See also p. 565, where he discusses hostages for safe passage.

[81] 'estoyent par les ennemis mesmes absous de leurs promesses, attendu qu'il auoyent garends par deuers eux, & qu'ils ne se fioyent pas au serment de leurs prisonniers' (5.6, p. 560; cf. Latin, p. 932). For James of Cyprus, see above, p. 164, n. 3.

[82] Ayala, *De iure et officiis bellicis et disciplina militari*, fol. 59r–v (1.6.5).

Alberico Gentili addressed these issues in considerably more depth in his *De iure belli* of 1598, in which he devotes a full chapter to the question of hostages; he, too, draws on ancient, medieval, and contemporary examples, but adds references to Roman law texts and commentary (particularly Baldus). He first argues that hostages are distinct from captives and slaves, despite the similarities in condition. He then moves on to the question of the legitimacy of killing hostages, agreeing ultimately with Bodin over Vitoria. The killing of hostages was legitimate under the law of war (*ius belli*). Like Bodin, Gentili notes cases where hostages were spared—Narses again, and Charlemagne—suggesting that it was 'seen as cruel by the best commanders to exact punishment from innocent hostages'. It would not be cruel if they were guilty. Similarly, hostages can legitimately be killed for the crimes of other hostages, as if some of a group attempt to escape, if such joint responsibility has been agreed upon. If it was not the hostages themselves who were guilty but others, it is in fact, Gentili confesses, cruel, but nonetheless it is also just and fitting.[83] Legal principles are certainly violated by hostageship: that people do not have *dominium* over their own bodies and lives; that a person cannot bind himself to corporal punishment for another's offence; that agreements to hand oneself over to an enemy are not valid; that people cannot be bound against their will. But these are principles of civil law. Hostageship is a part of the law of war, and such rules do not apply, despite attempts of commentators to harmonize the two. Gentili also addresses more technical questions arising from hostageship: how they are to be guarded (in whatever way is necessary to secure the agreement); whether they can be kept for an agreement other than the one for which they were originally granted (no); and whether they are released at the death of their principal (it depends). In these discussions, the connection of the issue of hostages to the more general issues of surety that interested the medieval jurists is still apparent. It was, however, the question of the execution of hostages that was for him, as for his fellow commentators, the most pressing.

It was not Gentili, or even Bodin, whose thinking dominated later thought on the question. That role fell to Hugo Grotius, whose *De jure belli ac pacis* became the foundation of the modern laws of war.[84] Grotius first addresses hostages in his chapter (3.4) treating of the right to kill an enemy in a lawful war; here he is engaged in historical description, and acknowledges—citing solely ancient examples—that the very broad licence to kill extended to hostages. When in the middle of the third book he turns from description to his counsels of moderation, however, the analysis of hostages changes. The idea that a guiltless hostage could be killed belonged to a time when it was thought that individuals had a property right over their own lives, a right that could be transferred to the political community of which he was a part (*civitas*). The hostage was justly killed not because of his individual guilt, but because of corporate guilt. But, argues Grotius, now that *dominium* over life is known to belong to God alone, an individual cannot transfer

---

[83] Gentili, *De iure belli*, pp. 393–401 (2.19): 'Et atrox tamen visum optimis imperatoribus, supplicium de innoxiis sumere obsidibus.'

[84] Grotius, *De jure belli ac pacis*, pp. 461, 524, 587–8, 606 (3.4.14, 11.18, 20.52–8, 23.16).

the right to his own life, and the community cannot transfer the right to the life of one of its members (*civis*)—precisely the argument rejected by Gentili as being inapplicable during wartime. This is the reason (*ideo*), Grotius argues somewhat weakly, why Narses found it cruel to kill an innocent hostage (he also cites Scipio, and unnamed others). If a hostage had been among the seriously delinquent (*in numero graviter delinquentium*) before being granted, or broke his word as a hostage over something serious (*in re magna*), it may be that punishment is not unjust. The double negative reveals the author's unease.

Grotius revisits the question of hostages again in his chapter on treaties that end wars, passing judgment on previous arguments and offering an influential synthesis of laws concerning the institution. He repeats here that if the killing of hostages is permitted by the external law of nations, it is not in accord with the internal (moral) law, unless the hostage is guilty. The fact that an individual does not have ownership over his own life only means that innocent hostages cannot be killed, not that they cannot be granted. They are granted either by their own will or that of the political community. If the latter, however, the community or its ruler had to compensate the hostage (or his relatives) for the inconvenience suffered. Compensation was, as we have seen, common for medieval hostages; here it is elevated to a principle. Vassals could not be forced to serve as hostages for their lords, unless they were also subjects; the obligation to serve as a hostage for one's lord was part of the medieval tradition, here rejected. Roman law held that hostages could not make wills and that their property devolved to the fisc; by the law of nations, Grotius argues, this is not the case. Gentili had argued that hostages, unlike captives, had no right to escape. Grotius modifies this position as well, limiting it to cases where the hostage had made some sort of promise by which he would be held more loosely; he may have been thinking of the sorts of oaths and pledges of behaviour in accordance with chivalry given by hostages from the later Middle Ages on. In the absence of such a promise, however, he could escape, for in handing the hostage over, the state gave a right to the enemy to detain the individual; it did not intend to bind its citizen not to flee. Like Gentili, Grotius addresses the question of whether hostages may be retained to guarantee agreements other than the ones for which they were initially granted. His answer here is particularly revealing of his overall view: 'The obligation of hostages is odious both because it is inimical to liberty (*libertas*), and because it arises from another's action.'[85] If hostages are retained, it is not as hostages but as subjects of reprisals.

The striking thing about these discussions is that during the Middle Ages the execution of hostages was a rarity, and by the period when these authors were writing it was all but unknown. It was the ancient tales of execution of hostages that drove their interest, along with the theological implications of substitution—Grotius penned an anti-Socinian tract, arguing (at odds with his findings in *De jure*) that in the case of Jesus it was permissible to punish an innocent for sins he did not

---

[85] 'Odiosa autem est obsidum obligatio, tum quia libertati inimica, tum quia ex facto alieno venit' (3.20.55, p. 588).

commit.[86] Their interest in dead hostages is very much responsible, however, for how hostages are viewed today. The idea that there was something wrong with killing innocent hostages—although voiced on occasion—was never much of a medieval concern, unlike the superiority of unsecured fidelity. It was medieval canonists who introduced the issue of freedom into discussions of hostageship, tying Justinian's sixth-century ban on the practice of debt-hostageship to the *obsides* of Roman and medieval law. Grotius does not take the final step of explicitly linking his prohibition on the killing of hostages to the idea of freedom, but the elements of a thoroughly modern critique of hostageship were certainly present in his work. The leap was not great to the characterization by Emer de Vattel in 1758 of the execution of treaty hostages as a 'barbarous cruelty, based on error' and 'a barbarism offensive to human nature', contrary to both natural law and the law of nations.[87]

Just as some aspects of early medieval hostageship, such as the role of hostages as markers of submission or as vectors of cultural influence, continue into the later Middle Ages, so too aspects of later medieval hostageship persist into the early modern era. The Treaty of Madrid of 1526 and the attendant hostageship of the sons of Francis I played such a significant role in the arguments of early modern jurists because it was such a notorious affair, but it was far from the only example of the continued use of hostages in peacemaking. They also appear in the treaties of Amiens (1475), Rome (1495), Cambrai (1529), Cateau-Cambrésis I (1559), Vervins (1598), and Pruth (1711), among others.[88] They continued, too, to be used for wartime engagements, such as capitulations (Dijon in 1513, Fassano in 1536, Thionville in 1558), or promises of safe passage (Louis XII to Philip of Hapsburg in 1502, Francis I to Charles V in 1539).[89] One of the few known examples of Mercedarian substitution for a Christian captive dates from the seventeenth century, a century after the obligation first appears in the order's statutes.[90] Nor were hostages limited to war and diplomacy: as noted, the *Einlager* persisted in

---

[86] Debora Kuller Shuger, *The Renaissance Bible: Scholarship, Sacrifice, and Subjectivity* (Berkeley, 1994), 67–73.

[87] Vattel, *Le droit des gens*, 1:451–9 (2.16, §§245–61): 'Cruauté barbare, fondée sur l'erreur', 'une barbarie injurieuse à la nature humaine'.

[88] *Corps universel de diplomatique du droit des gens*, 3.1:501 (no. 347, art. 2, a. 1475), 3.2:318 (no. 170, a. 1495), 4.2:8–9 (no. 2, art. 3, a. 1529), 5.1:32 (no. 21, a. 1559), 562 (no. 255, art. 18, a. 1598), 8.1:275 (no. 114, a. 1711); also 7.1:65 (no. 24, art. 26, a. 1667), 77 (no. 29, add. art. 6, a. 1668); *A Collection of Treaties... Malabar*, 1:76 (no. 96, art. 2, a. 1790), 2:1 (no. 1, art. 4, a. 1792), 3 (no. 2, art. 3, a. 1792). See Albert Desjardins, 'Les otages dans le droit des gens au XVIᵉ siècle', *Séances et travaux de l'Académie de sciences morales et politiques (Institut de France), Compte rendu*, ns 49 (1889), 238–50; Randall Lesaffer, 'Peace Treaties from Lodi to Westphalia', in Lesaffer, ed., *Peace Treaties and International Law in European History: From the Late Middle Ages to World War One* (Cambridge, 2004), 28–9; Heinz Durchhart, 'Peace Treaties from Westphalia to the Revolutionary Era', in Lesaffer, ed., *Peace Treaties*, 48–9; Karl-Heinz Ziegler, 'The Peace Treaties of the Ottoman Empire with European Christian Powers', in Lesaffer, ed., *Peace Treaties*, 352; J. H. W. Verzijl, *International Law in Historical Perspective*, vol. 6: *Juridical Facts as Sources of International Rights and Obligations* (Leiden, 1973), 293–4; C. H. Alexandrowicz, *An Introduction to the History of the Law of Nations in the East Indies (16th, 17th and 18th Centuries)* (Oxford, 1967), 167.

[89] Desjardins, 'Les otages'; Lutteroth, *Der Geisel*, 210–12.

[90] Above, p. 120.

isolated areas of Switzerland through the nineteenth century, and a communal ordinance of the Jews of Fez (Morocco) in 1568 prohibits using women as hostages for loans taken from Muslims.[91] If early modern jurists were drawing the bulk of their evidence from classical sources, it was more out of humanist impulses than lack of direct knowledge.

But as in the eleventh and twelfth centuries, hostageship had changed. The hostage as a mode of surety is seen to have disappeared from European law generally over the course of the fifteenth and sixteenth centuries, while the *Einlager* was abolished in imperial lands by the *Reichspolizeiordnung* of 1577 and in most Swiss jurisdictions by the seventeenth century.[92] Francis I's sons were the last hostages granted for a captive European king.[93] Ransoming—and the attendant hostages to guarantee ransoms—generally declined in favour of systems of prisoner exchange over the course of the sixteenth century, as the notion of *bonne guerre* and the responsibility of a state for its soldiers took hold.[94] The last hostages granted for a treaty between European states were the earl of Suffolk and Baron Cathcart, who served to guarantee English obligations under the treaty of Aix-la-Chapelle (1748). They were already a diplomatic archaism.[95]

The Lieber Code (1863) from the United States Civil War defines wartime hostages according to the old model, but describes them as 'rare in the present age'.[96] Lieber ignored the fact, however, that the term hostage was being used in a new way, to refer to captives seized to force certain behaviour. The new trend was noted as early as 1724 by Barbeyrac in his French translation of Grotius. The French revolutionary 'loi des otages' of 1799 is a precocious example of the use of hostages for the repression of civilian unrest; the Treaty of Belgrade of 1739, which allowed for hostages to be taken by each side from neutral border territory 'for no other reason than to maintain order', may be another.[97]

The explanation for these developments merits its own study, but some preliminary hypotheses may be proposed. The pieties of nineteenth- and early twentieth-century commentators, who posited the 'universal reprobation' of 'civilized countries' that accompanied the 'march of civilization' beyond the 'savage eras

---

[91] Ankawa, *Kerem Chemer*, 2:5r (no. 28) (ערבות).

[92] Above, p. 131, n. 3; *SP* 1:52; Walliser, *Bürgschaftsrecht*, 368–70.

[93] Although in 1791 hundreds of people offered themselves as hostages for the captive Louis XVI; the plan never came to fruition, and they were prosecuted three years later. See Thomas-Pascal Boulage, *Les otages de Louis XVI et de sa famille* (Paris, 1814); Hippolyte Sauvage, *Mortain pendant le terreur*, vol. 13: *Les otages du roi* (Avranches, 1901), 17–22.

[94] Philippe Contamine, 'The Growth of State Control. Practices of War 1300–1800: Ransom and Booty', in Contamine, ed., *War and Competition between States* (Oxford, 2001), 163–93.

[95] *Major Peace Treaties of Modern History*, 1:279 (art. 9); cf. 1:273 (art. 4).

[96] Irène Herrmann and Daniel Palmieri, 'A Haunting Figure: The Hostage through the Ages', *International Review of the Red Cross*, 87 (2005), 139; Lieber, *Instructions for the Government of Armies*, 16 (art. 54; cf. art. 55). The Treaty of Paris (1763) still referred to 'the hostages carried away, or given during the war' (*Major Peace Treaties of Modern History*, 1:308 [art. 3]).

[97] Grotius, *Le droit de la guerre et de la paix*, trans. Barbeyrac, 2:967 n., 968 n., citing Battier, *Disputatio politica de obsidibus et eorum jure* (1695), which discusses both hostages granted and hostages seized. See Desjardins, 'Les otages', 248–50; *Codex iuris gentium recentissimi*, 1:377 ('non per altro, che per mantenerli quieti').

of the Middle Ages or Antiquity' may be rejected, if only because it had been centuries since someone could point to a dead hostage.[98] 'The waning of the code of chivalry as the basis for conduct in war' may be closer to the mark.[99] Gentili cites Bodin as arguing that parties stopped killing hostages when trust began to be scorned: too many hostages would be killed if that were how deceit was punished. (Gentili himself thought that it was the opposite: trust began to be scorned when deceit ceased to be punished.) A general decline of trust in warfare and diplomacy in the early modern period is more likely to have been the impression of the jurists than a fact; it is true, however, that the collapse of papal claims to universal jurisdiction in the wake of the Reformation undermined the perceived utility of the oath, and thus pledges of fidelity, generally.[100]

But simpler explanations are at hand. Already Panormitanus (d. 1445) had linked the question of the right to grant hostages to just war theory, which identified those rulers who were capable of declaring war.[101] With the emergence of powerful nation-states in the early modern era, the number of parties who might legitimately grant and receive hostages was reduced, while the same process began to make the enforcement of agreements by other means more feasible. Thus in diplomacy, the individual treaty hostage was increasingly replaced by the granting of entire towns or regions as a guarantee and the promises of third-party states to enforce agreements.[102] Hostages for financial transactions were replaced by more efficient contract enforcement and, if necessary, public debtors' prisons.[103] The domain of private ordering, to return to the language of contract theory, became smaller. Medieval hostageship, especially in contrast to the Roman model from which it grew, was—like medieval political life generally—fundamentally multifocal; early modern politics and hostageship were much less so. Furthermore, the roles of hostageship beyond guarantee that were so prominent in the medieval period, particularly the way in which it established connections, were fulfilled in this new environment by other institutions. The transformation of diplomacy in the early modern period, for example, with its networks of ambassadors, resident and otherwise, made the hostage less necessary as a focus for communication and union. The same could be said of the development of increasingly complex commercial entities that tied individuals and families together in business, or political systems that bound populations to rulers more closely than before, transforming agreements between individual rulers into agreements between sovereign states.[104]

---

[98] Lutteroth, *Der Geisel*, 206 ('wilden Zeiten des Mittelalters oder des Altertums'); Calvo, *Le droit international*, 4:204–5.
[99] Lesaffer, 'Peace Treaties', 29.
[100] Lesaffer, 'Peace Treaties'.
[101] Tedeschi, *Commentaria secundæ partis in secundum librum decretalium* (ed. Anello de Botti and Corsetti, fol. 200v).
[102] Lutteroth, *Der Geisel*, 206–10; Durchart, 'Peace Treaties', 48–9; Verzijl, *International Law*, 285–98.
[103] Claustre, *Geôles*, esp. 194, 425, 428–9.
[104] Lesaffer, 'Peace Treaties'; Durchart, 'Peace Treaties'.

The execution of hostages and the attendant charge of barbarity[105] were still under discussion at 1947 at Nuremberg. In the so-called 'Hostages Case' (*United States of America* v.*Wilhelm List,* et al.), eleven German generals stood accused of war crimes and crimes against humanity.[106] One of the counts specified that 'the defendants issued, distributed, and executed orders for the execution of 100 "hostages" in retaliation for each German soldier killed and 50 "hostages" in retaliation for each German soldier wounded'. In its decision, the court stated: 'Under the ancient practice of taking hostages they were held responsible for the good faith of the persons who delivered them, even at the price of their lives. This barbarous practice was wholly abandoned by a more enlightened civilization. The idea that an innocent person may be killed for the criminal act of another is abhorrent to every natural law. We condemn the injustice of any such rule as a barbarous relic of ancient times.'[107]

The court condemned the relic, but found the newer sort of hostageship to be perfectly legal. Although 'killing of hostages' was explicitly defined as a war crime in Control Council Law No. 10,[108] which provided the statutory basis for the Nuremburg tribunals, the court found that it was acceptable practice because it had not been expressly prohibited by international law. Numerous authorities had lamented this fact following World War I; Oppenheim-Lauterpacht, the leading textbook on international law, stated bluntly, 'The experience of the World War shows that the taking of hostages is a matter urgently demanding regulation; the Hague Regulations do not mention it.'[109] Both the *British Manual of Military Law* and the *United States Basic Field Manual* then in force permitted the taking and killing of hostages in certain circumstances.[110] It was only the Fourth Geneva Convention of 1949 that banned the practice of taking hostages in the context of warfare.[111]

The tribunal fully accepted that hostages might 'be taken in order to guarantee the peaceful conduct of the populations of occupied territories and, when certain conditions exist and the necessary preliminaries have been taken...be shot'. All that it felt that it could do was to put limits on the practice, creating a list of steps that were to precede the resort to hostages: registration of inhabitants; passes and identification certificates; curfews; prohibition of assembly; and so on. It also determined that hostages could only be taken 'provided it can be shown that the population generally is a party to the offense'. (The prosecution had explicitly cited Grotius in making the argument that 'there must be some connection between the population from whom the hostages are taken and the crime committed'.[112]) The

[105] Desjardins, 'Les otages', 249, and 248, citing Calvo, *Le droit international,* 4:204. Cf. Gentili, *De iure belli,* pp. 395, 398 (2.19), who applies the term *atrox*; Vattel, in 1758 (above, p. 219), is the first I have found to use the term.
[106] *United States of America* v.*Wilhelm List,* et al. ('The Hostages Case'), 11:757–1332.
[107] *US* v. *List,* 11:1233, 1249.
[108] II.1 (b) (Taylor, *Final Report... Control Council Law no. 10,* 250).
[109] Oppenheim, *International Law,* 5th edn. (1935–7), 2:463–4.
[110] *US* v. *List,* 11:1251.
[111] *Convention (IV) Relative to the Protection of Civilian Persons in Time of War,* III.1 (b), art. 34 (ed. 75:310). See Claude Pilloud, 'La question des otages et les Conventions de Genève', *Revue internationale de la Croix-Rouge,* 32 (1950), 430–47.
[112] United Nations War Crimes Commission, *Law Reports,* 8:82; *US* v. *List,* 11:1249–50.

court proceeded to tinker with the machinery: 'it is essential to a lawful taking of hostages under customary law that proclamation be made, giving the names and addresses of hostages taken, notifying the population that upon the recurrence of stated acts of war treason that the hostages will be shot. The number of hostages shot must not exceed in severity the offenses the shooting is designed to deter.'[113] Hostageship was to be controlled, not eliminated. 'It is not our province to write international law as we would have it', the court held. '[W]e must apply it as we find it.'[114]

The court's conclusion may have been legally sound, but it was based on poor history. 'In former times', the court wrote, 'prominent persons were accepted as hostages as a means of insuring observance of treaties, armistices, and other agreements, the performance of which depended on good faith. This practice is now obsolete. Hostages under the alleged modern practice of nations are taken (a) to protect individuals held by the enemy, (b) to force the payment of requisitions, contributions, and the like, and (c) to insure against unlawful acts by enemy forces or people.'[115] But it was precisely the barbarity of modern practices, rather than the ancient ones, that the court was struggling with. It acknowledged that 'taking of reprisals against the civilian population by killing members thereof in retaliation for hostile acts against the armed forces or military operations of the occupant seems to have been originated by *Germany in modern times*', specifically during the Franco-Prussian war.[116] As seen above, this sort of hostageship began to be designated as such a century earlier than the court thought. Moreover, the court's characterization of 'ancient' practice was flawed. In its view, as noted, ancient hostageship involved prominent persons granted to guarantee treaties, armistices, and other agreements; this form of hostageship was now obsolete. But on the one hand this 'ancient' type of transaction was still being used, for example, in French colonial administration in the early twentieth century,[117] and on the other, it is hardly the case that this was the only possible model of historical hostageship. All three of the court's categories of 'modern' hostageship—those aimed at protecting individuals held by the enemy, those aimed at forcing payment, and those aimed at insuring against unlawful acts—have analogues in the medieval sources. We can imagine that the nameless hostages repeatedly granted by the Saxons to Charlemagne in the late eighth century, for example, were in practice closer to the twentieth-century

---

[113] *US* v. *List*, 11:1249–50.
[114] *US* v. *List*, 11:1249; cf. 1251, 1253.
[115] *US* v. *List*, 11:1248–9.
[116] *US* v. *List*, 11:1251 (my empahsis).
[117] Avon, 'Monographies centre-africaines' (1906), 302; Christian Roche, *Conquête et résistance des peuples de Casamance (1850–1920)* (Dakar, 1976), 111–13. English: *Documents Relative to the Colonial History of the State of New-York*, 7:622 (Seneca treaty, art. 8, a. 1764). In 1779, the English granted hostages *to* a local Indian ruler: *A Collection of Treaties... India*, 7:41 (no. 1.8); Alexandrowicz, *Introduction*, 167. Dutch: Richard Price, *To Slay the Hydra: Dutch Colonial Perspectives on the Saramaka Wars* (Ann Arbor, 1983), 159–65 (Saramacca treaty, a. 1762); Price, *Alabi's World* (Baltimore, 1990), 48–9, 98, 103–4, 123. Several of these examples are part of a traditional set of topoi in scholarship on hostages, which seems to be influenced by the unsigned article 'Hostage', in *The Encyclopaedia Britannica*, 11th edn. (New York, 1911), 13:801–2.

victims of the German army than to the two English nobles who guaranteed the treaty of Aix-la-Chapelle.

Finally, there is the matter of killing. Unlike their early modern predecessors, the Nuremberg court was operating in a world in which hostages were regularly killed. It is that fact, rather than the fact that they were taken, that bothered the court: 'The idea that an innocent person may be killed for the criminal act of another is abhorrent to every natural law.'[118] The prosecution pressed on the distinction between taking and killing a hostage, attempting to assimilate hostages to prisoners of war, who were already protected from execution by the Geneva Convention. They could point, for example, to Control Council Law No. 10, which banned not the *taking* of hostages, but the *killing* of hostages. But, as seen, the court rejected this argument, implicitly siding with the position taken by some authors cited—perhaps unwisely—by the prosecution: 'there is a fundamental absurdity in taking hostages if they cannot be executed'.[119] As has been demonstrated throughout this study, medieval hostageship, in which executions were extremely rare, was anything but absurd.

In short, the tribunal's teleological account of hostageship, in which an ancient, barbaric practice is overcome by the forces of Enlightenment, was wrong. There were few fundamental differences between the court's 'ancient' and 'modern' hostageship: specifically, the conventional high-ranking hostage-as-guarantee and the war hostage, whose status as granted rather than taken was more theoretical than practical, existed in the eighth as in the twentieth century. Furthermore, even if one were to accept a clear distinction between voluntary treaty hostages who are granted and involuntary hostages who are seized—a distinction that the evidence does not support—the court's chronology, with a more barbarous giving way to a less barbarous variety, would be backward. For the killing of hostages—surely the most barbaric aspect of the institution—was much more of a modern than an ancient problem... or a medieval one. The notion of relentless progress in law, and in history, once again fails. The Nuremberg tribunal's attempt to regulate an institutionalized hostageship is perfectly consonant with the history that the court itself rejected.

A pair of international lawyers writing in 1944 observed that, 'Where expediency and legality have coincided, acceptable examples of hostage-taking may be found. But these result more from circumstance than from deference to International Law... By destroying the basic legal relationship between the occupant and the civilian, the Germans have created a reign of terror.'[120] When the Fourth Geneva Convention of 1949 outlawed wartime hostages outright, terror was all that remained. Terrorism did not begin in 1949, of course, but the close association of hostages with terrorism is clearly a late twentieth-century phenomenon.

[118] *US* v. *List*, 11:1249.
[119] United Nations War Crimes Commission, *Law Reports*, 8:82.
[120] Ellen Hammer and Marina Salvin, 'The Taking of Hostages in Theory and Practice', *The American Journal of International Law*, 38 (1944), 27.

The famous cases—from Munich in 1972 and Entebbe in 1976 to Ingrid Betan-court in 2002—are just the tip of the iceberg. One study identifies 549 terrorist hostage-taking episodes between 1968 and 1986 alone.[121] The response of the international community was the 1979 International Convention Against the Tak-ing of Hostages.[122] The principal debates surrounding this treaty did not concern the question of whether there might be such a thing as legal hostageship outside the context of warfare, but rather the status of national liberation forces struggling against colonial regimes. A leader of a racist power captured by an opposition group was not, it was claimed, an innocent hostage, but rather a prisoner of war. The compromise that led to the final treaty allowed for a categorical ban on hos-tages, one grounded in universal human rights theory. And by claiming no conflict with the 1949 Geneva accord and its later protocols, the convention moved all debate out of the realm of the definition of hostages, and into that of the definition of warfare.[123]

As late as the Nuremberg tribunals, then, hostages were an acceptable part of the laws of war. Through the eighteenth century, if not later, they were an acceptable part of the laws of international relations. The explicit association of hostages with barbarity can be traced back only to the eighteenth century. But other forms per-sisted, and it was only German excesses in the two World Wars that led to the legal abolition of hostages in 1949. Then, terrorist activity in the second half of the twentieth century made it impossible to imagine that hostages were ever a legiti-mate institution.

But hostages, whether granted voluntarily or given under duress, had an evident utility in the Middle Ages, and hostageship was certainly viewed as a legitimate institution. Legal historians may be surprised to find hostageship still in use in societies that clearly do not qualify as primitive or archaic, and shocked to see it outlast the legal transformations of the central Middle Ages, but it was very much there. Despite the development in this same period of sophisticated theories of representation and identity in the realms of both politics and philosophy,[124] actual or potential physical control over a human being remained essential to crucial aspects of political and economic life. The persistence of the forms of hostageship studied here in the face of profound changes in medieval politics, economy, and society across a millennium, mark the institution as a defining feature of the Euro-pean Middle Ages. Why hostageship is no longer legitimate has to do with the newly powerful universal human rights claims that were implicit in the Geneva

---

[121] Todd Sandler and John L. Scott, 'Terrorist Success in Hostage-Taking Incidents: An Empirical Study', *Journal of Conflict Resolution*, 31 (1987), 37. See now the RAND Database of Worldwide Ter-rorism Incidents (www.rand.org/nsrd/projects/terrorism-incidents.html).

[122] *International Convention*; see Joseph J. Lambert, *Terrorism and Hostages in International Law: A Commentary on the Hostages Convention 1979* (Cambridge, 1990).

[123] Wil D. Verwey, 'The International Hostages Convention and National Liberation Movements', *American Journal of International Law*, 75 (1981), 69–92.

[124] A theme brilliantly explored in Brigitte Miriam Bedos-Rezak, 'Medieval Identity: A Sign and a Concept', *American Historical Review*, 105 (2000), 1489–533; for political representation, see Gaines Post, *Studies in Medieval Legal Thought: Public Law and the State, 1100–1322* (Princeton, 1964).

Conventions and explicit in the 1979 Hostage Convention.[125] But the increasing 'barbarism' of hostageship, which makes the medieval niceties surrounding the institution seem quaint, hints at what an individualist morality forced out. The history of hostageship in the Middle Ages highlights the communal foundations of medieval society that left a place for what the Nuremberg court thought of as a barbarous relic.

---

[125] In the 1980s, however, when nuclear war between the United States and the Soviet Union was the greatest geopolitical concern, individuals in the peace movement actually proposed a perfectly medieval hostage exchange: See J. Kenneth Smail, 'The Giving of Hostages', *Politics and the Life Sciences*, 16 (1997), 77–85.

Works Cited

I. MANUSCRIPT SOURCES

Barcelona, Arxiu de la Corona de Aragó
  Cancelleria
    Pergamins
    Registres 1377, 1569
Bruges, Stadsarchief
  99, 272
Ghent, Rijksarchief
  1
London, National Archives
  C 81
  E 30, 36, 101
  SC 8
Manresa, Arxiu històric de la ciutat
  AM, I-5
Paris, Archives nationales
  JJ 7, 100
  X/1a/1480
Paris, Bibliothèque nationale de France
  ms. lat. 17760, 13904
  Coll. Bourgogne 103
  Coll. Lorraine 238
Sankt Paul im Lavanttal, Stiftsbibliothek
  cod. 6/1
Toulouse, Archives municipales
  AA 5, 35, 45

II. PRINTED PRIMARY SOURCES

II Æthelred, ed. Liebermann, *Die Gesetze* (q.v.), 1:220–7.

Accounts of the Constables of Bristol Castle in the Thirteenth and Early Fourteenth Centuries, ed. Margaret Sharp (Gloucester, 1982).

Acta imperii inedita seculi XIII: Urkunden und Briefe zur Geschichte des Kaiserreichs und des Königreichs Sicilien in den Jahren 1198 bis 1273, ed. Eduard Winkelmann (Innsbruck, 1880).

Acta sanctorum quotquot toto orbe coluntur, 68 vols. (Antwerp, 1643–1940).

Actes de la famille Porcelet d'Arles (972–1320), ed. Martin Aurell (Paris, 2001).

Actes des comtes de Flandre: 1071–1128, ed. Fernand Vercauteren (Brussels, 1938).

Actes des comtes de Namur de la première race, 946–1196, ed. Félix Rousseau (Brussels, 1936).

Actes et documents anciens intéressant la Belgique, ed. Charles Duvivier (Brussels, 1898).

The Acts of David II, King of Scots, 1329–1371, ed. Bruce Webster (Edinburgh, 1982).

The Acts of Welsh Rulers, 1120–1283, ed. Huw Pryce (Cardiff, 2005).

Advice to a Prince [Diambad messe bad rí réil], ed. and trans. T. O'Donoghue, *Ériu*, 9 (1921–3), 43–54.

Æthelweard, *Chronicon*, ed. and trans. A. Campbell (London, 1962).

Agathias, *Historiae*, ed. Rudolf Keydell, CFHB 2 (1967); trans. Joseph D. Frendo, CFHB 2A (1975).

Ágrip af Nóregskonungasogum, ed. and trans. M. J. Driscoll (London, 1995).

Ajbar machmuã, ed. and trans. Emilio Lafuente y Alcántara (Madrid, 1867).

al-Balādhurī, *Origins of the Islamic State* [Kitāb futūh al-Buldān], trans. Philip Khuri Hitti and Francis Clark Murgotten, 2 vols. (New York, 1916–24).

al-Makrīzī, *Histoire d'Égypte* [Kitāb al-Sulūk li-ma'rifat al-mulūk], trans. E. Blochet (Paris, 1908).

al-Mawardi, *The Ordinances of Government* [Kitab al-Ahkam al-Sultaniyya], trans. Wafaa H. Wahba (Reading, 1996); trans. E. Fagnan, *Les statuts gouvernementaux, ou, Règles de droit public et adminstratif* (Algiers, 1915).

al-Sarakhsi, *Le grand livre de la conduite de l'État* [Kitab al-Siyar al-Kabir], trans. Muhammad Hamidullah, 4 vols. (Ankara, 1989–91).

al-Tabarī, *The History* [Ta'rīkh al-rusul wa-al-muluk], trans. Franz Rosenthal et al., 40 vols. (Albany, 1985–2007).

Albert of Aachen, *Historia Ierosolimitana*, ed. and trans. Susan B. Edgington, OMT (2007).

Alexander III, *Epistolae et privilegia*, PL 200:69–1320 (1855).

Alfonso II rey de Aragón, conde de Barcelona y marqués de Provenza: Documentos (1162–1196), ed. Ana Isabel Sánchez Casabón (Zaragoza, 1995).

Alfred and Guthrum, ed. Liebermann, *Die Gesetze* (q.v.), 1:126–8.

Alpert of Metz, *De diversitate temporum*, ed. Georg Heinrich Pertz, MGH SS 4:700–23 (1841).

Álvarez, João, *Trautado da vida e feitos do muito vertuoso senhor Ifante Dom Fernando*, ed. Adelino de Almeida Calado, *Obras*, vol. 1 (Coimbra, 1960).

Amadi, Francesco, *Chronique*, ed. René de Mas Latrie, *Chroniques d'Amadi et de Strambaldi*, vol. 1 (Paris, 1891).

Amatus of Montecassino, *Storia de' Normanni*, ed. Vicenzo De Bartholmaeis (Rome, 1935).

Analecta hymnica medii aevi, ed. Clemens Blume and Guido M. Dreves, 55 vols. (Leipzig, 1886–1920).

Andreas of Bergamo, *Historia*, ed. Georg Heinrich Pertz, MGH SS 3:232–8 (1839).

Andrew of Wyntoun, *The Original Chronicle*, ed. F. J. Amours, 6 vols. (Edinburgh, 1903–14).

'The Anglo-Flemish Treaty of 1101', trans. Elisabeth Van Houts, *Anglo-Norman Studies*, 21 (1998), 169–74.

Anglo-Norman Letters and Petitions from All Souls MS. 182, ed. M. Dominica Legge (Oxford, 1941).

Anglo-Scottish Relations, 1174–1328: Some Selected Documents, ed. and trans. E. L. G. Stones, OMT (1970).

Ankawa, Abraham, *Kerem Chemer*, 2 vols. (Livorno, 1869).

Annales Alamannici, ed. Georg Heinrich Pertz, MGH SS 1:22–30 (1826).

Annales Altahenses maiores, 2nd edn., ed. Edmund L. B. von Oefele, MGH SrG 4 (1891).

Annales Brixiensis, ed. Ludwig Bethmann, MGH SS 18:811–20 (1863).

Annales Cambriae, ed. John Williams, RS 20 (1860).

Annales Casinenses, ed. Georg Heinrich Pertz, MGH SS 19:303–20 (1866).

Annales de Saint-Bertin, ed. Félix Grat et al., SHF (1964).

Annales Elmarenses, ed. Philip Grierson, *Les annales de Saint-Pierre de Gand et de Saint-Amand* (Brussels, 1937), 74–115.

Annales Fuldenses, ed. Friedrich Kurze, MGH SrG 7 (1891); trans. Timothy Reuter, *The Annals of Fulda* (Manchester, 1992).

Annales Gandenses, ed. and trans. Hilda Johnstone (London, 1951).

Annales Laureshamenses, ed. Georg Heinrich Pertz, MGH SS 1:22–39 (1826).

Annales Lobienses, ed. G. Waitz, MGH SS 13:224–35 (1881).

Annales Marbacenses, ed. Hermann Bloch, MGH SrG 9 (1907).

Annales Mettenses priores, ed. B. von Simson, MGH SrG 10 (1905).

Annales Monasterii de Waverleia, ed. Henry Richards Luard, *Annales monastici*, vol. 2, RS 38.2:127–411 (1865).

Annales Mosellani, ed. I. M. Lappenberg, MGH SS 16:491–9 (1859).

Annales Otakariani, ed. Rudolf Köpke, MGH SS 9:181–94 (1851).

Annales Petaviani, ed. Georg Heinrich Pertz, MGH SS 1:7–18 (1826).

Annales qui dicuntur Einhardi, ed. Friedrich Kurze, MGH SrG 6 (1895).

Annales regni Francorum, ed. Friedrich Kurze, MGH SrG (1895).

Annales S. Amandi, ed. Georg Heinrich Pertz, MGH SS 1:6–14 (1826).

Annales S. Columbae Senonensis, ed. Georg Heinrich Pertz, MGH SS 1:102–9 (1826).

Annales S. Iustinae Patavini, ed. Philipp Jaffé, MGH SS 19:148–93 (1866).

Annales Vedastini, ed. B. von Simson, MGH SrG 12:40–82 (1909).

Annales Wormatienses, ed. Georg Heinrich Pertz, MGH SS 17:34–73 (1861).

Annales Xantenses, ed. B. von Simson, MGH SrG 12:1–39 (1909).

Annalista Saxo, ed. Klaus Nass, MGH SS 37 (2006).

Annals of Clonmacnoise, trans. Conell Mageoghagan, ed. Denis Murphy (Dublin, 1896).

Annals of the Four Masters, ed. and trans. John O'Donovan, *Annals of the Kingdom of Ireland by the Four Masters from the Earliest Period to the Year 1616*, 2nd edn., 7 vols. (Dublin, 1856).

Annals of Ulster, ed. and trans. W. M. Hennessy and B. MacCarthy, 4 vols. (Dublin, 1887–1901).

Anonymous Syriac Chronicle, trans. A. S. Tritton, with notes by H. A. R. Gibb, 'The First and Second Crusades from an Anonymous Syriac Chronicle', *Journal of the Royal Asiatic Society of Great Britain and Ireland* (1933), 69–101, 273–305.

Ansbert, *Historia de expeditione Friderici imperatoris*, MGH SrG ns 5:1–115 (1928).

Arnold of Lübeck, *Chronica Slavorum*, ed. Georg Heinrich Pertz, MGH SrG 14 (1868).

Asser, *Life of King Alfred*, ed. William Henry Stevenson, *Asser's Life of King Alfred, together with the Annals of Saint Neots Erroneously Ascribed to Asser* (Oxford, 1904), 1–96; trans. Simon Keynes and Michael Lapidge, *Alfred the Great: Asser's Life of King Alfred and Other Contemporary Sources* (Harmondsworth, 1983), 65–110.

Le Assise di Ariano, ed. and trans. Ortensio Zecchino (Cava dei Tirreni, 1984).

Astronomer, *Vita Hludowici imperatoris*, ed. and trans. Ernst Tremp, MGH SrG 64:279–555 (1995).

Atto of Vercelli, *Epistolae*, PL 134:95–123 (1884).

—— *Polipticum quod appellatur Perpendiculum*, ed. Georg Goetz (Leipzig, 1922).

Avon, [Capitaine], 'Monographies centre-africaines', *Bulletin du Comité de l'Afrique française*, 16 (1906), 300–4.

Ayala, Balthazar, *De iure et officiis bellicis et disciplina militari* (Douai, 1582; repr. Washington, DC, 1912).

Baldric of Dol [Baudri de Bourgueil], *Historia Jerosolymitana*, RHC Occ. 4:9–111 (1879).

Bar Hebraeus, *Chronography*, ed. and trans. Ernest A. Wallis Budge, 2 vols. (London, 1932).

Barnwell Chronicle, ed. William Stubbs, *The Historical Collections of Walter of Coventry*, vol. 2, RS 58.2:196–279 (1873).

Bartholomeo de Neocastro, *Historia Sicula*, ed. Giuseppe Paladino, RIS² 13.3 (1921–2).

Battier, Jean-Jacques, *Disputatio politica de obsidibus et eorum iure* (Basel, 1695).

The Battle of Maldon, ed. D. G. Scragg (Manchester, 1981).

Beaumanoir, Philippe de, *Coutumes de Beauvaisis*, ed. Am. Salmon, 2 vols., CTH 24, 30 (1899–1900).

Belli, Pierino, *De re militari et bello tractatus* (Venice, 1563; repr. Oxford, 1936).

Benzo of Alba, *Ad Heinricum IV. Imperatorem*, ed. and trans. Hans Seyffert, MGH SrG 65 (1996).

[Bernard of Angers], *Liber miraculorum sanctae Fidis*, ed. A. Bouillet, CTH 21 (1897).

Bernard of Clairvaux, *Sermones in nativitate Domini*, 5, ed. J. LeClerq and H. Rochais, *Opera*, vol. 4: *Sermones I* (Rome, 1966), 244–70.

Bernold of Konstanz, *Chronicon*, ed. Ian S. Robinson, MGH SrG ns 14:383–540 (2003).

Bertran de Born *lo fils*, *Quan vei lo temps renovelar* (razo), ed. Albert Stimming, *Bertran von Born*, 2nd edn. (Halle, 1913), 146–8.

Blondel, Robert, *De reductione Normanniæ*, ed. Joseph Stevenson, RS 32:1–238 (1863).

Bodin, Jean, *Les six livres de la republique* (Lyon, 1579); *De republica libri sex*, 3rd edn. (Frankfurt, 1594).

Bonizo of Sutri, *Liber ad amicum*, ed. Ernest Dümmler, MGH Libelli de lite imperatorum et pontificum saeculis XI. et XII. conscripti 1:568–620 (1891).

The Book of the Himyarites, ed. and trans. Axel Moberg (Lund, 1924).

Book of Prests of the King's Wardrobe for 1294–5, ed. E. B. Fryde (Oxford, 1962).

Bouton, Claude, *Miroir des dames*, ed. E. Beauvois, *Un agent politique de Charles-Quint: Le Bourgignon Claude Bouton, seigneur de Corberon* (Paris, 1882), 3–30.

Bower, Walter, *Scotichronicon*, ed. and trans. D. E. R. Watt, 9 vols. (Aberdeen, 1987–98).

The Brut, ed. Friedrich W. D. Brie, 2 vols. (London, 1906–8).

Brut y Tywysogyon or The Chronicle of the Princes (Red Book of Hergest Version), ed. and trans. Thomas Jones (Cardiff, 1955).

Caffaro, *Annales*, ed. Georg Heinrich Pertz, MGH SS 18:1–39 (1863).

Calendar of Documents Preserved in France, Illustrative of the History of Great Britain and Ireland, vol. 1 (only): *A.D. 918–1206*, ed. John Horace Round (London, 1899).

Calendar of Documents Relating to Scotland Preserved in Her Majesty's Public Record Office, London, ed. Joseph Bain, 5 vols. (Edinburgh, 1888–1987).

Calendar of Inquisitions Miscellaneous (Chancery) Preserved in the Public Record Office, vol. 2 (London, 1916).

Calendar of the Patent Rolls Preserved in the Public Record Office: Henry III, A.D. 1258–1266 (London, 1910).

Calvo, Carlos, *Le droit international théorique et pratique, précédé d'un exposé historique des progrès de la science du droit des gens*, 4th edn., 5 vols. (Paris, 1887–8).

Cartes de poblament medievals valencianes, ed. Enric Guinot Rodríguez (Valencia, 1991).

Cartulaire de Béziers (Livre noir), ed. J. Rouquette (Paris, 1918–22).

Cartulaire de l'abbaye bénédictine de Notre-Dame et Saint-Jean-Baptiste de Chalais au diocèse de Grenoble, ed. Em. Pilot de Thorey (Grenoble, 1879).

Cartulaire de l'abbaye de Saint-André-le-Bas de Vienne, ordre de Saint-Benoît, suivi d'un appendice de chartes inédites sur le diocèse de Vienne (IXᵉ–XIIᵉ siècles), ed. Ulysse Chevalier (Lyon, 1869).

Cartulaire de l'abbaye de Saint-Aubin d'Angers, ed. Bertrand de Broussillon, 3 vols. (Angers, 1896–1903).

Cartulaire de l'abbaye de Saint-Victor de Marseille, ed. Benjamin Guérard, 2 vols. (Paris, 1857).

Cartulaire de l'abbaye de Savigny, suivi du petit cartulaire de l'abbaye d'Ainay, ed. Auguste Bernard (Paris, 1853).

Cartulaire de l'abbaye de Silvanès, ed. P. A. Verlaguet (Rodez, 1910).

Cartulaire de l'abbaye royale de Notre-Dame de Saintes de l'ordre de Saint-Benoit, ed. Th. Grasilier (Niort, 1871).

Cartulaire de l'église Notre-Dame de Paris, ed. [Benjamin] Guérard, 4 vols. (Paris, 1850).

Cartulaire de Maguelone, ed. J. Rouquette and A. Villemagne (Montpellier, 1912).

Cartulaire de Saint-Jean d'Angely, 2 vols. (Paris, 1901–3).

Cartulaire de Sainte-Croix d'Orléans, 814–1300, ed. Joseph Thillier and Eugène Jarry (Orleans, 1906).

Cartulaire du chapitre de Saint-Étienne de Limoges (IXe–XIIe siècles), ed. Jacques de Font-Réaulx (Limoges, 1922).

Cartulaire historique et généalogique des Artevelde, ed. Napoléon de Pauw (Brussels, 1920).

Cartulaires des abbayes d'Aniane et de Gellone, ed. Léon Cassan and Édouard Meynial, 2 vols. (Montpellier, 1898–1900).

Cassiodorus, *Variae*, ed. Theodor Mommsen, MGH AA 12 (1894); trans. S. J. B. Barnish (Liverpool, 1992).

Catalogus comitum Capuae, ed. Georg Waitz, MGH SrL 498–501 (1878).

Catalunya Carolíngia, vol. 3: *Els comtats de Pallars i Ribagorça*, ed. Ramon d'Abadal i de Vinyals (Barcelona, 1955).

Cert cech rïg co réil, ed. and trans. T. O'Donoghue, in *Miscellany Presented to Kuno Meyer...*, ed. Osborn Bergin and Carl Marstrander (Halle, 1912), 258–77.

Charters of Saint Paul's, London, ed. Susan Kelly (Oxford, 2004).

'Chartes angevines des onzième et douzième siècles', ed. Paul Marchegay, *Bibliothèque de l'École des chartes*, 36 (1875), 381–441.

'Les chartes de l'abbaye de Saint-Pierre de Corbie (988–1196)', ed. Laurent Morelle, PhD thesis, École nationale des chartes, 1982.

Chartes de coutume en Picardie: XIe–XIIIe siècle, ed. Robert Fossier (Paris, 1974).

Chartier, Jean, *Chronique de Charles VII*, ed. [Auguste] Vallet de Viriville, 3 vols. (Paris, 1858).

Chartularium Sangallense, 11 vols. to date, ed. Otto P. Clavedetscher (Sigmaringen, 1983–).

Chastellain, Georges, *Chronique*, ed. [Joseph M. B. C., baron] Kervyn de Lettenhove, *Œuvres*, vols. 1–5 (Brussels, 1863–4).

Choniates, Nicetas, *Historia*, ed. Jan Louis van Dieten, 2 vols., CFHB 11 (1975).

Chronica Adefonsi imperatoris, ed. Antonio Maya Sánchez, CCCM 71:109–248 (1990).

Chronica de gestis consulum Andegavorum, ed. Louis Halphen and René Poupardin, *Chroniques des comtes d'Anjou et des seigneurs d'Amboise*, CTH 48:25–72 (1913).

Chronica monasterii Casinensis, ed. Hartmut Hoffmann, MGH SS 34 (1980).

Chronica monasterii de Mesla, ed. Edward A. Bond, 3 vols., RS 43.1–3 (1866–8).

Chronica regia Coloniensis, ed. Georg Waitz, MGH SrG 18 (1880).

The Chronicle of Morea, ed. John Schmitt (London, 1904).

The Chronicle of Zuqnïn, Parts III and IV, trans. Amir Harrak (Toronto, 1999).

Chronicon Dubnicense, ed. M. Florianus (Leipzig, 1894).

Chronicon Moguntinum, ed. Karl Hegel, MGH SrG 20 (1885).

Chronicon Moissacense, ed. Georg Heinrich Pertz, MGH SS 1:280–313 (1826).

Chronicon S. Martini Turonensis, ed. O. Holder-Egger, MGH SS 26:458–76 (1882).

Chronicon Salernitanum, ed. Ulla Westerbergh (Stockholm, 1956).

Chronicon Sancti Petri Vivi Senonensis, ed. and trans. Robert-Henri Bautier and Monique Gilles (Paris, 1979).

Chronicon Urspergensium, ed. Otto Abel and Ludwig Weiland, MGH SS 23:333–83 (1874).

Chronicon Venetum, ed. Georg Heinrich Pertz, MGH SS 7:4–38 (1846).

Chronique de la Pucelle, ed. [Auguste] Vallet de Viriville (Paris, 1859).

Chronique de Saint-Pierre de Bèze, ed. Joseph Garnier, in *Chronique de l'abbaye de Saint-Bénigne de Dijon suivie de la Chronique de Saint-Pierre de Bèze*, ed. E. Bougard and Joseph Garnier, Analecta Divionensia 9 (Dijon, 1875), 231–503.

Chronique de Saint-Pierre du Puy, ed. Ulysse Chevalier, *Cartulaire de l'abbaye de St-Chaffre du Monastier, Ordre de Saint-Benoît, suivi de la Chronique de Saint-Pierre du Puy et d'un appendice de chartes* (Paris, 1884), 151–66.

Chronique des Cordeliers, ed. L. Douët-d'Arcq, *Extrait d'une chronique anonyme pour le règne de Charles VI, 1400–1422*, in Monstrelet, *Chronique* (q.v.), 6:191–327.

Chronique des quatre premiers Valois (1327–1393), ed. Siméon Luce, SHF (1862).

Cijar, Pedro, *Opusculum tantum quinque super commutatione votorum in redemptione* (n.p.: Petrus Posa, impens. Johannis Urgellensis, 1491).

Close Rolls of the Reign of Henry III, A.D. 1231–1234 (London, 1905).

Codagnello, Giovanni, *Annales Placentini*, ed. Oswald Holder-Egger, MGH SrG 23 (1901).

Codex Carolinus, ed. Wilhelm Gundlach, MGH Epp. 3:469–657 (1892).

Codex diplomaticus Flandriae, inde ab anno 1296 ad usque 1325, ed. Thierry Limburg-Stirum, 2 vols. (Bruges, 1879–89).

Codex iuris gentium recentissimi, ed. Friedrich August Wilhelm Wenck, vol. 1 (Leipzig, 1781).

Lo codi in der lateinischen Übersetzung des Ricardus Pisanus, ed. Hermann Fitting (Halle, 1906).

Codice diplomatico della Repubblica di Genova dal MCLXIII al MCLXXXX, ed. Cesare Imperiale di Sant'Angelo, vol. 2 (Rome, 1938).

Colección de documentos inéditos del Archivo General de la Corona de Aragón, ed. Próspero de Bofarull y Mascaró et al., 50 vols. (1847–1992).

Collectio monumentorum…, ed. Simon Friedrich Hahn, vol. 1 (Brunswick, 1724).

A Collection of Treaties, Engagements and Other Papers of Importance Relating to British Affairs in Malabar, ed. W. Logan (Calcutta, 1879).

A Collection of Treaties, Engagements, and Sunnuds, Relating to India and Neighbouring Countries, ed. C. U. Aitchison, vol. 7 (Calcutta, 1865).

Comnena, Anna, *Alexiade*, ed. and trans. Bernard Leib, 3 vols. (Paris, 1937–45).

Commynes, Philippe de, *Mémoires*, ed. [L. M. Émille] Dupont, 3 vols., SHF (1840–7); trans. Michael Jones (Harmondsworth, 1972).

'Les confiscations dans la Châtellanie du Franc de Bruges après la bataille de Cassel', ed. J. A. Mertens, *Bulletin de la Commission royale d'histoire* (1968), 239–84.

Constantine VII, *De administrando imperio*, new edn., ed. G. Moravcsik, trans. R. J. H. Jenkins, CFHB 1 (1967; repr. 1985).

Les constitucions de Pau i Treva de Catalunya (segles XI–XIII), ed. Gener Gonzalvo i Bou (Barcelona, 1994).

Consuetudines et iusticie, ed. Charles Homer Haskins, *Norman Institutions* (Cambridge, Mass., 1918), 277–84.

Convention (IV) Relative to the Protection of Civilian Persons in Time of War (Geneva, 12 August 1949), in United Nations, *Treaty Series*, vol. 75 (New York, 1950), 287–416 (no. 973).

Conventum inter Guillelmum Aquitanorum comitem et Hugonem Chiliarchum, ed. Jane Martindale, *English Historical Review*, 84 (1969), 528–48.

Conversio Bagoariorum et Carantanorum, ed. Fritz Lošek, MGH Studien und Texte 15 (1997).

Corps universel de diplomatique du droit des gens, ed. Jean Dumont, 8 vols. (Amsterdam, 1726–31).

Corpus inscriptionum semiticarum, vol. 4.2.3 (Paris, 1920).

Corpus iuris civilis, 5 vols. (Venice, 1487–9; repr. *Corpus glossatorum iuris civilis*, vols. 7–11, Turin, 1968–9).

Corpus iuris Hibernici, ed. D. A. Binchy (Dublin, 1978).

Corpus juris canonici emendatum et notis illustratum, 4 vols. (Rome, 1582).

Cotton, Bartholomew, *Historia anglicana*, ed. Henry Richards Luard, RS 16:1–344 (1859).

Crónica Albeldense, ed. Juan Gil Fernández, *Cronicas Asturianas* (Oviedo, 1985), 151–88.

' "Cronica de Wallia" and Other Documents from Exeter Cathedral Library MS. 3514', ed. Thomas Jones, *Bulletin of the Board of Celtic Studies* 12 (1948), 27–44.

Curia regis Rolls of the Reign of Henry III Preserved in the Public Record Office: 4 and 5 Henry III (London, 1952).

De expugnatione Lyxbonensi, ed. and trans. Charles Wendell David (New York, 1936; repr. 2001).

De' Mussi, Giovanni, *Chronicon Placentinum*, RIS 16 (1730).

De ortu Waluuanii nepotis Arturi, ed. and trans. Mildred Leake Day (New York, 1984).

Dhuoda, *Liber manualis*, ed. and trans. Marcelle Thiébaux (Cambridge, 1998); trans. Carol Neel, *Handbook for William* (Washington, DC, 1999).

Dietrich of Nieheim, *Cronica*, ed. Katharina Colberg and Joachim Leuschner, MGH Staatsschriften des späteren Mittelalters 5.2:143–292 (1980).

Diplomatarium Danicum, vol. 1.6: *1224–1237*, ed. Niels Skyum-Nielsen (Copenhagen, 1979); vol. 2.10: *1328–1332*, ed. C. A. Christensen (Copenhagen, 1948).

Diplomatic Documents Preserved in the Public Record Office, vol. 1 (only): *1101–1272*, ed. Pierre Chaplais (London, 1964).

'Documenti sulla prigonia di Carlo II d'Angiò principe di Salerno', ed. Luisa D'Arienzo, in *La società mediterranea all'epoca del Vespro (XI Congresso di storia della Corona d'Aragona, Palermo-Trapani-Erice, 25–30 aprile 1982)*, vol. 2: *Comunicazioni* (Palermo, 1983), 489–555.

Documentos sobre relaciones internacionales de los Reyes Católicos, vol. 1: *1479–1483*, ed. Antonio de la Torre (Barcelona, 1949).

'Documents concernant divers pays de l'Orient Latin', ed. L. de Mas Latrie, *Bibliothèque de l'École des chartes*, 58 (1897), 78–125.

Documents and Records Illustrating the History of Scotland and the Transactions between the Crowns of Scotland and England Preserved in the Treasury of Her Majesty's Exchequer, ed. Francis Palgrave, vol. 1 (London, 1837).

Documents relatifs au comté de Champagne et de Brie, 1172–1361, ed. Auguste Longnon, 2 vols. (Paris, 1901–4).

Documents Relative to the Colonial History of the State of New-York, ed. E. B. O'Callaghan, 15 vols. (Albany, 1853–87).

Ducas, *Historia byzantina*, ed. Immanuel Bekker, CSHB 16 (1834).

Du Clercq, Jacques, *Mémoires*, ed. Frédéric, baron de Reiffenberg, 4 vols. (Brussels, 1823).

Dudo of Saint-Quentin, *De moribus et actis primorum Normanniæ ducum*, ed. Jules Lair (Caen, 1865).

Dunsæte, ed. Liebermann, *Die Gesetze* (q.v.), 1:374–9.

Eadmer, *Historia novorum in Anglia*, ed. Martin Rule, RS 81:1–302 (1884).

Ecbasis cuiusdam captivi per tropologiam, ed. and trans. Edwin H. Zeydel (Chapel Hill, 1964).

Edward and Guthrum, ed. Liebermann, *Die Gesetze* (q.v.), 1:128–35.

Einhard, *Vita Karoli Magni*, 6th edn., ed. O. Holder-Egger, MGH SrG 25 (1911).

Encomium Emmae Reginae, ed. and trans. Alistair Campbell (London, 1949; repr. Cambridge, 1998).

'L'enquête de Bruges après la bataille de Cassel, documents inédits publiés', ed. N. de Pauw, *Compte rendu des séances de la Commission royale d'histoire ou recueil des ses bulletins*, 68 (1899), 665–704.

Erchempert, *Historia Langobardorum Beneventanorum*, ed. G. Waitz, MGH SrL 230–64 (1878).

Ermoldus Nigellus, *Poème sur Louis le Pieux*, ed. and trans. Edmond Faral, *Poème sur Louis le Pieux et Épitres au roi Pépin* (Paris, 1932), 1–201.

Escouchy, Mathieu d', *Chronique*, ed. G. Du Fresne de Beaucourt, 3 vols., SHF (1863–4).

L'Estoire de Eracles empereur, RHC Occ. 2:1–481 (1859).

Eunapius, *Fragmenta historiarum*, trans. R. C. Blockley, *The Fragmentary Classicizing Historians of the Later Roman Empire: Euanpius, Olympiodorus, Priscus, and Malchus*, 2 vols. (Liverpool, 1981–3), 2:1–150.

Eventus infortunii transmarini secundum Templariorum mandatum, in Paris, *Chronica majora* (q.v.), 6:191–7 (Additamenta 95).

The Exchequer Rolls of Scotland: Rotuli scaccarii regum Scotorum, ed. G. Burnett et al., 23 vols. (Edinburgh, 1878–1908).

Falco of Benevento, *Chronicon Beneventanum*, ed. Eduardo D'Angelo (Florence, 1998).

Fenin, Pierre de, *Mémoires*, ed. [L. M. Émille] Dupont, SHF (1837).

Fiscal Accounts of Catalonia under the Early Count-Kings (1151–1213), ed. Thomas N. Bisson, 2 vols. (Berkeley, 1984).

Flodoard, *Annales*, ed. Ph. Lauer, CTH 39 (1905).

—— *Historia Remensis ecclesiae*, ed. Martina Stratmann, MGH SS 36 (1998).

Foedera…, ed. Thomas Rymer, new edn., 4 vols. in 7 (London, 1816–69); 2nd edn., ed. George Holmes, 17 vols. (London, 1727–9).

Formulae imperiales, ed. Karl Zeumer, MGH Formulae Merowingici et Karolini aevi 285–328 (1886).

Fredegar, *Chronica*, ed. B. Krusch, MGH SrM 2:1–193 (1888).

Froissart, Jean, *Chroniques*, ed. Siméon Luce et al., 15 vols., SHF (1869–75); ed. [Joseph M. B. C., baron] Kervyn de Lettenhove, 25 vols. in 26 (Brussels, 1867–77); ed. Denis Sauvage, *Histoire et cronique*, 4 vols. (Lyon, 1559–61). [Abbreviated as Froissart]

Fuero de Cuenca, ed. Rafael de Ureña y Smenjaud (Madrid, 1935).

El fuero de Teruel, ed. Max Gorosch (Stockholm, 1950).

Fulcher of Chartres, *Historia Hierosolymitana*, ed. Heinrich Hagenmeyer (Heidelberg, 1913).

Gaguin, Robert, *Les croniques de France…*, trans. Pierre Desrey (Paris: Galliot Du Pré, 1515).

Galbert of Bruges, *De multro, traditione, et occisione gloriosi Karoli comitis Flandriarum*, ed. Jeff Rider, CCCM 131 (1994).

Galíndez de Carvajal, Lorenzo, *Crónica de Enrique IV*, ed. Juan Torres Fontes, *Estudio sobre la 'Crónica de Enrique IV' del Dr. Galíndez de Carvajal* (Murcia, 1946), 67–460.

Gallus Anonymus, *Cronica et gesta ducum sive principum Polonorum*, ed. Karol Maleczyński (Cracow, 1952).

Gautier [of Chalon], *Diplomata*, PL 160:1165–72.

Genealogia ducum Northmannorum, ed. André Duchesne, *Historiae Normannorum scriptores antiqui* (Paris, 1619), 213.

Gentili, Alberico, *De iure belli libri tres* (Hanover, 1612; repr. Oxford, 1933).

Geoffrey of Clairvaux, *Vita et res gesta Sancti Bernardi, PL* 185:321–50.

Georgian Chronicles (Armenian), trans. Robert W. Thomson, *Rewriting Caucasian History: The Medieval Armenian Adaptation of the Georgian Chronicles* (Oxford, 1986).

Gerald of Wales, *Expugnatio Hibernica*, ed. James F. Dimock, RS 21.5:205–411 (1867).

Gerbert of Reims, *Die Briefsammlung*, ed. Fritz Weigle, MGH Briefe der deutschen Kaiserzeit 2 (1966).

Gerhard of Steterburg, *Annales Stederburgenses*, ed. Georg Heinrich Pertz, MGH SS 16:197–231 (1859).

Gervase of Canterbury, *Gesta regum*, ed. William Stubbs, RS 73.2:3–324 (1880).

Gesta Dagoberti I. regis Francorum, ed. Bruno Krusch, MGH SrM 2:396–425 (1888).

Gesta Edwardi de Carnarvan, ed. William Stubbs, RS 76.2:25–92 (1883).

Gesta episcoporum Cameracensium, ed. Ludwig C. Bethmann, MGH SS 7:393–525 (1846).

Gesta Federici I. imperatoris in Lombardia, ed. Oswald Holder-Egger, MGH SrG 27:14–64 (1892).

Die 'Gesta Hungarorum' des anonymen Notars, ed. and trans. László Veszprémy and Gabriel Silagi (Sigmaringen, 1991).

Gesta Innocenti papae III, PL 214:xv–ccxxviii.

Gesta Ludovici VIII, RHF 17:302–11 (1878).

Gesta Stephani, ed. and trans. K. R. Potter, with a new introduction and notes by R. H. C. Davis, OMT (1976).

Gesta Treverorum, ed. G. Waitz, MGH SS 8:111–260 (1848).

La geste des nobles françois, ed. [Auguste] Vallet de Viriville, in *Chronique de la Pucelle* (q.v.), 105–204.

Die Gesetze der Angelsachsen, ed. Felix Liebermann, 3 vols. (Halle, 1903–16).

Gislebert of Mons, *Chronique*, ed. Léon Vanderkindere (Brussels, 1904).

Gottfried of Viterbo, *Gesta Heinrici VI.*, continuatio Funiacensis et Eberbacensis, ed. Georg Waitz, MGH SS 22:342–9 (1872).

Les grands traités de la Guerre de Cent Ans, ed. E. Cosneau, CTH 7 (1889).

Gray, Thomas, *Scalacronica*, [ed. Joseph Stevenson] (Edinburgh, 1836).

The Great Roll of the Pipe for the Fifth Year of the Reign of King Richard the First, Michaelmas 1193, ed. D. M. Stenton (London, 1927).

The Great Roll of the Pipe for the Sixth Year of King Richard the First, Michaelmas 1194, ed. D. M. Stenton (London, 1928).

The Great Roll of the Pipe for the Seventh Year of the Reign of King Richard the First, Michaelmas 1195, ed. D. M. Stenton (London, 1929).

The Great Roll of the Pipe for the Twenty-Third Year of the Reign of King Henry the Second, A.D. 1176–1177 (London, 1905).

Gregory I, *Registrum epistolarum*, ed. Paul Ewald and Ludwig M. Hartmann, 2 vols., MGH Epp. 1–2 (1887–99).

——*Dialogues*, ed. Adalbert de Vogüé, trans. Paul Antin, 3 vols., SC 251, 260, 265 (1978–80).

Gregory of Tours, *Historiae*, 2nd edn., ed. Bruno Krusch and Wilhelm Levison, MGH SrM 1.1 (1951).

——*Liber in gloria martyrum*, ed. Bruno Krusch, MGH SS rer. Merov. 1.2:34–111 (1885; repr. 1969).

Grotius, Hugo, *De jure belli ac pacis libri tres* (Amsterdam, 1646; repr. Washington, DC, 1913); trans. Jean Barbeyrac, *Le droit de la guerre et de la paix*, 2 vols. (Amsterdam, 1724).

Gruel, Guillaume, *Chronique d'Arthur de Richemont*, ed. Achille Le Vavasseur, SHF (1890).

Guillaume de Nangis, *Chronique latine*, ed. H. Géraud, 2 vols., SHF (1843).

Guillaume le Breton, *Gesta Philippi Augusti*, ed. H. François Delaborde, *Oeuvres de Rigord et de Guillaume le Breton, historiens de Philippe-Auguste*, vol. 1, SHF (1882), 168–320.

——*Philippidos*, ed. H. François Delaborde, *Oeuvres de Rigord et de Guillaume le Breton histoiens de Philippe Auguste*, vol. 2, SHF (1885).

Gunther the Poet, *Ligurinus*, ed. Erwin Assmann, MGH SrG 63 (1987).

Harðar saga, ed. Þórhallur Vilmundarson and Bjarni Vilhjálmsson, Íslenzk fornrit 13 (Reykjavik, 1991), 1–97; trans. Robert Kellogg, *The Complete Sagas of the Icelanders*, ed. Viðar Hrinsson et al., 5 vols. (Reykjavik, 1997), 2:193–236.

Heinrich Taube von Selbach, *Chronica*, ed. Harry Bresslau, MGH SrG ns 1 (1922).

Helmold, *Cronica Slavorum*, ed. Bernhard Schmeidler, MGH SrG 32:1–218 (1937).

Hemingi chartularium ecclesiæ Wigorniensis, ed. Thomas Hearne, 2 vols. (Oxford, 1723).

Henry IV, *Die Briefe*, ed. Carl Erdmann (Leipzig, 1937).

Henry of Huntingdon, *Historia Anglorum*, ed. and trans. Diana Greenway, OMT (1996).

Henry of Livonia, *Chronicon Livoniae*, 2nd edn., ed. Leonid Arbusow and Albert Bauer, MGH SrG 31 (1955).

Hermannus Contractus, *Chronicon*, ed. Georg Heinrich Pertz, MGH SS 5:67–133 (1844).

Histoire des ducs de Normandie et des rois d'Angleterre, ed. Francisque Michel, SHF (1840).

Historia Compostellana, ed. Emma Falque Rey, CCCM 70 (1988).

Historia Francorum Senonensis, ed. Georg Waitz, MGH SS 9:364–9 (1851).

Historia peregrinorum, ed. A. Chroust, MGH SrG ns 5:116–72 (1928).

Historia Selebiensis monasterii, ed. J. T. Fowler, *The Coucher Book of Selby*, 2 vols. (York, 1891–3), 1:1–54.

History of William Marshal, ed. A. J. Holden, trans. S. Gregory, with notes by D. Crouch, 3 vols. (London, 2002–6).

Honorius II, *Epistolae et privilegia*, PL 166:1217–320.

Hugh of Poitiers, *Chronicon*, ed. R. B. C. Huygens, CCCM 42:395–607 (1976).

Ibn 'Abd al-Hakam, *Conquête de l'Afrique du Nord et de l'Espagne (Futûh' Ifrîqiya wa'l-Andalus)*, ed. and trans. Albert Gateau (Algiers, 1942).

Ibn 'Abd Rabbih, *al-'Iqd al-farid* [The Unique Necklace], selections, ed. and trans. James T. Monroe, *Hispano-Arabic Poetry: A Student Anthology* (Berkeley, 1974), 74–129.

Ibn al-'Adīm [Kamāl al-Dīn], *Chronique d'Alep* [Zubdat al-ḥalab fī ta'rīkh Ḥalab], ed. and trans. Charles Barbier de Meynard, RHC Or. 3:571–690 (1884).

Ibn al-Athīr, *The Chronicle*... [al-Kāmil fi'l-ta'rīkh], trans. D. S. Richards, 3 vols. (Aldershot, 2006–8).

Ibn al-Qalānisī, *The Damascus Chronicle of the Crusades* [Dhayl tarikh Dimashq], trans. H. A. R. Gibb (London, 1932).

Ibn al-Qūtīya, *History*, trans. David James, *Early Islamic Spain: The History of Ibn al-Qutiya* (London, 2009).

Ibn Wāsil, *Mufarrij al-kurūb fī akhbār banī Ayyūb* [The Dissipator of Cares in the Account of the Ayyubid Dynasty], trans. Peter Jackson, *The Seventh Crusade, 1244–1254: Sources and Documents* (Aldershot, 2009), 47, 128–54, 213–23.

'Inscriptions sud-arabes: Dixième série', ed. G. Ryckmans, *Le Muséon*, 66 (1953), 267–317.

International Convention against the Taking of Hostages (New York, 17 December 1979), in United Nations, *Treaty Series*, vol. 1316 (New York, 1983), 205–80 (no. 21931).

Inventaire analytique et chronologique des chartes et documents appartenant aux Archives de la ville d'Ypres, ed. I. L. A. Diegerick, 7 vols. (Bruges, 1853–77).

Itinerarium peregrinorum et gesta regis Ricardi, ed. William Stubbs, RS 38.1 (1864).

Jaume I, *Llibre dels feits del rei En Jaume*, ed. Ferran Soldevila, rev. Jordi Bruguera and M. Teresa Ferrer i Mallol, *Les quatre grans cròniques*, vol. 1 (Barcelona, 2007).

Jean de Saint-Victor, *Memoriale historiarum*, *RHF* 21:630–76 (1855).

Jiménez de Rada, Rodrigo, *Historia de rebus Hispaniae sive Historia Gothica*, ed. Juan Fernández Valverde, CCCM 72 (1987).

Johannes Andreae, *Novella in Decretales*, in *Corpus juris canonici* (q.v.).

John VIII, *Epistolae*, ed. E. Caspar and G. Laehr, MGH Epp. 7:313–29 (1912–28).

John of Fordun, *Chronica gentis Scotorum*, ed. William F. Skene (Edinburgh, 1871).

John of Ibelin, *Le livre des assises*, ed. Peter W. Edbury (Leiden, 2003).

John of Salisbury, *Letters*, ed. and trans. W. J. Millor, H. E. Butler, and C. N. L. Brooke, 2 vols., OMT (1979–86).

John of Trokelowe, *Annales*, ed. Henry Thomas Riley, RS 28.3:61–127 (1866).

John of Worcester, *Chronicle*, ed. R. R. Darlington and P. McGurk, trans. Jennifer Bray and P. McGurk, 2 vols. to date, OMT (1995–8).

Joinville, Jean de, *Vie de Saint Louis*, ed. and trans. Jacques Monfrin (Paris, 1995).

Les journaux du trésor de Philippe IV le Bel, ed. Jules Viard (Paris, 1940).

Konrad von Megenberg, *Yconomica*, ed. Sabine Krüger, 3 vols., MGH Staatsschriften des späteren Mittelalters 3.1–3 (1973–84).

Die Kreuzzugsbriefe aus den Jahren 1088–1100, ed. Heinrich Hagenmeyer (Innsbruck, 1901).

Kudrun, ed. Karl Bartsch (Leipzig, 1865).

Lambert of Hersfeld, *Annales*, ed. Oswald Holder-Egger, MGH SrG 38:1–304 (1894).

Laurent de Liège, *Gesta episcoporum Virdunensium*, ed. Georg Waitz, MGH SS 10:489–516 (1852).

Laxdæla Saga, ed. Einar Ól. Sveinsson, Íslensk fornrit 5 (Reykjavik, 1934), 1–248.

Layettes du Trésor des chartes, ed. Alexandre Teulet et al., 5 vols. (Paris, 1863–1909).

Le Fèvre, Jean, *Chronique*, ed. François Morand, 2 vols., SHF (1876–81).

Le Muisit, Gilles, *Chronique*, ed. Henri Lemaître, *Chronique et annales*, SHF (1906), 1–219.

Leo the Deacon, *Historiae*, ed. Karl Benedict Hase, CSHB (1828).

Lex Frisionum, ed. Karl August Eckhardt and Albrecht Eckhardt, MGH Fontes iuris Germanici antiqui in usum scholarum separatim editi 12 (1982).

Lex Visigothorum, ed. Karl Zeumer, MGH Leges nationum germanicarum 1:33–456 (1902).

Liber Eliensis, ed. E. O. Blake (London, 1962).

Liber feudorum maior: Cartulario real que se conserva en el Archivo de la Corona de Aragón, 2 vols. (Barcelona, 1945).

Liber instrumentorum memorialium: Cartulaire des Guillems de Montpellier, ed. Alexandre Germain (Montpellier, 1884–6).

Liber monasterii de Hyda, ed. Edward Edwards, RS 45 (1866).

Le Liber pontificalis, 2nd edn., ed. L. Duschesne, 3 vols. (Paris, 1955–7).

Lieber, Francis, *Instructions for the Government of Armies of the United States in the Field* (New York, 1863).

Lignages d'Outremer, ed. Marie-Adélaïde Nielen (Paris, 2003).

Liutprand of Cremona, *Antapodosis*, 3rd edn., ed. Joseph Becker, MGH SrG 41:1–158 (1915).

Le livre au roi, ed. Myriam Greilsammer (Paris, 1995).

Livre des assises de la cour des bourgeois, ed. E. H. Kausler, *Les livres des assises et des usages dou reaume de Jérusalem*, vol. 1 (only) (Stuttgart, 1839), 1–352.

Livre des Miracles de Sainte-Catherine-de-Fierbois: 1375–1470, ed. Yves Chauvin (Poitiers, 1976).

Lupus Protospatarius, *Annales*, ed. Georg Heinrich Pertz, MGH SS 5:52–63 (1844).

Machairas, Leontios, *Chronikon Kyprou*, ed. and trans. E. Miller and Constantin Sathas, 2 vols. (Paris, 1881–2).

Machiavelli, Niccolò, *Discorsi sopra la prima deca di Tito Livio*, ed. Corrado Vivanti, *Opere*, vol. 1 (Turin, 1997), 193–525.

Magni rotuli scaccarii Normanniæ sub regibus Angliæ, vol. 1, ed. Thomas Stapleton (London, 1840).

Mainzer Urkundenbuch, vol. 2: *Die Urkunden seit dem Tode erzbischof Adalberts I. (1137) bis zum Tode Erzbischof Konrads (1200)*, part 2: *1176–1200*, ed. Peter Acht (Darmstadt, 1971).

Major Peace Treaties of Modern History, 1648–1967, ed. Fred L. Israel, 4 vols. (New York, 1967).

Malalas, John, *Chronographia*, ed. Hans Thurn, CFHB 35 (2000).

Malaspina, Saba, *Die Chronik*, ed. Walter Koller and August Nitschke, MGH SS 35 (1999).

Malaterra, Goffredo, *De rebus gestis Rogerii Calabriae et Siciliae comitis et Roberti Guiscardi ducis fratris eius*, ed. Ernesto Pontieri, RIS² 5.1 (1928).

Mandements et actes divers de Charles V (1364–1380), ed. Léopold Delisle (Paris, 1874).

Matthew of Edessa, *Chronique*, trans. Édouard Dulaurier (Paris, 1858).

Matthias of Neuenburg, *Chronica*, ed. Adolf Hofmeister, MGH SrG ns 4:1–501 (1924–40).

Mecklenburgisches Urkundenbuch, vol. 1: *786–1250* (Schwerin, 1863).

Mémoires pour servir de preuves à l'histoire ecclésiastique et civile de Bretagne, ed. Hyacinthe Morice, 3 vols. (Paris, 1742–6).

Merobaudes, Flavius, *Panegyricus II*, ed. Friedrich Vollmer, MGH AA 14:11–18 (1905); trans. Frank M. Clover (Philadelphia, 1971), 13–15.

Michael the Syrian, *Chronique*, ed. and trans. J.-B. Chabot, 4 vols. in 7 (Paris, 1899–1910).

Miracula S. Wandregisili abbatis, in *Acta Sanctorum* (q.v.), Julii V (1868), 281–91.

Molina, Luis de, *De justitia et jure*, new edn. (Mainz, 1659).

Molinet, Jean, *Chroniques*, ed. J.-A. Buchon, 5 vols. (Paris, 1827–8).

Monumenta Henricina, vol. 6 (Coimbra, 1964).

Monuments historiques (cartons des rois, 528–1789), ed. Jules Tardif (Paris, 1966).

Monstrelet, Enguerrand de, *Chronique*, ed. L. Douët-d'Arcq, 6 vols., SHF (1857–62). [Abbreviated as Monstrelet]

Morena, Otto, *Historia*, ed. Ferdinand Güterbock, MGH SrG ns 7:1–129 (1930).

Morigia, Bonincontro, *Chronicon Modoetiense*, RIS 12:1061–184 (1728).

Das Nibelungenlied, ed. Karl Bartsch and Helmut de Boor, 13th edn. (Wiesbaden, 1956).

Nicolas de Brai, *Gesta Ludovici VIII, francorum regis*, RHF 17:311–45 (1878).

Nithard, *Histoire des fils de Louis le Pieux*, ed. Ph. Lauer (Paris, 1926).

Northern Petitions Illustrative of Life in Berwick, Cumbria and Durham in the Fourteenth Century, ed. C. M. Fraser (Gateshead, 1981).

'Nouvelles preuves de l'histoire de Chypre', ed. L. de Mas Latrie, *Bibliothèque de l'École des chartes*, 32 (1871), 341–78; 34 (1873), 47–87.

'Nuova serie di documenti sulle relazione di Genova coll'impero Bizantino', ed. Angelo Sanguineti and Gerolamo Bertolotto, *Atti della Società ligure di storia patria*, 28 (1896), 337–573.

Obertus, *Annales*, ed. Georg Heinrich Pertz, MGH SS 18:56–96 (1863).

Odo of Cluny, *De vita S. Geraldi comitis*, PL 133:649–704.

Oliver of Paderborn, *Historia Damiatina*, ed. [Hermann] Hoogeweg (Tübingen, 1894).

De oorkonden der graven van Vlaanderen (Juli 1128–September 1191), vol. 2.1: *Regering van Diederik van de Elzas (Juli 1128–17 Januari 1168)*, ed. Thérèse de Hemptinne and Adriaan Verhulst (Brussels, 1988).

Oorkondenboek van Holland en Zeeland tot 1299, vol. 2: *1222 tot 1256*, ed. J. G. Kruisheer (Assen, 1986).

Oppenheim, Lassa, *International Law: A Treatise*, 5th edn., ed. Hersch Lauterpacht (London, 1935–7).

Orderic Vitalis, *Historia ecclesiastica*, ed. and trans. Marjorie Chibnall, 6 vols., OMT (1969–80).

Ordonnances des roys de France de la troisième race..., vol. 1, ed. [Eusèbe Jacob] de Laurière (Paris, 1723).

Orestes of Jerusalem, *De historia et laudibus Sabae et Macarii Siculorum*, ed. J. Cozza-Luzi, *Studi et documenti di storia e diritto*, 12 (1891), 33–56, 135–68, 311–23.

Original Documents Relating to the Hostages of John, King of France, and the Treaty of Brétigny, in 1360, ed. G. F. Duckett (London, 1890).

Orville, Jean Cabaret d', *La chronique du bon duc Loys de Bourbon*, ed. A.-M. Chazaud, SHF (1876).

Otto of Saint-Blasien, *Chronica*, ed. Adolf Hofmeister, MGH SrG 47:1–88 (1912).

Paris, Matthew, *Chronica majora*, ed. Henry Richards Luard, 7 vols., RS 57.1–7 (1872–83).

Passio S. Pelagii, ed. Celso Rodríguez Fernández, *La Pasión de S. Pelayo* (Santiago de Compostela, 1991).

Passio SS. Acepsimae episcopi, Ioseph presbyteri et Aeithalae diaconi, ed. and trans. Hippolyte Delehaye, *Les versions grecques des actes des martyrs persans sous Sapor II*, Patrologia Orientalis 2.4 (Paris, 1907), 478–557.

Patent Rolls of the Reign of Henry III Preserved in the Public Record Office, A.D. 1216–1225 (London, 1901).

Patrologia cursus completus, series Latina, 221 vols. (Paris, 1841–64). [Abbreviated as *PL*]

Paul of Bernried, *Vita Gregorii VII*, PL 148:39–104.

Paul the Deacon, *Historia Langobardorum*, ed. L. Bethmann and G. Waitz, MGH SrL 12–187 (1878).

Paulinus of Pella, *Eucharisticos*, ed. and trans. Claude Moussy, *Poème d'action de grâces et prière*, SC 209 (1974).

Els pergamins de l'arxiu comtal de Barcelona de Ramon Borrell a Ramon Berenguer, ed. Gaspar Feliu et al., 3 vols. (Barcelona, 1999).

Philostorgius, *Kirchengeschichte*, ed. Jospeh Bidez, 3rd edn., ed. Fridhelm Winkelmann (Berlin, 1981).

Pierre des Vaux-de-Cernay, *Hystoria Albigensis*, ed. P. Guébin and E. Lyon, 3 vols., SHF (1926–39).

Pina, Rui de, *Crónicas*, ed. M. Lopes de Almeida (Porto, 1977).

[Pintoin, Michel], *Chronique du religieux de Saint-Denys*, ed. and trans L. Bellaguet, 6 vols. (Paris, 1839–52).

Politische Verträge des frühen Mittelalters, ed. Peter Classen (Germering, 1966).

Preußisches Urkundenbuch, vol. 1.1, ed. Rudolf Philippi (Königsberg, 1882).

Procopius, *Works*, ed. and trans. H. B. Dewing, 7 vols. (Cambridge, Mass., 1914–40).

Psellos, Michael, *Chronographie*, Émile Renauld, 2 vols. (Paris, 1967).

Pseudo-Isidore, *Crónica*, ed. Antonio Benito Vidal (Valencia, 1961).

Pseudo-Joshua the Stylite, *Chronicle*, trans. Frank R. Twombley and John W. Watt (Liverpool, 2000).

Pulgar, Hernando del, *Crónica de los señores reyes católicos Don Fernando y Doña Isabel*, ed. Cayetano Rosell, *Crónicas de los reyes de Castilla*, 3 vols. (Madrid, 1875–8), 3:223–511.

'A Question about the Succession', ed. A. A. M. Duncan, *Miscellany of the Scottish Historical Society*, 12 (1994), 1–57.

Rahewin of Freising, *Gesta Friderici I. imperatoris*, 3rd edn., ed. G. Waitz and B. von Simson, MGH SrG 46:162–346 (1912).

Ralph of Diceto, *Ymagines historiarum*, ed. William Stubbs, RS 68.2:1–174 (1876).

Ralph of Coggeshall, *Chronicon Anglicanum*, ed. Joseph Stevenson, RS 66:1–208 (1875).

RAND Database of Worldwide Terrorism Incidents [website] (www.rand.org/nsrd/projects/terrorism-incidents.html).

The Ransom of John II, King of France, 1360–1370, ed. Dorothy M. Broome, Camden Miscellany 14 (London, 1926).

Raoul de Cambrai, ed. and trans. Sarah Kay (Oxford, 1992).

Raoul of Saint-Trond, *Gesta abbatum Trudonensium*, ed. C. De Borman, *Chronique de l'Abbaye de Saint-Trond*, 2 vols. (Liège, 1877).

Récits d'un ménestrel de Reims au treizième siècle, ed. Natalis de Wailly, SHF (1876).

Recueil des actes de Henri II, roi d'Angleterre et duc de Normandie, concernant les provinces françaises et les affaires de France, ed. Léopold Delisle, rev. Élie Berger, 3 vols. (Paris, 1916–27).

Recueil des actes de Jean IV, duc de Bretagne, ed. Michael Jones, 3 vols. (Paris, 1980–2001).

Recueil des actes de Louis VI, roi de France (1108–1137), ed. Robert-Henri Bautier and Jean Dufour, 4 vols. (Paris, 1992–4).

Recueil des actes de Philippe Auguste, roi de France, ed. Élie Berger et al., 6 vols. (Paris, 1916–2005).

Recueil des actes des comtes de Provence appartenant à la maison de Barcelona: Alphonse II et Raimond Bérenger V, ed. Fernand Benoît, 2 vols. (Monaco, 1925).

Recueil des chartes de l'abbaye de Cluny, ed. Auguste Bernard and Alexander Bruel, 6 vols. (Paris, 1876–1903).

Recueil des historiens des croisades, 16 vols. (Paris, 1841–1906). [Abbreviated as *RHC*]

Recueil des historiens des Gaules et de la France, 24 vols. in 25 (Paris, 1738–1904). [Abbreviated as *RHF*]

Recueil des monuments inédits de l'histoire du tiers état, ed. Augustin Thierry, vol. 1 (Paris, 1850).

Regesta pontificum romanorum ab condita ecclesia ad annum post Christum natum MCXCVIII, ed. Philipp Jaffé, 2nd edn., ed. S. Loewenfeld, F. Kaltenbrunner, and P. Ewald, 2 vols. (Leipzig, 1885–8). [Abbreviated as JE/JL]

Regesta pontificum romanorum inde ab a. post Christum natum MXCXVIII ad a. MCCCIV, ed. August Potthast, 2 vols. (Berlin, 1874–5). [Abbreviated as Potthast]

Regesta regum Anglo-Normannorum, 1066–1154, ed. R. H. C. Davis, Charles Johnson, and Henry A. Cronne, 3 vols. (Oxford, 1913–69).

Regesten des Kaiserurkunden des oströmischen Reiches, ed. Franz Dölger, 5 vols. (Munich, 1924–77).

Régestes de la cité de Liège, vol. 4: *1456 à 1482*, ed. Émile Fairon (Liège, 1939).

Regino of Prüm, *Chronicon*, ed. Friedrich Kurze, MGH SrG 50:1–153 (1890).

Die Register Innocenz' III., ed. Othmar Hageneder et al., 9 vols. in 12 to date (Graz, 1964–).

'Le registre de la "Loi" de Tournai, de 1302 et listes des otages de Bruges (1301) et de Courtrai: Documents inédits', ed. Léo Verriest, *Bulletin de la Commission royale d'histoire*, 80 (1911), 369–584.

Les registres d'Honorius IV, ed. Maurice Prou (Paris, 1888).

Les registres de Grégoire IX, ed. Lucien Auvray, 4 vols. (Paris, 1896–1955).

Les registres de Nicolas IV, ed. Ernest Langlois (Paris, 1886).

Les registres de Philippe Auguste, ed. John Baldwin, 1 vol. to date (Paris, 1992–).

Registrum honoris de Morton: A Series of Ancient Charters of the Earldom of Morton with Other Original Papers, 2 vols. (Edinburgh, 1853).

Regnier, Jean, *Livre de la prison*, ed. E. Droz, *Les fortunes et adversitez de Jean Regnier* (Paris, 1923), 1–169.

Regula Magistri, ed. and trans. Adalbert de Vogüé, 3 vols., SC 105–7 (1964–5).

De rekeningen der stad Gent: Tijdvak van Jacob van Artevelde, 1336–1349, vol. 3.1, ed. Napoléon de Pauw and Julius Vuylsteke (Ghent, 1882).

Renier of Saint-Laurent de Liège, *Triumphale Bulonicum*, ed. Wilhelm Arndt, MGH SS 20:583–92 (1868).

Rennes Dindšenchas, ed. and trans. Whitley Stokes, 'The Prose Tales in the Rennes Dindšenchas', *Revue celtique*, 15 (1894), 277–336.

Richard of San Germano, *Chronica*, ed. Georg Heinrich Pertz, MGH SrG 53 (1864).

Richer, *Gesta Senoniensis ecclesiae*, ed. G. Waitz, MGH SS 25:249–345 (1880).

——*Historiae*, ed. Hartmut Hoffmann, MGH SS 38 (2000).

Rigord, *Gesta Philippi Augusti*, ed. H. François Delaborde, *Oeuvres de Rigord et de Guillaume le Breton, historiens de Philippe-Auguste*, vol. 1, SHF (1882), 1–167.

Rimbert, *Vita Anskarii*, ed. G. Waitz, MGH SrG 55:5–79 (1884).

Robert of Avesbury, *De gestis mirabilibus regis Edwardi Tertii*, ed. Edward Maunde Thompson, RS 93:277–471 (1889).

Robert of Torigni, *Chronica*, ed. R. Howlett, RS 82.4 (1889).

[Roger of Howden], *Gesta Henrici II et Ricardi I*, ed. William Stubbs, 2 vols., RS 49.1–2 (1867).

——*Chronica*, ed. William Stubbs, 4 vols., RS 51.1–4 (1868–71).

Roger of Wendover, *Flores historiarum*, ed. Henry G. Hewlett, 3 vols., RS 84.1–3 (1886–9); ed. Henry O. Coxe, 4 vols. (London, 1841–2).

Rolandino of Padua, *Chronica*, ed. Philipp Jaffé, MGH SS 19:32–147 (1886).

Rôles gascons, ed. Francisque Michel, 3 vols. in 4 (Paris, 1885–1906).

Romuald of Salerno, *Annales*, ed. Wilhelm Arndt, MGH SS 17:387–461 (1866).

Rotuli chartarum in turri Londinensi asservati, vol. 1.1 (only): *Ab anno MCXCIX. ad annum MCCXVI*, ed. Thomas Duffus Hardy (London, 1837).

Rotuli de oblatis et finibus in turri Londinensi asservati, tempore regis Johannis, ed. Thomas Duffus Hardy (London, 1835).

Rotuli litterarum clausarum in turri Londinensi asservati, ed. Thomas Duffus Hardy, 2 vols. (London, 1833–4).

Rotuli litterarum patentium in turri Londinensi asservati, ed. Thomas Duffus Hardy (London, 1835).

Rotuli Scotiæ in turri Londinensi et in domo capitulari Westmonasteriensi asservati, 2 vols. (London, 1814–19).

Royal and Other Historical Letters Illustrative of the Reign of Henry III, ed. Walter Waddington Shirley, 2 vols., RS 27.1–2 (1862–6).

The Russian Primary Chronicle, trans. Samuel H. Cross (Cambridge, Mass., 1930).

Sabaean Inscriptions from Mahram Bilqîs (Mârib), ed. A. Jamme (Baltimore, 1962).

Sachsenspiegel: Landrecht, 2nd edn., ed. Karl August Eckhardt, MGH Fontes iuris Germanici antiqui, ns 1.1 (1955).

Sacrorum conciliorum nova et amplissima collectio, ed. Giovanni Domenico Mansi, 53 vols. (Florence, 1759–1927).

Sālih ibn Yahyā, *Histoire de Beyrouth et des émirs d'al-Garb* [Tārīkh Bayrūt], appendix, ed. and trans. Louis Cheikho, 'Un dernier écho des Croisades', *Mélanges de la faculté orientale* (Université Saint-Joseph, Beirut), 1 (1906), 303–75.

Salimbene de Adam, *Cronica*, ed. Giuseppe Scalia, 2 vols., CCCM 125–125A (1998–9).

Die Salzburger Briefsammlung, ed. Günther Hödl and Peter Classen, MGH Briefe der deutschen Kaiserzeit 6:149–97 (1983).

Saxo Grammaticus, *Gesta Danorum*, ed. J. Olrik and H. Ræder, 2 vols. (Copenhagen, 1931–57).

Sicard of Cremona, *Cronica*, in Salimbene de Adam, *Cronica* (q.v.).

Siete Partidas, ed. Meynardo Ungut Alamano and Lançalao Polo (Seville, 1491; facsim. ed. Gonzalo Martínez Díez, Valladolid, 1988).

Sigebert of Gembloux, *Chronica*, ed. Ludwig Conrad Bethmann, MGH SS 6:300–474 (1844).

Simeon of Durham, *Historia regum*, ed. Thomas Arnold, RS 75.2:1–283 (1885).

Skylitzes, John, *Synopsis historiarum*, ed. Hans Thurn, CFHB 5 (1973).

Snorri Sturluson, *Heimskringla*, ed. N. Linder and K. A. Haggson, 3 vols. (Uppsala, 1869–72).

The Song of Roland, ed. and trans. Gerard J. Brault, 2 vols. (University Park, 1978).

Some Documents Regarding the Fulfilment and Interpretation of the Treaty of Brétigny, 1361–1369, ed. Pierre Chaplais (London, 1952).

Le soulèvement de la Flandre maritime, 1323–1328: Documents inédites, ed. Henri Pirenne (Brussels, 1900).

Spicilegium Liberianum, ed. Francesco Liverani, vol. 1 (Florence, 1863).

Statuta capitulorum generalium ordinis Cisterciensis ab anno 1116 ad annum 1786, ed. A. Trilhe and Joseph-Marie Canivez, 8 vols. (Louvain, 1933–41).

Statuto del comune di Perugia del 1279, ed. Severino Caprioli et al., 2 vols. (Perugia, 1996).

Symeon Logothetes, *Chronicon*, ed. Stephan Wahlgren, CFHB 44 (2006).

Taylor, Telford, *Final Report to the Secretary of the Army on the Nuernberg War Crimes Trials Under Control Council Law no. 10* (Washington, DC, 1949).

Tedeschi, Niccolò [Panormitanus], *Commentaria secundæ partis in secundum librum decretalium*, ed. Jacopo Anello de Botti and Antonio Corsetti (Venice, 1588).

Theophanes Confessor, *Chronographia*, ed. Carl de Boor, 2 vols. (Leipzig, 1883–5).

Theophanes continuatus, ed. Immanuel Bekker, CSHB (1838).

Thesaurus novus anecdotorum, ed. Edmond Martène and Ursin Durand, 5 vols. (Paris, 1717).

Thietmar of Merseburg, *Chronicon*, ed. Robert Holzmann, MGH SrG ns 9 (1935).

'Le Traité de Gaillon (1196): Édition critique et traduction', ed. and trans. Emmanuel Rousseau and Gilles Désiré dit Gosset, *Tabularia: Sources écrites de la Normandie médiévale* (www.unicaen.fr/mrsh/craham/revue/tabularia/).

Translatio S. Alexandri, ed. H. Bresslau, MGH SS 30.2:954–7 (1934).

Translatio S. Liborii, ed. Georg Heinrich Pertz, MGH SS 4:149–57 (1841).

Translatio S. Viti, ed. Philipp Jaffé, *Bibliotheca rerum Germanicarum*, vol. 1: *Monumenta Corbeiensia* (Berlin, 1864), 3–26.

The Treaty of Bayonne (1388) with Preliminary Treaties of Trancoso (1387), ed. John Palmer and Brian Powell (Exeter, 1988).

Triumphus Sancti Lamberti de castro Bollonio, ed. Wilhelm Arndt, MGH SS 20:497–511 (1868).

Two of the Saxon Chronicles Parallel, ed. Charles Plummer and John Earle, 2 vols. (Oxford, 1892–9); trans. Dorothy Whitelock, David C. Douglas, and Susie I. Tucker, *The Anglo-Saxon Chronicle: A Revised Translation* (London, 1961). [Abbreviated as *ASC*]

Ulrich von Zatzikhoven, *Lanzelet: Eine Erzählung*, ed. K. A. Hahn (Frankfurt am Main, 1845).

United Nations War Crimes Commission, *Law Reports of the Trials of War Criminals*, vol. 8 (London, 1949).

United States of America v. Wilhelm List, et al. ('The Hostages Case'), in *Trials of War Criminals before the Nurenberg Military Tribunals under Control Council Law No. 10, Nurenberg, October 1946–April 1949*, vol. 11 (Washington, DC, 1950), 757–1332.

Urban III, *Epistolae et privilegia*, PL 202:1331–532.

Urkundenbuch zur Geschichte der Babenberger in Österreich, ed. Heinrich Fichtenau and Erich Zöllner, vol. 4.1: *Ergänzende Quellen, 976–1194* (Vienna, 1968).

Urkundenbuch zur Geschichte der, jetzt die Preussischen Regierungsbezirke, Coblenz und Trier bildenden mittelrheinischen Territorien, ed. Heinrich Beyer, vol. 1: *Von den älteren Zeiten bis zum Jahre 1169* (Koblenz, 1860).

Urkundliche Beiträge zur Geschichte des Hussitenkrieges in den Jahren 1419–1436, ed. Franz Palacký, 2 vols. (Prague, 1873).

Usāma ibn Munqidh, *An Arab-Syrian Gentleman and Warrior in the Period of the Crusades: Memoirs of Usamah ibn-Munqidh* [Kitāb al-i'tibār], trans. Philip K. Hitti (New York, 1929; repr. 2000).

Vattel, Emer de, *Le droit des gens*, 2 vols. (London, 1758).

La vie de Seint Auban, ed. Arthur Robert Harden (Oxford, 1968).

Vincent of Prague, *Annales*, ed. Wilhelm Wattenbach, MGH SS 17:658–83 (1861).

Vita Arnoldi archiepiscopi Moguntini, ed. Philipp Jaffé, *Bibliotheca rerum Germanicarum*, vol. 3: *Monumenta Moguntina* (Berlin, 1866), 604–75.

Vita Petri Iberi, ed. and trans. Richard Raabe, *Petrus der Iberer: ein Charakterbild zur Kirchen und Sittengeschichte des fünften Jahrhunderts* (Leipzig, 1895).

Vita S. Caelestini V, in *Acta sanctorum* (q.v.), Maii IV (1685), 437–61.

Vita S. Hermenegildi, in *Acta sanctorum* (q.v.), Aprilis II (1675), 134–8.

Vita S. Laurentii archiepiscopi Dublinensis, ed. Charles Plummer, 'Vie et miracles de S. Laurent, archevêque de Dublin', *Analecta Bollandiana*, 33 (1914), 121–86.

Vitoria, Francisco de, *De Indis et de iure belli relectiones*, ed. Ernest Nys and Herbert Francis Wright, trans. John Pawley Bate (Washington, DC, 1917).

—— *Comentarios a la Secunda secundae de santo Tomás*, 6 vols., ed. Vicente Beltrán de Heredia (Salamanca, 1932–52).

Walsingham, Thomas, *Historia anglicana*, ed. Henry Thomas Riley, RS 28.1 (London, 1863–4).

Waltharius, ed. Karl Strecker, MGH Poetae Latini medii aevi 6.1:1–85 (1951).

Wavrin, Jehan de, *Recueil des croniques...*, ed. William Hardy and Edward L. C. P. Hardy, 5 vols., RS 39.1–5 (1864–91).

Westschweizer Schiedsurkunden bis zum Jahre 1300, ed. Emil Usteri (Zurich, 1955).

Widukind of Corvey, *Res gestae Saxonicae*, 5th edn., ed. Paul Hirsch and H.-E. Lohmann, MGH SrG 60:1–154 (1935).

William of Apulia, *La geste de Robert Guiscard*, ed. and trans. Marguerite Mathieu (Palermo, 1961).

William of Jumièges, [Orderic Vitalis, and Robert of Torigni], *Gesta Normannorum ducum*, ed. and trans. Elisabeth M. C. Van Houts, 2 vols., OMT (1992–5).

William of Malmesbury, *El libro De laudibus et miraculis Sanctae Mariae*, 2nd edn., ed. José Maria Canal (Rome, 1968).

—— *Historia novella*, ed. Edmund King, trans. K. R. Potter, OMT (1998).

—— *Gesta regum Anglorum*, ed. and. trans. R. A. B. Mynors, R. M. Thomson, and M. Winterbottom, 2 vols., OMT (1998–9).

William of Newburgh, *Historia rerum Anglicarum*, ed. Richard Howlett, 2 vols., RS 82.1–2[:583] (1884–5).

William of Poitiers, *Gesta Guillelmi*, ed. and trans. R. H. C. Davis and Marjorie Chibnall, OMT (1998).

William of Tyre, *Chronicon*, ed. R. B. C. Huygens, 2 vols., CCCM 63–63A (1986); Rothelin continuation, *RHC* Occ. 2:483–639 (1859).

Wykes, Thomas, *Chronicon*, ed. Henry Richards Luard, RS 36.4:6–352 (1869).

Zonaras, John, *Epitoma historiarum*, ed. Moritz Pinder and Theodor Buttner-Wobst, 3 vols., CSHB (1841–97).

III. SECONDARY SOURCES

(An asterisk denotes studies that print primary sources used.)

Abels, Richard, 'Paying the Danegeld: Anglo-Saxon Peacemaking with the Vikings', in Philip de Souza and John France, eds., *War and Peace in Ancient and Medieval History* (Cambridge, 2008), 173–92.

Ahmadijan, Christina, and Oxley, Joanne, 'Using Hostages to Support Exchange: Dependence and Partial Equity Stakes in Japanese Automotive Supply Relationships', *Journal of Law, Economics, and Organization*, 22 (2005), 213–33.

Alexandrowicz, C. H., *An Introduction to the History of the Law of Nations in the East Indies (16th, 17th and 18th Centuries)* (Oxford, 1967).

Algazi, Gadi, Groebner, Valentin, Jussen, and Bernhard, eds., *Negotiating the Gift: Pre-Modern Figurations of Exchange* (Göttingen, 2003).

Allen, Joel, *Hostages and Hostage-Taking in the Roman Empire* (Cambridge, 2006).

Allsen, Thomas T., *Culture and Conquest in Mongol Eurasia* (Cambridge, 2004).

Althoff, Gerd, *Family, Friends, and Followers: Political and Social Bonds in Medieval Europe*, trans. Christopher Carroll (Cambridge, 2004 [1990]).

—— *Spielregeln der Politik im Mittelalter: Kommunikation in Frieden und Fehde* (Darmstadt, 1997).

Amira, Karl von, *Nordgermanisches Obligationenrecht*, vol. 2: *Westnordisches Obligationenrecht* (Leipzig, 1895).

Amit, M., 'Hostages in Ancient Greece', *Rivista di filologia e di istruzione classica*, 3rd ser., 98 (1970), 129–47.

Angenendt, Arnold, *Kaiserherrschaft und Königstaufe: Kaiser, Könige und Päpste als geistliche Patrone in der abendländischen Missionsgeschichte* (Berlin, 1984).

Anon., 'Hostage', in *The Encyclopaedia Britannica*, 11th edn. (New York, 1911), 13:801–2.

Atkinson, Clarissa W., *The Oldest Vocation: Christian Motherhood in the Middle Ages* (Ithaca, 1991).

Aubrun, Michel *L'ancien diocèse de Limoges des origines au milieu du XIe siècle* (Clermont-Ferrand, 1981).

Aymard, André, 'Les otages barbares au début de l'Empire', *Journal of Roman Studies*, 51 (1961), 136–42.

Bachrach, Bernard S., *Fulk Nerra, the Neo-Roman Consul, 987–1040* (Berkeley, 1993).

Balfour-Melville, E. W. M., *James I, King of Scots, 1406–1437* (London, 1936).

——— *Edward III and David II* (London, 1954).

Barante, [Amable-Guillaume-Prosper Brugière, baron] de, *Histoire des ducs de Bourgogne de la maison de Valois, 1364–1477*, new edn., ed. [Louis-Prosper] Gachard, vol. 2 (Brussels, 1838).

Barker, John W., *Manuel II Palaeologus (1391–1425): A Study in Late Byzantine Statesmanship* (New Brunswick, 1969).

Barlow, Frank, *William Rufus* (Berkeley, 1983).

Barratt, Nick, 'The English Revenue of Richard I', *English Historical Review*, 116 (2001), 635–56.

Barthélemy, Dominique, *L'an mil et la paix de Dieu: La France chrétienne et féodale, 980–1060* (Paris, 1999).

Bartlett, Robert, *England under the Norman and Angevin Kings, 1075–1225* (Oxford, 2000).

Bedos-Rezak, Brigitte Miriam, 'Medieval Identity: A Sign and a Concept', *American Historical Review*, 105 (2000), 1489–533.

*Bémont, Charles, *Simon de Montfort, comte de Leicester, sa vie (120?–1265), son rôle politique en France et en Angleterre* (Paris, 1874).

*Benet i Clarà, Albert, *La família Gurb-Queralt (956–1276): Senyors de Sallent, Oló, Avinyó, Gurb, Manlleu, Voltregà, Queralt i Santa Coloma de Queralt* (Sallent, 1993).

Benham, Jenny, *Peacemaking in the Middle Ages: Principles and Practice* (Manchester, 2001).

Berger, Raoul, 'From Hostage to Contract', *Illinois Law Review*, 5 (1940), 154–74, 281–92.

Bériac-Lainé, Françoise, and Given-Wilson, Chris, *Les prisonniers de la bataille de Poitiers* (Paris, 2002).

Bernard, Auguste, 'Excommunication de l'abbaye de Savigny au XIIe siècle', *Revue du Lyonnais*, ns 6 (1853), 177–90.

Beyerle, Franz, 'Der Ursprung der Bürgschaft: Ein Deutungsversuch vom germanischen Rechte her', *Zeitschrift der Savigny-Stiftung für Rechtsgeschichte*, Germanistische Abteilung, 47 (1927), 567–645.

Bisson, Thomas N., 'The Organized Peace in Southern France and Catalonia, ca. 1140–ca. 1233', *American Historical Review*, 82 (1977), 290–311.

——— *The Crisis of the Twelfth Century: Power, Lordship, and the Origins of European Government* (Princeton, 2009).

Bonnassie, Pierre, 'Hagiographie et Paix de Dieu dans le Sud-Ouest de la France (X^e–début XIIe siècle)', in Bonnassie, *Les sociétés de l'an mil: Un monde entre deux âges* (Brussels, 2001), 317–35.

Boom, Ghislaine de, *Marguerite d'Autriche-Savoie et la Pré-Renaissance* (Paris, 1935).

*Boselli, Vicenzo, *Delle storie piacentine* (Piacenza, 1793; repr. Bologna, 1976).

Bossuat, André, 'Les prisonniers de Beauvais et la rançon du poète Jean Regnier, bailli d'Auxerre', in *Mélanges d'histoire du Moyen Âge dédié à la mémoire de Louis Halphen* (Paris, 1951), 27–32.

——— 'Les prisonniers de guerre au XVe siècle: La rançon de Guillaume, seigneur de Châteauvillain', *Annales de Bourgogne*, 23 (1951), 7–35.

——— 'Les prisonniers de guerre au XVe siècle: La rançon de Jean, seigneur de Rodemack', *Annales de l'Est*, 5th ser., 2 (1951), 145–62.

*Boswell, John, *The Royal Treasure: Muslim Communities under the Crown of Aragon in the Fourteenth Century* (New Haven, 1977).

——— *The Kindness of Strangers: The Abandonment of Children in Western Europe from Late Antiquity to the Renaissance* (New York, 1988).

*Boswell, John, *Same-Sex Unions in Premodern Europe* (New York, 1994).

Boulage, Thomas-Pascal, *Les otages de Louis XVI et de sa famille* (Paris, 1814).

Brand, Paul, 'Aspects of the Law of Debt, 1189–1307', in P. R. Schofield and N. J. Mayhew, eds., *Credit and Debt in Medieval England, c.1180–c.1350* (Oxford, 2002), 19–41.

Brodman, James W., *Ransoming Captives in Crusader Spain: The Order of Merced on the Christian-Islamic Frontier* (Philadelphia, 1986).

*Broussillon, Arthur Bertrand de, *La maison de Laval: Étude historique accompagnée du cartulaire de Laval et de Vitré*, vol. 5 (Paris, 1903).

Brown, Elizabeth A. R., 'Philip V, Charles IV, and the Jews of France: The Alleged Expulsion of 1322', *Speculum*, 66 (1991), 294–329.

——Rapp, Claudia, and Shaw, Brent D., 'Ritual Brotherhood in Ancient and Medieval Europe: A Symposium', *Traditio*, 52 (1997), 261–381.

Brown, Michael, *James I*, rev. edn. (East Linton, 2000).

Bruder, Reinhold, *Die germanische Frau im Lichte der Runeninschriften und der antiken Historiographie* (Berlin, 1974).

Brundage, James A., *Law, Sex, and Christian Society in Medieval Europe* (Chicago, 1987).

Buisson, Ludwig, 'Formen normannischer Staatsbildung (9. bis 11. Jahrhundert)', in *Studien zum mittelalterlichen Lehenswesen* (Sigmaringen, 1960; repr. 1972), 95–184.

*Calmet, Augustin, *Histoire ecclésiastique et civile de Lorraine*, vol. 3 (Nancy, 1728).

Cameron, Averil, *Agathias* (Oxford, 1970).

Campbell, James W., 'England, Scotland and the Hundred Years War in the Fourteenth Century', in J. R. Hale, J. R. L. Highfield, and B. Smalley, eds., *Europe in the Late Middle Ages* (Evanston, 1965), 184–216.

*Carini, Isidoro, *Gli archivi e le bibliotheche di Spagna in rapporto alla storia d'Italia in generale e di Sicilia in particolare*, 2 vols. (Palermo, 1884–97).

Carolus-Barré, L., 'Recherches sur les otages de Beauvais et de Compiègne', *Mémoires de la Société académique d'archéologie, sciences et arts du département de l'Oise*, 25 (1926), 165–91.

Caucanas, Sylvie, Cazals, Rémy, and Payen, Pascal, eds., *Les prisonniers de guerre dans l'histoire: Contacts entre peuples et cultures* (Toulouse, 2003). [Abbreviated as *Les prisonniers*]

Cazelles, Raymond, *Société politique, noblesse et couronne sous Jean le Bon et Charles V* (Geneva, 1982).

Chaisemartin, A., *Proverbes et maximes du droit germanique* (Paris, 1891).

Chantraine, Pierre, *Dictionnaire étymologique de la langue grecque: Histoire des mots* (Paris, 1984–90).

Charles-Edwards, T. M., *Early Irish and Welsh Kinship* (Oxford, 1993).

——'Alliances, Godfathers, Treaties and Boundaries', in Mark A. S. Blackburn and D. N. Dumville, eds., *Kings, Currency, and Alliances: History and Coinage of Southern England in the Ninth Century* (Woodbridge, 1998), 47–62.

Cheyette, Fredric L., 'The "Sale" of Carcassonne to the Counts of Barcelona (1067–1070) and the Rise of the Trencavels', *Speculum*, 63 (1988), 826–64.

*Chrimes, S. B., 'Some Letters of John of Lancaster as Warden of the East Marches towards Scotland', *Speculum*, 14 (1939), 3–27.

Christys, Ann, ' "How Can I Trust You, Since You Are a Christian and I Am a Moor?" The Multiple Identities of the Chronicle of Pseudo-Isidore', in Richard Corradini et al., eds., *Texts and Identities in the Early Middle Ages* (Vienna, 2006), 359–72.

Cipollone, Giulio, ed., *La liberazione dei 'captivi' tra Cristianità e Islam: Oltre la Crociata e il Ğihād: Tolleranza e servizio umanitario: Atti del Congresso interdisciplinare di studi storici (Roma, 16–19 settembre 1998) organizzato per l'VIII centenario dell'approvazione della regola dei Trinitari da parte del Papa Innocenzo III il 17 dicembre 1198/15 safar, 595 H* (Vatican City, 2000).

Claustre, Julie, *Dans les geôles du roi: L'emprisonnement pour dette à Paris à la fin du Moyen Âge* (Paris, 2007).

Cocard, Hugues, *L'Ordre de la Merci en France, 1574–1792: Un ordre voué a la liberation des captifs* (Paris, 2007).

Colley, Linda, *Captives: Britain, Empire and the World, 1600–1850* (New York, 2004).

Contamine, Philippe, 'The Growth of State Control. Practices of War 1300–1800: Ransom and Booty', in Contamine, ed., *War and Competition between States* (Oxford, 2001), 163–93.

Corbier, Mireille, ed., *Adoption et fosterage* (Paris, 1999).

Corominas, Joan, and Pascual, José A., *Diccionario crítico etimológico castellano e hispánico* (Madrid, 1991–2).

Coviaux, Stéphane, 'Baptême et conversion des chefs scandinaves du IXe au XIe siècle', in Pierre Bauduin, ed., *Les fondations scandinaves en Occident et les débuts du duché de Normandie* (Caen, 2005), 67–80.

Cowdrey, H. E. J., *Pope Gregory VII, 1073–1085* (Oxford, 1998).

*Craster, H. H. E., *A History of Northumberland*, vol. 10: *The Parish of Corbridge* (London, 1914).

Crouch, David, *William Marshal: Knighthood, War and Chivalry, 1147–1219*, 2nd edn. (London, 2002).

Cutler, Kenneth E., 'The Godwinist Hostages: The Case for 1051', *Annuale medievale*, 12 (1972), 70–7.

Cuttino, George Peddy, *English Medieval Diplomacy* (Bloomington, 1985).

Davies, Rees, 'The Medieval State: The Tyranny of a Concept', *Journal of Historical Sociology*, 16 (2003), 280–300.

*Davis, R. H. C., 'Treaty between William Earl of Gloucester and Roger Earl of Hereford', in *A Medieval Miscellany for Doris May Stenton* (London, 1962), 139–46.

De Angulo, Lucy, 'Charles and Jean d'Orléans: An Attempt to Trace the Contacts between Them during Their Captivity in England', in Franco Simone, ed., *Miscellanea di studi e ricerche sul quattrocento francese* (Turin, 1967), 59–92.

De Jong, Mayke, *In Samuel's Image: Child Oblation in the Early Medieval West* (Leiden, 1996).

Débax, Hélène, *La féodalité languedocienne, XIe–XIIe siècles: Serments, hommages et fiefs dans le Languedoc des Trencavel* (Toulouse, 2003).

Delachenal, R., *Histoire de Charles V*, 5 vols. (Paris, 1909–31).

Depreux, Philippe, 'Princes, princesses et nobles étrangers à la cour des rois mérovingiens et carolingiens: Alliés, hôtes ou otages?', in *L'étranger au Moyen Âge: XXXe congrès de la Société des historiens médiévistes de l'enseignement supérieur (Göttingen, juin 1999)* (Paris, 2000), 133–54.

*Dept, Gaston G., *Les influences anglaise et française dans le comté de Flandre au début du XIIIme siècle* (Ghent, 1928).

Derrida, Jacques, *Apories: Mourir–s'attendre aux 'limites de la vérité'* (Paris, 1996).

Desjardins, Albert, 'Les otages dans le droit des gens au XVIe siècle', *Séances et travaux de l'Académie de sciences morales et politiques (Institut de France), Compte rendu*, ns 49 (1889).

Diago Hernando, Máximo, 'Un noble entre tres reinos en la España del siglo XIV: Juan Ramírez de Arellano', *Príncipe de Viana*, 230 (2003), 523–56.

*Didot, Ambroise Firmin, *Études sur la vie et les travaux de Jean Sire de Joinville*, vol. 1 (Paris, 1870).

*Digard, Georges, *Philippe le Bel et le Saint-Siège de 1285 à 1304*, 2 vols. (Paris, 1936).

*Dinis, António Joaquim, 'Carta do Infante Santo ao regente D. Pedro, datada da masmorra de Fez a 12 de junho de 1441', *Anais da Academia Portuguesa da História*, 2nd ser., 13 (1965), 151–74.

Douglas, David C., *William the Conqueror: The Norman Impact upon England* (Berkeley, 1964).

Duby, Georges, ed., *A History of Private Life: Revelations of the Medieval World*, trans. Arthur Goldhammer (Cambridge, Mass., 1993 [1985]).

Du Cange, Charles Du Fresne, sieur, *Glossarium mediae et infimae latinitatis*, ed. Léopold Favre, 10 vols. (Niort, 1883–7).

Dunbabin, Jean, *Captivity and Imprisonment in Medieval Europe, 1000–1300* (Basingstoke, 2002).

Duncan, A. A. M., '*Honi soit qui mal y pense*: David II and Edward III, 1346–52', *Scottish Historical Review*, 67 (1988), 113–41.

Dupont-Ferrier, Gustave, 'La captivité de Jean d'Orléans, comte d'Angoulême (1412–1445)', *Revue historique*, 62 (1896), 42–74.

Durchhart, Heinz, 'Peace Treaties from Westphalia to the Revolutionary Era', in Lesaffer, ed., *Peace Treaties* (q.v), 45–58.

Edwards, J. G., 'The Treason of Thomas Turberville, 1295', in R. W. Hunt et al., eds., *Studies in Medieval History Presented to Frederick Maurice Powicke* (Oxford, 1948), 296–309.

El-Hajji, A., 'The Andalusian Diplomatic Relations with the Vikings during the Umayyad Period (138–366/755–796)', *Hespéris-Tamuda*, 8 (1967), 67–105.

Elbern, Stephan, 'Geiseln in Rom', *Athenaeum*, 78 (1990), 97–140.

Encyclopedia of Islam, 2nd edn., 13 vols. (Leiden, 1960–2005).

Epp, Verena, *Amicitia: Zur Geschichte personaler, sozialer, politischer und geistlicher Beziehungen im frühen Mittelalter* (Stuttgart, 1999).

Erler, Adalbert, *Der Loskauf Gefangener: Ein Rechtsproblem seit drei Jahrtausenden* (Berlin, 1978).

Evans, Stephen S., *The Lords of Battle: Image and Reality in the Comitatus in Dark Age Britain* (Woodbridge, 1997).

Evergates, Theodore, *The Aristocracy in the County of Champagne, 1100–1300* (Philadelphia, 2007).

Feliu, Eduard, 'Mots catalans en textos hebreus medievals: Els dictàmens de Salamó ben Adret', *Calls* (Tàrrega), 3 (1988), 53–73.

Ferrer i Mallol, Maria Teresa, and Durán i Duelt, Daniel, 'Una ambaixada catalana a Constantinoble i el matrimoni de la princesa Eudòxia', *Anuario de estudios medievales*, 30 (2000), 963–78.

Fildes, Valerie A., *Wet-Nursing: A History from Antiquity to the Present* (Oxford, 1988).

Forey, A. J., 'The Military Orders and the Ransoming of Captives from Islam (Twelfth to Early Fourteenth Centuries)', *Studia monastica*, 33 (1991), 259–79.

Forte, Antonio, *The Hostage: An Shigao and His Offspring* (Kyoto, 1995).

Fouracre, Paul, 'Merovingian History and Merovingian Hagiography', *Past & Present* 127 (1990), 3–38.

*Fraser, William, *The Douglas Book*, 4 vols. (Edinburgh, 1885).

Frey, Siegried, *Das öffentlich-rechtliche Schiedsgericht in Oberitalien im XII. und XIII. Jahrhundert: Beitrag zur Geschichte völkerrechtlicher Institutionen* (Lucerne, 1928).

Friedlaender, Ernst, *Das Einlager: Ein Beitrag zur deutschen Rechtsgeschichte* (Münster, 1868).

Friedman, Yvonne, *Encounter between Enemies: Captivity and Ransom in the Latin Kingdom of Jerusalem* (Leiden, 2002).

Fryde, E. B., 'Financial Resources of Edward III in the Netherlands, 1337–40', *Revue belge de philologie et d'histoire*, 45 (1967), 1142–216.

Ganshof, François Louis, 'Les traités des rois mérovingiens', *Tijdschrift voor Rechtsgeschiedenis*, 32 (1964), 163–92.

—— 'The Treaties of the Carolingians', *Medieval and Renaissance Studies*, 3 (1967), 23–52.

—— *The Middle Ages: A History of International Relations*, trans. Rémy Inglis Hall (New York, 1970 [1968]).

—— 'The Use of the Written Word in Charlemagne's Administration', in Ganshof, *The Carolingians and the Frankish Monarchy: Studies in Carolingian History*, trans. J. Sondheimer (Ithaca, 1971), 125–42 [*Le Moyen Âge*, 57 (1951), 1–25].

—— Van Caenegem, Raoul, and Verhulst, Adriaan, 'Note sur le premier traité anglo-flamand de Douvres', *Revue du Nord*, 40 (1958), 245–57.

Geltner, Guy, *The Medieval Prison: A Social History* (Princeton, 2008).

Gierke, Otto von, *Schuld und Haftung im älteren deutschen Recht: Insbesondere die Form der Schuld- und Haftungsgeschäfte* (Breslau, 1910).

Gillespie, James L., 'Richard II's Knights: Chivalry and Patronage', *Journal of Medieval History*, 13 (1987), 143–59.

Gillingham, John, *Richard I* (New Haven, 1999).

—— 'The Kidnapped King: Richard I in Germany, 1192–1194', *German Historical Institute London Bulletin*, 30 (2008), 5–34.

Giordanengo, Gérard, *Le droit féodal dans les pays de droit écrit: L'exemple de la Provence et du Dauphiné, XIIᵉ–début XIVᵉ siècle* (Rome, 1988).

Giraud, Charles, *Essai sur l'histoire du droit français au Moyen Âge*, 2 vols. (Paris, 1846).

*Giraud, [Paul-Emile], *Essai historique sur l'abbaye de S. Barnard et sur la ville de Romans: Complément textuel du cartulaire* (Lyon, 1869).

Given-Wilson, Chris, 'The Ransom of Olivier du Guesclin', *Bulletin of the Institute of Historical Research*, 54 (1981), 17–28.

Goffart, Walter, 'Roman Taxation to Mediaeval Seigneurie: Three Notes (Part I)', *Speculum*, 47 (1972), 165–87.

*Góngora Alcasar e Pempicileón, Luis de, *Real grandeza de la serenissima República de Genova*, trans. Carolo Speroni (Genoa, 1669).

*González, Julio, *El Reino de Castilla en la época de Alfonso VIII*, 3 vols. (Madrid, 1960).

Gougenheim, Georges, 'La fausse étymologie savante', *Romance Philology*, 1 (1947–8), 277–86 [repr. Gougenheim, *Études de grammaire et de vocabulaire française* (Paris, 1970), 219–28].

Grand, Roger, 'La prison et la notion d'emprisonnement dans l'ancien droit', *Revue historique de droit français et étranger*, 4th ser., 19–20 (1940–1), 58–87.

Green, Judith A., *The Aristocracy of Norman England* (Cambridge, 1997).

Greenfield, Jonas C., '*Kullu nafsin bimā kasabat rahīnā*: The Use of *rhn* in Aramaic and Arabic', in Alan Jones, ed., *Arabicus Felix: Luminosus Britannicus: Essays in Honour of A. F. L. Beeston on his Eightieth Birthday* (Oxford, 1991), 221–7.

*Griffiths, John, 'The Revolt of Madog ap Llywelyn, 1294–5', *Transactions/Trafodion* (Caernarvonshire Historical Society), 16 (1955), 12–24.

Guilhiermoz, Paul, *Essai sur l'origine de la noblesse en France au Moyen Âge* (Paris, 1902).

*Güterbock, Ferdinand, 'Alla vigilia della Lega Lombarda', *Archivio storico italiano*, 95.1 (1937), 188–217; 95.2 (1937), 64–77, 181–92.

*—— 'Le lettere del notaio imperiale Burcardo intorno alla politica del Barbarossa nello scisma ed alla distruzione di Milano', *Bullettino dell'Istituto storico italiano per il Medio Evo e Archivio Muratoriano*, 61 (1949), 1–65.

Halecki, Oskar, *Un empereur de Byzance à Rome* (Warsaw, 1930; repr. London, 1972).

Hammer, Ellen, and Salvin, Marina, 'The Taking of Hostages in Theory and Practice', *American Journal of International Law*, 38 (1944), 20–33.

Hanawalt, Barbara A., 'Medievalists and the Study of Childhood', *Speculum*, 77 (2002), 440–60.

Handwörterbuch zur deutschen Rechtsgeschichte, 5 vols. (Berlin, 1971–98).

Harvey, L. P., *Muslims in Spain, 1500–1614* (Chicago, 2006).

Head, Thomas, 'The Development of the Peace of God in Aquitaine (970–1005)', *Speculum*, 74 (1999), 656–86.

—— and Landes, Richard, eds., *The Peace of God: Social Violence and Religious Response around the Year 1000* (Ithaca, 1992).

*Hefele, Karl Josef von, *Histoire des conciles d'après les documents originaux*, trans. Henri Leclercq, vol. 4.2 (Paris, 1911).

Henneman, John Bell, *Royal Taxation in Fourteenth-Century France: The Captivity and Ransom of John II, 1356–1370* (Philadelphia, 1976).

—— *Olivier de Clisson and Political Society in France under Charles V and Charles VI* (Philadelphia, 1996).

Herrmann, Irène, and Palmieri, Daniel, 'A Haunting Figure: The Hostage through the Ages', *International Review of the Red Cross*, 87 (2005), 135–45.

*Historical Manuscripts Commission, *Report on Manuscripts in Various Collections*, vol. 1 (London, 1901).

Hoffman, Hartmut, *Gottesfriede und Treuga Dei* (Stuttgart, 1964).

Holdsworth, Christopher, 'Peacemaking in the Twelfth Century', *Anglo-Norman Studies*, 19 (1996), 1–17.

Hollister, C. Warren, *The Military Organization of Norman England* (Oxford, 1965).

—— 'Magnates and "Curiales" in Early Norman England', *Viator*, 4 (1973), 115–22.

—— *Henry I* (New Haven, 2001).

Holmes, Oliver Wendell, *The Common Law* (Boston, 1881).

*Holt, J. C., *Magna Carta*, 2nd edn. (Cambridge, 1992).

Hoppe, Helmut R., 'Die Geiselschaft: Ihre Entwicklung und Bedeutung', Dr. iur. dissertation, Georg-August-Universität Göttingen, 1953.

Huillard-Bréholles, Jean-Louis-Alphonse, 'La rançon du duc de Bourbon Jean Iᵉʳ (1415–1436)', *Mémoires présentés par divers savants à l'Académie des inscriptions et belles-lettres de l'Institut de France*, 1st ser., vol. 8, part 2 (Paris, 1874), 37–91.

Iglesia Ferreirós, Aquilino, *La prenda contractual: Desde sus orígenes hasta la recepción del Derecho Común* (Santiago de Compostela, 1977).

Innes, Matthew, ' "A Place of Discipline": Carolingian Courts and Aristocratic Youth', in Catherine Cubitt, ed., *Court Culture in the Early Middle Ages: The Proceedings of the First Alcuin Conference* (Turnhout, 2003), 59–67.

Ites, M., 'Zur Bewertung des Agathias', *Byzantinische Zeitschrift*, 26 (1926), 273–85.

Jankrift, Kay Peter, 'Aus der Heimat in die Fremde: Geiseln und Kriegsgefangene im frühen Mittelalter', in Hardy Eidam and Gudrun Noll, eds., *Radegunde: Ein Frauenschicksal zwischen Mord und Askese* (Erfurt, 2006), 50–4.

Jones, Michael, *Ducal Brittany, 1364–1399: Relations with England and France during the Reign of Duke John IV* (Oxford, 1970).

—— 'The Ransom of Jean de Bretagne, Count of Penthièvre', *Bulletin of the Institute of Historical Research*, 45 (1972), 7–24.

Jussen, Bernhard, *Spiritual Kinship as Social Practice: Godparenthood and Adoption in the Early Middle Ages*, rev. edn., trans. Pamela Selwyn (Newark, Del., 2000 [1991]).

Kamp, Norbert, 'Konsuln und Podestà, *balivus comunis* und Volkskapitän in Viterbo im 12. und 13. Jahrhundert, mit einem Verzeichnis der Konsuln, Podestà, *balivi comunis* und Volkskapitäne 1099–1300)', in Augusto Pepponi, ed., *Biblioteca degli ardenti della città di Viterbo: Studi e ricerche nel 150° della fonadazione* (Viterbo, 1960), 49–127.

Keen, M. H., *The Laws of War in the Late Middle Ages* (London, 1965).

Kelly, Fergus, *A Guide to Early Irish Law* (Dublin, 1988).

Kerlouegan, François, 'Essai sur la mise en nourriture et l'éducation dans les pays celtiques d'après le témoignage des textes hagiographiques latins', *Études celtiques*, 12 (1968–9), 101–46.

Kershaw, Paul J. E., *Peaceful Kings: Peace, Power, and the Early Medieval Political Imagination* (Oxford, 2011).

*Kervyn de Lettenhove, [Joseph M. B. C.], *Histoire de Flandre*, vol. 2: *Époque communale* (Brussels, 1847).

Kessler, Ulrike, *Richard I. Löwenherz: König, Kreuzritter, Abenteurer* (Graz, 1995).

Kiesewetter, Andreas, *Die Anfänge der Regierung König Karls II. von Anjou: Das Königreich Neapel, die Grafschaft Provence und der Mittelmeerraum zu Ausgang des 13. Jahrhunderts* (Husum, 1999).

King, A., ' "According to the Custom Used in the French and Scottish Wars": Prisoners and Casualties on the Scottish Marches in the Fourteenth Century', *Journal of Medieval History*, 28 (2002), 263–90.

Kister, M. J., 'Al-Hira: Some Notes on Its Relations with Arabia', *Arabica*, 15 (1968), 143–69.

Kitzinger, Martin, 'Geiseln und Gefangene im Mittelalter: Zur Entwicklung eines politischen Instruments', in Andreas Gestrich, Gerhard Hirschfeld, and Holger Sonnabend, eds., *Ausweisung und Deportation: Formen der Zwangsmigration in der Geschichte* (Stuttgart, 1995), 41–59.

Kosto, Adam J., *Making Agreements in Medieval Catalonia: Power, Order, and the Written Word, 1000–1200* (Cambridge, 2001).

—— 'Hostages in the Carolingian World (714–840)', *Early Medieval Europe* 11 (2002), 123–47.

—— 'Hostages during the First Century of the Crusades', *Medieval Encounters* 9 (2003), 3–31.

—— 'L'otage, comme vecteur d'échange culturel du IVe au XVe siècle', in *Les prisonniers*, 171–81.

—— 'Hostages and the Habit of Representation in Thirteenth-Century Occitania', in Robert F. Berkhofer, Alan Cooper, and Adam J. Kosto, eds., *The Experience of Power in Medieval Europe, 950–1350* (Aldershot, 2005), 181–91.

—— 'Les otages conditionnels en Languedoc et en Catalogne au XIe siècle', *Annales du Midi*, 118 (2006), 387–403.

—— 'Hostages in Late Antiquity' (unpublished paper).

Koziol, Geoffrey, *Begging Pardon and Favor: Ritual and Political Order in Early Medieval France* (Ithaca, 1992).

Kronman, Anthony T., 'Contract Law and the State of Nature', *Journal of Law, Economics, and Organization*, 1 (1985), 5–32.

Laat, Paul B. de, 'Dangerous Liaisons: Sharing Knowledge within Research and Development Alliances', in Anna Grandori, ed., *Interfirm Networks: Organization and Industrial Competitiveness* (London, 1999), 208–33.

Lambert, Joseph J., *Terrorism and Hostages in International Law: A Commentary on the Hostages Convention 1979* (Cambridge, 1990).

Landon, Lionel, *The Itinerary of King Richard I* (London, 1935).

Lapôtre, Arthur, *L'Europe et le Saint-Siège à l'époque carolingienne*, vol. 1: *Le pape Jean VIII (872–882)* (Paris, 1895).

Laske, Walther, 'Zwangsaufenthalt im frühmittelalterlichen Kloster: Gott und Mensch im Einklang und Widerstreit', *Zeitschrift der Savigny-Stiftung für Rechtsgeschichte*, Kanonistische Abteilung, 64 (1978), 321–30.

Lauer, Philippe, *Le règne de Louis IV d'Outre-mer* (Paris, 1900).

Laurason-Rosaz, Christian, *L'Auvergne et ses marges (Velay, Gévaudan) du VIIIᵉ au XIᵉ siècle: La fin du monde antique?* (Le Puy-en-Velay, 1987).

Lauwereyns de Roosendaele, L. de, *Les otages de Saint-Omer, 1360–1371: Épisode de la Paix de Brétigny* (Saint-Omer, 1879).

Lavelle, Ryan, 'The Use and Abuse of Hostages in Later Anglo-Saxon England', *Early Medieval Europe*, 14 (2006), 269–96.

Lawn, Elizabeth, *'Gefangenschaft': Aspekt und Symbol sozialer Bindung im Mittelalter, dargestellt an chronikalischen und poetischen Quellen* (Frankfurt am Main, 1977).

Le Baud, Pierre, *Histoire de Bretagne...*, ed. Pierre D'Hozier (Paris, 1638).

Le Fort, Charles, 'L'otage conventionnel d'après des documents du Moyen Âge', *Revue de législation ancienne et modèrne française et étrangère* (1874), 408–33.

Le Patourel, John, 'The Treaty of Brétigny, 1360', *Transactions of the Royal Historical Society*, 5th ser., 10 (1960), 19–39.

Lebeuf, Jean, *Histoire de la ville et de tout le diocèse de Paris*, 5 vols. (Paris, 1883).

Lechner, Adolf, *Das Obstagium oder die Giselschaft nach schweizerischen Quellen* (Bern, 1906).

*Lecoy de la Marche, A., *Le roi René: Sa vie, son administration, ses travaux artistiques et littéraries, d'après les documents inédits des archives de France et d'Italie*, 2 vols. (Paris, 1875).

Leguai, André, 'Le problème des rançons au XVᵉ siècle: La captivité de Jean Iᵉʳ, duc de Bourbon', *Cahiers de l'histoire*, 6 (1961), 42–58.

Leroy-Molinghen, Alice, 'Les fils de Pierre de Bulgarie', *Byzantion*, 42 (1972), 405–19.

Lesaffer, Randall, 'Peace Treaties from Lodi to Westphalia', in Lesaffer, ed., *Peace Treaties* (q.v), 9–44.

——— ed., *Peace Treaties and International Law in European History: From the Late Middle Ages to World War One* (Cambridge, 2004).

Leu, Jean-Jacques, *Le cautionnement dans le pays de Vaud (XIIᵉ–XVIᵉ siècle)* (Lausanne, 1958).

Levillain, Léon, 'Études sur l'abbaye de Saint-Denis à l'époque mérovingienne, III, *Privilegium et immunitas* ou Saint-Denis dans l'Église et dans l'État', *Bibliothèque de l'École des chartes*, 87 (1926), 20–97.

Levy, Ernst, *'Captivus redemptus'*, *Classical Philology*, 38 (1943), 159–76.

Livingstone, Amy, *Out of Love for My Kin: Aristocratic Family Life in the Lands of the Loire* (Ithaca, 2010).

Lonis, Raoul, 'Les otages dans les relations internationales en Grèce classique: Insuffisances et ambiguïtés d'une garantie', in *Mélanges offerts à Léopold Sédar Senghor: Langues–littérature–histoire anciennes* (Dakar, 1977), 215–34.

López, Jerónimo, 'En torno al cuarto voto mercedario', *Estudios* (Madrid), 12 (1956), 361–400.

Lotter, Friedrich, 'Methodisches zur Gewinnung historischer Erkenntnisse aus hagiographischen Quellen', *Historische Zeitschrift*, 229 (1979), 298–356.

Luchaire, Achille, *Louis VI le Gros: Annales de sa vie et de son règne (1081–1137) avec une introduction historique* (Paris, 1890).

——*Manuel des institutions françaises: Période des Capétiens directs* (Paris, 1892).

Lupoi, Maurizio, *The Origins of the European Legal Order*, trans. Adrian Belton (Cambridge, 2000 [1994]).

Lutteroth, Ascan, *Der Geisel im Rechtsleben: Ein Beitrag zur allgemeinen Rechtsgeschichte und dem geltenden Völkerrecht* (Breslau, 1922).

Lynch, Joseph H., *Godparents and Kinship in Early Medieval Europe* (Princeton, 1986).

——*Christianizing Kinship: Ritual Sponsorship in Anglo-Saxon England* (Ithaca, 1998).

Lyon, Bryce D., *From Fief to Indenture: The Transition from Feudal to Non-Feudal Contract in Western Europe* (Cambridge, Mass., 1957).

McCormick, Michael, *Origins of the European Economy: Communications and Commerce, A.D. 300–900* (Cambridge, 2001).

McCullough, Roy L., *Coercion, Conversion and Counterinsurgency in Louis XIV's France* (Leiden, 2007), 21–34.

*McFarlane, K. B., 'A Business-Partnership in War and Administration, 1421–1445', *English Historical Review*, 78 (1963), 290–310.

McKechnie, William Sharp, *Magna Carta: A Commentary on the Great Charter of King John with an Historical Introduction*, 2nd edn. (Glasgow, 1914).

McKitterick, Rosamond, 'Paul the Deacon and the Franks', *Early Medieval Europe*, 8 (1999), 319–39.

Maddicott, J. R., *Simon de Montfort* (Cambridge, 1996).

Malafosse, Jehan de, 'Contribution à l'étude du crédit dans le Midi aux Xᵉ et XIᵉ siècles: Les sûretés réelles', *Annales du Midi*, 63 (1951), 105–48.

*Malo, Henri, *Un grand feudataire: Renaud de Dammartin et la coalition de Bouvines: Contribution a l'étude du règne de Philippe-Auguste* (Paris, 1898).

*Manteyer, Georges de, 'Les origines de la maison de Savoie en Bourgogne (910–1060): La paix en Viennois (Anse [17 juin?] 1025) et les additions à la Bible de Vienne (ms. Bern. A 9)', *Bulletin de la Société des sciences naturelles et des arts industriels du département de l'Isère*, 4th ser., 7 (1904), 87–192 (published separately, Grenoble, 1904; repr. 1978).

*Marchegay, P., 'La rançon d'Olivier de Coëtivy, seigneur de Taillebourg et sénéchal de Guyenne, 1451–1477', *Bibliothèque de l'École des chartes*, 38 (1877), 5–48.

*Marichalar, Amalio, and Manrique, Cayetano, *Historia de la legislacion y recitaciones del derecho civil de España*, vol. 5 (Madrid, 1862).

Martin, W. A. P., 'Traces of International Law in Ancient China', *International Review*, 14 (1883), 63–77.

*Mata Carriazo, Juan de, 'Los moros de Granada en las actas del concejo de Jaén de 1479', in Mata Carriazo, *En la frontera de Granada* (Seville, 1971; repr. Granada, 2002), 265–310 [*Miscelánea de Estudios Arabes y Hebráicos*, 4 (1955), 81–125].

Matthei, A., 'Das Geiselwesen bei den Römern', *Philologus*, 64 (1905), 224–47.

Mauss, Marcel, *The Gift: The Form and Reason for Exchange in Archaic Societies*, trans. W. D. Halls (New York, 1990 [1950]).

Meron, Theodor, *Henry's Wars and Shakespeare's Laws: Perspectives on the Law of War in the Later Middle Ages* (Oxford, 1993).

Millán Rubio, Joaquín, 'El voto mercaderio de dar la vida por los cautivos cristianos', in *Los consejos evangelicos en la tradición monastica: XIV Semana de estudios monasticos, Silos, 1973* (Silos, 1975), 113–41.

Miller, Reuben, 'Game Theory and Hostage-Taking Incidents: A Case Study of the Munich Olympic Games', *Conflict Quarterly*, 10 (1990), 12–33.

Miller, William Ian, *Bloodtaking and Peacemaking: Feud, Law, and Society in Saga Iceland* (Chicago, 1990).

Miller, William Ian, *Audun and the Polar Bear: Luck, Law, and Largesse in a Medieval Tale of Risky Business* (Leiden, 2008).

Mitteis, Heinrich, *Lehnrecht und Staatsgewalt: Untersuchungen zur mittelalterlichen Verfassungsgeschichte* (Weimar, 1933; repr. Darmstadt, 1958).

Moeglin, Jean-Marie, *Les bourgeois de Calais: Essai sur un mythe historique* (Paris, 2002).

Molinier, Auguste, 'Étude sur l'administration féodale dans le Languedoc (900–1250)', *HGL* 7:132–213.

Morschauser, Scott, '"Hospitality," Hostiles and Hostages: On the Legal Background to Genesis 19.1–9', *Journal for the Study of the Old Testament*, 27 (2003), 461–85.

Moscovich, M. James, '*Obsidibus traditis*: Hostages in Caesar's *De bello Gallico*', *Classical Journal*, 75 (1979–80), 122–8.

Mulchrone, Kathleen, 'The Rights and Duties of Women with Regard to the Education of Their Children', in Rudolf Thurneysen et al., eds., *Studies in Early Irish Law* (Dublin, 1936), 187–205.

Munz, Peter, *Frederick Barbarossa: A Study in Medieval Politics* (Ithaca, 1969).

Ndiaye, Saliou, 'Le recours aux otages à Rome sous la République', *Dialogues d'histoire ancienne*, 21 (1995), 149–65.

Nelson, Janet L., 'Charlemagne and Empire', in Jennifer R. Davis and Michael McCormick, eds., *The Long Morning of Medieval Europe: New Directions in Early Medieval Studies* (Aldershot, 2008), 223–34.

Neuman de Vegvar, Carol, 'Images of Women in Anglo-Saxon Art: I. Hostages: Women in the "Titus" Scene on the Franks Casket', *Old English Newsletter*, 24 (1990), 44–5.

Newman, Charlotte A., *The Anglo-Norman Nobility in the Reign of Henry I: The Second Generation* (Philadelphia, 1988).

Nicholas, David, *Medieval Flanders* (London, 1992).

—— *The Growth of the Medieval City: From Late Antiquity to the Early Fourteenth Century* (London, 1997).

Nicholson, Ranald, *Scotland: The Later Middle Ages* (Edinburgh, 1974).

Niermeyer, J. F., *Mediae latinitatis lexicon minus* (Leiden, 1993).

Nip, Renée, 'The Political Relations between England and Flanders (1066–1128)', *Anglo-Norman Studies*, 21 (1998), 145–67.

Novum glossarium mediae latinitatis ab anno DCCC usque ad annum MCC (Copenhagen, 1957–).

Nutini, Hugo G., and Bell, Betty, *Ritual Kinship*, 2 vols. (Princeton, 1980–4).

Ogris, Werner, 'Die persönlichen Sicherheiten im Spätmittelalter: Versuch eines Überblickes', *Zeitschrift der Savigny-Stiftung für Rechtsgeschichte*, Germanistische Abteilung, 82 (1965), 140–89.

Oost, Stewart Irvin, *Galla Placidia: A Biographical Essay* (Chicago, 1968).

Osiek, Carolyn, 'The Ransom of Captives: Evolution of a Tradition', *Harvard Theological Review*, 74 (1981), 365–86.

Paludan-Müller, C., *Studier til Danmarks Historie i det 13de Aarhundrede*, 1, *Underhandlingerne om Kong Valdemar den Andens Fangenskab. Grevskabet Nørrehalland* (Copenhagen, 1869).

Panagopoulos, Andreas, *Captives and Hostages in the Peloponnesian War* (Amsterdam, 1989 [1978]).

Papon, Jean Pierre, *Histoire générale de Provence*, 4 vols. (Paris, 1777–86).

Parkes, Peter, 'Celtic Fosterage: Adoptive Kinship and Clientage in Northwestern Europe', *Comparative Studies in Society and History*, 48 (2006), 359–95.

Parks, Annette P., 'Living Pledges: A Study of Hostageship in the High Middle Ages, 1050–1300', PhD dissertation, Emory University, 2000.

——'Rescuing the Maidens from the Tower: Recovering the Stories of Two Female Political Hostages', in Belle S. Tuten and Tracey L. Billado, eds., *Feud, Violence, and Practice: Essays in Medieval Studies in Honor of Stephen D. White* (Aldershot, 2010), 279–91.

Paul, James Balfour, ed., *The Scots Peerage*, vol. 2 (Edinburgh, 1905).

Penman, Michael A., *David II, 1329–71* (East Linton, 2004).

*——and Tanner, David, 'An Unpublished Act of David II, 1359', *Scottish Historical Review*, 83 (2004), 59–69.

Perroy, Edouard, 'Gras profits et rançons pendant la Guerre de Cent Ans: L'affaire du comte de Denia', in *Mélanges d'histoire du Moyen Âge dédiés à la mémoire de Louis Halphen* (Paris, 1951), 573–80.

Pfaff, Carl, 'Der gefangene König', *Basler Zeitschrift für Geschichte und Altertumskunde*, 71 (1971), 9–35.

Phillipson, Donald E., 'Development of the Roman Law of Debt Security', *Stanford Law Review*, 20 (1968), 1230–48.

Pilloud, Claude, 'La question des otages et les Conventions de Genève', *Revue internationale de la Croix-Rouge*, 32 (1950), 430–47.

Poly, Jean-Pierre, *La Provence et la société féodale: Contribution à l'étude des structures dites féodales dans le Midi* (Paris, 1976).

Post, Gaines, *Studies in Medieval Legal Thought: Public Law and the State, 1100–1322* (Princeton, 1964).

Prawer, Joshua, *Crusader Institutions* (Oxford, 1980).

*Price, Richard, *To Slay the Hydra: Dutch Colonial Perspectives on the Saramaka Wars* (Ann Arbor, 1983).

——*Alabi's World* (Baltimore, 1990).

Pugh, Ralph B., *Imprisonment in Medieval England* (Cambridge, 1970).

Racine, Pierre, 'Plaisance du Xᵉᵐᵉ à la fin du XIIIᵉᵐᵉ siècle: Essai d'historie urbaine', PhD dissertation, Université de Paris–I, 1977.

Rapin de Thoyras, Paul, *The History of England*, trans. N. Tindal, 3rd edn., 4 vols. in 5 (London, 1743–7).

Reuter, Timothy, *Medieval Polities and Modern Mentalities*, ed. Janet L. Nelson (Cambridge, 2006).

Reynolds, Susan, 'The Historiography of the Medieval State', in Michael Bently, ed., *Companion to Historiography* (London, 1997), 109–29.

——*Fiefs and Vassals: The Medieval Evidence Reinterpreted* (Oxford, 2001).

——'The Emergence of Professional Law in the Long Twelfth Century', *Law and History Review*, 21 (2003), 347–66.

Riches, Theo M., 'Episcopal Historiography as Archive: Some Reflections on the Autograph of the *Gesta episcoporum Cameracensium* (MS Den Haag KB 75 F 15)', *Jaarboek voor middeleeuwse geschiedenis*, 10 (2007), 7–46.

Rintelen, Max, *Schuldhaft und Einlager im Vollstreckungsverfahren des altniederländischen und sächsischen Rechtes* (Leipzig, 1908).

Roche, Christian, *Conquête et résistance des peuples de Casamance (1850–1920)* (Dakar, 1976).

Rodón Binué, Eulalia, *El lenguaje técnico del feudalismo en el siglo XI en Cataluña (Contribución al estudio del latín medieval)* (Barcelona, 1957).

Rodriguez, Jarbel, *Captives and Their Saviors in the Medieval Crown of Aragon* (Washington, DC, 2007).

Roger, Paul, *Noblesse et chevalerie du comté de Flandre, d'Artois et de Picardie* (Amiens, 1843).

*Rogers, A., 'Hoton versus Shakell: A Ransom Case in the Court of Chivalry, 1390–5', *Nottingham Medieval Studies*, 6 (1962), 74–108; 7 (1963), 53–78.

Rogers, Clifford J., *War Cruel and Sharp: English Strategy under Edward III, 1327–1360* (Woodbridge, 2000).

——'The Anglo-French Peace Negotiations of 1354–1360 Reconsidered', in J. S. Bothwell, ed., *The Age of Edward III* (Rochester, NY, 2001), 193–213.

Rowan, Steven W., 'Ulrich Zasius and the Baptism of Jewish Children', *Sixteenth Century Journal*, 6 (1975), 3–25.

Ruffi, Antoine de, *Histoire de la ville de Marseille...*, 2nd edn., ed. Louis-Antoine de Ruffi (Marseille, 1696).

Runciman, Steven, *History of the Crusades*, 3 vols. (Cambridge, 1951–4).

——*The Sicilian Vespers: A History of the Mediterranean World in the Later Thirteenth Century* (Cambridge, 1958).

Sandler, Todd, and Scott, John L., 'Terrorist Success in Hostage-Taking Incidents: An Empirical Study', *Journal of Conflict Resolution* 31 (1987), 35–53.

Santaniello, Giovanni, 'La prigionia di Paolino: Tradizione e storia', in A. Ruggiero, H. Crouzel, and G. Santaniello, *Paolino di Nola: Momenti della sua vita e delle sue opere* (Nola, 1983), 221–49.

Sauvage, Hippolyte, *Mortain pendant le terreur*, 13, *Les otages du roi* (Avranches, 1901).

Schacht, Joseph, 'Foreign Elements in Ancient Islamic Law (I)', *Mémoires de l'Académie internationale de droit comparé*, 3.4 (1955), 127–41.

Schelling, Thomas C., 'An Essay on Bargaining', *American Economic Review*, 46 (1956), 281–306.

Scott, Robert E., 'A Relational Theory of Secured Financing', *Columbia Law Review*, 86 (1986), 901–77.

Seabourne, Gwen, 'Eleanor of Brittany and Her Treatment by King John and Henry III', *Nottingham Medieval Studies*, 51 (2007), 73–110.

Sellert, Wolfgang, 'Geiselnahme und Pfändung als Gegenstand spätmittelalterliche Landfrieden', in Arno Buschmann and Elmar Wadle, eds., *Landfrieden: Anspruch und Wirklichkeit* (Paderborn, 2002), 231–52.

Shatzmiller, Joseph, *Shylock Reconsidered: Jews, Moneylending, and Medieval Society* (Berkeley, 1990).

Shepard, Jonathan, 'Manners Maketh Romans? Young Barbarians at the Emperor's Court', in Elizabeth Jeffreys, ed., *Byzantine Style, Religion and Civilization: In Honour of Sir Steven Runciman* (Cambridge, 2006), 135–58.

Shideler, John, *A Medieval Catalan Noble Family: The Montcadas, 1000–1230* (Berkeley, 1983).

Shuger, Debora Kuller, *The Renaissance Bible: Scholarship, Sacrifice, and Subjectivity* (Berkeley, 1994).

Siems, H., *Studien zur Lex Frisionum* (Ebelsbach, 1980).

Sivery, Gérard, 'L'enquête de 1247 et les dommages de guerre en Tournaisis, en Flandre gallicante et en Artois', *Revue du Nord*, 59 (1977), 7–18.

Slater, Colleen, ' "So Hard Was It to Release Princes Whom Fortuna Had Put in Her Chains": Queens and Female Rulers as Hostage- and Captive-Takers and Holders', *Medieval Feminist Forum*, 45 (2009), 12–40.

——' "Virile Strength in a Feminine Breast": Women, Hostageship, Captivity, and Society in the Anglo-French World, *c.*1000–*c.*1300', PhD dissertation, Cornell University, 2009.

Smail, J. Kenneth, 'The Giving of Hostages', *Politics and the Life Sciences*, 16 (1997), 77–85.

Smith, Llinos Beverley, 'Fosterage, Adoption, and God-Parenthood: Ritual and Fictive Kinship in Medieval Wales', *Welsh History Review*, 16 (1992), 1–35.

*Smyrl, Edwin, 'La famille des Baux', *Cahiers du Centre d'études des sociétés méditerranéennes*, 2 (1968), 7–108.

Stacey, Robin Chapman, *The Road to Judgment: From Custom to Court in Medieval Ireland and Wales* (Philadelphia, 1994).

Starostine, Dmitri, 'Hostage by Agreement and the Language of Dependence in the Eleventh Century: Mutation or Corruption?', in Michael W. Herren, Christopher J. McDonough, and Ross G. Arthur, eds., *Latin Culture in the Eleventh Century: Proceedings of the Third International Conference on Medieval Latin Studies, Cambridge, September 9–12, 1998* (Turnhout, 2002), 965–79.

Stein, Ernst, *Histoire du Bas-Empire*, 2 vols. (Paris, 1949–59).

*Stein, Henri, 'Les conséquences de la bataille de Cassel pour la ville de Bruges et la mort de Guillaume de Deken, son ancien bourgmestre', *Compte rendu des séances de la Commission royale d'histoire ou recueil de ses bulletins*, 68 (1899), 647–64.

Steinmeyer, Elias, *Althochdeutsches Wörterbuch* (Berlin, 1952–).

Strickland, Matthew, *War and Chivalry: The Conduct and Perception of War in England and Normandy, 1066–1217* (Cambridge, 1996).

Sumption, Jonathan, *The Hundred Years War*, vol. 2: *Trial by Fire* (London, 1999).

Les sûretés personnelles, 3 vols., Recueils de la Société Jean Bodin pour l'histoire comparative des institutions 28–30 (Brussels, 1969–74). [Abbreviated as *SP*]

Tabuteau, Emily Zack, *Transfers of Property in Eleventh-Century Norman Law* (Chapel Hill, 1988).

Taube, Michel de, 'Les origines de l'arbitrage international: Antiquité et Moyen Âge', *Recueil des cours* (Académie de droit international), 42 (1932), 1–115.

Taviani-Carozzi, Huguette, *La principauté lombarde de Salerne (IXᵉ–XIᵉ siècle): Pouvoir et société en Italie lombarde méridionale*, 2 vols. (Rome, 1991).

TeBrake, William, *A Plague of Insurrection: Popular Politics and Peasant Revolt in Flanders, 1323–1328* (Philadelphia, 1993).

Thesleff, Holger, 'Notes on the Name of Homer and the Homeric Question', in *Studia in honorem Iiro Kajanto* (Helsinki, 1985), 293–314.

Tiefenbach, Heinrich, 'Sprachliches zum Namenverzeichnis in der Handschrift St. Paul 6/1', in Uwe Ludwig and Thomas Schilp, eds., *Nomen et fraternitas: Festschrift für Dieter Geuenich zum 65. Geburtstag* (Berlin, 2008), 115–29.

*Timbal, Pierre-Clément, *La Guerre de Cent Ans vue à travers les registres du Parlement (1337–1369)* (Paris, 1961). [Abbreviated as *GCA*]

Tobler, Adolf, 'Romanische Etymologien', *Zeitschrift für romanische Philologie* 3 (1879), 568–76.

—— and Lommasch, Erhard, *Altfranzösisches Wörterbuch* (Berlin, 1925–).

*Tournadre, Guy de, *Histoire du Comté de Forcalquier (XIIᵉᵐᵉ siècle)* (Paris, 1930).

Tournier, Maurice, 'De hôte à otage: comment en est-on venu là?', *Mots: Les langages du politique*, 25 (1990), 95–8.

Toynbee, Margaret, *S. Louis of Toulouse and the Process of Canonisation in the Fourteenth Century* (Manchester, 1929).

Trabut-Cussac, Jean Paul, *L'administration anglaise en Gascogne sous Henry III et Edouard I de 1254 à 1307* (Geneva, 1972).

Tuchman, Barbara W., *A Distant Mirror: The Calamitous Fourteenth Century* (New York, 1978).

Turlan, Juliette, 'Prisonniers et otages des pays de Loire pendant la Guerre de Cent Ans (1337–1369) d'après les registres du Parlement', *Mémoires de l'Academie des sciences et arts de Touraine*, 4 (1991), 23–32.

Van Caenegem, R. C., *Geschiedenis van het strafrecht in Vlaanderen van de XI' tot de XIV' eeuw* (Brussels, 1954).

Van den Auweele, D., 'De Brugse gijzelaarslijsten van 1301, 1305 en 1328: Een komparatieve analyse', *Handelingen van het Genootschap voor geschiedenis gesticht onder de benaming 'Société d'émulation' te Brugge*, 110 (1973), 105–67.

Van Houts, Elisabeth M. C., 'The State of Research: Women in Medieval History and Literature', *Journal of Medieval History*, 20 (1994), 277–92.

Vanden Bussche, Émile, 'Flamands et Danois', *La Flandre*, 11 (1880), 253–326.

Vandermaesen, Maurice, 'De rekening der Brugse gijzelaars, 1328–9/1338–41', *Handelingen van het Genootschap voor geschiedenis gesticht onder de benaming 'Société d'émulation' te Brugge*, 115 (1978), 1–16.

*—— 'Brugse en Ieprse gijzelaars voor koning en graaf, 1328–1329: Een administratief dossier', *Handelingen van het Genootschap voor geschiedenis gesticht onder de benaming 'Société d'émulation' te Brugge*, 130 (1993), 119–44.

Vatin, Nicolas, *Sultan Djem: Un prince ottoman dans l'Europe du XV' siècle d'après deux sources contemporaines: Vâk'iat-i Sultân Cem, Œuvres de Guillaume Caoursin* (Ankara, 1997).

Vaughan, Richard, *Charles the Bold: The Last Valois Duke of Burgundy* (London, 1973).

Verbruggen, J. F., *The Battle of the Golden Spurs (Courtrai, 11 July 1302): A Contribution to the History of Flanders' War of Liberation, 1297–1305*, ed. Kelly DeVries, trans. David Richard Ferguson (Woodbridge, 2002 [1952]).

Verlinden, Charles, *L'esclavage dans l'Europe médiévale*, vol. 2: *Italie. Colonies italiennes du Levant. Levant latin. Empire byzantin* (Ghent, 1977).

Verwey, Wil D., 'The International Hostages Convention and National Liberation Movements', *American Journal of International Law*, 75 (1981), 69–92.

Verzijl, J. H. W., *International Law in Historical Perspective*, vol. 6: *Juridical Facts as Sources of International Rights and Obligations* (Leiden, 1973).

*Vic, Cl. de, and Vaissete, J.; *Histoire générale de Languedoc avec des notes et les pièces justificatives*, 15 vols. (Toulouse, 1872–93). [Abbreviated as *HGL*]

*Vignati, Cesare, *Storia diplomatica della Lega Lombarda con XXV documenti inediti* (Milan, 1866).

*Villanueva, Jaime, *Viage literario a las iglesias de España*, 22 vols. (Madrid, 1803–52).

Walker, Cheryl L., 'Hostages in Republican Rome', PhD dissertation, University of North Carolina–Chapel Hill, 1980; chs.harvard.edu/publications.sec/online_print_books.ssp (Washington, DC, 2005).

Walliser, Peter R., *Das Bürgschaftsrecht in historischer Sicht dargestellt im Zusammenhang mit der Entwicklung des Schuldrechts in den schweizerischen Kantonen Waadt, Bern und Solothurn bis zum 19. Jahrhundert* (Basel, 1974).

Warlop, Ernest, *The Flemish Nobility before 1300*, 2 vols. in 4 (Kortrijk, 1975–6).

Warren, W. L., *Henry II* (Berkeley, 1978).

Wartburg, Walther von, *Französisches etymologisches Wörterbuch* (Bonn, 1928–).

Watt, J. A., 'Gaelic Polity and Cultural Identity', in Art Cosgrove, ed., *A New History of Ireland*, vol. 2: *Medieval Ireland, 1169–1534* (Oxford, 1987), 314–51.

Weber, Max, *Economy and Society: An Outline of Interpretative Sociology*, ed. Guenther Roth and Claus Wittich, 2 vols. (Berkeley, 1987).

Weiler, Björn, *Kingship, Rebellion, and Political Culture: England and Germany, c.1215–c.1250* (Basingstoke, 2007).

Wemple, Suzanne Fonay, *Women in Frankish Society: Marriage and the Cloister, 500 to 900* (Philadelphia, 1985).

Wielers, Margaret, *Zwischenstaatliche Beziehungsformen im frühen Mittelalter (Pax, Foedus, Amicitia, Fraternitas)* (Munich, 1959).

Williamson, Oliver E., 'Credible Commitments: Using Hostages to Support Exchange', *American Economic Review*, 73 (1983), 519–40.

Winroth, Anders, *The Making of Gratian's Decretum* (Cambridge, 2000).

Wolff, Robert Lee, 'Mortgage and Redemption of an Emperor's Son: Castile and the Latin Empire of Constantinople', *Speculum*, 29 (1954), 45–84.

Wood, Ian, 'Beyond Satraps and Ostriches: Political and Social Structures of the Saxons in the Early Carolingian Period', in D. H. Green and Frank Siegmund, eds., *The Continental Saxons from the Migration Period to the Tenth Century: An Ethnographic Perspective* (Woodbridge, 2003), 271–98.

Wormald, Patrick, *The Making of English Law: King Alfred to the Twelfth Century*, vol. 1: *Legislation and Its Limits* (Oxford, 1999).

Wylie, J. H., and Waugh, W. T., *The Reign of Henry the Fifth*, 3 vols. (Cambridge, 1914–29).

Xhayet, Geneviève, *Réseaux de pouvoir et solidarités de parti à Liège au Moyen Âge (1250–1468)* (Geneva, 1997).

Yarbrough, Beth V., and Yarbrough, Robert M., 'Reciprocity, Bilateralism, and Economic "Hostages": Self-Enforcing Agreements in International Trade', *International Studies Quarterly*, 30 (1986), 7–21.

Ziegler, Karl-Heinz, 'The Peace Treaties of the Ottoman Empire with European Christian Powers', in Lesaffer, ed., *Peace Treaties* (q.v), 338–64.

Zimmermann, Michel, ' "Et je t'empouvoirrai" (*Potestativum te farei*): À propos des relations entre fidélité et pouvoir en Catalogne au XIᵉ siècle', *Médiévales*, 10 (1986), 17–36.

Index

Peoples are generally indexed under corresponding places, e.g., 'Saxons' under 'Saxony'. Medieval individuals are generally indexed by given name; surnames/toponymics that appear more than once are given separate entries with cross-references to given names; individuals are generally cross-referenced to relatives identified as such. Sources are indexed only where authors or titles appear in the text (excluding Appendix). England, France/Francia, Iberia/Spain, and Italy have not been given global entries. Entries marked * are found under the main heading 'hostages'. Abbreviations: emp. (emperor), k. (king), q. (queen), pr. (prince), d. (duke/duchess), e. (earl), c. (count/ess), abp. (archbishop), bp. (bishop), ab. (abbot), vc. (viscount/ess), slt. (sultan), em. (emir), f. (son/daughter).

Louis I the Pious, k. Aquitaine, emp., *(cont.)*
— III, k. Naples 80
— I, d. Anjou 108–10, 163–5, 200, 202
—, d. Bourbon 37
— I, c. Flanders 96–7
— II de Mâle, c. Flanders 96
—, c. Saint-Pol 80, 204–5
—, St, bp. Toulouse, f. Charles II, k. Naples 36–7, 177–8
—, f. John I, d. Bourbon 118
Louvain, c. 140
Luca Savelli 26
Lucca, siege of (553) 45, 203, 216
Ludwig I, d. Bavaria 48, 208
— II, d. Bavaria 123
Lutteroth, Ascan 5–6, 139, 143, 146, 148
Luxembourg, *see* Conrad I, John II
Lynch, Joseph 76–7
Lyon 165; *see also* Hugh

Mabel of Clare 88
Madrid, Treaty of (1526) 216, 219
Maelgwyn ap Rhys, pr. Deheubarth 51
Magna Carta 4, 27, 168
Magnus I, k. Norway 35
— IV, k. Sweden 124
Maguire, *see* Domnall, Thomas
Magyars 70, 207
Mahel, f. Miles, e. Hereford 155
Maine 149
Mainz 29, 43, 66
abp. — 43, 124, 171, 207; *see also* Adalbert, Christian
Malcolm Fleming 196; *see also* Wigtown
Malcolm III, k. Scotland 31, 80
Malik Ghazi, em. 80
Malise, e. Menteith 195
Malise Graham 196–7
Mallorca 108
Malvasletus 96
Mannassel Arsic 153
Manresa 124, 127
Mansura, Battle of (1250) 169–70
Mantua 93
Manuel II, emp. 10, 79n, 91
manulevator 17–18, 158
Mar, e. 191, 196
March, e. 194n, 196; *see also* Patrick
Mardin, *see* Ilghazi, Sukman, Timurtash
Margaret of Austria 84n
Margery, f. Robert the Bruce 90
Marguerite (f. protostrator) 90
de Monnay 91
— de Passavant 128
Marmande 180; *see also* Arnold
marriage 45, 76, 84, 92, 122–3, 143n, 154, 159–60, 168, 171–2, 174, 193
Marseille 30, 159–60, 178–81
Saint-Victor of —, abbey 136–8, 145

Marshal, *see* John, William
Martigues 180–1
Mathieu de Roye 127n
Matilda, emp. 79
— (f. Richard of Clare) 88
(f. Simon fitz Walter) 89
— (f. William of Avranches) 89
— of Braose 202
Maurice Fitzgerald 51
Maurisio 212
Mawdud, atabeg of Mosul 50, 82, 202
Maximilian I, k. Romans, emp. 164n
Meaux 105
Mediterranean (region) 3, 9, 74, 102–3, 115, 121, 148, 160
Melaghlin O'Donnell 51
Melun 58, 98, 105
Mercedarians 120, 219
merchant 111, 118, 124, 157, 160; *see also* guild, Symon Musonus, Trepelezinus
Merobaudes, Flavius 36, 64–5
Merpins 211
Messina, Treaty of (1191) 154, 156
Metz 59; *see also* Arnulf
Michael VIII Paleologus, emp. 90
Miesko I, d. Poland 31
— II, d. Poland 26, 112
Milan 13, 29, 40, 50, 94–5, 126
abp. — 94
Miles, e. Hereford 155–6; *see also* Mahel
— Crispin 153
Milo fitz Bishop 126
miracle 19n, 26; *see also* *hagiography
Miracles of Saint Wandregisil 68
Modena 93
Moissac 110
Molina, Luis de, *De iustitia et iure* 216
Monchas 107, 110
Monells 158
Mongols 79n
Monstrelet, Enguerrand de 19, 105, 108, 202
Montcada, *see* Ramon, Guillem
Monte Cassino 18–9, 115
Montereau 202
Montgomery (John, of Ardrossan) 194n; *see also* Arnulf
Montolieu, abbey 141
Montpellier 141, 158–60; *see also* Guilhem V/ VII/VIII
Montségur 106
Monza 39
Moors, *see* North Africa
Moravia 55
d. — 56; *see also* Zwentibold
Mortemer 106
Mosul 166; *see also* Âk Sunkur al-Bursukî, Djawâlî, Mawdud
Mu'âwiya, caliph 215
Mu'in al-Din, atabeg of Damascus 81

Somerset, d. 123
Sora 115
Sorbs 55; *see also* Semela
Soviet Union 226n
Speyer 173
Spoleto, d., *see* Ariulf, Conrad I, Hildebrand,
    Lambert I
sponsorship 60, 72–3, 75–7
Stade, *see* Henry, Siegfried
state 4, 6, 10, 20, 41, 131n, 133, 146, 214–15,
    218, 220–1
Stederburg Annals, 175
Stephen, c. Mortain, k. England 1, 14, 41–3,
    45, 47–8, 79, 85–6, 112, 155, 203,
    205
    III, d. Naples 33, 83
    — II, pope 61
    — of Richmond, 'count of Brittany' 153
Stewart, *see* Albany, Angus, John, Robert
Strickland, Matthew 162
Suana 211
Suffolk, e. 220
Sukman, em. Mardin, 166
Suleiman Celebi 88; *see also* Fatima
surety, personal 4, 13, 69, 72, 78, 81, 92n, 120,
    125–6, 130n, 148, 156, 162, 185,
    217, 220; *see also* *as origin of surety,
    *distinguished from other surety,
    fideiussor, guarantor, *guarantee/
    surety, *manulevator*
    —, real 4n, 6–7, 31, 34, 42, 47, 78, 81,
    120n, 131, 146–8, 151
Susa 44, 50
Sutherland, e. (Robert) 196; *see also* William
Swabia, d., *see* Erchagner, Philip
Sweden 55, *see* Magnus IV, Olaf
Switzerland 161, 219–20
Symon Musonus 38, 111
Syria (Roman) 45

Tabomuizl, d. Obodrites 32n
Tacitus 21, 83
Talbot, John, lord 47
Tancred, k. Sicily 154
    —, pr. Galilee 50, 82, 202
Taranto, pr. 80
Tarascon 180–1
Tarragona 120
Tartas 105, 107
Tassilo III, d. Bavaria 31, 58–9, 63; *see also*
    Theodo
Teck, p. 39
Templars 169
Terracino 62
Terricus Squelpe 93
terrorism 1, 4, 10, 224–5
Teruel, see *fuero*
Tervingi 64
Teutonic Knights 79

Tewkesbury, abbey 153
Thebes 3
Theinard, castellan of Bourbourg 152–3
Theoderic, k. Ostrogoths 49
Theodo, f. Tassilo III, d. Bavaria 31
Theophano, emp. 206
Theuderic I, k. Austrasia 27
Thierry, c. Flanders 150, 154, 156
Thietmar, bp. Merseberg 32–3, 49; *see also*
    Henry, Siegfried
Thionville 59, 219
Thomas Óg Maguire, k. Fermanagh 91
    —, f. Robert Erskine 187, 190
    —, f. William Hay of Locherworth
    187, 190
    Bisset 187, 189–90; *see also* William
    — de Turberville 111
    — Fleming, grandson of e. Wigtown
    186–7, 190
    — Hay of Yester 194n
    — Murray, brother of John Murray of
    Bothwell 183, 186–92
    — Muschamp 201
    — Somerville 187, 190; *see also* William
Thorfinn, f. Harald Maddadsson 51
Thorkell 49
Thouars 104n
Thrasco, d. Obodrites 31n
Thucydides 2
Thuringia 49
Tighearnan Ua Ruairc, k. Breifne 50
Timurtash, ruler of Mardin 86, 167
Toirdhealbhach, k. Connacht 50
Tongeren 205
Tongres 98
Tortosa 102, 160
Toulon 180–1
Toulouges, council of 134–5
Toulouse 47, 79, 161n, 165; *see also* Louis,
    Raimond II/IV,
Tournai 96
Tours, council of 134–5
    Treaty of — (1392) 123; *see also* Gregory
town, *see* guild, law (municipal), *townsman
Translation of Saint Vitus 68
Transylvania 18
treason 40, 49, 60, 102, 111, 168, 202,
    212–13, 223
Trencavel 141–4
    —, vc. Béziers 158; *see also*
    Raimond-Bernard
Trepelezinus 159–60
Treviso 94
trial by combat, *see* duel
tribute 27, 30, 56, 70–1, 141, 206
Trier, abp. 79; *see also* Eberhard, Ekbert
Trinquetaille 157
triumph 3
Troia, siege of (1022) 209

CPSIA information can be obtained at www.ICGtesting.com
Printed in the USA
LVOW10*0047010214

371879LV00006B/25/P